INVENTING THE MIDDLE EAST

INVENTING THE MIDDLE EAST

Britain and the Persian Gulf in the Age of Global Imperialism

Guillemette Crouzet

McGill-Queen's University Press
Montreal & Kingston · London · Chicago

First published in French as *Genèses du Moyen-Orient. Le Golfe Persique à l'âge des impérialismes (vers 1800-vers 1914)*, © Champ Vallon 2015

ISBN 978-0-2280-1405-8 (cloth)
ISBN 978-0-2280-1406-5 (paper)
ISBN 978-0-2280-1500-0 (ePDF)
ISBN 978-0-2280-1501-7 (ePUB)

Legal deposit fourth quarter 2022
Bibliothèque nationale du Québec

This book has been published with the help of a grant from the Centre National du Livre.

Library and Archives Canada Cataloguing in Publication

Title: Inventing the Middle East : Britain and the Persian Gulf in the age of global imperialism / Guillemette Crouzet.
Other titles: Genèses du Moyen-Orient. English
Names: Crouzet, Guillemette, author.
Description: Revised version of the French book: Genèses du Moyen-Orient: le golfe Persique à l'âge des impérialismes (vers 1800-vers 1914). | Includes bibliographical references and index.
Identifiers: Canadiana (print) 20220245940 | Canadiana (ebook) 20220246017 | ISBN 9780228014058 (cloth) | ISBN 9780228014065 (paper) | ISBN 9780228015000 (ePDF) | ISBN 9780228015017 (ePUB)
Subjects: LCSH: Persian Gulf Region—History—19th century. | LCSH: Imperialism—History—19th century. | LCSH: British—Persian Gulf Region—History—19th century. | LCSH: Persian Gulf Region—Strategic aspects—History—19th century. | LCSH: Persian Gulf Region—Foreign relations—Great Britain. | LCSH: Great Britain—Foreign relations—Persian Gulf Region. | LCSH: Great Britain—Colonies—Asia—History—19th century.
Classification: LCC DS326 .C76513 2022 | DDC 953.6—dc23

Set in 11/14 Minion Pro
Book design & typesetting by Garet Markvoort, zijn digital

CONTENTS

FIGURES AND MAPS

Figures

Maps

PREFACE

THIS BOOK WAS BORN OUT OF A SENSE that an important dimension was missing in existing accounts of the genesis of the "Middle East." Whole library shelves of scholarly literature have been dedicated to describing how Western powers drew lines in the sand in the wake of the First World War and thereby recast the political borders of the region. This conjuncture saw the disaggregation of the territories of the old Ottoman Empire and their reformulation into a new and complex territorial mosaic conceived largely around the geopolitics of oil. It is usually assumed that the concept of the Middle East, with all the territorial and strategic upheavals it promoted, was launched from this early twentieth-century juncture. In the pages that follow, I seek to tell instead the history of *another* Middle East, one at a significant remove – not only chronologically but also geographically – from this conventionally ascribed starting point. For while "Middle East" has long been an ubiquitous term in world affairs, its own antecedents and early invocations have remained curiously underexplored. When in fact was this label first imagined, and why? What geographical spaces did it first denote? And what entanglements of actors, conflicts, and processes underpinned these shifts, which made the coining of that geographical term both meaningful and necessary?

By pursuing such questions, this book offers a new account of the Middle East's invention. The answers it proposes explore how the idea of the "Middle East" emerged not from the First World War and its aftermath but rather from much earlier conflicts centred on the nineteenth-century Persian Gulf. Even before the oil boom of the twentieth century, the Gulf region had taken on strategic importance for competing global empires, and the fundamental dynamic in this was how the Gulf came to form a terraqueous crossroads and borderland guarding British India's western flank. The origins of the term "Middle East" can be traced precisely to Britain's long hegemony over the Indian subcontinent and to its violent overspill into the Gulf and its hinterlands.

This pattern of British encroachment into the Persian Gulf region began by degrees under the expansionist East India Company in the later eighteenth century. It would be catalyzed by the geostrategic shock generated by Napoleon's invasion of Egypt in 1798; in the decades after that, it would be further ratcheted up by gunboat attacks conducted under British auspices in the name of pacifying Arab "pirates." Throughout the 1800s, this crucial geopolitical arena was then secured and transformed to become the bulwark of an informal imperial system erected around British India. The creation of this sphere of influence was piecemeal and multifaceted, involving a triangle of actors in London, on the Indian subcontinent, and in the Gulf region itself. Cartographical expeditions imposed a geographical logic on this "British" Gulf, whose political economy – geared toward the globalizing trade in pearls, date palms, and slaves – was reordered to favour imperial priorities. Officials and speculators sought new passages to India running through Mesopotamia, archaeologists unearthed artifacts of the region's ancient empires, and ideologues envisaged the rebirth of this cradle of civilizations under British oversight. By the end of the nineteenth century, amid renewed waves of inter-imperial competition, this nexus of British interests and narratives in the Gulf region would occasion the appearance of a new appellation, the "Middle East."

Around this same period, apologists for empire would propagate celebratory retrospective narratives of this century-long unfolding of British interventionism and overlordship in the Persian Gulf and its environs with a view to justifying its transformation into a kind of British "lake," while also seeking to sustain the wider region's open-ended continuation under imperial tutelage. Such accounts often fêted Britain's history of informal empire in the region as one characterized by fair and benevolent custodianship. Yet the realities of how the British – and, more particularly, the emergent semiautonomous imperial administration of British India – had projected themselves into this contested Gulf region emerge in this book in a markedly different light. A critical interrogation of the historical record – notwithstanding that the available archives and other sources are largely of British official origin – strongly suggests that the policies of intervention in the region only belatedly resembled a grand design, and at no point a disinterested one. Indeed, in the later eighteenth and early nineteenth centuries there had been significant seesawing and sclerosis among British officials regarding what the most efficacious policy to adopt in the region might be. Even when an informal imperial agenda did begin to take shape, its enactment remained fraught, and included periods of conflict involving considerable violence and some notable military setbacks at the hands of local actors in the Gulf. Nevertheless, these decades of British "imperial meridian" in the region would gradually coalesce into a distinct pattern of indirect rule.[1] As accretively elaborated and systematized from the mid-nineteenth century on, this ensured regional security and pacification – conditions of immense knock-on benefit to British India – with relatively low running costs. The early globalization of the Gulf economy, with the local shaykhs and other rulers instrumentalized as brokers under British auspices, would prove to be of central importance in these developments.

British influence in the region that would thenceforth be dubbed the Middle East ebbed in the final decades of the nineteenth century. New interloper powers, Germany the most prominent among them, sought to insert themselves into the strategic crucible of the Gulf, threatening to weaken Britain's position there. In the event, however, the informal empire the British had constructed in the Gulf's waters and sands would be supplanted and transformed in quite rapid and unexpected ways during the fallout from the First World War as the Middle East came to be "reinvented" around oil. In the ensuing years, a new kind of British colonial regime administered from London across a swathe of former Ottoman territories quickly overshadowed what had come before. Given this peak of British direct rule across a very different iteration of the Middle East down to the middle of the twentieth century, it has become all the more difficult to comprehend that there had in fact been a much longer history of British imperial entanglement and interventionism in the Gulf region dating back to the age of Napoleon.

Finally, the origins of this book require a few words of explanation. Its first iteration was as a French-language book, published in 2015 by the French academic publisher Champ Vallon.[2] This new English-language version was made possible by a substantial grant from the Centre National du Livre in France. This work represents not just a translation and a slimming down of the original French text, but also a significant updating and revision. Over the several years since the publication of the French version of this book, the scholarship around different aspects of the intertwined histories of Britain, the Indian subcontinent, and inter-imperial competition in the Gulf region has blossomed significantly. Taking stock of this wave of important new work has been an additional element of preparing this new English version.[3] In a host of other ways, too, this book has been changed by the author's own transplantation from a francophone to an anglophone context, with a change of academic home from France to Britain. My many debts in this respect are described more fully in this book's Acknowledgments.

ACKNOWLEDGMENTS

THIS BOOK IS AN EXTENSIVELY REVISED VERSION of a book published in French in 2015, *Genèses du Moyen-Orient. Le Golfe Persique à l'âge des impérialismes (vers 1800–vers 1914)*. It was a privilege to work on that first book manuscript with Patrick Beaune and Joël Cornette at Champ Vallon. Richard Baggaley at McGill-Queen's University Press then made possible the transformation of this work from its original French form into the present English-language version. He was the ideal editor, and I cannot thank him enough for his boundlessly generous and tireless work on this book. I also would like to thank Kathleen Fraser and Carol Bonnett at McGill-Queen's University Press for their assistance with the manuscript at a later stage. The translation of the French manuscript into English was itself enabled by a grant from the Centre National du Livre and from several further sources in both France and the United Kingdom. These included the Laboratoire d'excellence "Ecrire une histoire nouvelle de l'Europe"; the Fond d'intervention pour la recherche of Lettres Sorbonne Université; and, at Warwick University, the Global History and Culture Centre, the Early Modern and Eighteenth Century Centre, the Humanities Research Fund, and the Institute of Advanced Study. The initial French manuscript was translated by Juliet Sutcliffe, whom I wish to thank. The long process of revising and copy editing the text was then assisted by the late Meredith Sherlock, whom I wish could have seen the final result, and by Kelly Bimbry Midura. Deborah Schwartz then reviewed the entire manuscript and further assisted me with the transliterations of Arabic and Persian words. Thanks also to Matthew Kudelka for rescuing me from innumerable errors and to Tere Mullins for her help with the index.

This text began its life as a doctoral thesis at the Sorbonne launched in 2008. I thank my supervisor, Eric Bussière, and the members of the examining committee. My research greatly benefited from spending two years as a visiting doctoral student in Britain. The first of these years was spent at King's College London, with the mentorship of David Todd, to whom I am most grateful. The second was at the University of Cambridge, where I was welcomed by Chris Bayly, who went on to become an external examiner for my thesis and would ultimately write the foreword to the French version of this book. His enthusiastic support for my research was boundless, and the largest of my intellectual debts is to him. He passed away before I completed this book, and I hope he would have been pleased that I followed the encouragement he gave me to publish a version of my work in English.

This book is not merely a translation but an updated version of its French-language iteration. Over the past several years, I have been fortunate to spend time at a series of institutions that have allowed my work to develop in new directions. At the European University Institute in Florence, where I was lucky enough to have an office "with a view" for a year, I am indebted to Youssef Cassis, Laura Lee Downs, Ann Thomson, and Stéphane Van Damme. From my subsequent time as a fellow at the Graduate Institute in Geneva, I thank Gopalan Balachandran and Davide Rodogno. Above all, however, this book is the product of my time at Warwick University, where I have been exceptionally lucky to be based as a postdoctoral fellow in the History Department. My greatest debt at Warwick is to the wonderful Maxine Berg, without whom this book would not have been possible. I have also accrued many further debts, above all to Anne Gerritsen and Rebecca Earle. Exchanges with members of the Global History and Culture Centre and the Early Modern and Eighteenth Century Centre have shaped this book in a multitude of ways, and I have been fortunate to be part of a thriving community of fellow postdocs and researchers. Particular thanks for all manner of help and support go to Dan Branch, Giorgio Riello, Robert Fletcher, Penny Roberts, Charles Walton, Mark Philp, Mark Knights, and Guido van Meersbergen. My time at Warwick would not have been as pleasant had it not been for the support of some of the administrators of the History Department and the Faculty of Arts, especially Claudia Gray, Amy Evans, Robert Horton, David Duncan, Liese Perrin, and Jean Noonan.

As this project developed, it benefited from opportunities to present and discuss my work at numerous conferences, seminars, and other forums, and from the help and encouragement of many scholars and friends. I wish particularly to thank Sunil Amrith, Maureen Attali, On Barak, Fabrice Bensimon, Francisco Bethencourt, Noëlline Castagnez, Philippe Chassaigne, Nandini Chatterjee, William Gervase Clarence-Smith, Olivier Dard, Jean-Pierre Dormois, Jean-François Dunyach, Margot Finn, Mark Greengrass, Simon Jackson, Colin Jones, Lawrence Klein, Marie-Clarté Lagrée, Simon Layton, Vincent Lemire, Michel Leymarie, Josephine McDonagh, Jacob Norris, James Onley, Pierre Purseigle, John Slight, Elizabeth Elbourne, Jon Parry, Laila Parsons, Yann Rodier, Eugene Rogan, Radhika Singha, Sujit Sivansundaram, Herman van Der Vee, and Myriam Yacoubi. Special thanks go to Laurie Macdonald. I am also grateful for the assistance of the staff of numerous libraries, archives, and research centres, notably the India Office Records at the British Library and Warwick University Library.

I grew up in a family obsessed with history. My two grandmothers, Françoise Crouzet and Paulette Pavan, shared their memories of the Second World War in France, one as a Jew subject to persecution and forced into hiding, and the other as a young woman who, together with her parents, joined a Resistance network that helped shelter downed American and British airmen. My grandfather François Crouzet was a virtuoso historian, and hearing recollections of a career in which he had met Lucien Febvre, Fernand Braudel, and many other giants of the historian's craft helped me develop my own taste for history. My parents, Denis and Elisabeth Crouzet, have done for me more than I can express in words. They are models for me, as parents and as historians.

When I met Simon, *Genèses* had just been published. He has been with me at every step of the process of preparing this English-language version of the book and has read every word I wrote. He has been my biggest support. I could not have done all this without him and his endless love and patience. Our daughter Alice arrived while I was completing this book. I hope that one day she reads it and, instead of finding it too dull, perceives between its lines some of the joy I felt while writing it and imagining her imminent arrival in our lives. This book is for her and for Simon.

Note on Transliteration

Arabic and Persian words and names have been transliterated into English according to a simplified system based on that used by the *International Journal of Middle East Studies* (*IJMES*). To facilitate reading for the non-specialist, all diacritical marks have been omitted, with a few exceptions (Shatt al-ʿArab, FathʿAli Shah). For Arabic and Persian names and words that have a common transliteration in English (Muhammad, Mecca), this spelling has been used. According to the *IJMES* transliteration system, British capitalization rules have been applied to transliterated Arabic titles and the article *al-* is not capitalized unless it begins a sentence or endnote.

All translations from French are my own, unless otherwise noted.

THE PERSIAN GULF IN THE 19TH CENTURY

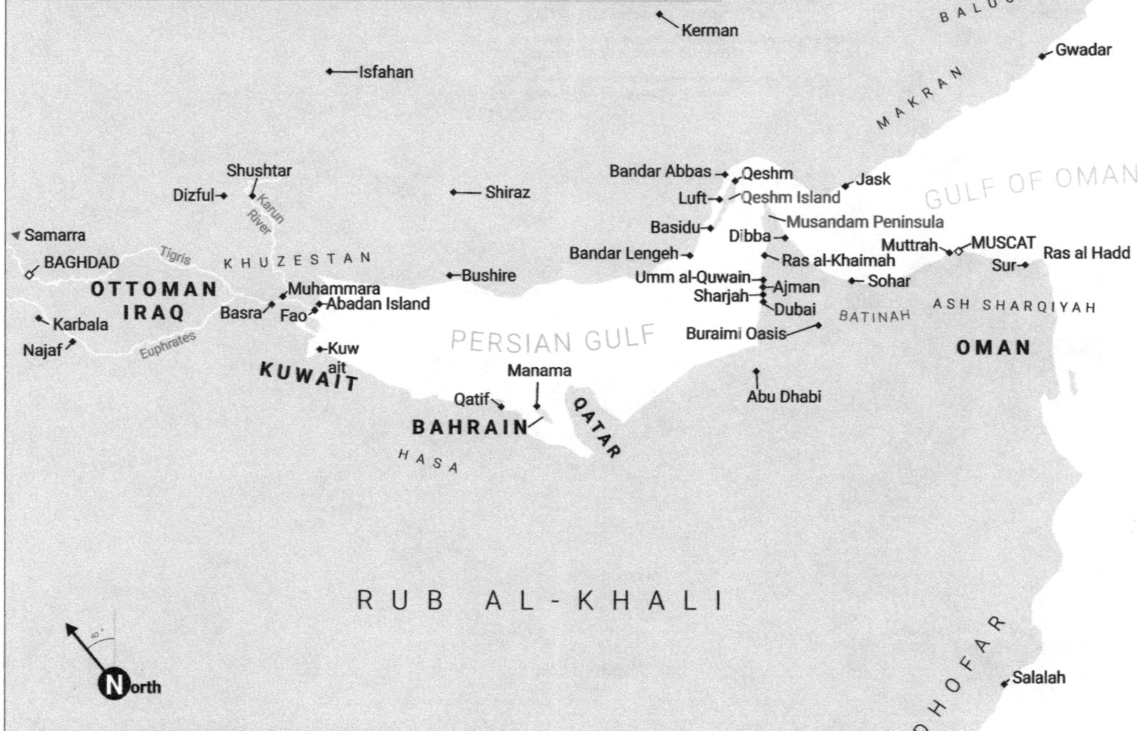

Source: John B. Kelly, *Britain and the Persian Gulf, 1795-1880* (Oxford: Clarendon, 1968)
Design: Joshua Vachon (Cyberfjord Studio)

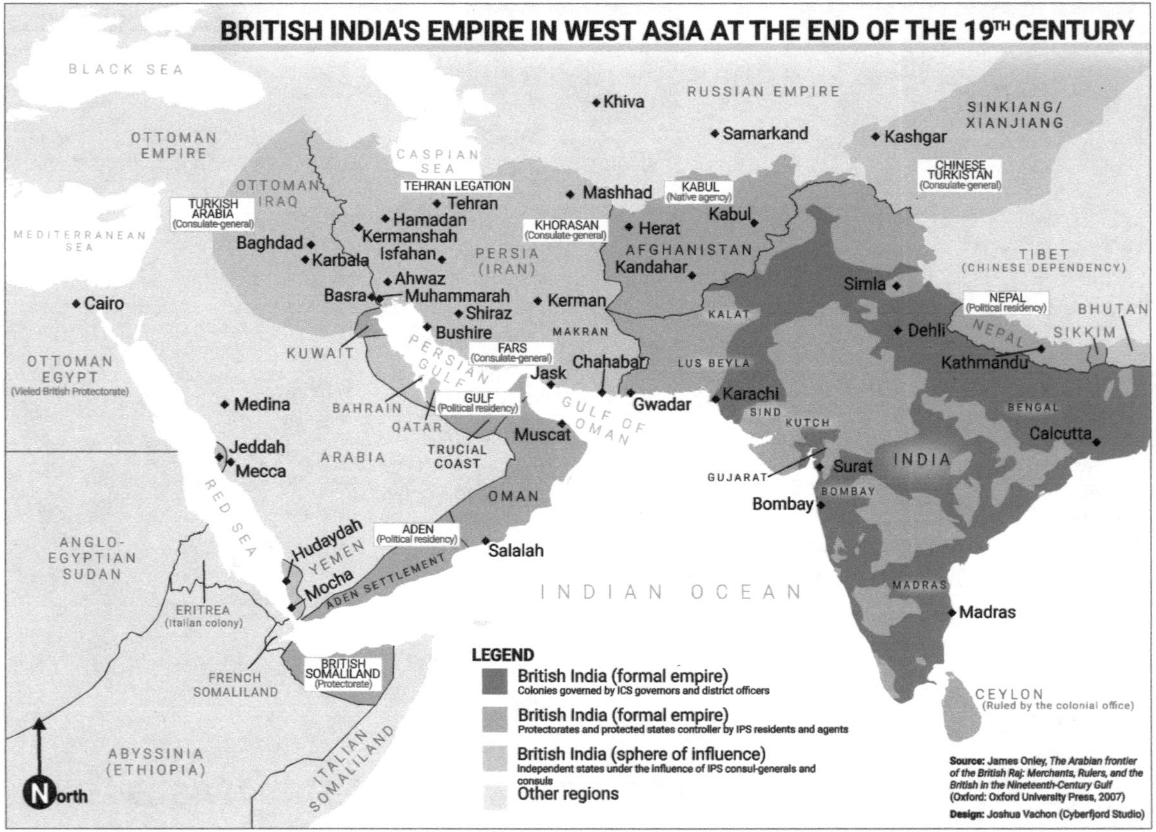
BRITISH INDIA'S EMPIRE IN WEST ASIA AT THE END OF THE 19TH CENTURY
BLACK SEA
OTTOMAN EMPIRE
MEDITERRANEAN SEA
Cairo
OTTOMAN EGYPT
(Vieled British Protectorate)
TURKISH ARABIA
(Consulate-general)
OTTOMAN IRAQ
Baghdad
Karbala
Basra
CASPIAN SEA
TEHRAN LEGATION
Tehran
Hamadan
Kermanshah
Isfahan
Ahwaz
Muhammarah
Shiraz
Bushire
PERSIA (IRAN)
KHORASAN
(Consulate-general)
Mashhad
Kerman
MAKRAN
FARS
(Consulate-general)
Khiva
RUSSIAN EMPIRE
Samarkand
KABUL
(Native agency)
Kabul
Herat
AFGHANISTAN
Kandahar
Kashgar
SINKIANG/ XIANJIANG
CHINESE TURKISTAN
(Consulate-general)
TIBET
(CHINESE DEPENDENCY)
Simla
NEPAL
(Political residency)
BHUTAN
SIKKIM
NEPAL
Dehli
Kathmandu
KALAT
LUS BEYLA
Karachi
SIND
KUTCH
BENGAL
Calcutta
INDIA
GUJARAT
Surat
BOMBAY
Bombay
MADRAS
Madras
CEYLON
(Ruled by the colonial office)
KUWAIT
PERSIAN GULF
Jask
Chahabar
Gwadar
GULF OF OMAN
BAHRAIN
GULF
(Political residency)
QATAR
Muscat
TRUCIAL COAST
ARABIA
Medina
Jeddah
Mecca
RED SEA
OMAN
ADEN
(Political residency)
Salalah
Hudaydah
YEMEN
Mocha
ADEN SETTLEMENT
INDIAN OCEAN
ANGLO-EGYPTIAN SUDAN
ERITREA
(Italian colony)
FRENCH SOMALILAND
BRITISH SOMALILAND
(Protectorate)
ABYSSINIA (ETHIOPIA)
ITALIAN SOMALILAND
North
LEGEND
British India (formal empire)
Colonies governed by ICS governors and district officers
British India (formal empire)
Protectorates and protected states controller by IPS residents and agents
British India (sphere of influence)
Independent states under the influence of IPS consul-generals and consuls
Other regions
Source: James Onley, The Arabian frontier of the British Raj: Merchants, Rulers, and the British in the Nineteenth-Century Gulf (Oxford: Oxford University Press, 2007)
Design: Joshua Vachon (Cyberfjord Studio)

INVENTING THE MIDDLE EAST

INTRODUCTION

IN NOVEMBER 1903, George Nathaniel Curzon, the Viceroy of India, set sail from Bombay for the Persian Gulf to begin a carefully choreographed official tour of the region. Accompanied by an impressive naval flotilla, Curzon – who as viceroy was Britain's chief administrator of India and the sovereign's representative – his wife, and their entourage travelled on the *Argonaut*, which was accompanied by four other ships with more than one thousand men on board. As Lucien Laronce, the French vice-consul in Oman, noted, such a deployment of force in the Gulf waters had not been seen since a fleet of vessels belonging to the British Royal Navy and to the East India Company – the trading company turned territorial power that had spearheaded the British presence in India since 1600 – had sailed from Bombay to attack the "pirate" city of Ras al-Khaimah on the Strait of Hormuz in 1809. Curzon's descent on the Gulf in 1903, by contrast, was framed not as a military intervention but rather as a kind of triumphal marker of the imperial role that the British had constructed for themselves in the Gulf over the intervening century. Indeed, the tour was elaborately structured so as to commemorate but also to consolidate the seamless map of alliances Britain had forged with local powers in a process dating back to 1798, when a treaty had been signed with the Sultanate of Oman – the first of many accords reached with regional potentates on both sides of the Gulf. Over the same period, the British regime in India had itself changed markedly, the East India Company proxy government having been replaced by the Government of India in 1858 and British direct and indirect imperial rule having been extended over ever greater swathes of the subcontinent. Curzon's three-week tour through the Gulf involved the staging of ceremonialized encounters with all the major rulers of the Arabian side of the Gulf, coupled with a more abbreviated program of visits and meetings in Persia. The tour as a whole redeployed an array of pomp-and-circumstance techniques of diplomacy and indirect rule whose efficacy had already been proven in the context of British India itself.

In geopolitical terms, the viceroy's 1903 tour of the Gulf may be said to have been symbolic of a fundamental strategic fact: in parallel with the development of the British Empire in India, the Gulf and its hinterlands was perceived to be a vital arena of imperial defence and had been treated as such. In speeches he gave during the tour, Curzon set out a historical grand narrative lionizing Britain's imperial mission – one that he asserted to be a mission accomplished – of securing peace and prosperity in the Gulf region. At the same time, however, his very presence in the area highlighted the fact that the ultimate purpose served by this long-term program of British interventions in the region had been a highly pragmatic one of safeguarding the western flank of British India. The importance to British India of the frontier zone of sea and sand composed by the Gulf and its hinterlands was, indeed, such that a corresponding new spatial concept had evolved over the course of the nineteenth century to describe the region. For much of that century, this was a concept without a definitive label. At precisely the same period in which Curzon's tour was being planned and undertaken, however, a retrospective name for it was found, and it began to achieve a degree of critical mass: the "Middle East." This book is a history of the entangled relationships between Britain, the Indian subcontinent, and the Gulf, which culminated in that new moniker – one coined with reference to geopolitical circumstances set in place over the nineteenth century, but which would go on to have a much-transformed afterlife, down to the present day.

The Middle East: "A term which I have not seen"

Curzon does not appear to have used the term "Middle East" – neither during his 1903 tour of the Gulf nor in his correspondence about it – when referring to the land and sea territories to the west of India. But the term was rapidly gaining currency at precisely this juncture. In 1902, one year before the viceroy's squadron dropped anchor at Muscat on the first stage of the viceregal tour, the influential British journalist Valentine Chirol published twenty essays in *The Times* dedicated to "The Middle Eastern Question." These were subsequently republished as a book titled *The Middle Eastern Question; or, Some Political Problems of Indian Defence* (1903), whose main subject was, to quote the author, "the Indian frontier."[1] According to Chirol, the Middle East consisted of "those regions of Asia which extend to the borders of India or command the approaches to India, and which are consequently bound up with the problems of Indian political as well as military defence."[2] From Egypt and the Red Sea to Afghanistan, India was protected by an immense frontier composed of land and sea territories that were centred around the Gulf. This was the Middle East.

Chirol was an influential publicist, and his intervention gave the term "Middle East" a great boost. But he was not in fact the first commentator to have come up with this concept. In 1900, Thomas Gordon, a former British Army officer, had written an article on the "Middle East" region, where, according to him, the concerns of the "external policy" of the British Empire in India were especially "sensitive."[3] Gordon, who had spent most of his military career on the subcontinent, did not claim ownership of the term "Middle East."[4] In fact, he pointed out that the term had been in use for several years in administrative circles in British India, as well as in Persia at the British legation in Tehran (where Gordon had been an attaché).[5] Despite these early instances, however, the launching of the term "Middle East" is often credited to the American admiral Alfred T. Mahan, with the publication of his article titled "The Persian Gulf and International Relations" in the *National Review*, a London periodical, in September 1902.[6] There, Mahan defined the Middle East – which he described as his original coinage, "a term which I have not seen" – as a zone with fluid borders situated between South and West Asia and centred around the Gulf. More specifically, he described a space where Britain's domination of the strategic land and sea communication routes between London and India was increasingly being threatened by the encroachments of imperial rivals, especially Russia and Germany.[7] In 1908 the first cartographical projection of this Middle East evoked by Gordon, Chirol, and Mahan was printed. This map, titled "Map of Arabia and the Persian Gulf," did not use the term "Middle East," yet it represented what were in effect its imagined territories, extending from Egypt to Afghanistan and encompassing the Arabian Peninsula, the Gulf, and the Sea of Oman.[8]

The definitions of the Middle East posited by Chirol, Mahan, and Gordon were not precisely the same. Indeed, it might appear that at the beginning of the twentieth century imaginary geographies were beginning to appear, not just of a single Middle East, but of multiple possible Middle Easts. From the very first uses of the term, there was a significant lack of consistency over the exact location of this space. Where *was* the Middle East, if not by default east of Europe and west of India?

For Gordon and Chirol, the existence of the Middle East was determined by that of the British Empire in India, while for Mahan it was instead a terraqueous zone of confrontation where British supremacy at sea – the foundation of its global power – was encountering imperial challenges from Russia and Germany. To some extent, what is most salient is the overlap in these positions: in particular, a unifying characteristic of the Middle East concept as envisaged by Chirol, Mahan, and Gordon was its definition by geopolitics rather than by any particular cultural or religious identity, or indeed by reference to the Bible or to ancient history. It is also worth emphasizing that in the accounts of these three authors, the term was not developed primarily in relation to the Ottoman Empire or the "Eastern Question" (a long-standing European debate about the Ottoman Empire's decline and potential dismemberment), but with reference to the British Empire.[9]

From all this we can see that the early twentieth century constituted a turning point at which various observers felt the need to name or define a space that was still geographically fluid yet understood to be of key strategic importance and which thus began to be cautiously referred to as the Middle East. From that point onward the world map no longer seemed to make sense without this intermediary space.

Why did this macroregion begin to take form on maps and begin to be written about by journalists, geographers, and imperial administrators just at the beginning of the twentieth century? Why was the existence of the Middle East, for Chirol and Gordon, linked to that of the British colonies in the Indian subcontinent?

Seeking to answer these questions, this book proposes to study the invention of one Middle East, namely the British Middle East, the one that first occasioned the term's appearance in English. In this study readers will find the genesis of this metageographical concept not in the West in the twentieth century, but rather in the relationship between India and an inland sea that was part of the Indian Ocean – the Persian Gulf – during the nineteenth century.[10] This Middle East is not the space that was created in the aftermath of the First World War, comprising a mosaic of territories with different administrative statuses and rooted in the deserts of Palestine, Jordan, and Iraq. In these pages there is nothing on the Sykes-Picot Agreement signed by France and Britain in 1916, on the system of mandates whose borders were drawn in the aftermath of the war, or on the oil wells that were so coveted by Western powers. *Inventing the Middle East* instead tells the history of a Middle East focused on a maritime world, the Gulf, which the British imagined in the nineteenth century as a fulcrum of their empire and as a bridge between Europe and the Mediterranean on the one hand, and India and the wider Indian Ocean world on the other. Around this space and its hinterlands the British developed a complex tapestry of interventionist practices and imperial fantasies. In these dynamics the region was envisioned as the site of a transformation, to be overseen by Britain, that would both target the supposedly endemic lawlessness and unproductivity of its seas and deserts and foster a kind of renewal that might somehow reconnect this space with its own lost glory as a site of great ancient empires, thus bringing back to life something of the lost grandeur of the Hanging Gardens of Babylon.

In other words, in seeking to interpret this *new* conception – of the "Middle East" as first envisaged around 1900 – this book explores a set of *past* practices for which the term furnished a label. It may thus be considered a term that – to draw on the theoretical language proposed by the historian Reinhart Koselleck – provided a solution to a set of needs, or organized an area of uncertainty. In this sense its conception offers an example of "a historical concept oriented to the future." It was certainly a concept that offered itself up to multiple reuses and refurbishments against changing contexts, as illustrated by its subsequent and enduring history down to the present.[11] Conversely, it also contained an inheritance from the past, for "Middle East," as launched in the years around 1900, referred to a set of already long-standing circumstances – a triangle of entanglements between Britain, the Gulf, and the British Empire in India.

Indeed, to borrow again from Koselleck's analytical framework, "Middle East" might itself be used retrospectively in consciously teleological ways, offering as it does a later concept extended "to cover earlier periods" so as to establish "a minimum of common ground" for analysis.[12] Indeed, for the nineteenth century at least, such uses of "Middle East" may be teleological only in a strict sense, for the term did not emerge out of nowhere; rather, there was in fact a series of predecessor terms (such as "East," "Orient," and "Near East") that extensively – although only ever partially – conceptually prefigured it. To put the case more cautiously, "Middle East" may be said to be interestingly poised between two levels of thinking historiographically about the past: first, that which "investigates circumstances already articulated at an earlier period in language" (albeit here not yet in the precise formulation "Middle East"), and second, that which "reconstructs circumstances which were not articulated into language earlier but which can be worked up with the help of specific methods and indices."[13]

A guiding principle of the present book is that when the term "Middle East" is taken to be a starting point for an analysis geared around the post-1900 period, something important is lost from view – namely the nineteenth-century history of which the term was a kind of culmination. The reconstitution of that history so as to link together Britain, India, and the Gulf is the primary purpose of this account. Accordingly, it presents a multifaceted exploration. The remainder of this introduction briefly evokes three main elements that underpin the following chapters. First, a survey is made of the ways the space now known as the Middle East was considered discursively in imperial imaginaries before the term "Middle East" was coined. Second, discussion is given to the question of the structure of the British Empire in India and its significant autonomy in relation to the government in London. Last, attention turns to the spaces of the Gulf and the globally connected maritime and terrestrial crossroads it formed.

East, Orient, Near East, Nearer East: The Impossible Middle East

The decades after 1900 saw the enactment, in Britain and other imperial regions, of an aspiration on the part of geographers, administrators, and publicists to divide the world into vast macroregions that would transcend political, cultural, geophysical, and social borders.[14] Mahan and Chirol appear to have been part of this dynamic. Other examples from around the same time include the concepts of "pivot area" and "heartland of Euro-Asia," invented in 1904 by the British geographer Halford Mackinder; "Central Europe," invented by Friedrich Naumann in 1915; and Ewald Banse's attempt to fix a specific definition of "the Orient" in 1908.[15]

Such designations were neither preordained nor uncontested: "Middle East" was in fact a late arrival in the search for terminology to describe the space stretching from the eastern Mediterranean and the Black Sea to the Indian Ocean and the subcontinent. Despite the cluster of invocations of "Middle East" around 1900, the term in fact struggled to gain traction in Britain during the early twentieth century. More favour was accorded to the term "Near East," which had been much in fashion since the mid-nineteenth century and was still being used by Curzon on the eve of the First World War.[16] Even Chirol had long preferred Near East to Middle East, notably in his book *The Far Eastern Question*, published seven years before *The Middle Eastern Question*.[17] In Britain around 1900, alongside "Near East," the looser terms "Orient" and "East" were also used, rather than "Middle East."[18]

What were the outer limits of this "East," or this "Orient," notions that were endlessly evoked in Victorian and Edwardian Britain? Where were they located? For some British travellers, writers, and diplomats, the East and the Orient included Syria, Egypt, the Arabian Peninsula, and Palestine. For others who favoured a more maximalist definition, these terms might also encompass the territories of the Ottoman Empire in the Balkans and Asia Minor, as well as Persia, Russia, and other yet more distant horizons. Among the Victorian and Edwardian elite, this fluctuating geography of the Orient and the East was strongly influenced by ancient history, both as recounted by classical authors and as reinterpreted in more recent canonical British works such as Edward Gibbon's monumental *The Decline and Fall of the Roman Empire*.[19] The borders of "the East" thus corresponded, from one point of view, to those of the ancient Roman Empire in the Orient. Equally, for the British historical imagination of the late nineteenth century, the Orient referred even further into the classical past, evoking the empire of Darius the Great, which was centred around Persia and had threatened what was recognized as one of the origins of European civilization, Greece. Biblical narratives were another key point of reference. For British travellers in the nineteenth century, a journey in the Orient or in the East often traced a route to Jerusalem, and this might be combined with visits to a series of other famed historical centres, including Cairo, cities in the Levant such as Aleppo and Damascus, and Persian cities such as Shiraz and Isfahan, as well as Baghdad and Constantinople. India, however, was not part of this paradigmatic map, tending to be considered as a separate destination in its own right.[20]

The East and the Orient were thus associated with a kaleidoscope of different images, reflecting multiple and much-mythologized pasts, making these terms a kind of palimpsest of memory and culture. They variously evoked the cradle of civilization, the Holy Land, and the fulcrum of prosperous empires described by ancient historians and geographers such as Ptolemy, Pliny, and Strabo. Nor was this all: in the British imagination, these representational strata were overlaid by still others, with the Orient or the East also evoking the Bedouin civilization of the deserts of the Arabian Peninsula where Islam was born.[21] Partly as a result of this evocative power, the terms "East" and "Orient" continued in the early twentieth century to dominate in the press, in literature, and in political and diplomatic circles.

In 1902 the British archaeologist David Hogarth published *The Nearer East*, thereby popularizing another new term – and yet another rival to "Middle East" for terminological prominence.[22] The "Nearer East" was specified as being an expanse of territories extending from the Adriatic Sea to the Black and Caspian Seas and even to the Indian Ocean. This label enjoyed a brief vogue in the early twentieth century, probably initially because of the events that shook the Balkans between 1900 and 1914, but perhaps also because, given its geographical definition, it provided a way of reformulating the Eastern Question.[23]

Between 1914 and 1918, Mesopotamia and the wider Ottoman Empire were major theatres of the war, yet the term "Middle East" was only rarely invoked in Britain. Only in the 1920s did this twenty-year-old term gain official status.[24] Most auspiciously, in 1921 a new Middle East Department was established within the Colonial Office at the instigation of its then secretary of state, Winston Churchill. This Middle East Department was charged with administering Palestine, Aden,

Iraq, and Transjordan. This was different from Chirol's Middle East in that it did not include the Gulf, Persia, Egypt, or Afghanistan. But like Chirol's, Churchill's Middle East reached the shores of the Indian Ocean and the Mediterranean. There is another significant testimony to the relevance of the "Middle East" concept around the same period: in 1920 the Royal Geographical Society's Permanent Committee on Geographical Names, a quasi-official body charged with standardizing geographical nomenclature for use by British institutions, set out a new position on the question. It vouchsafed that from then on, with the dissolution of the Ottoman Empire, the term "Near East" would refer only to the Balkans; "Middle East" would refer to the regions between the Bosporus and India.[25] In 1922 an influential historian, Arnold Toynbee, adopted the terminology espoused by the RGS, thereby giving it a degree of scholarly legitimation. The Greeks, the Romans, and the Bulgars were, in his view, "Near Eastern nations"; the adjective "Middle Eastern" should, however, be used in reference to Arabs, Turks, and Persians.[26] It may be said, then, that by the interwar period, "Middle East" was gaining discursive ground in Britain. But it was not until the Second World War, with the creation of the British Middle East Command based in Cairo, or perhaps even as late as the Cold War, that the terminological ascendancy of "Middle East" in Britain was completed.[27]

What should we conclude from this genealogy of concepts forged from the end of the nineteenth century onward to designate this intermediate but indeterminate space located between the Occident and the Far East? What can be deduced from the existence of so many competing and fluid names, all of them trying to encapsulate a geographical grey area?

From one point of view, the Middle East may be understood as emphatically an invention of "the West," that is, an Orient set in binary terms against an Occident. This Middle East, seen as a cultural and intellectual construction and the site of an absolute alterity, has been influentially explored in the work of Edward Said.[28] Seen in these terms, the Middle East appears conceivable only in relation to the West and a geography centred on Europe. Its genesis in cartographic form beginning in 1908 and the remaking of its borders during and after the First World War are to be understood as projections of Western imperialism and, more specifically, of competition over access to oil resources, exemplified in the division of the spoils of victory in 1918 between France, Britain, and the United States. In this light the notion of the Middle East amounts, as one scholar of the region's historical geography has noted, to a "capricious colonial artifact" reflecting "the geopolitical and economic interests of the European powers who created it."[29] As summarized by the historian Roderic H. Davison, "the power and parochial outlook of the western nations are responsible" for the birth of this space. And one Western power had particular responsibility: Britain, "the villain in the piece."[30]

From this point of view, the First World War and the interwar period saw the effective inception of the Middle East, principally orchestrated by Britain, which had become the dominant power there.[31] The Middle East was erected on the territorial ruins of the Ottoman Empire, which was dismantled after 1919. At the postwar peace conferences at Versailles, San Remo, and Sèvres, heads of state drew borders in the sands of the former Ottoman provinces, assigning mandates and oil deposits mainly to Britain and, to a lesser extent, France. In 1928 a round of oil business negotiations, known as the Red Line Agreement, continued this dynamic. Between 1918 and the 1930s, a new Middle East was thus emerging, organized around the geographies of mandates and of oil, rooted in the deserts of Iraq, Jordan, Syria, and Palestine and forged by British diplomacy, notably as steered in the early twentieth century by figures such as Arthur Balfour, Winston Churchill, George Curzon, George Sykes, and David Lloyd George.[32] From these starting points, an extensive scholarship has been dedicated to the transformations wrought in the Middle East and in wider global geopolitics by the "oil revolution" over the past century.

Yet at the same time, as scholars have noted, "the genesis of the term" Middle East has received significantly less scrutiny.[33] In focusing on the twentieth century, historians have largely overlooked how the region had fulfilled a different function – and a specific imaginary – within the British Empire during the nineteenth century, and that both were different from what followed in the wake of the First World War. This, then, is the basis of the present book. It is of course possible to overstate the importance of a watershed moment around 1900 in the history of the region now termed the "Middle East": in the sweep of nineteenth- and twentieth-century history, the region saw many continuities as well as changes in the interventionist policies of Britain and other imperial powers. Yet it remains the case that "Middle East" was coined *before* oil was discovered in industrial-scale and commercially viable quantities in the region (beginning in southwestern Persia in 1908). In investigating the nineteenth-century British Middle East, this book takes seriously the first definitions created by Chirol and Gordon, for whom the Middle East was organized around the maritime world of the Gulf and around the purpose of providing a defensive buffer zone for India. Hence this book's title, which highlights the direct links between British imperialism in the Gulf and the creation of the Middle East. The Middle East was invented by British imperialists and had two goals. One was to protect and defend India from potential invasion; the other was to link not only different parts of the British Empire but also three continents: Europe, Asia, and Africa; and three bodies of water: the Mediterranean, the Indian Ocean, and the Red Sea.

More specifically, this book contends that we should not look solely to the West and specifically to London to understand the creation of the Middle East. On the contrary, we also need to look east, to the British Empire in India in the nineteenth century. *Inventing the Middle East* thus proposes to recast the history of the Middle East by reversing the historical and the geographical perspectives so often adopted in the past. That is the essence of the present work's originality. This is not, however, to claim that the invention of the Middle East was rooted solely in South and West Asia. To do so would be to replace one kind of determinism with another. Accordingly, while this account seeks to avoid an excessively Eurocentric vision of the phenomenon of British expansionism in West Asia, it does not seek flatly to replace this with a blunt claim for the overriding salience of a "peripheral view" rooted in India.[34] The relevant history is more complex and more nuanced.

As its central argument, *Inventing the Middle East* contends that a key phase of the history of the conceptualization of the Middle East occurred during the long nineteenth century, in British India and in the Persian Gulf, and in constant dialogue with the various imperial institutions in London. Starting in the early nineteenth century, various figures in India's two key administrative capitals, Bombay and Calcutta, as well as in the Gulf and London, began to flesh out a range of practices and ideas regarding this space between the Mediterranean and the Indian Ocean, in the "middle" of Britain's eastern possessions, which would ultimately make it possible to evoke a "Middle East." The Middle East was thus a co-production of the policies of, on the one hand, the Indian presidencies from the early nineteenth century and the Government of India after 1858 and, on the other hand, the imperial administrations based in London.

The History of the Middle East Seen through the Prism of India's History

Inventing the Middle East takes up the call made by Christopher Bayly for "reintegrating 'west Asia' with the history of the Indian 'subcontinent,'" while also taking into account the role of the government in London.[35] By analyzing the complexities of British imperialism in the Persian Gulf and its coastal regions, with particular reference to the role of India, this book allows us to untangle the history of the invention of the concept of the Middle East. What was the nature of British colonial power on the Indian subcontinent, and to what extent was that colonial power a force in its own right in its own macroregion rather than simply a tool of the government in London?

At the outset of the time frame studied in this book, the British had been a presence in India for two centuries already. The East India Company, a monopoly trading firm based in London, had been established in 1600; its initial tangible form in India had come in the shape of trading outposts on the Coromandel Coast, a privilege granted by the Mughal emperors who then dominated part of the subcontinent. By the mid-eighteenth century, a densification of its network of outposts on the subcontinent and an intensification of its interests there saw the Company transformed into a political actor. This involved an expanding territorial presence, profiting from Mughal decline: the Company achieved dominance first in Bengal; then in the centre of India, through a series of wars with the Sultanate of Mysore ending in 1799; and then through a series of further conflicts with Maratha and Sikh antagonists in the north. Many other territories were co-opted into the Company's sphere of influence as a consequence of treaties with local powers. The Company's footing in India was administered via three "presidencies," each headed by a governor, located at Bombay, Madras, and Calcutta, with the latter gradually gaining an ascendant position in the Company's governing structure over the course of the late eighteenth and early nineteenth centuries. Below the presidencies were a descending series of other Company trading and administrative outposts (notably "residencies" and "agencies"). The colonies of the East India Company on the subcontinent thus played a major role in the foundation of what is sometimes referred to as a "second" British Empire, firmly rooted in South Asia, created in the aftermath of the loss of the North American colonies.[36]

After the Indian Rebellion of 1857, a sweeping reform of the governing structure on the subcontinent was undertaken. The Company was abolished and replaced with a new structure through the Government of India Act (1858). In London the key figure would thereafter be a government minister, the Secretary of State for India, while on the subcontinent the colonial administration would be directed by a governor general (or viceroy). Lands previously governed by the Company passed to the British Crown and were ruled directly; however, large swathes of the subcontinent remained governed only indirectly, after the signing of accords with the local princely rulers.

Be it under the East India Company or through the Government of India, the influence of this British colonial presence on the subcontinent also played out in territories farther afield. From its earliest days, the Company had developed a network of trading outposts across the Indian Ocean, from the African coast to Southeast Asia.[37] Notably, it established a presence in Penang in 1786, in Singapore in 1819, and in Malacca in 1824. These far-flung sites were administered by the various presidencies on the subcontinent. In the Gulf, an epicontinental sea in the Indian Ocean world, operations would be conducted largely under the auspices of the Bombay Presidency. From small beginnings in the seventeenth century, the Company went on to develop "factories" (or trading posts) across a series of sites in the Gulf, essentially in Persia and along the Persian coast, at Shiraz, Isfahan, Jask, and Bandar Abbas. By the end of the eighteenth century, there were two residencies in the Gulf, one at Bushire in Persia and the other at Basra in Ottoman territory. With the growing politicization of the East India Company, the Bushire Residency would become of paramount importance for the

British presence in the Gulf. The Bushire Residency in turn administered various other outposts, notably an agency in Muscat, and worked in close cooperation with the various British diplomatic envoys sent to the Persian court.

The policies toward the Persian Gulf of the administrations in India – the presidencies up until 1858, the Government of India thereafter – are at the heart of the analysis here. The chapters that follow reconstruct the chronology and methods of British India's imperial interventions in the Gulf from the late eighteenth century to the eve of the First World War. This history has not previously been the subject of a full study.[38] Indeed, the Gulf has long been something of a poor relation in the historiography of the territories and border zones that were part of the orbit of British India; other spaces, such as Burma, Ceylon, and Southeast Asia, have been studied in detail.[39]

Inventing the Middle East contends that however little scholarly attention has been paid to it, the Gulf was in fact hugely important for British India. Seen at first, at the end of the eighteenth century, as a peripheral region subject to the depredations of pirates, the Gulf would become transformed in the coming decades into India's sand-and-water border, one with a vital protective function. This book shows that the existence of a perennial threat to India – first incarnated by the French and the Wahhabis and Gulf-based "pirates" in the decades around 1800, then by the Russians from 1820 to 1830, and ultimately by the Germans between 1870 and 1880 – allowed Britain to justify a long century of imperial interventionism in the Gulf.[40] The Gulf was turned into a protective buffer zone over the course of the nineteenth century by an ensemble of political practices that are detailed in this book: these included treaties signed with local powers, maritime patrols, a strengthening of the role of the Indian government's representatives in the region, the undertaking of surveys and mapping ventures, and the fostering of a political economy in the Gulf linked to two booming global commodities, pearls and dates.

From the 1790s to the middle of the nineteenth century, the East India Company's efforts focused first on the south of the Gulf, on the region around the Strait of Hormuz, between the northern part of the Sultanate of Oman and the southern part of Bahrain, which would later be known to the British as the "Lower Gulf." This sphere of influence then expanded, so that by 1900 it extended from Muscat to the Shatt al-ʿArab and encompassed both the Persian and Arabian shores of the Gulf. From 1880 to 1899, when Britain and Kuwait signed a treaty, relations with the micropowers in the southern Gulf and Oman were strengthened, while part of the upper Gulf was absorbed into the Government of India's sphere of dominance. In 1914 the Gulf was the most important part of the network of directly and indirectly ruled territories that formed British India's sphere of influence in the western Indian Ocean, which also extended to Aden, Oman, and Zanzibar, as well as to Hadramaut, the African coast, and the shores of the Red Sea.[41] Comparative attention to other spaces on the edge of Britain's Indian empire demonstrates that the Gulf was a terraqueous border zone: both a link and a gap, both peripheral and central, and capable of connecting several worlds.[42]

Ultimately, then, by analyzing the example of the Gulf, *Inventing the Middle East* demonstrates that a British sub-imperialism existed in western Asia, initiated in part from the imperial centre of India. This perspective draws on a body of scholarship that has highlighted the existence of an element of autonomy in the government of the British colonies on the Indian subcontinent, dating back to the middle of the eighteenth century. Especially after the Battle of Plassey in 1757, British interests on the subcontinent gained ascendancy over those of France and the colonies of the East India Company engaged in an intense maritime expansion policy in the Indian Ocean world.[43] This more or less continuous expansion would be carried out by the presidencies and then the Government of India throughout the nineteenth century.[44]

A History of the Space

As with "Middle East" and "British India," the term "Gulf," or "Gulf region," is not without problems. To what exactly does this geographic term refer? A clarification is necessary. The terms Gulf, Persian Gulf, Arabian-Persian Gulf, and Arabo-Persian Gulf in the following pages are used interchangeably. They are here used to evoke the subject of this study – that is to say, the British Gulf and its different boundaries as conceived of in the nineteenth century by the British. They designate a zone with fluctuating borders, centred around a maritime world where London's and India's imperial policies were rolled out: the space evoked here is not the geographically more precise "Gulf" understood as an epicontinental sea within the Indian Ocean. Space, as imagined and as constructed historically, is the basis of study here.[45]

The British Gulf was constructed around a shallow, warm-water maritime expanse surrounded by rocky and sandy coasts, scattered with islands and shallows, and connected to the Indian Ocean world by the Strait of Hormuz and the Sea of Oman. In the late eighteenth century this space was characterized by extreme political fragmentation. By this point, the Persian and Ottoman empires exercised only limited authority in these waters and along these shores. The Sultanate of Oman and Zanzibar, the Qasimi from Ras al-Khaimah, and the local micropowers arrayed along the Gulf's Arabian coast – Qatar, Kuwait, Bahrain, Abu Dhabi, and Dubai – were engaged in power struggles and rivalries. This was the fragmented space that the British attempted, in an accretive process, to unify under their imperial purview. This "British" Gulf was, then, a composite space, encompassing both the Persian and Arabian littorals and the northern coasts of Oman, but also islands such as Hormuz and inland waterways connecting the Gulf to interior regions. In particular the Gulf's influence could be felt far inland through the delta of the Shatt al-ʿArab, a river system formed by the juncture of the Euphrates and Tigris Rivers and joined farther along its course by the Karun River.

Reconstructing this British Gulf makes it possible to consider this space not as a backwater of nineteenth-century history but as a region that was a key crucible of larger global and imperial conjunctures. In particular this study of the Gulf highlights two global processes that reached far beyond the edges of the Shatt al-ʿArab and the Strait of Hormuz: the emergence of a global economic market, and the "conquest" of vast swathes of the globe by European imperial powers. While this was an "age of global imperialism," the present account also highlights that in the case of the British Gulf, the guiding dynamics were not simply metropolitan, that is to say centred on London, but also involved a sub-imperialism directed from the Indian subcontinent itself. Accordingly, this book seeks to enable comparisons and connections with other spaces – governed both formally and informally – of the British Empire as a whole, as well as with the distinctive arc of influence and interventionism that emanated around the terrestrial and maritime edges of British India.

Even after the Suez Canal was opened in the late nineteenth century, the Gulf retained a special place in the British imperial system. It kept its strategic importance as a flank on which the Indian subcontinent might become vulnerable, and it continued to offer a parallel travel route to India. It also remained a potent site of imperial fantasy. The world of the Gulf was a horizon of different histories and possible futures, reaching to the Shatt al-ʿArab region and Mesopotamia, centres of prosperous ancient empires such as the Babylonian and Assyrian empires, which had been envied throughout the period of antiquity for their fertility and wealth. These histories, which were being excavated by British scholars – and appropriated in the name of metropolitan science – at precisely this period, gave the region a vivid and enduring place in imperial imaginaries. The British dreamed that by establishing themselves in this vast region, they would become successors to Nebuchadnezzar, Darius, and Alexander. All the while, they hoped to create their own empire, a perduring empire that, unlike the ones that preceded it, might never disappear.

The British Gulf was part of a layered spatial invention, one that was seen through the prism of India's perceived vulnerability, and one around which in turn the Middle East would come to be envisaged. The various aspects of this study tap into a range of different sources, historiographies, and methodologies.[46] This involves interlinking the approaches scholars have taken to studying the history of empire with those developed for investigating maritime spaces from a global perspective. In particular, viewing the Gulf through the lens of its being India's maritime border provides a powerful point of reference in relation to the historiographical renewal that has been happening in recent decades in the field of the history of the Indian Ocean world. The "oceanic turn," of which such histories are an example, presents a valuable way forward for rethinking the history of the Middle East.[47] More specifically, this book relates to recent critical scholarship that has proposed thinking, according to the formulation proposed by Nile Green, in terms of a vast "Indian Ocean arena" defined by "social geographies" and "mobile societies" and transcending the frontiers of multiple conventional areas of analysis (notably South Asia, Central

Asia, the Arabian Peninsula, and the Middle East).[48] This "arena" was one that transcended Eurocentric and imperial geographies and one in which the Gulf was a key component.

A considerable body of scholarship now exists on the impact of globalization on the societies of the Indian Ocean, a process that was inseparable from European imperialism in this terraqueous space.[49] These studies reveal the history of the Indian Ocean over many centuries, thus showing how this space offers a vast parallel to the historical canvas of the Mediterranean as explored in the pioneering *longue durée* scholarship of Fernand Braudel.[50] As early as the medieval period, the Indian Ocean was linked through various flows to other maritime and land spaces near and far; by then, it was already integrated into the world economy and its different markets.[51] Far from being a closed-off space at the time of the arrival of European powers, the Indian Ocean was a connected arena, criss-crossed by the movements of merchants, pilgrims, travellers, sailors, and workers from South Asia, Malaysia, and the Arabian Peninsula.[52] The consequences of imperialism and the arrival of steamships in this maritime space over the course of the nineteenth century – which resulted in the destruction of some of the Indian Ocean's existing economic and human networks, the transformation of others, and the development of new forms of globalization – therefore require nuanced appraisals and form the subject of ongoing inquiry and scholarly debate.[53]

Study, in this light, of the British Gulf of the nineteenth century is made possible by a great number of historical sources. As noted earlier with regard to the launching in the public sphere of the term "Middle East," there exists a considerable published record about the British Gulf, dating from the period itself: these records include travel accounts, journalism and pamphlets, memoirs, maps, and other representations such as photographic images. Even more important for this account, however, the period saw the creation of a range of archival records stemming from imperial policy-making and administration. Much of this material was produced by the colonial bureaucracy on the Indian subcontinent, before 1858 with the various presidencies, then after that year by the Government of India.[54] These in turn can be considered alongside British government records, notably from departments such as the Foreign Office and the Admiralty; key materials here are the archives of consular posts in Persia (Bushire) and Ottoman Iraq (Baghdad and Basra). Areas of agreement, but also of tension and divergence, between the two governing poles at play here – the authorities in India, and those in the British metropole – can be traced by confronting the records produced by each side. Some critical sidelights are shed on this by reference to the archives of French consular posts in the Gulf region (Oman and Baghdad). Overall, however, this is a study of the British Gulf rather than an attempt at a complete history of all of the different powers invested in the region, some of whose histories have already been the subject of valuable scholarship, and the picture here is reconstructed largely via British sources. By the same token, this work is by no means a history of the Gulf populations of the nineteenth century; when the voices of the people of the Gulf are heard in the British sources, this is in fragmentary and polemicized ways, requiring reading against the grain rather than at face value.

Inventing the Middle East is thus an aquatic or amphibious history of the Middle East, a space whose maritime character and connections with the Indian Ocean world invite re-evaluation. It seeks to depart from the terracentrism of some studies of the Middle East, which are overly focused on the landward aspects of the Ottoman Empire; it proposes instead a history of this macroregion as centred on a maritime edge, the Gulf.[55] Paying heed to the Gulf's terraqueous environment here reveals the nineteenth-century emergence of one Middle East, the British Middle East, which was integrated during the nineteenth century into a larger Indian Ocean arena. To be sure, this is but one among a host of other Middle Easts. Yet the history traced here also suggests a broader need to consider the histories of different Middle Easts – before and after the invention of the term itself – as being concerned with a maritime space. The Middle East, though organized around a maritime space, the Gulf, remains too often envisaged, even today, as a terrestrial space rooted in deserts. While opening new horizons, the present study also invites us to escape a landlocked vision of the history of this region.[56]

The opening chapter of this history traces the rivalries between several powers – the French, the British, the Wahhabis (who were expanding significantly in the Arabian Peninsula at this juncture), the Qasimi of

Ras al-Khaimah and their allies along the Persian and Arabian shores, and the Sultanate of Oman – in the waters of the Gulf between 1780 and 1820. It sets the beginning of British intervention in the Gulf in local, regional, and global contexts and analyzes the discourse about "pirates" that developed in British India from the end of the eighteenth century. It contends that accusations of piracy against the Gulf tribes, particularly the Qasimi, were largely a pretext for the Bombay and Calcutta Presidencies to launch their first attack, in 1809, against Ras al-Khaimah, the "pirate" city that commanded the maritime entrance to the Gulf at the Strait of Hormuz. Behind such pretexts lay the larger fear of a French threat to India, felt especially in the aftermath of Napoleon Bonaparte's 1798 expedition to Egypt. The Gulf was thus beginning to be perceived as a frontier space that, if secured and "pacified," would protect India's western flank. This chapter highlights how the spectre of a French threat developed in British India when Napoleon Bonaparte created a menacing network of local and global alliances with the sultan of Oman, the shah of Persia, and the tsar of Russia. Discourses about piracy and pacification, it is argued here, may be best understood as merely the foam on the waves caused by Bonaparte's half-real, half-fantastical ambitions in West and South Asia and by the East India Company's own expansive agenda on the subcontinent and in the wider arena formed by the Indian Ocean world.

The second chapter examines the debates about how to manage the Gulf that were conducted in British India in the years after the attack against Ras al-Khaimah. British imperialism in the Gulf region was marked by significant hesitation on the part of the Bombay and Calcutta Presidencies. How extensive a continuing role should they play in the Gulf region? Should British involvement in the Gulf revert to an economic presence only, as had previously obtained? In this view, notably articulated by influential colonial figures in Bombay, to be dragged into an ongoing confrontation with the tyranny represented by Oriental potentates – which in British discourse included Napoleon – would be to fall into a trap. According to the opposing view, an ongoing policy of political interventionism and semiformal empire in the Gulf appeared to be the best tack to follow for protecting British interests in India. As uncertainty continued regarding which strategy to pursue, an important testing of the waters occurred when an envoy,

Captain George Sadleir, was sent from Bombay in 1819 to strengthen relations with regional powers: Sadleir would cross the Arabian Peninsula by land – traversing what was new terrain for the British – to meet Ibrahim, son of Mehmed Ali Pasha, the Ottoman viceroy of Egypt. Ultimately, in the light of a continued sense of threat to India, embodied by the French up till 1815 and by Russia thereafter, a policy of interventionism was chosen. This provided the backdrop to a second attack on Ras al-Khaimah in 1819. It also informed the gradual politicization of the East India Company's administration in the Gulf, notably the increasing power of the resident officials it maintained there. Forging this new, more interventionist policy in the Gulf was among the larger shifts in the policy of the Bombay and Calcutta Presidencies, especially under the leadership of Mountstuart Elphinstone and the Marquess of Hastings. This particular shift involved a step change in the expansion of British colonies on the subcontinent, as well as a particular focus on securing India's borderlands. The chapter also analyzes the maritime truce system, which was a decisive element in the process of constructing the Gulf as India's sand-and-water border.

Chapter 3 tracks another dimension of the creation of a borderland for British India in the Gulf by examining how the space was made the object of multiple geographical expeditions, maritime survey programs, and varieties of mapmaking over the course of the nineteenth century. This constituted the geographical invention of a British Gulf, a phenomenon that should also be understood as the creation of a border zone for India. These efforts were structured around a maritime space encompassing both the Persian and Arabian shores of the Gulf, one that stretched laterally from east to west, from the Sultanate of Oman and the Strait of Hormuz to the Shatt al-ʿArab. This chapter describes how surveyors, engineers, topographers, and sailors sent out from India created an imperial topography, naming and standardizing space. It also underscores the importance of interactions with the local Gulf populations and highlights the question of how greatly this ambitious imperial geographical project may have relied on pre-existing local topographical knowledge.

Chapter 4 examines how the nineteenth-century Gulf became integrated into the expanding world economy, especially through the globalization of trade in two regional products, pearls and dates. With both pearls and dates becoming the objects of a market boom among European and American consumers, this had a powerful impact on the Gulf's economy. This chapter argues that the consolidation over this same period, under the auspices of British India, of practices of political oversight and interventionism in the Gulf – an example of a wider phenomenon that historians have labelled "informal" empire – created a context that was favourable to the development of the date and pearl booms. In British imperial ideology, fostering legal trade centred around these two global commodities was envisaged as key to ending piracy and other forms of regional conflict, with the resulting prosperity serving to establish peace in the Gulf waters. By the same token, it would also offer a tangible endorsement of the virtues of imperial tutelage (or "Pax Britannica," as it was beginning to be characterized around this time). Ideology aside, the instrumental value of establishing a political economy built around globalized trade in dates and pearls may be underscored, for this was an integral element of the larger process of transforming the Gulf's status as a dangerous peripheral area menacing British India: the larger payoff of prosperity in the Gulf would be the safeguarding of India's western flank. This chapter also explores how the globalization of dates and pearls was deeply invested in slave trade networks in the western Indian Ocean world. The two booms were powered by an increase in slave labour in pearl fishing and date cultivation. Efforts on the part of the authorities in India to curb the slave trade in this macroregion, it is argued here, remained limited precisely because this trade was crucial to the functioning of these two economic sectors and so to maintaining the British system in the Gulf. Conversely, a final trade in the Gulf around the turn of the twentieth century, namely that in arms, often transported via smuggling networks, highlights how not all patterns of exchange in the region proved amenable to British interests, in that the final destinations of such military equipment included frontier zones of conflict with British India.

Chapter 5 moves the focus of analysis northward in the Gulf world to consider a beguiling sphere in its hinterlands, Mesopotamia (to apply the historicizing term used for this area by the British in the nineteenth century). Beginning in the 1830s, the archaeological excavations of Austen Layard and Claudius Rich unearthed historical traces of ancient Mesopotamia, providing new materials for mythologized visions of the past as well as spurring fantasies of contemporary reconstruction. While new steam navigation routes linking London and the Indian subcontinent via the Gulf were becoming the objects of experiment and debate, the transformations associated with bringing steam technology into the Shatt al-ʿArab delta and its related river system were being seen as a powerful projection of imperial achievement and a reordering of the natural world. This held out the symbolically saturated promise of thereby breathing new life into ancient Mesopotamia, thus restoring a neglected realm of collapsed ancient empires under the banner of British imperial modernity. This would see modern technology forge a new economic empire in the north of the Gulf, making a hub that could bring together and multiply the wealth of Syria, Persia, the Arabian Peninsula, and India. Archaeology, the opening up of steam lines in the Shatt al-ʿArab, and the development of the British residency in Baghdad were some of the key manifestations of this developing informal imperialism in Mesopotamia. Ultimately, this chapter argues, this Mesopotamian moment in the Gulf furnished a kind of first instantiation of concepts that would later be bundled under the category of "Middle East," namely, a space conceived of as linking together multiple continents, seas, and oceans, on whose fortunes hung the safety of the western approaches to India.

The book concludes with an analysis of the final phase of British imperialism in the Gulf, during the late nineteenth and early twentieth centuries. In a period of renewed imperial ambition and international tensions – conventionally labelled as the "New Imperialism" – the British faced heightened competition in the Gulf. These dynamics included a renewal of French efforts to position themselves in Oman and in the northern Indian Ocean, a more assertive role played by the Ottoman authorities in the north of the Gulf, and new efforts by Russia and Germany to insert themselves into this space. Conflict tended to be restricted to disputes over commerce and economic interests, but for all the competing actors in the Gulf and its hinterlands, including the British, these masked larger strategic and national competitions. The Government of India and the political bodies in London in charge of imperial policies sometimes disagreed about which strategies to adopt in response to these competing threats. Ultimately, however, the result was a far more assertive policy in the Gulf, tending toward further formalizing and territorializing a presence that had previously been more loosely asserted but that had also been under less pressure from other actors. Mainly under the auspices of the Government of India, a series of treaties were signed with Oman and the tribal chiefs along the Trucial Coast, instituting what were disguised protectorates; in parallel with this, Bahrain and Kuwait were effectively absorbed into the jurisdiction of British India. A major architect of this policy step change toward greater implantation and securitization of what was becoming as much a formal as an informal empire in the Gulf was George Curzon, the Viceroy of India, who identified the region as key to the protection of British India. While this backdrop of heightened tensions and renewed interventionism marked continuity as much as change in the triangle linking together Britain, the Indian subcontinent, and the Gulf, dating over the previous century, it would be at this juncture that a new geopolitical terminology, the "Middle East," would be coined. This term would acquire lasting influence in the twentieth century and beyond, albeit in ways that often transformed – and in doing so lost sight of – its original referent.

1

Edge of Empire

Britain, the East India Company, and Early Interventions in the Gulf

FOR ANY RETROSPECTIVE EXPLORATION of British involvement in the region that would later be dubbed the "Middle East," the major attack launched under the auspices of the East India Company administration in Bombay on the city of Ras al-Khaimah in 1809 represents a key episode. An Arabian port on the Strait of Hormuz, Ras al-Khaimah commanded access to the Persian Gulf from the western Indian Ocean. The military action launched from Bombay in 1809 was ostensibly undertaken in response to a years-long series of "pirate" attacks on trade in the region, above all insofar as these affected British and East India Company ships. According to British accounts, Ras al-Khaimah was a veritable pirates' nest, home to marauders of the sea whose dhows had for too long attacked peaceful shipping and massacred crews. Attempts to halt this maritime lawlessness by negotiating agreements having failed, the only option remaining, it was claimed, was a punitive expedition. Described as a pacification exercise, the British venture involved a sizable naval flotilla and a large landing force, manned by a mix of British and Indian sailors and soldiers. The Ras al-Khaimah attack, together with several secondary attacks on other ports in the same campaign, would be commemorated in visual form in a set of engravings produced in the wake of the expedition on the basis of sketches made by the British soldier Richard Temple. Echoing larger imperial narratives of the Ras al-Khaimah campaign, these engravings pictured the venture as one that meted out calibrated violence in order to achieve a kind of retributive justice in the Gulf, seen here as

Figure 1.1 John Clark after Richard Temple, "Ras ul Khymah from the S.W. and the Situation of the Troops," from *Sixteen views of places in the Persian Gulph taken in the years 1809–10: illustrative of the proceedings of the forces employ'd on the expedition sent from Bombay [...] against the Arabian pirates.*

a lawless frontier zone that had become something of a sea of trouble for British India (Figure 1.1).

Having intervened at Ras al-Khaimah in 1809, both the East India Company administrations on the subcontinent, and beyond them the government in London, would over the following decades become gradually ensconced in an ongoing political and military role in the Gulf region. Crucial questions, however, remain about the critical conjuncture around 1809. What was the phenomenon in and around Gulf waters that the British termed as "piracy"? Did the British suddenly become interested in the Gulf region at this point, or was the turn to military interventionism the culmination of larger processes? Looking beyond the 1809 attack in particular, this chapter seeks to set this episode in wider contexts by reviewing and deconstructing the momentous geopolitical conjunctures that framed it, exploring these both with and against the grain of the body of sources from the time – a documentation very largely of British origin, making for a very largely one-sided historical record.

As will be seen, there were a series of polemics around the issue of "piracy," and this in turn raises the question of how much commonality there was in the terms of discourse between the British on the one hand and their antagonists on the other. Looming above this, however, an overarching stimulus to the 1809 intervention may have been less the immediate theme of "piracy" and more the global war under way over these years between Britain and Napoleonic France. This conflict had itself extended to the Persian Gulf to a significant degree, notably through British fears of French instrumentalization of local powers in the region. From this perspective, the Gulf was a potential stepping stone in an overarching French ambition to undermine British power in India – perhaps even through military invasion. Accordingly, "piracy" in the Gulf might amount to the thin end of a wedge of unrest in the region that would enable Napoleonic interventionism on the subcontinent itself.

With India in his distant sights, Napoleon certainly fancied himself to some extent as a kind of symbolic heir to ancient precursors on this mythologized continent-crossing path, such as Alexander the Great. Moreover, after France's surprise Egyptian campaign in 1798, almost anything seemed possible in terms of grand strategy. The Egyptian episode, led in person by Napoleon, had been a profound shock to the existing strategic balance in the Orient, and it raised critical questions about British dominance on the Indian subcontinent. Viewed from this perspective, then, the British intervention at Ras al-Khaimah begins to look less like a conflict specific to the region and more like the local iteration of a much larger and longer-term clash of strategies. Seen in these terms, the Ras al-Khaimah raid was to some extent a British gambit to ward off not just "pirates" but also the long reach of an enemy empire based in Paris.

In the final analysis, however, it may well be that neither "piracy" nor the idea of a French threat alone explains, or was a necessary precondition to, an ever-greater British imprint on the Gulf region. Certainly, both influenced the timing, the shape, and the narratives involved around this increased British role in the Gulf. Yet this British role so suddenly and violently announced by the raid on Ras al-Khaimah in

1809 did not arise out of nowhere; rather, it was a long time in the making. Given the dynamics of British expansionism in India and its peripheries over the course of the eighteenth century, and continuing thereafter, some kind of active British shading into the Gulf may have been already overdetermined.

As a means to approach these sequentially wider explanatory frameworks, this chapter is divided into three parts. The first explores the polemics around the question of "piracy" in the Gulf and the entanglement of the British in this issue, which culminated in the raid on Ras al-Khaimah. The second turns to the question of a supposed French threat in and around the Gulf region, especially as this took shape in the decade or so following Napoleon's Egyptian campaign. In the third part, attention shifts to some of the broader dynamics around British colonial expansionism and the "imperial meridian" around this period, as well as how these trends radiated around the Indian subcontinent and its peripheral regions.[1]

Pirates of the Gulf?

In September 1809, the *Bombay Gazette*, an influential early colonial newspaper printed in the East India Company's territories on the subcontinent, reported on a horrific pirate attack. A merchant ship, the *Minerva*, captained by John Hopwood, had been the victim of Gulf-based raiders. That ship's heroic resistance and the massacre that followed made for grim reading. Casualties had been suffered during a days-long running battle between dozens of dhows, filled with pirates, and the beleaguered merchantman. More still were killed during the boarding and capture of the *Minerva*. Particularly shocking was the massacre of survivors, apart from a few who were forced to change religion or who were taken as slaves or as captives for ransom. As enumerated in the *Bombay Gazette*, the ship's captain was killed and the "2nd Officer Wounded slightly afterwards shot himself." Listed after these were other crew members, "Mr. Bijaun, David the Purser," the supercargo "Mr. John Martyne," and the passenger "Mr. Chatoor Ter Arathoon," all of whom "were massacred," along with about forty lascar sailors.[2]

News of the *Minerva*'s fate also reached the press in London and the wider British media. The *Caledonian Mercury* provided one of the fullest accounts:

> Letters from Bombay . . . mention, that the pirates in the Persian Gulph, owing to the supineness of the local government in that quarter, had increased to a most formidable body, and had carried on their depredatory warfare with unusual success, and more than usual barbarity. The Minerva, Hopwood, had been recently captured, and her passengers and crew most inhumanly treated. The list of captures [i.e., the number of ships being captured around this point] was so extensive as to force the consideration of the subject on the attention of the Bombay Government. A naval and military force had in consequence been ordered to proceed to the Gulph.[3]

As this report indicates, plans for an attack on Ras al-Khaimah – alluded to obliquely in the last sentence – had been under way even before the *Minerva* incident. News of that further outrage perpetrated on a merchant ship now furnished a fresh pretext for sending out the intervention force. When the British attack group arrived at Ras al-Khaimah, it found the captured *Minerva* in port there – a final demonstration, it seems, that this was indeed the pirates' lair.

What was the geopolitical complexion of this Gulf into which this British intervention was launched, and who were the "pirates" who were the object of this exercise in projecting imperial military power and violence, one that its sponsors framed as both punitive and pacificatory?

In the late eighteenth century, the Gulf region was awash with political upheavals, and its waters were an arena of increasingly explosive rivalries between different powers. Competition between local micropowers had characterized the region for centuries and had resulted in occasional wars at sea.[4] But by around 1800, the powers that had formerly controlled the Gulf and exercised a regulatory role in the region, namely the Ottoman Empire and the Persian Qajar dynasty, had been significantly weakened,[5] and this cleared the field for competition between aggressively expansionist micropowers. Moreover, longer-term demographic shifts had been transforming the littoral of the Arabian Peninsula as previously nomadic tribes increasingly underwent sedentarization. Additionally, the peninsula's interior had been marked over recent decades by the emergence of the Wahhabis (see below), who were now seeking to expand their influence in the coastal regions.

One group that emerged prominently in this context were the so-called Qasimi (often referred to as the "Joasmees" or "Joassamees" by the British). It was the Qasimi whose maritime power the 1809 expedition from Bombay set out to annihilate. However, the term "Qasimi" and related designations tended to be employed by the British in somewhat broad-brush terms to describe the total population of the small port towns between Ras al-Khaimah and Abu Hail (today a neighbourhood of Dubai) in the northwest of the present-day United Arab Emirates. The Qasimi were themselves composed of several subgroups, and they in turn belonged to a larger tribal confederation, the Hawalah.[6] Historians believe that several tribal groups belonging to this tribal confederation migrated from the oases of the interior of the Arabian Peninsula to the shores of the Gulf. The "Qasimi" who emerge from British discourse may therefore best be understood not as a single tribe, but rather as a group of tribes inhabiting the Musandam Peninsula and its coasts.[7]

By the end of the eighteenth century, Ras al-Khaimah, a thriving port, formed the base of Qasimi power. However, some Qasimi groups had settled in the eighteenth century along the Persian coast, notably at Bandar Lengeh. Around 1800, branches of the Qasimi tribe ruled Ras al-Khaimah and Sharjah on the Arabian coast and Bandar Lengeh on the Persian Coast. With these settlements on both shores of the Strait of Hormuz, the Qasimi commanded a strategic location in the mouth of the Gulf, enabling them to play a prominent role in the wider regional political landscape. Furthermore, since the mid-eighteenth century, the Qasimi had been pursuing an expansionist policy in the Gulf. In 1755 they established themselves on the island of Qeshm, on the Persian side of the strait, and around 1765 they also tried, without success, to seize control of Bandar Abbas and Hormuz in Persia itself. In 1777, they launched a failed attack on Bahrain.[8]

Historians estimate that around 1800, 50,000 people were living in Ras al-Khaimah, Sharjah, and Bandar Lengeh under the Sultan of Ras al-Khaimah's authority.[9] According to a British reckoning in 1808, the sheikh's forces numbered 18,000 and 20,000 men and "they possess[ed] in dhows and buglas" (i.e., large dhows), a force amounting to between one or two hundred vessels.[10] At this point around twenty-five port towns of varying size on the Persian and Arabian coasts were allied with Ras al-Khaimah.[11] The Qasimi formed what one scholar has described as an "elastic maritime confederation," one that at its height in the late eighteenth century stretched from Khor Kalba to Umm al-Quwain on the Arabian coast and from Bandar Lengeh to Bandar Abbas on the Persian coast.[12]

Ras al-Khaimah was a quintessentially maritime power. The Qasimi played a crucial role in the trading networks of the Indian Ocean. Qasimi ships transported dates to Basra, returning with silk, wood, cloth, and other products, which they traded with Yemen, India, and the African coast. Other goods traded by the Qasimi included horses from Basra and Bahrain, pearls from the Gulf, coffee from Yemen, carpets, rifles, and tobacco from Persia, and wheat from Hormuz. The Qasimi also earned their livelihood from fishing, including pearl fishing.[13]

In the correspondence between the authorities in Bombay and their representatives at Bushire in the decades prior to 1809, the Qasimi and the Gulf tribes were frequently branded as "fanatical."[14] The Gulf tribes were described as resembling a seagoing branch of the Wahhabis, in that they were conducting a holy war on the high seas against British ships. Connections were made between Islam and piracy. For instance, it was said that in 1808, during the attack on the *Sylph*, some of the "pirates" "performed a religious ceremony in thanks for their having had an opportunity to put so many Christians to death."[15]

Who were the Wahhabis? The beginning of the eighteenth century saw the birth in the Najd of Muhammad ibn'Abd al-Wahhab, whose fiery sermons would have a profound impact on the Arabian Peninsula. Around 1740, Muhammad ibn'Abd al-Wahhab began preaching a sort of Islamic orthodoxy, a return to a pristine Islam, to the Islam preached by the Prophet Muhammad himself, purged of all moral and religious corruption and accretions. In 1744, Muhammad ibn 'Abd al-Wahhab signed an alliance with the Al Saud house. Muhammad ibn

Saud agreed to help propagate the Wahhabi doctrine; in return, he and his successors were promised that their political ambitions would be fulfilled. Muhammad ibn Saud and his followers began rapidly expanding and strengthening their power in Najd while propagating the religious teachings of Muhammad ibnʿAbd al-Wahhab. Groups of Bedouin tribes began spreading terror in the Najd, leading terrifying raids that involved massacres, pillaging, destruction of religious monuments, and forced conversions. By 1785, Muhammad ibn Saud's armies were strong enough to begin raiding beyond central Arabia. They conquered the Hijaz province in western Arabia. The holy cities of Mecca and Medina fell to them in 1803. The Wahhabi army also threatened Ottoman Iraq by raiding the city of Kerbala, the site of one of Shiite Islam's holiest shrines, in 1802.[16]

By 1800, the entire Arabian coast of the Gulf was feeling the force of Wahhabi expansionism to varying degrees. Kuwait resisted, but Qatar and Bahrain suffered raids. In southeastern Arabia, Wahhabi influence was felt on the coast between Abu Dhabi and Ras al-Khaimah and also in Oman. Saudi armies raided Oman and the Musandam Peninsula from their regional base at the oasis of Buraimi, in the interior of Oman, which they had seized in 1800.[17] By the beginning of the nineteenth century the Wahhabi had become major political players in the Gulf region. Around this time, during this surge of Wahhabi expansionism, Qasimi attacks on British and East India Company ships reached their zenith, according to British sources. Had the Qasimi formed an alliance with the Wahhabi? Had the Qasimi converted to Wahhabism? Were the pirate attacks against British vessels a form of religious war at sea, an extension of the Wahhabi-led campaigns in the Arabian Peninsula and on the Gulf coast? Interpretations like these were advanced at the time, but they could not be wholly verified, because – as historians have emphasized – "the precise relationship between Wahhabis and Qawasim has not been fully established."[18]

The precise contours of the alliances and loyalties of the actors in the region remain unclear to this day, but in broader terms, the general shape of the Gulf region's politics at the time are easily discernable. The region was in upheaval; rival groups were continually clashing with one another. Meanwhile, British India was becoming increasingly powerful and would soon assert that power in this contested world, ultimately becoming a central actor. Its profile in the Gulf had expanded gradually, and with relative ease, over much of the later eighteenth century. By the century's final decades, however, a discourse had developed in India that labelled the Qasimi and by extension the Gulf tribes as "pirates." That discourse would ultimately be invoked to justify the organization by the Bombay Presidency, and the approval by Calcutta, of the 1809 expedition against Ras al-Khaimah.

What are we to make of the discourse around those phenomena in the Gulf region that the British termed "piracy"? A good deal of scholarly ink has been spilt on the question of piracy in and around the Gulf. Much of it has been conducted as an argument around nailing down empirical data, as if this alone would offer heuristic clarity and resolution. To be sure, this work is often of considerable scholarly interest in its own terms. From such studies, we know there were indeed many attacks on British and East India Company shipping in the region. The rate of such attacks was uneven, but it was broadly rising up until the British responded with their raid on Ras al-Khaimah in 1809. Some of these attacks involved horrific violence, at least occasionally with a religious dimension. Moreover, that maritime violence was sometimes meted out by groups living on the Arabian coast who had promised the British, more or less formally, to desist from piratical practices.

Beginning in the late 1770s, British documents mention numerous attacks by Qasimi ships against East India Company vessels. In late 1778, an East India Company vessel en route from Bombay to Basra was captured by the Qasimi. In January 1779 the *Success*, sailing from Basra to Muscat, was chased by ten dhows, escaping them only with difficulty. A month later, another attack against a Company vessel in the Gulf, the *Assistance*, resulted in a twenty-five-minute battle. Thereafter, periods when numerous vessels were attacked might be followed by years-long periods when attacks receded. In 1790, the Company ship *Beglerbeg*, bound from Bengal to Bushire, was captured by the Qasimi off the Musandam Peninsula. It has been calculated that between 1797 and 1819, eighty-seven ships were boarded and pillaged in the Gulf. During the same period, more than one hundred met a similar fate along the west coast of India and twenty-nine more were looted off the coast of southern Arabia.[19] British residents' reports state clearly that some of these attacks involved the "Joassamees"; in other cases, the evidence that the Qasimi were responsible was more tenuous. In two separate incidents in 1797, two Company ships, the *Bassein* and the *Viper*, were attacked by Qasimi dhows.[20] In 1802 and 1805 the correspondence between Bombay and Bushire mentioned "the troubled state" of the Gulf because of "formidable pirates" and "troublesome piratical dhows."[21] Among the British ships targeted in 1805 were two privately owned trading brigs, the *Shannon* and the *Trimmer*, both of which were captured.[22] The *Queen* was attacked in April 1805, and an unsuccessful attack was made that same year on a Company cruiser, the *Mornington*. The *Shannon* would be targeted again in 1807. A series of attacks in 1808 targeted the *Lively*, the *Fury*, the *Minerva*, the *Sylph*, and the *Nautilus*.[23] Where these attacks succeeded, events often reportedly unfolded in a similar manner, with the same seemingly ritualized violence: the entire crew, or part of it, was massacred; Britain was denounced; the British flag was burnt or lowered and the Qasimi flag raised.

In British imperial discourse, the Qasimi were identified as responsible for disturbing the Gulf's trading economy, including the commerce linking the region with India. Besides launching specific attacks, they were also alleged to have sought to enforce a larger extortion, in British eyes, namely by instituting a tax at the Strait of Hormuz. In 1802, the British agent in Oman, David Seton, noted that the Qasimi opposed "the free passage of these merchant dhows, carrying our flag."[24] In 1801, he stated that all the British merchants who disembarked or who were in transit at the port of Bandar Abbas, on the Persian coast east of Hormuz, had been obliged to pay for permission to enter the Gulf.[25] Both Francis Warden, Chief Secretary to the Bombay Government, and Arnold B. Kemball, the assistant to the resident at Bushire in Persia, claimed in the 1820s that taxes had been levied by the Qasimi at the beginning of the nineteenth century on anyone wanting to travel through the Strait of Hormuz or to enter ports on the Persian shore.[26] A final charge laid by the British against these antagonists was treaty-breaking: a limited treaty had been agreed to in 1806, arranged through David Seton, British agent in Oman, that involved some restitution for British losses and a Qasimi undertaking to desist from such attacks in the future. This agreement would soon be conspicuously broken.

Reconstructing the record of "pirate" attacks and the larger charge sheet the British compiled against the Qasimi allows us to explore some of the specific frictions in the Gulf that lay behind the 1809 intervention. However, this empirical approach may only take us so far, given that much of this conflict between the British and their antagonists in the Gulf may be said to have involved differing systems of signification. As various critiques have highlighted, much of the existing historiography retains a notably "Eurocentric" view of Gulf maritime activities.[27] The scholar Patricia Risso has argued, for example, that it is important to note that the word "piracy" has no real equivalent in either Arabic or Farsi.[28] The Arabic word closest to the English "piracy" is best translated as "maritime warfare" but has a broader meaning, signifying a variety of hostilities at sea. Given all this, we may well query whether British ascriptions of "piracy" are appropriate for describing the maritime violence of the Gulf in which British India became enmeshed.

The word "piracy" is used in British sources, as are "maritime warfare," "maritime violence" and "sea violence." Also mentioned are the terms "pirates," "robbers," "thieves," "looters," "freebooters," "dangerous," and "fanatical." The variety of terms suggests a struggle to define the maritime activities of the Gulf populations. This may also indicate a failure or inability on the part of the British to engage conceptually with the specific nature of the maritime societies that inhabited the Gulf and the Indian Ocean world. To some degree, the British seem to have transferred their understanding of piracy from other parts of the globe, such as the Caribbean, the Mediterranean, and the Atlantic, where there were long-established patterns of piracy, buccaneering, privateering, and "pirate" states (for example, the Barbary Coast). Seen from this perspective, the British had tied the customs of the maritime societies of the Gulf to a conceptual framework that was alien to those societies.

At a broader level, indeed, it can be said that conflicts over definitions went to the heart of the larger struggle for hegemony in the Gulf region. Military interventions undertaken there in the early nineteenth century by the British administration in India, and the latter's claims to ongoing authority over the region that issued from this, were based in part on a rhetoric about protecting free trade and the freedom of the seas. But the Gulf was not a sphere of interaction where all parties were committed to a shared set of notions along these lines, let alone a broader framework of international law. Indeed, those principles may be considered less as neutral yardsticks and more as instruments the British took up to leverage a position for themselves in the Gulf. More specifically, such discourses cannot be separated from the wider expansionist agenda of British India. As a recent study by the historian Simon Layton has concluded, the suppression of piracy in the Gulf had "as much to do with territorial expansion" as it did with the freedom of trade and navigation, with "the emerging universalisms of economic liberalism" being bound up with "a process of direct and indirect conquest" on the part of the Company polity in India. Such findings are congruent with a larger recent historiography, notably the work of Christopher Bayly, on the emerging Company state in India itself and the ideologies and imperial political economy that developed around it and thereby sustained it.[29] In this light, Layton further argues that, given there existed "a close correlation between the territorial conquest of India and the establishment of maritime power across the waterways of Indian Ocean trade," the discourse on piracy "clearly serviced each process concomitantly."[30]

Deconstructing discourses of piracy in this way opens up new possible ways to think about the conflict between British India and the so-called pirates of the Persian Gulf. In particular, it makes it feasible to consider the antagonistic parties less as polar opposites than as sharing certain affinities. For there were, arguably, significant parallels between these two actors in the region. The historical record regarding the population of the Arabian littoral of the Gulf prior to the late eighteenth century remains scantily documented and highly moot. But one plausible hypothetical scholarly reconstruction of the region's history during this period would suggest that it was precisely during the 1700s that nomadic tribalism was giving way to sedentarism, in substantive and transformative ways. This may well have brought about a demographic boom and an ensuing nexus of political and religious upheavals, notably Wahhabism. Put another way, we might view the late eighteenth-century Gulf as space where two expanding regional actors increasingly overlapped, competed, and then violently collided – with those actors being, on the one hand, the so-called pirate polities such as Ras al-Khaimah, and, on the other hand, the aggressively expanding British presence in India.

In this context, what the British labelled piracy may be better understood as a method by which the Qasimi signalled their claims to this space against perceived challenges. Seen in that light, such attacks would appear to have been a way for the Qasimi to "mark" their power over the Gulf's waters and to strengthen their domination in a context of increased political and economic competition. They were symbolic acts by which the Qasimi made it clear that they viewed the passage of British ships through Gulf waters as a threat or as competition; that is, they were communicating that they intended to play a leading role in the Gulf and to defend that role. Note, in this context, that the British were not the only targets of "pirate" attacks; it seems that Qasimi expansionism also aimed to encroach on Omani interests through similar attacks. Indeed, different actors had for centuries resorted to maritime warfare in the Gulf and the wider Indian Ocean so as to signal their power at the expense of other regional players.[31] Thus, patterns of maritime plunder can be viewed as having been historically endemic in the Gulf and as part of the broader rhythms of economic life and survival for its societies.

This phenomenon of "piracy" may further be illuminated, at least in comparative perspective, through the use of terms proposed by the cultural anthropologist Jatin Dua, who recently described a political economy of piracy in the twenty-first-century western Indian Ocean as an "economy of protection"; thus, piracy should be understood as "a form of work" and a "claim to political authority," albeit one that may operate only when there are no other forms of subsistence. In Dua's account, this contemporary picture has close echoes with what prevailed in the region in the early nineteenth century.[32] In this reading, attacks and maritime warfare may in fact signal significant socio-economic stress. Indeed, Gulf maritime economies were particularly sensitive to environmental changes as well as to economic downturns and demographic shifts. A move toward compensatory predation activities may therefore have been in some measure a response to economic stress. By way of comparison, we know that during times of resource stress in the Arabian Peninsula, tribes engaged in raids on neighbouring tribes to procure basic commodities.[33]

Seen from this perspective, the increase in pirate raids at the end of the eighteenth century as described in British sources might be read as indicating not just geopolitical rivalry but also a highly unstable socio-economic situation in the Gulf. In this respect, the somewhat later testimony of one woman who was well-placed to observe British policy in the Gulf may be cited: during the second attack on Ras al-Khaimah in 1819, Anne Thompson accompanied her husband, Captain Thomas P. Thompson, who was an interpreter for the expedition's commander, Major General William G. Keir. From the deck of the *Orient*, an East India Company warship, Thompson witnessed Ras al-Khaimah's destruction. She described the "Qawasim" as a "race of devout robbers" but added that this was not their usual activity: "they fish, both for food and pearls, and cultivate dates; piracy was only a save-all."[34]

The French Threat

While "piracy" was the immediate pretext the British gave for intervening in the Gulf in 1809, a larger spectre lay behind this: the global rivalry with France and a sense of the specific threats this might entail for India. As recent scholarship on the Napoleonic Wars has emphasized, these were conflicts with global dimensions. They encompassed spaces such as the Ottoman Empire, Persia, the fringes of the Russian Empire in the Caucasus, the Indian Ocean world, and, not least, the Gulf and its micropowers. As the Napoleonic conflict seeped into this region, new strategic importance was taken on by points on the map such as Oman, the Arabian hinterlands, and a host of the Gulf's maritime and littoral spaces such as its islands, straits, and ports – Ras-El Khaimah being one of them.[35]

The key moment in all these developments was France's Egyptian expedition of 1798. The French capture of Alexandria and then Cairo in July of that year, and their subsequent military occupation of Egypt and campaigning onwards as far as Syria, constituted a spectacular surprise that upended the existing strategic map of the world. One element of this new conjuncture was that it appeared to leave British India suddenly exposed.[36] The sudden and unexpected occupation of Egypt was a demonstration of France's newly aggressive foreign policy. The British saw the events in Egypt, which came less than a decade after the storming of the Bastille, as a sign that the French Revolution had crossed not only France's borders but also those of Europe.[37] Also notable was that the expedition went against France's traditional policy in the Levant of "defending" the Ottoman Empire. From this new vantage point, a world of new ambitions for France – and of dangers for British India – appeared possible. A letter sent to the governor general of India, Wellesley, by an East India Company official in late 1798 testifies to the anxiety caused by the French incursion into Egypt: "We cannot doubt for a moment that the French Republic would try to exploit this situation to introduce into India the revolutionary machinations she has successfully employed in almost all parts of Europe. We have to extirpate the French presence in Egypt and as quickly as possible."[38] Finally, another wild card thrown down by this new situation was the man of the moment, Napoleon Bonaparte, the young general who had led the French expedition. His rapid victories in Egypt, and his military campaigns in Syria, put a seal on his fast-growing reputation as a strategic factor in his own right; indeed, within a few years he would hold dictatorial powers in France and launch a program of imperial expansion.

At the time, it had almost been forgotten that French operations on the subcontinent had once posed a plausible threat to British India: the brief heyday of French fortunes there had come in the first half of the eighteenth century, notably under the leadership of General Dupleix. Most recent French incursions directed toward India had relied instead on the French navy and had been staged from French-occupied islands in the Indian Ocean, where French-held strategic points included especially Mauritius and Réunion in the Mascarene Islands.[39] The British had been able to counter these efforts with relative ease. But after the summer of 1798, with a powerful French army occupying Egypt, India seemed at risk not just from the familiar pattern of French naval threats, but potentially also from land invasion along a corridor of attack through the Red Sea or the Gulf region. From there, encroachment on India would be an obvious next step, and indeed Napoleon might theoretically use this axis to despatch an invasion force. Such a project would directly threaten the British presence in India and in the Indian Ocean world. As a leading Company official in India, James Augustus Grant, would write in May 1799 in a letter to

Duncan, the Governor of Bombay, "General Buonaparte's" expedition into Egypt was developing "the dangerous machinations of the French Directory against the English Power in India."[40]

This menacing context led British government ministers and the East India Company's leaders to reassess both land and maritime approaches to India. The precautionary investigations they undertook provided various indications suggesting that Egypt might indeed be just one step in Napoleon's broader plans and that his true aim might be the destruction of British power in India. Following the arrival of news of the landing of French forces in Egypt, Captain Samuel Wilson, a Company official, was despatched from Bombay to Arabia with a view to monitoring and influencing developments in the region. This paid dividends in early 1799 when he intercepted a bundle of letters sent by Napoleon to a number of rulers in Arabia and the Gulf region and on the Indian subcontinent. One of these letters was addressed to the Sharif of Mecca, Amir Ghalib, with whom Napoleon had already been engaged in correspondence for some months.[41] In another of the letters, written at Cairo on 25 January 1799, Napoleon sought to establish links with a new interlocutor, the Sultan of Oman. His letter sought to foster diplomatic amity and to encourage maritime commerce between Oman and French-occupied Suez. More explosively still, it included a request that the sultan arrange the forwarding onwards of an enclosed letter addressed to Tippu Sahib, the Sultan of Mysore.

Tippu Sahib had long been the Company's most feared opponent on the subcontinent. In writing to him, Napoleon announced himself to be at Suez with an "innumerable and invincible army." He proclaimed his wish "of delivering you from the Iron yoke of England."[42] By seeking contact with Tippu Sahib, Napoleon was fulfilling a part of the mission designed by the Directory government in Paris. Egypt was just a step: according to his instructions, "as soon as he became master of Egypt," Napoleon was to "establish relations with the Indian princes, and, together with them, attack the British in their possessions."[43] Indeed, in a letter to the Directory in December 1798, Napoleon indicated that he had received reports that the mere presence of the French in Egypt was already having an influence on events on the subcontinent: "It seems that our arrival in Egypt has given a high idea

Figure 1.2 John Clark after Richard Temple, "Muskat, from the Harbour," from *Sixteen views of places in the Persian Gulph taken in the years 1809–10.*

of our power in India and has produced a very unfavourable effect on the English; fighting is underway there."[44]

Fears of a French threat would rapidly catalyze a nascent sub-imperialism of British India in the Gulf. In the aftermath of events in Egypt in 1798, the administration in British India moved quickly to reinforce its diplomatic and military arrangements in the region. In particular, the governor of the Bombay Presidency, Jonathan Duncan, asked Mirza Mahdi Ali Khan Bahadur, the British resident at Bushire, to travel to Muscat to sign a treaty with the Sultan of Oman.[45] The sultan's possessions at that time included not only Oman itself but also Zanzibar and parts of the African coast; all these territories represented potential staging points for any French expedition aimed at India. These negotiations bore fruit with an agreement signed on 12 October 1798 declaring that if French vessels attacked East India Company ships, the sultan's fleet would help the British.[46] The treaty with Oman would become a keystone of the Company's policy of seeking alliances with local powers in the Gulf.[47] Duncan tasked Mirza Mahdi Ali Khan Bahadur with a further mission in the autumn of 1798: he was to negotiate an agreement with Fath'Ali Shah of Persia. This attempt was a failure, as the shah merely promised to detain any Frenchmen found along the Persian coast.[48] Yet the effort provides a further indication of broader attempts by officials in British India at this juncture to strengthen their influence in the Gulf region. Oman would become an important military ally, and its ports, such as Muscat, would offer key staging posts for subsequent British interventions in the region (Figure 1.2).

Military countermeasures were another aspect of British efforts. One focus of attention was the Red Sea, to which a naval squadron commanded by Rear-Admiral John Blankett would be sent from Britain. It arrived in the spring of 1799 with a view to deterring further French advances beyond Egypt. Another expedition was organized from Bombay in early 1799 to occupy the island of Perim in the Bab-el-Mandeb, the strait that controlled the mouth of the Red Sea. It was anticipated that a garrison and naval force at Perim would be able to block any French move to send forces from Egypt through the Red Sea for an attack on India. This proved to be an exaggeration of Perim's strategic value, however, and the troops sent there would ultimately be withdrawn.[49]

Around the same time, Napoleon's efforts to contact Tippu Sahib led to major military endeavours on the subcontinent itself. Rumours of Tippu Sahib's sympathy for Napoleon and the French Revolution caused alarm in India; there were concerns that he might provide a powerful force in furtherance of French designs. Such concerns were not restricted to Mysore: another powerful Indian ruler, the Nizam of Hyderabad, was known for having once had French officers in his army, and some of them were still present at his court in 1798.[50] To block French ambitions in India, Wellesley targeted their supposed key ally on the subcontinent, Tippu Sahib. That conflict reached its apogee in mid-1799, when Tippu Sahib died during the capture of Mysore's capital, Seringapatam. From Wellesley's perspective, this was a major victory for Britain, one that made the success of any French expedition to the subcontinent far less likely. As he wrote, "If Bonaparte should now choose to visit Malabar, I trust he will find supper prepared for him before he has reached Calcutta."[51] Discoveries among documents captured at Seringapatam suggested that Tippu Sahib had permitted the establishment by French expatriates there of a club whose activities included celebrating the French Revolution and planting a Tree of Liberty. For the British, this served to confirm their assessment that attempts had been under way to bring revolutionary subversion to the subcontinent, which would have favoured French interests.[52]

Another response by the government in India to the French threats in Egypt came later in 1799. Wellesley sent an emissary, John Malcolm, to sign a treaty of alliance with Persia in order to continue reinforcing the Company's influence in the Gulf region. Wellesley's instructions were to "counteract the possible attempts of those villainous but active democrats, the French."[53] Malcolm would become a significant figure in the history of Britain's involvement in the Gulf.[54] Travelling with an extensive entourage, he was received at the court of Fath'Ali Shah in November 1800, and went on to negotiate a series of political and commercial accords.[55] These treaties, agreed in January 1801, were never fully validated, since Hajj Khalil Khan, the Persian envoy who travelled to India to undertake their ratification, was killed in a riot in Bombay in 1802 before they could be concluded. When news of this Persian envoy's accidental death reached Paris, it was a boon to French propaganda: in the Napoleonic press, the episode was cast as a "murder" and as yet another instance of British misgovernment in India.[56] Nonetheless, these exchanges between Persia and British India marked a significant diplomatic overture.

Malcolm also succeeded in reinforcing links with Oman. On the way to Tehran, he stopped at Muscat, where in January 1800 he convinced Sultan bin Ahmad to accept a resident Company representative.[57] During his stay in Muscat, he and Sultan bin Ahmad also signed a treaty in which the sultan recognized France as an "enemy." This treaty was a reaffirmation of that of 1798.[58]

As part of this mission, Malcolm also toured the Gulf in search of sites of strategic interest. Notably, he focused on Bundar Abbas in the Strait of Hormuz, Bushire on the Persian coast in the upper Gulf, and the islands of Bahrain, Kharg, Hormuz, and Larak. In letters he sent to Wellesley, Malcolm compared the respective advantages of these various ports and islands, advocating for one or another of them to be adopted as the seat of a major new base in the Gulf for the East

India Company. Malcolm identified the need for a new linchpin for British interests in the Gulf region, one that would not be geared just toward commerce but would also have strategic importance. In many ways, then, the correspondence between Malcolm and Wellesley demonstrates how, around 1800, a perceived French threat to India was triggering a change in thinking among officials from Britain's Indian empire regarding use of the Gulf as a space of forward defence.[59]

France's Egyptian expedition would end in failure: its forces there were defeated in the summer of 1801. That defeat notwithstanding, a second phase in the history of the perceived French threat to British India can be traced over the following years. The immediate threat had been headed off, yet it was obvious that the British colonies on the subcontinent remained vulnerable. So too did the threat posed by France and Russia against the Ottoman Empire, which was a key buffer state for British India.[60] For Wellesley, the failure of French endeavours in Egypt and Syria would not of itself put a stop to France's ambitions for India; indeed, it might reactivate them. As Wellesley declared in the autumn of 1801, the French remained intent on positioning themselves in the Red Sea, the Indian Ocean, and the "countries adjacent to the Arabian Gulf." From these places, they could threaten British colonies on the subcontinent.[61] Occasional episodes in the Gulf chimed with such British fears. On 8 September 1801, for instance, a French frigate was spotted cruising off Kharg Island.[62]

While the idea of a French encroachment on India, organized from the Gulf or from one of the French islands in the Indian Ocean, was becoming a kind of received wisdom among East India Company officials, the sense of threat went beyond this. A moment of real crisis occurred, and from an unexpected angle, in the wake of a major diplomatic shift in alliances that saw Russia turn from being Britain's ally against France during much of the 1790s to become France's ally against Britain by the end of 1800. This change of heart of the Russian tsar, Paul I, culminated in secret negotiations with Napoleon with a view to a joint invasion of British India. This plan envisaged sending 70,000 men on this distant expedition, half of whom were to be provided by France. French troops would travel down the Danube River and cross the Black Sea, then await Russian reinforcements at Astrakhan. In February 1801, on the orders of the tsar, an army of Don Cossacks set off on a march to Astrakhan. However, Paul I's murder in March 1801 put an end to this whole project.[63]

The Treaty of Amiens between Britain and France brought a pause in outright hostilities over 1802–3.[64] But this fourteen-month interlude was also a time of escalating diplomatic tensions and jockeying for position in the Orient. In 1802, the French ambassador at Constantinople signed a treaty with Sultan Selim III that mutually guaranteed the integrity of the French and Ottoman possessions and granted France various privileges in the Ottoman Empire. Alarm in India about French ambitions was compounded by a high-profile episode that played out around the French general Horace Sebastiani. On 30 January 1803 a special extended edition was published of France's newspaper of record, the *Moniteur*, featuring a lengthy report regarding a tour Sebastiani had just undertaken of North Africa, Egypt, and the Levant.[65] Sebastiani had been ordered on this mission with a view to reviving French commercial interests in various parts of the Ottoman Empire; at the same time, he would be surveying these regions from a military perspective. But the venture's larger purpose, and the point of publicizing it so prominently, was to impress upon the British that France had lost none of its interest in the Orient and to underscore that renewed French interventionism in Egypt and beyond was entirely plausible.[66] With this British audience in mind, the *Moniteur* text was conspicuously republished in the recently launched *Argus*, a Paris-based newspaper written in English that served as a propaganda vehicle for the French regime.[67] Leading British officials, including the prime minister, William Pitt, perceived Sebastiani's mission as a demonstration that Napoleon's designs on British colonies in India had not faded.[68]

Following the collapse of the Treaty of Amiens in May 1803, Napoleon launched a multipronged diplomatic and military effort to apply pressure against British India. One aspect of this involved maritime warfare. A French naval squadron commanded by Admiral Charles-Alexandre Linois and comprising the flagship *Marengo*, the frigates *Atalante*, *Belle-Poule* and *Sémillante*, and various transport and ancillary vessels had departed from Brest in March 1803 for the Indian Ocean.[69] This force would be stationed at Mauritius, where it would provide the basis for a French strategy of sending naval raiders to harry the shipping and commerce of British India. The French ships engaged in this effort – some of them from Linois's force and others privateers – had some notable successes in the resulting campaign.[70] British naval forces had a fundamental numerical advantage, but given the enormous maritime spaces involved, they had considerable difficulty in stopping the French attacks. The Gulf was a notable theatre of these conflicts, and French ships often caused great damage before finally being intercepted. For example, the privateer *La Fortune* was captured in late 1804 in the waters off Muscat by HMS *Concorde* after a twelve-hour pursuit. Satisfied, the British ship's captain, John Wood, declared that he was "particularly happy in taking *La Fortune*" and thereby putting an end to the damage this French vessel had been inflicting: "She must have done great damage to the Trade on this coast, being a remarkable fast vessel, and her command well acquainted with every part thereof."[71] Indeed, *La Fortune*, under its Captain Le Même, had struck hard in the Gulf over recent months, capturing a series of British ships, notably the Company brig *Fly*.[72] In 1805, another French privateer, the *Bellone*, armed with thirty-six cannons, was seen in the Bay of Muscat.[73]

French representatives also attempted to suborn British India's network of diplomatic alliances in the region. General Charles-Mathieu-Isidore Decaen was based in the Mascarenes from early 1803. Napoleon had originally charged him to lead an expedition to restore French authority in Pondicherry, which the British had seized in 1793. This initial mission had proved to be a dead letter, however, for the British had no intention of restoring this Indian enclave to France at a time when the Treaty of Amiens was fast unravelling.[74] With the renewal of hostilities, Decaen, based in Mauritius, would instead seek to challenge British India via its alliance with Oman. He sent a French representative named Jean-Baptiste Cavaignac to Muscat with a view to setting him up as consul there. But when Cavaignac arrived at Muscat in October 1803, on the French warship *Atalante*, Sultan bin Ahmad refused to receive the French envoy.[75] Accepting a French consul in Oman would have breached the treaty that Oman and Britain had signed in 1798. This potential French representation in Muscat was seen as sufficiently dangerous a prospect to India that the Governor of the Bombay Presidency issued a pointed warning to the sultan, declaring that "if the

French obtain a footing at Muscat on any terms or in any situation, all communications between Muscat and India must cease."[76]

Around this time, rumours spread in 1805 and 1806 that Napoleon was aiming to establish a French toehold on the strategically positioned island of Kamaran in the Red Sea.[77] If true, this French project would be a genuine threat: from Kamaran and the Mascarenes, the French might be able to launch a naval expedition at India. Other French activities may have been unknown to the British: in 1804, for example, Decaen had welcomed in Mauritius two envoys from Mocha, both of them Bania merchants.[78] Adding to British fears, French efforts in Oman in 1806 and 1807 appeared to be gathering pace. Indeed, in June 1807 Decaen would sign a "perpetual and inviolable" peace treaty with Sayyid Majid, Sayyid Said's envoy. In the end, Paris did not ratify this treaty; even so, that Decaen had negotiated it indicated a favourable turn in French fortunes after Cavaignac's failure.[79]

Ultimately, however, Persia would become the strongest focus of Napoleon's efforts in the region. One secondary effect of the Egyptian expedition had been to highlight the importance of Qajar Persia for European powers. Could Persia become a foothold for the French? Malcolm's mission to Tehran in 1800–1 demonstrated that Wellesley and other Company representatives in India feared as much, although Napoleon's retreat from Egypt gave the British a brief respite.[80] On the face of it, such fears were far-fetched. France and Persia had not maintained formal diplomatic ties since the fall of the Safavid dynasty in 1722. A diplomatic mission had been sent by Paris in 1795, but it had failed, with the two French envoys, Jean Guillaume Bruguière and Guillaume Antoine Olivier, returning empty-handed.[81] But from 1803, Napoleon would seek a diplomatic rapprochement, with a series of new contacts with Tehran launched via French officials in Constantinople, Baghdad, and Aleppo.[82] This was part of an imperial strategy to build an alliance against two of his enemies: Britain of course was targeted, but so too was Russia. Napoleon envisaged an alliance with Persia, building on a rapprochement with the Ottoman Empire he was pursuing at the same time, as a way of asserting French influence in the East.

In 1805, two diplomatic missions were organized from Paris, involving respectively Pierre Amédée Jaubert, a specialist in oriental languages, and Antoine-Alexandre Romieu, an army general. Travelling to Tehran by separate routes, they each had the task of collecting information on Persia and gaining the favour of Fath'Ali Shah. Romieu's mission was short-lived, for he died soon after his arrival. But before his death he had sent a report to Paris that emphasized the shah's frustration with Britain and his readiness to negotiate with France.[83] Jaubert, who arrived in Tehran later, then picked up the baton of negotiations.[84]

Next, a Persian envoy, Mirza Mohammed Reza-Qazvini, was despatched to sign a formal alliance with Napoleon. He travelled via Constantinople, where he met in late 1806 with the French ambassador, Sebastiani; after that meeting, several French officers were despatched to Tehran to advise the Persian army. The Persian envoy then travelled on to meet Napoleon, who was at that point in Prussia, and their subsequent negotiations resulted in the signing of the Treaty of Finckenstein in May 1807. This important agreement marked a new formal relationship between France and Persia.[85] The treaty demonstrated the extent of Napoleon's ambitions in the East, extending from Russia to India, and his ultimate desire to leverage Persia's position in order to threaten the western flank of the British Empire on the subcontinent. Notably, Fath'Ali Shah promised to provide bases for a French naval squadron in the Persian Gulf.[86] The event would later be commemorated in visual form as a French diplomatic triumph and as a symbol of the world stage on which the Napoleonic empire had come to operate (Figure 1.3).

By signing the Treaty of Finckenstein, Fath'Ali Shah had effectively placed himself in contradiction with the never-formalized treaty that Malcolm had negotiated with him in 1801, which had laid out "conditions of mutual aid and assistance" between Britain and Persia, including that "all causes of hatred and hostility shall be banished between the two countries."[87] British India appeared to have lost a crucial diplomatic battle for Persian alliance. In the wake of the treaty, Napoleon tasked one of his generals, Gardane, with leading a French military mission to Persia. Gardane was the grandson of Ange de Gardane, Louis XIV's envoy to the Savafid court in the early eighteenth century. The build-up to his arrival in Persia was carefully orchestrated.[88] Napoleon's detailed instructions to Gardane illustrated the scope and ambition of France's imperial projects in the East. He underscored that

Figure 1.3 François-Henri Mulard, *Napoleon receiving the ambassador of Persia*, 1810.

Persia was important to France for two main reasons, first its enmity with Russia, and second its strategic location for a potential invasion of India.[89] Gardane's main task was to gather information about Persia's armies and about communication routes and ports in the Qajar Empire and the Persian Gulf.

French machinations in Persia, real or imagined, came under close surveillance by British India. From 1806 the rumour spread in Bushire and in India that Fath'Ali Shah would be likely to sell or cede the Persian port of Bandar Abbas in the Strait of Hormuz to the French.[90] As fears of an alliance between Persia, France, and the Ottoman Empire threatened to become a reality, the British sent an expeditionary force to Egypt, occupying Alexandria in early 1807. Later that year, the government in India was greatly alarmed by the signing of the Treaty of

Finckenstein between France and Persia. A French invasion of India seemed to be looming via Persia and the Gulf. In the autumn of 1807, the Governor of the Bombay Presidency received reports from Muscat that the French had received a promise from Fath'Ali Shah that he would cede two strategic footholds, Bandar Abbas in the Strait of Hormuz and Kharg in the upper Gulf.[91] In November 1807, the British resident in Bushire, Nicholas Hankey Smith, reiterated his concern that the French might be strengthening their presence in the Gulf, possibly as a prelude to an expedition against India. The French were also said to be surveying the Gulf waters, particularly around the island of Hormuz.[92]

However, by the time of Gardane's arrival in Tehran in December 1807, with more than forty people in his diplomatic party, wider geopolitical transformations meant that the Treaty of Finckenstein no longer held much strategic value.[93] Napoleon had defeated the Russians at the Battle of Friedland in June 1807; the two powers had signed the Treaty of Tilsit the following month. The diplomatic situation had thus completely changed, and Gardane's mission was therefore refocused on the more limited objective of modernizing the Persian armies.[94] Two French infantry officers, Lamy and Verdier, were tasked with training the "New Army," or Nezame Jadid. At the same time, Gardane sent two artillery officers, Fabvier and Reboul, to Isfahan to establish a cannon foundry intended to strengthen the Persian artillery.[95]

Gardane's mission, so ambitiously conceived, had lost much of its original animating purpose; nevertheless, the presence of Napoleon's envoys at Tehran in and of itself was a source of great anxiety for the East India Company. In 1807 rumours reached Bombay and Calcutta that part of a French army stationed in eastern Europe had set off across Turkey in the direction of the Gulf and that a French naval flotilla had left La Rochelle and was heading toward the Gulf. Another sensational account purported to reveal that the French had assembled 50,000 men in Persia, notably at Bandar Abbas and on the island of Kharg, and that they were preparing to move on India.[96] From this vantage point, Napoleon's troops might within a matter of weeks be shipped to the Malabar Coast, or alternatively might attack India via a land route through Sindh. The Earl of Minto, recently installed in India as governor general in place of Wellesley, was in October 1807 expressing anxiety about France's "great diligence" in developing "subversions" and "intrigues."[97] Furthermore, noted Minto, "the western side of India" was the "most important and immediate object of vigilance."[98] In January 1808 he expanded on this theme, writing that one favoured project of the French in Persia was "believed to be to take possession of a port on the coast of the Persian Gulf, by which they may communicate with the Mauritius, and receive supplies by sea, and from whence they may attempt an invasion of the western coast of India."[99]

Although none of these anticipated attacks ultimately materialized, the threat long continued to be felt. In November of that year, the British resident at Bushire maintained that the French delegation was far more numerous than Gardane's mere presence suggested and that the scheme in which the French were engaged at Fath'Ali Shah's court was far more menacing than first appeared.[100] For the East India Company, the Franco-Persian rapprochement and the presence of French envoys in Tehran seemed to have rendered anything possible, and Napoleon's project of invading India now seemed tangibly close. In the words of Mountstuart Elphinstone, a future Governor of the Bombay Presidency, at this juncture "it appeared as if the French intended to carry the war into Asia."[101]

Shortly after Gardane's arrival in Persia, a small naval squadron from Bombay was despatched to the Gulf to present a show of strength, arriving there in February 1808. Minto originally wanted to send a far larger naval and military force to emphasize British power. But he ultimately dropped this plan as one which, given that Persia was not a maritime power, would have had little effect.[102] The commander of this naval expedition reported having observed the activities around the coast of a number of French individuals who were assumed to be working for Gardane. These Frenchmen had supposedly obtained a Persian *firman*, or decree, that allowed them to move freely, and they had headed toward strategic sites such as Bandar Abbas, Qeshm, Shiraz, and Muscat. The British assumed that their intention was to sign trade agreements and to make political contacts. In particular, two of these men, "Messieurs Frezél et Dupré," were seeking to advance France's economic and political interests; one of them introduced himself as the brother of the French ambassador at the shah's court.[103] British efforts in this respect had produced intelligence that seemed reliable. Adrien

Figures 1.4 and 1.5 Unknown Persian artist, *The Court of Fathʿ Ali Shah at the Nowrooz Salaam Ceremony*, details showing British (*above*) and French (*opposite*) ambassadors, c. 1830.

Dupré and Camille Alphonse Trézel were indeed two members of the French legation, and Trézel was an engineer and geographer tasked with surveying routes and ports.[104] At the very least, the news from Persia maintained the climate of fear in Bombay and Calcutta.

Minto's larger response to Gardane's presence was a diplomatic effort, with the sending of an envoy to Fathʿ Ali Shah's court. The man selected for this role was Malcolm, who was well-versed with Persian affairs on account of his earlier career there and who had since 1803 been the resident in Mysore. Invested with plenipotentiary powers that would

enable him to negotiate both with Shah of Persia and with powers elsewhere in the Gulf, Malcolm had a complicated task. London had at the same time appointed its own representative in Persia in 1807, Sir Harford Jones, who was also familiar with Gulf affairs, having served as East India Company resident in Baghdad from 1798 to 1806.[105] The overlap between these two missions might reinforce both but might also cause friction. It was with reference to this context of rival diplomatic parties courting the Shah of Persia for preference that a series of commemorative wall murals would later be made for the palace at Nigaristan, depicting successive rival French and British diplomatic visitors (Figures 1.4 and 1.5).[106]

Minto's instructions to Malcolm demonstrate the anxieties instilled by the French presence in Persia and the Company's growing desire to become a political force in the Gulf. Malcolm's first task was to "detach the Court of Persia from the French alliance, and to prevail on that Court to refuse the passage of French troops through the territories subject to Persia."[107] That meant he would have to obstruct the progress of the French in Persia, prevent the signing of alliances between France and local powers in the Gulf and Oman, and impede the creation of French establishments on any of the Gulf islands. Malcolm was also instructed to obtain information regarding the true nature of the treaties and engagements signed between France and Persia and to assess the attitude of Fath'Ali Shah's government toward the French. If he found that a French expedition to India actually was in train, he was also to seek intelligence as to the route that Napoleon's armies would take and how much aid the shah had promised. A final task for Malcolm was to prepare Kharg for occupation by a small garrison. Minto regarded Kharg as a useful forward British base in the event of military operations against Persia and France, should conflict prove unavoidable.[108]

Malcolm arrived at Bushire in May 1808 with an impressive escort of around five hundred sepoys, conducted by three frigates. Gardane threatened to leave Persia if the British envoy was allowed at the shah's court. Fath'Ali Shah was keen to preserve his alliance with France, which seemed to offer greater advantages in Persia's conflict with Russia. Accordingly, he refused to receive Malcolm in Tehran and permitted him to communicate only with provincial authorities. Malcolm's second mission thus ended in considerable tensions with Persia, with the British envoy taking Fath'Ali Shah to task for not upholding provisions of the 1801 treaty and threatening a British military intervention if Gardane were not expelled. In short, Malcolm's second mission to Persia was a notable failure.

However, Sir Harford Jones's mission met with a measure of success. Unlike Malcolm, he was regarded by the shah as embodying the authority of the British government, so he was allowed to proceed to Tehran. He arrived there in February 1809, laden with gifts, and received a favourable reception. Emphasizing the advantages of an

Anglo-Iranian alliance, Jones promised the shah an annual subsidy of £120,000 for as long as the war with Russia lasted.[109] The envoy also offered the shah British expertise in training Persian troops. These negotiations resulted in a second Anglo-Iranian treaty, signed by Jones and Fath'Ali Shah in March 1809. This diplomatic success relieved the pressure that the East India Company had been feeling for several years. Britain promised to train and equip the Persian army and to intervene if Persia were attacked by a European power. For Persia, the signing of this treaty led to the cancellation of all earlier treaties signed with European powers, first and foremost the one with France.[110]

This new treaty, even if signed by a diplomat sent by London and not by Minto's envoy, would be part of a process whereby the Company's territories in India were secured on their western flank in the Gulf region. Fath'Ali Shah had promised not to undertake any "engagements inimical to Britain" or "pregnant with injury and disadvantage" to British territories in India.[111] The treaty also confirmed an earlier 1763 trade agreement under which British and Indian merchants of the East India Company had received permission to establish themselves at Persian ports and were exempted from taxes.[112] With the conclusion of this Anglo-Persian alliance, the Franco-Persian rapprochement had become void. Shortly before Jones obtained his treaty with the shah, Gardane left Tehran. Jones had thus succeeded in strengthening diplomatic ties between Britain and Persia and in effectively displacing the French.[113] In May 1809, Jones's secretary James J. Morier left Tehran for London with a Persian envoy, Mirza Abul Hasan, to ratify the treaty at the court of George III.[114]

For Minto, even if the prospect of a Franco-Persian expedition directed at India appeared to have receded, the contrast between Jones's success and Malcolm's crushing failure raised difficulties in its own right. The inability of the two envoys to present a united front at the Persian court created tensions between India and London. Minto would send Malcolm on a third mission to Persia in 1810 with a view to restoring the Company's prestige at the shah's court; yet Jones was confirmed the same year as the official envoy of the British government. Nevertheless, all the efforts the French had put into forging a relationship with Persia had ultimately come to nothing.

The Attack on Ras al-Khaimah and British India's Expansionism

With Gardane's departure from Tehran, Napoleon had in effect retreated from West Asia. The possibility of a French encroachment in the region, aimed ultimately at India, seemed therefore to vanish in late 1808 and 1809. With the collapse of Napoleon's projects, the London press was able to express self-congratulatory relief regarding a strategic turnaround in the Gulf region. An article in the *Morning Post* at the end of 1809 spelled out this view:

> The manner in which the intrigues of the French at the Court of Ispahan [i.e., Persia] were defeated, and their efforts, not only to fix their influence over the Persian Councils, but to establish themselves in the Persian Gulph, rendered abortive, does great credit to our Government. The French had actually succeeded in negociating a treaty with Persia, by which an island in the Persian Gulph was to be ceded to them, the possession of which would have been of the greatest detriment to us … – A glance at the Map will suffice to shew the great value we ought to set upon the friendship of Persia.[115]

Around the same juncture, Napoleon's armies were bogged down in Spain. The year 1809 also seemed to mark a break in French expansionist efforts beyond Europe: territorial losses included Guiana, Martinique, Saint-Domingue (Haiti), and Senegal. From one point of view, then, it seems that the tide had turned on the previously ascendant Napoleonic empire, putting paid to its hopes of aggrandizement at British expense in pivotal spaces such as West Asia.

Why, then, was the attack on Ras al-Khaimah undertaken, if "the intrigues of the French" in the region had been defeated? Perhaps a lingering sense of danger from Napoleonic surprises helped precipitate British India's shift toward direct military intervention in the Gulf region. In December 1808, after the failure of Malcolm's second mission, Calcutta and Bombay had agreed in outline on the need to despatch a punitive expedition against the "Joassamees" of Ras al-Khaimah. At this point memories remained fresh of the Franco-Russian peace treaty signed at Tilsit in 1807 and of Napoleon's rapprochement in

Persia. The aims of the planned Gulf expedition and its immediate context, as described by its architects in the British administrations on the subcontinent, were clear enough: it was intended to enforce British influence in regions west of the "British territories in India" that their "European enemies" – including France, of course – might threaten to dominate.[116] At the same time, the instructions regarding the expedition's wider scope were significantly more hazy. Notably, it was envisaged that, as a further task, the expedition might permanently station troops on an appropriate (but unspecified) island off the coast of Persia. This was seen as a possible solution to the challenge of ensuring safe passage on the seas to guarantee future communication between Basra and India.[117]

As this latter and more inchoate aspect of the plans developed by British India suggests, the sense of a threat from France around the Gulf can be seen as a key ingredient, but not the only one, in Britain's rising ambitions in the region. French machinations in Persia, rather than being a single issue that faded away once it had been overcome, had stimulated a wider discussion in Bombay about the Company's presence in the Gulf. Since his first mission in Persia, Malcolm had reflected on the need to reform the Company's system of residencies and agencies in the Gulf. In December 1808, he proposed to Minto that the residencies of Basra and Bushire be transferred to Kharg, the strategic island of which he had failed to take possession during his second mission. He also advocated closing the agency in Muscat. These measures, he argued, would help reduce the costs of the Company's presence in the Gulf and would also ensure greater coordination and influence. Kharg was ideally located and would allow easy communications with Basra and Bushire as well as Bahrein. Malcolm conceived Kharg both as a commercial entrepôt on the trade routes criss-crossing the Persian and Ottoman Empires and the Arabian Peninsula, and as a strategic and political outpost. A single resident, seconded by two assistants and a surgeon, would be stationed there permanently and would represent the Company in the Gulf. The Residency would be fortified and guarded by a significant detachment of sepoys and artillery.

In the end, this proposed expedition to Kharg envisaged as part of Malcolm's 1808 mission to Persia never happened, even though Minto and Duncan had set preparations in motion to this end, assembling a force of two thousand men in the harbour of Bombay when Malcolm had left for Persia. Why did Minto and Duncan subsequently agree on attacking Ras al-Khaimah instead of pursuing that earlier plan of occupying Kharg and reforming the Company's system in the Gulf region? In the words of Minto, in 1809, the Company could not risk taking possession of Kharg: "We cannot commit hostilities on Persia when the King of England is negotiating with the King of Persia."[118] The occupation of the island by East India Company troops would have amounted to a declaration of war against a country that was now bound in a diplomatic agreement with Britain. Attacking Ras al-Khaimah offered an alternative means for Bombay and Calcutta to demonstrate strength in the Gulf waters and to impress Fathʿ Ali Shah, whose choices from 1806 to favour the French over the British as allies had seemed to place Britain's colonies on the subcontinent at risk of Napoleonic impingements and even invasion.

The campaign that ultimately took shape around the Ras Al-Khaimah expedition was brief but intense, and its history can be reconstructed in some detail. The Bombay Presidency confirmed on 7 September 1809 its plan to target Ras al-Khaimah, having received the green light from Calcutta some weeks earlier. The expedition was declared as being directed "exclusively against the piratical branch of that tribe which has so long infested the commerce of India and the Gulf."[119] On 14 September 1809 the British expedition left Bombay under the command of Captain John Wainwright. Lieutenant-Colonel Lionel Smith was in charge of the large force of infantry and cavalry that boarded the ships *Chiffon*, *Caroline*, *Minerva*, *Friendship*, *Duncan*, and *Mary*. Eight East India Company fighting ships completed the flotilla. After stopping at Muscat for provisions on 23 October, the squadron burned between fifty and seventy Qasimi ships in the bay of Ras al-Khaimah on 11 November. The next day, the town itself was subjected to a three-hour bombardment. On 13 November, British troops disembarked and launched a land-based assault on the town, which surrendered after a few hours. British losses were minor, with three killed and ten wounded; in all these conflicts, the casualty rate among their outgunned opponents appears to have been much higher.

The British squadron then rapidly set sail for other "pirate" lairs along the Persian side of the Strait of Hormuz. These smaller operations mainly involved destroying flotillas in lesser ports allied with the Qasimi sultan. Notably, on 17 November at Bandar Lengeh, twenty dhows were destroyed. The *Chiffon*, the *Caroline*, and the cruisers *Mornington*, *Ternate*, *Nautilus*, and *Fury*, as well as two troop transport ships carrying around five hundred men, next sailed for Luft, on the northern coast of the island of Qeshm. In the battles that led to Luft's surrender, the British lost eight men, with twenty-three wounded.

Along with allied troops from the Sultan of Oman, on 3 January 1810 Wainwright and Smith's forces attacked the port of Shinas on the Batinah coast, north of Muscat. The inhabitants put up a noteworthy resistance, but Shinas ultimately capitulated on 4 January. Khor Fakkan, a port on the Sea of Oman, remained in Wahhabi hands because the British were reluctant to attack it after being resisted so strongly at Shinas. Thus, at the beginning of February 1810, Lieutenant-Colonel Smith's troops were able to return to Bombay. The operation was over.

Reconstructing the history of the Ras al-Khaimah campaign allows us to place it in the context of wider military and diplomatic efforts being undertaken by British India, whether on the subcontinent itself or more widely in its peripheral regions and indeed at a global level encompassing South and Southeast Asia and the Indian Ocean as a whole. Reviewed from this perspective, the sense of the French threat may be seen as inextricably interwoven with a larger policy of expansionism on the part of the Indian presidencies. Tracing any precise line between these two elements may be an impossible task. Yet what may be most significant is how far the dynamics of aggrandizement observable in the actions of the administrations of British India were such as to overstep significantly the realities and the chronology of actual French threats in this part of the globe. While certainly the attack on Ras al-Khaimah and the Qasimi strongholds must be associated with the perceived need to maintain alliance with Persia, and to dissuade it from any future rapprochement with France, it needs also to be understood within a broader geopolitical vision. This wider context involved the creation by the Indian presidencies, through diplomatic and military means, of an immense buffer zone intended to protect the British colonies on the subcontinent. But the creation of such a buffer zone also amounted to a policy of imperial expansion in both direct and indirect ways. By attacking Ras al-Khaimah, the British were pursuing an expansionist policy on the Arabian side of the Gulf even while continuing their policy of selectively targeting perceived opponents and building a system of alliances.

Seen from this point of view, the Gulf fits within a much larger realm of activities stretching across the Indian Ocean and touching many of its hinterlands. One early focus of these efforts was the sea routes connecting Europe to India, especially the key strategic nexus around the Cape of Good Hope. The British had occupied the Cape Colony for the first time between 1795 and 1803, at which point the Treaty of Amiens had required that it be returned to the Batavian Republic. In January 1806, however, after a brief blockade, the British seized the Cape and occupied it anew. The invasion in 1795 had ended nearly a century and a half of the Dutch East India Company's rule there.[120] As it safeguarded the route to India, the Cape became key to the exercise of British naval power in the East, just like Gibraltar ensured Britain a privileged position in the Mediterranean. The Cape would form a sort of midpoint for the British Empire, between its old territorial interests in the Atlantic and the new centre of empire in India, West Asia, and the Indian Ocean.

The East India Company also concentrated its efforts from the late 1790s around the Indian Ocean itself. The Seychelles were taken in 1794, and Ceylon was taken from the Dutch in 1796 by troops sent from Madras. In addition, Malacca was occupied in 1795, given back after the Treaty of Amiens in 1802, and then reoccupied in 1807.[121] Other diplomatic and military endeavours led by the presidencies then took place in West Asia connected to the East India Company's strategy for protecting India against a French land attack. Besides attempting to secure India's maritime approaches, Calcutta and Bombay made concentrated efforts to bolster its territorial approaches. Military actions were combined with diplomatic attention encompassing, as Minto wrote in 1808, "the countries of several independent chiefs situated between Persia and the Company's possessions."[122]

First, there was a diplomatic mission to Afghanistan.[123] This was intended to block any invading French army that might attempt to invade India through Persia and Afghanistan. In July 1808 the British envoy Mountstuart Elphinstone travelled to Peshawar to meet Shah Shujah Durrani with an "unusually numerous escort" of four thousand men, six hundred camels, and thirteen elephants.[124] Since the late eighteenth century, the Durrani empire had suffered territorial losses. Even so, as of 1808 Shah Shujah still reigned over extensive territories northwest of the subcontinent corresponding more or less to present-day Afghanistan. The mission's aim was to elicit Afghan cooperation against Russia and France, with these being obtained in exchange for a promise to provide weapons. Elphinstone highlighted the desirability of preventing "that country falling into the hands of the French; for if they were once in possession of it, their invasion of our territories would no longer be a great and desperate enterprise."[125] The convoy arrived in Peshawar in February 1809, and the two sides signed a treaty in April.[126]

Around the same time as Elphinstone's mission, a further diplomatic venture against the background of the perceived French threat involved the sending of another Company official, Charles Metcalfe, to secure the cooperation of the Punjab ruler Ranjit Singh.[127] Meanwhile, also in late 1808, just as Malcolm had left Bombay for Persia for his second mission, the East India Company's representative in Muscat, Captain David Seton, would set out for Hyderabad and the court of the Sindh emirs with a small detachment of the Bombay Infantry. Rumours had spread that the three Sindh emirs who ruled over swathes of territories located north of the Bombay Presidency had made contact with the French and with the Shah of Persia against their mutual enemy, Afghanistan. While in Hyderabad, Seton obtained that the emirs would not allow the French into Sindh, with this again being negotiated in exchange for British support in arms and provisions. This treaty of friendship also allowed the Company to open factories in Sindh.[128] Yet another marker of the East India Company administration's attempt to secure the land approaches to India was Henry Pottinger's mission in Baluchistan in 1809–10. Pottinger and another Company officer, Charles Christie, travelled from Bombay to "explore the Baluch country and the east of Persia." The two lieutenants travelled from Nushki in Baluchistan to Isfahan in Persia and gathered significant information about these territories.[129]

A new series of military operations in the Indian Ocean world followed to complete these diplomatic rapprochements. The British plan expanded in 1809–11 with the conquest of the French Mascarenes. In

August 1809 the British seized the island of Rodrigues. From there, in July 1810, a large contingent of British soldiers and Indian sepoys landed on Île Bonaparte (Réunion). The island quickly capitulated and was placed under the authority of a British colonial governor, Robert Farquhar. One last island remained in French possession, Mauritius, where the French put up fierce resistance. In November 1810, Mauritius fell and Decaen surrendered, after a military operation involving more than 6,500 men and nearly seventy warships.[130] In May 1811, the fall of the two French trading outposts on Madagascar, Tamatave and Foulpointe, confirmed British dominance in the western Indian Ocean. Minto further extended his military efforts against the French presence east of the subcontinent, completing the system protecting the Indian colonies of the East India Company through strategic conquests in the Indonesian archipelago. Java, including present-day Jakarta, and various islands in Indonesia had been under the influence of the Dutch East India Company since the seventeenth century; but in 1795, with the French occupation of the Dutch Republic, the Dutch East Indies had fallen into the possession of France. From 1810, Minto organized naval operations that gradually seized all former Dutch colonies that were under French governance, such as the island of Amboyna, the Banda Islands, and the Dutch Spice Islands (Maluku Islands). In September 1811, Java and its dependencies (Timor, Macassar, and Palembang) fell to the British, and Stamford Raffles was appointed lieutenant-governor.[131]

Through these several efforts, a buffer zone was created around India, both on land and at sea, extending around 1810 – after the attack on Ras al-Khaimah – from the Gulf to territories located northwest of the subcontinent, and encompassing the western Indian Ocean. This was a huge protective cordon, intended to safeguard access to the subcontinent. Through military operations and diplomatic alliances, Wellesley and Minto had built a system for guarding the approaches to India. The Gulf already played a central role in this, connecting British strongholds in the western Indian Ocean with allied powers in West Asia.

An imperial discourse developed in India that conflated maritime hostilities in the Gulf with "piracy" was invoked to justify the attack on Ras al-Khaimah in 1809. Behind this, as this chapter has explored, may be seen the spectre that arose in 1798 of a French threat to India. Even if this menace was as much imagined as real, it helped stimulate a desire on the part of the Indian presidencies to gain a footing in the Gulf. More precisely, however, concerns over France may be said to have catalyzed a larger process by which the Company was increasingly concerned about affirming its authority in the Gulf region. This involved not only military operations against the Qasimi but also the forging of alliances with Oman and Persia; and all of this occurred against a backdrop of intense territorial conquests in India itself. Ultimately this logic of aggrandizement would continue even as the notion of a French threat faded away. This new policy of the East India Company in the Gulf region reflects the changing nature of the Company itself, which by the end of the eighteenth century had become a political power.[132] The Gulf region, seen in this light, was one of the territories protecting the emerging British Empire in India, one link in a long chain that included Afghanistan, the Mascarenes, and more.

Seen against the backdrop of these larger historical trends, therefore, the 1809 expedition centring on Ras al-Khaimah might appear to have been overdetermined. At the time, however, the Company's policies in the Gulf and beyond may have appeared to be far more contingent and uncertain; a significant degree of confusion and disagreement over policy would continue to mark debates among officials long after the expedition. It was also the case that, while ostensibly a success, the interventionism of 1809 had not eclipsed all potential rivals for domination in the Gulf region itself, nor had it resolved the question of the longer-term governance of this part of British India's peripheral regions. Within a few years, British sources would again begin mentioning new pirate attacks against Gulf shipping. Rapidly, in the context of a perceived renewal of the Qasimi threat, a debate around the nature of the involvement of the Company in the Gulf would began to take shape in Bombay and Calcutta. Thus, in 1809, the slow transformation of the Gulf into the border of water and sand of the British Empire in India was only beginning. This process would witness decisive steps over the following decades, which the next chapter examines.

2

"Pax Britannica" in the Gulf?

Strategies for Indirect Rule, 1810–1853

WHILE THE MILITARY INTERVENTION launched in 1809 from British India against Ras al-Khaimah had, in purely military terms, been frameable as a success, its aftermath was far less clear-cut. The intervention had occasioned a multitude of celebratory representations – drawings, prints, and written accounts – that applauded Britain's success in subduing by armed force a restive periphery of the rising British imperial power on the subcontinent. Revealingly, however, over the following decades, little attention would be paid to the Gulf region by British image-makers and publicists. The confused and uncertain situation of British India's imperial engagement in the Gulf over these years was not a subject that invited further celebration; indeed, it raised ideologically troubling questions about the nature, coherence, and sustainability of the imperial project.

Placed in a broader context, the 1809 expedition may be seen as Janus-faced in its repercussions. On the one hand, it was a powerful and bloody indication of just how far the interests of British imperial power had become tied up with the Gulf – or, put another way, how the British had encroached on this maritime space. This was a marker of the burgeoning colonial and trading nexus constituted by the East India Company's semi-independent polity on the subcontinent, a phenomenon that had grown to the point that it had acquired its own regional sphere of influence and vulnerability, of which the Gulf was a salient part. The punitive mission of 1809 had been efficiently carried out, achieving a symbolic reversal in response to the "pirate" attacks of previous years that had made British and East India Company shipping interests appear to be an easy target. On the other hand, however, the Ras al-Khaimah attack in many ways highlighted the effective lack, as yet, of any broader or long-term strategy on the part of the British administrations in India for dealing with this complex and unfamiliar region. Intervention had been a violent declaration of the extended purview and reach of British India into an increasingly important part of its periphery; however, the 1809 attack also bore testament to the inconsistencies and unevenness of British policy in the Gulf, which seemed to veer between extremes of neglect and sudden applications of force. Tellingly, there appeared to be no plan for what to do after the military intervention force had left the region.

Such a policy vision, which in 1809 remained remarkable mainly for its absence, did gradually coalesce over the following decades. This chapter explores how, over these years, expansionist British India, having stumbled into a role in the Gulf over the later eighteenth and early nineteenth centuries, engaged in an extended process of trial and error, and improvisation and debate, in a triangle involving multiple actors in London, on the subcontinent, and in the Gulf itself. The first part of the discussion presented here examines the aftermath of the 1809 expedition – which was quickly recognized by the British authorities in India as having gained them no lasting security in the Gulf region – as well as the debates about ideas of empire in the Gulf over the ensuing decade, which ultimately led to a second intervention against Ras al-Khaimah in 1819. In the second part, the Company's difficulties and setbacks in the 1820s are highlighted. The final section analyzes a key moment in the history of British imperialism, the engineering of the "trucial" system, which would be developed from initiatives starting in the mid-1830s and would establish and enforce peace at sea in the Gulf. The trucial template inaugurated at this juncture would be of profound importance for the Gulf's future, and its influence would last well into the twentieth century. It also marked the beginning of a process whereby a terraqueous region that had been the site of long-standing ambitions for the British, but also something of a sea of trouble for them, would be secured and transformed into a borderland guarding British India's western flank.

Through this process, the Gulf would become the object of a kind of indirect rule. Scholars have recognized how policies of imperial indirect rule owed a crucial debt of inspiration to the example of British

India.[1] Over the preceding decades, the British had developed a model for gathering the profits of empire in India while minimizing its costs and responsibilities, allowing local rulers to remain in place even while dominating and instrumentalizing them for the advantage of Britain's East India Company. The Company's involvement in the Gulf as this developed over the first half of the nineteenth century, as retraced here, may be seen as to some extent a borrowing of this indirect-rule template from British India. But as will be seen, the adaptation of the Company's practices in India to the context of managing the Gulf came about only belatedly, and almost haphazardly, after a range of other options had been tested and exhausted. Equally, the model of indirect rule could not simply be transplanted wholesale from the Indian context: it needed to be rethought and transformed for the particular situation and challenges of the Gulf. The focus here is on the key juncture of 1810–53, a period of intense debates in India over the Company's imperial policy in the Gulf. As will be seen, Company officials held a multitude of views about the governance of the Gulf, and there was no single, agreed-upon imperial objective. Instead, what may be observed is a range of often discordant strategic perspectives, and a correspondingly uneven range of interventions in the Gulf itself, which fluctuated depending on the date, on geographical and institutional context, and on ideological affinity.

Back to the Future: Intervening Anew in the Gulf, 1819

The Bombay Presidency's intervention in the Gulf in 1809 had been intended as a decisive counterstroke to the problem of "piracy" or maritime warfare in the region and the threat this posed to the interests of British India. But according to the correspondence conducted over ensuing years between the residents and Bombay, the expedition's aftermath was a disappointment to such hopes. Indeed, rather than being extinguished, piracy seemed to have taken on new shapes. After 1809 a series of independent "pirates" gained a high profile in the Gulf region. Sources mention one figure in particular, Sayyid Mohamed bin Akil, who by 1813 was being described as an "infamous Pirate" and as striking terror in Gulf waters.[2] Inquiries elicited the information that Bin Akil resided "at a place called Dofar" (i.e., Dhofar), with his situation there being one "perfectly independent of any other Arab state."[3]

More broadly, the 1809 expedition against Ras al-Khaimah had been only a very partial blow to Qasimi expansionism in the Gulf region; the Qasimi network of alliances had survived. After 1809, the Qasimi had rebuilt their fleet, which by 1815 amounted to 89 large dhows and 161 smaller ones, manned by more than 10,000 fighting men.[4] In a letter addressed to Bombay in August 1815, the resident at Bushire, William Bruce, described a catastrophic state of affairs in the Gulf. Qasimi attacks were being launched at "vessels bearing British flags and colour" and were "not confined to vessels belonging to Foreign States." Attacks that summer on ships in the Strait of Hormuz had included the targeting of an Omani dhow and a ship that had sailed from the Malabar Coast. The pirates had pillaged the two ships' cargoes of rice and wood before massacring the crews.[5] Also in 1815 the Qasimi captured a *baggala* belonging to the Sultan of Oman, Sayyid Said. The following year, there were multiple attacks: a French schooner and an American ship fell victim to the Qasimi, and four Company ships were also attacked.[6] The assault on one of the latter, the *Sylph*, was particularly shocking. After boarding the ship, the pirates ceremoniously killed almost the entire crew before seizing gunpowder and weapons.[7]

Even more remarkably, the Qasimi seemed to have extended the sphere of their operations. In 1813 they launched two attacks north of Bombay in the waters off Porbandar, a port city of the Kathiawar Peninsula in today's Gujarat state.[8] In 1816 the Qasimi ventured as far as the Red Sea, where they captured three ships flying the British flag.[9] Attacks continued over the following years, notably in the Gulf and the Arabian Sea.[10] Letters exchanged between the Company's representatives underscored the barbaric treatment of the ships' crews captured by the Qasimi. According to one report, the pirates were accustomed to "knocking out the Brains" of their victims with "a Hatchet or with a hammer" and to "cut[ting] the flesh off the Bones into small pieces" and "throw[ing] the Carcass overboard."[11]

In response to this surge in piracy, in December 1816 the Governor of Bombay, Sir Evan Nepean, raised the prospect of a second British expedition in the Gulf. He received approval for this from the governor general, Francis Rawdon Hastings, 2nd Earl of Moira (soon to be made Marquess of Hastings).[12] Hastings, however, delayed the intervention for various reasons. One was that by 1817 the Company had no spare troops for service outside of India because of the second war against the Maharatas (1817–19) and the Pindari War (1818–19).[13] Moreover, in January 1818 the Company's Court of Directors laid down that "a pacific and unambitious policy" was in the interests of "the Company's Government in India in the years ahead."[14] In other words, no new responsibilities were to be assumed beyond the limits of the Company's territories on the subcontinent.

But Nepean and Hastings still had to address what they perceived as the unfinished business of the 1809 Gulf expedition. Thus, in the autumn of 1818 Hastings suggested to Nepean that the Company invite Mehmed Ali's son, Ibrahim Pasha, to participate in a joint expedition against the Qasimi, with his troops converging with forces that would be sent from India. It was also hoped that after this second intervention, Ibrahim Pasha's men might garrison Ras al-Khaimah.[15] Who was Ibrahim Pasha, whom Hastings considered an ally against Qasimi expansionism? In the aftermath of the French occupation of Egypt, the Porte had welcomed the rise to power in Egypt of Mehmed Ali, a fine military strategist of Albanian origin and an active reformer. In 1805, he had become the *vali* (governor) of Egypt and had received the honorary title of pasha. Since 1813, on the Porte's behalf, he and his son Ibrahim Pasha had been leading a successful campaign against the Wahhabis to restore Ottoman power in the Arabian Peninsula.[16] In late 1818, a few weeks after Hastings put forward the idea of cooperation between Britain and Egypt, Bushire reported the fall of the Wahhabi capital, Dariya, and the arrival of Egyptian troops on the coast of eastern Arabia.[17] In January 1819, upon receiving the news of this major setback for the Wahhabis, Hastings wrote to Ibrahim Pasha, mentioning reports circulating in the Gulf and India that, after his success against the Wahhabis, he was now ready to defeat the latter's Qasimi allies. In his letter Hastings framed a potential intervention against the Qasimi as the logical follow-up to the Egyptian military operations in Arabia.[18] If Ibrahim shared this view, Hastings asked that he establish contact with Nepean.[19]

With this in mind, in April 1819 Nepean presented a plan to the Bombay Council for a political settlement in the Gulf after the envisaged intervention against the Qasimi. That plan promised to provide for the security of the Gulf waters without involving the Company in any unwelcome obligations. Nepean's project relied on the cooperation of the Company's oldest ally in the Gulf, the Sultan of Oman, on the assistance of Ibrahim Pasha, and on the establishment of a British base near the Strait of Hormuz, with Qeshm Island being the likely site.[20] The Arabian coast from Ras al-Khaimah to Kuwait would be placed under Egyptian authority; the coast north of Ras al-Khaimah, Bahrain, and the Musandam Peninsula would be under Sayyid Said's authority.

Nepean's plan did not receive the approval he expected. During discussions held in Bombay in April 1819, Nepean encountered fierce opposition from Francis Warden, Chief Secretary to the Bombay Government and a member of the Bombay Council. Warden thought that Nepean's political vision seemed risky. The Gulf region was unstable, and alliances were volatile. Nepean's plan would inevitably drag the Company into local political and territorial disputes. For instance, Nepean's idea of placing Bahrain under Sayyid Said's authority risked creating tensions with Persia, which regarded Bahrain as its exclusive domain.[21] For Warden, the eradication of piracy had to remain the presidency's top priority. As far as British interests were concerned, it was a "perfectly immaterial" matter, he argued, "to what Power or Powers the different islands and ports on the Persian and Arabian shores may devolve, provided the main and sole object of our solicitude, the complete suppression of piracy, be attained."[22] Some council members saw merit in Warden's arguments.

Faced with this divided opinion, Nepean agreed to delay any decision until Ibrahim Pasha's views on the Company's proposal that he participate in the future political settlement of the Gulf became known. He further agreed that the approach to Ibrahim Pasha should be made in person rather than in writing.[23] Nepean chose Captain George F. Sadleir of the British army to conduct a diplomatic mission to Ibrahim Pasha and determine "the nature of Ibrahim Pasha's views in the further prosecution of his conquests in the Arabian shores of the Persian Gulf."[24] Sadleir was familiar with the affairs of the Gulf region. He had taken part in the 1809 expedition, and in 1812 he and Gore Ouseley had been part of a small team of officers sent to Tehran to modernize the Persian army.[25]

Sadleir received his instructions in April 1819. That May, en route to the Arabian Peninsula, he stopped at Muscat to discuss with Sayyid Said the sultan's willingness to collaborate with the British and the Egyptians on a future expedition against Ras al-Khaimah. Sadleir failed to obtain Said's cooperation, which it had been hoped might be elicited on account of the 1798 treaty. Sayyid Said made it clear to Sadleir that he was suspicious of Nepean's scheme. He feared that if Ibrahim Pasha's sphere of influence in the Gulf reached as far as Ras al-Khaimah and the Musandam Peninsula, his own sultanate might be absorbed into the future pasha's domain. Also, Sayyid Said himself coveted Bahrain and so was not well disposed to the possibility that the island might be placed under Egyptian tutelage.[26]

In June, Sadleir sailed on to Qatif. From there, he departed on his mission.[27] His chances of success were probably quite slim, and in fact his mission was a failure. In the first place, Ibrahim Pasha and his father had no obvious interest in supporting the Company's imperialism in the Gulf; moreover, in spring 1819, having accomplished the mission entrusted to him by the Porte, Ibrahim and his troops were about to evacuate Arabia. Nevertheless, during Sadleir's 12,000-mile journey, which took him from Qatif in the Gulf to the Red Sea, the envoy gathered a considerable amount of geographical information about the Arabian Peninsula.[28] He followed Ibrahim and his troops as they retreated from the Hasa in eastern Arabia and marched toward the Hijaz and Medina. The Company's envoy was granted two meetings with Ibrahim Pasha on 8 and 9 September 1819, on the plain near Medina. Sadleir would recount that he had been "received courteously" by Ibrahim Pasha at the first meeting on 8 September. The following morning, he again met with Ibrahim, this time presenting him with a ceremonial sword he had brought from Bombay, as well as a letter from Nepean in which the Governor of Bombay suggested that the Company and the pasha cooperate against the Qasimi. Ibrahim responded that he could not give a definite answer until he had referred the matter to his father.[29]

While Sadleir was carrying out his mission, Nepean had independently concluded, based on information received from Bushire, that cooperation with Ibrahim Pasha in reducing Qasimi expansionism in the Gulf would not be forthcoming.[30] Sadleir's mission had thus been overtaken by events before it had even been completed. In the summer of 1819, Nepean drew up an alternative plan for securing the Arabian coast of the Gulf; this one omitted the Egyptian support he had envisaged in his previous calculations. This plan, which otherwise differed little from what had been proposed before, was laid before the Bombay Council on 21 July.[31] The placing of a garrison on Qeshm Island remained a priority. The plan favoured Sayyid Said, who would receive authority not only over the Arabian coast north of Ras al-Khaimah, but also over Bahrain. Once again, the council was divided over Nepean's ambitions.[32] Council members agreed, however, on one point, namely the need for a British base in the Gulf. Warden's intervention in relation to the wider thrust of this second plan was once again critical. To support his argument, he assembled a great many documents on the Gulf tribes, notably historical memoranda he had compiled from government records.[33] He particularly objected to Britain placing Bahrain under Sayyid Said's rule. In Warden's view, such a move would antagonize the Al Khalifa of Bahrain and would inevitably lead to a surge in maritime warfare in the Gulf. Furthermore, he felt that the Company should not support Sayyid Said's imperialism in the Gulf. In his view, Sayyid Said's ambitions in the Gulf, and those of his father, Sultan Bin Ahmad, had been responsible for much of the recent turmoil and violence in Gulf waters.[34]

Nepean dismissed Warden's arguments and forwarded his plan to Hastings, who wrote back in August 1819. Hastings expressed no opinion on the problem of Bahrain. On two points, however, the governor general was insistent: a permanent British military establishment was most undesirable, and equally undesirable was "all interference in the concerns of the Arab states," excepting only "what may be necessary for the suppression of piracy."[35] For Nepean, Hastings's response was quite disconcerting. On the sole point regarding which Nepean had received the approval of the council – a permanent military base in the Gulf – Hastings had expressed his disapproval. On the other points, the governor general had left Nepean without any guidance.

Nepean decided nonetheless to go ahead, and in October, British Major General Sir William G. Keir, who had been appointed commander-in-chief for this new expedition against Ras al-Khaimah, received his instructions. Keir was to sail to Ras al-Khaimah, capture the town, and annihilate the Qasimi fleet. He was then to proceed to the ports allied with the Qasimi on the Persian and Arabian coasts – Rams, Sharjah, Jazirat al-Hamra, and Ajman – and destroy their ships. After the capture of Ras al-Khaimah, the city was to be garrisoned by a small British force. Keir had one final task: to determine the best location for a permanent military base in the Gulf.[36] The objectives of Keir's mission were clear and detailed, but no instructions were provided regarding the aftermath of the operations. Months of discussions among Bombay Council members and lengthy exchanges between Hastings and Nepean had not solved the fundamental question of what the Company's future role in the Gulf was to be.

On 3 November 1819, the troops assembled by Keir set off from Bombay for Ras al-Khaimah. The military force that sailed for the Gulf consisted of 3,500 British soldiers and sepoys on board two Royal Navy ships and one belonging to the Company. These ships were joined in the Gulf by another navy vessel, HMS *Eden*, and seven more Company ships.[37] Sayyid Said had agreed to dispatch 4,000 men overland to Ras al-Khaimah to assist in the assault on the city and to participate in the attack with three warships. Further support from Sayyid Said would include fresh provisions for the troops and a sizable flotilla of small boats for landing troops.[38] This expedition was a powerful one, as powerful as the Indian expedition that had been despatched to Egypt in 1801 against Napoleon's troops.[39]

On 2 December the British fleet and two Omani frigates set sail for Ras al-Khaimah. Since 1809, Ras al-Khaimah's defences had been restored and significantly strengthened; the city was now protected by extensive fortifications.[40] Between four and seven thousand men were assembled at Ras al-Khaimah to resist the attack.[41] On 3 and 4 December, British troops disembarked and began the attack. On the morning of 5 December, bombardment of the city began. British forces met with strong resistance from the Qasimi for three days, but on 8 December, troops under Keir's command succeeded in breaking through the Qasimi defences and entering the city.[42] Further operations aimed against piracy continued immediately after the surrender of Ras al-Khaimah. The troops next sailed for Rams, north of Ras al-Khaimah, which they found abandoned. Its inhabitants had taken refuge at Dhayah, in the interior of the Musandam Peninsula, which was captured on 22 December.[43]

After this episode, much remained to be done according to Nepean's instructions: the fortifications of Ras al-Khaimah had to be razed, as well as all ships of a certain size.[44] Most important of all, a political settlement to end Qasimi expansionism in the Gulf had still to be reached. Time was pressing: the fleet had to leave the Gulf before the winter storms began. But Bombay's orders regarding the political settlement had yet to arrive. In the absence of clear instructions, Keir's role would be of determining importance. In early January 1820 he met with the shaykh of Ras al-Khaimah, Hasan bin-Rahmah, and told him he was being deposed by the British government. The shaykh of Sharjah, Sultan Bin Saqr, became the *de facto* ruler of Ras al-Khaimah.[45] Keir then summoned the various shaykhs of the "Pirate Coast" – as the British termed much of the Arabian littoral – with the result that Sultan Bin Saqr of Sharjah and Ras al-Khaimah, Tahnun bin Shakhbut (the shaykh of Abu Dhabi), Muhammad bin Hazza bin Zaal (the child-shaykh of Dubai, accompanied by his uncle), and the shaykhs of Ajman, Umm al-Quwain, and Jazirat al-Hamra all submitted to Keir's authority.[46] Keir also signed preliminary agreements with the shaykhs by which they agreed to deliver up all vessels in their ports other than fishing craft.[47]

To enforce the agreements he had obtained, Keir dispatched troops to search all of the ports along the "Pirate Coast," and a number of ships were burned. In January and February 1820, Keir's forces also conducted a few anti-pirate operations off the Persian coast, notably in Lingah, Asaluyeh, and Kharg Island.[48] The destruction of Ras al-Khaimah's fortifications was also undertaken: the shores of the Strait of Hormuz were denuded of what was left of its defensive walls and towers, thus extirpating the warlike infrastructure that had symbolized Qasimi expansionism in the Gulf in defiance of the Company. Just as in 1809, British "pacification" and victory had been inscribed on the land: by the beginning of 1820, Ras al-Khaimah lay in ruins and the landscape around the city was desolated, the date palm plantations having been burned. However, in a way again comparable to the aftermath of the expedition a decade earlier, the troops sent by Bombay to the Gulf had received no clear instructions on how to deal with the aftermath of their military operations or how to find a lasting political settlement with the regional powers.

Trial and Error: Improvising a Gulf Policy in the 1820s

Keir's solution to the larger policy dilemma of contriving a new model for securing the future of the Gulf under British tutelage was to organize, assisted by an Arabic interpreter, Captain Thomas P. Thompson of the British army, what became known as the General Maritime Treaty. This was signed with a series of shaykhs of the "Pirate Coast" over a period of weeks in January 1820.[49] The treaty's opening article banned "plunder and piracy by land and sea on the part of the Arabs who are parties to this contract." Plunder and piracy were very broadly defined, in the treaty's second article, as any attack committed without the sanction "of acknowledged War," which in turn was described as "that which is proclaimed, avowed, and ordered by Government against Government."[50] Articles 5 and 6 sought to establish close British control over the coasts and seas of the lower Gulf. Every vessel put to sea from the ports was to carry a register and port clearance, signed by the ruling shaykh and listing information, including the vessel's size, the names of its owner and captain, and its origin and destination. Registers and port clearances were to be produced by the boat's captain (*nakhoda*) and renewed annually, countersigned by an East India Company representative. The enforcement of the requirements for paperwork endorsed by the Company was a tool to control and discipline the tribes and monitor their movements at sea.

Yet this accord was much more than an anti-piracy treaty. It fostered a process of political unification of the Arabian coast of the Gulf. It also conferred semantic unity on that coast by labelling the different tribal groups as variously the "Arab tribes who are parties to this contract," "friendly Arabs," or "pacificated Tribes," thus erasing the tribal and political diversity of the powers arrayed along the coast from Ras al-Khaimah to Dubai. The various micro-tribal powers were considered in terms that made them almost an undifferentiated contracting party, with the treaty's opening lines declaring that "[t]here is established a lasting peace between the British Government and the Arab Tribes." Indeed, it was envisaged that in their dealings with the British government through the mediation of the resident in the Gulf, the tribes, considered in practical terms as one political entity, were to be represented by a single envoy, according to Article 6. This imperial endeavour for the ethnic and political unification of the Gulf's southwestern coast also appeared in Articles 3 and 4, which established a measure Keir hoped would restrain future piratical actions. These stipulated that a distinctive flag, red with a white border, was to be adopted by the signatory tribes, which would be required to fly it "by land and sea."

On 28 January 1820, too late to be of much use, Keir received instructions from Bombay on the policy to be followed in the Gulf. It had been sent by Mountstuart Elphinstone, who had succeeded Nepean as governor in December 1819.[51] Elphinstone urged strong measures, notably regular inspections by British cruisers of the ports and vessels of the signatory tribal powers. He also recommended that an agent be posted at Ras al-Khaimah to ensure that a piratical fleet would not be rebuilt. When he received a copy of the 1820 treaty as agreed by Keir, Elphinstone expressed his strong disapproval. He judged the maritime regulations introduced therein to be inadequate. In Elphinstone's opinion, Keir should have obtained from the signatory shaykhs both the consent to limit the size of their vessels and a more specific right of search.[52] As the scholar Patricia Risso has argued, Keir had probably deliberately avoided implementing harsh measures, such as prohibiting the import of shipbuilding timber, given that these might have curbed legitimate trade more than they did piracy. For Keir, peace could only reign in the Gulf if the Qasimi were able to reorient their activities toward non-violent trading, with this being seen as a resumption of a pattern of life that predated the disruptions occasioned by Wahhabi interference in the region.[53]

In the end, despite Elphinstone's initial reluctance, Hastings in April 1820 ratified the treaty. In the meantime, the treaty had received a further signatory, Bahrain, in February. Nevertheless, when Keir left for Bombay in March 1820, no progress had been made toward acquiring a base for the Company in the region. Keir left a small force at Ras al-Khaimah, under Thompson's command, which was transferred to Qeshm Island in July.[54] Thompson was given the title of political agent for the lower Gulf and charged with relations with the shaykhs in matters relating to the General Maritime Treaty.[55]

A serious incident in late 1820 reminded Bombay that the second expedition in the Gulf and the General Maritime Treaty had far from solved the question of piracy and maritime conflict and that the Company's relations with local powers and the degree of involvement of its delegates in local political matters remained inchoate. The background of this incident dated to a few weeks after the military detachment landed at Qeshm. Bombay at this time was planning an attack on the Bani buʿAli, a tribe in the Ash Sharqiyah region in Oman, southeast of Muscat. This tribe, which had a fighting strength of about 4,000 men, had thrown off its allegiance to Sayyid Said and embraced Wahhabism in 1818.[56] Reports from Bushire and Qeshm sent to Bombay in 1820 mentioned several Bani buʿAli "piratical" attacks committed off the coast of Oman against Omani and European vessels.[57] In the summer of 1820, Elphinstone asked Thompson to inquire about these piratical attacks and to remind the Bani buʿAli's chiefs of the Company's policy regarding piracy in the Gulf region.[58] In September 1820, Thompson sent a letter to the Bani buʿAli, expressing the Company's concern about piracy, which the shaykh of Ras al Hadd, a port in southern Oman, volunteered to carry to the tribe's chiefs.[59] On 20 September, having travelled on board a Company cruiser, the shaykh of Ras al Hadd arrived in the Ash Sharqiyah region off the port of Al Ashkharah, the place of residence of the shaykhs of the Bani buʿAli. Almost as soon as he landed, he was attacked and killed by a group of Bani buʿAli.[60] When news of the attack reached him, Thompson embarked for Muscat with a force of troops. Sayyid Said had already informed Thompson in August that he was planning a September expedition against the Bani buʿAli to reassert his authority in the Ash Sharqiyah.[61] In September 1820, Sayyid Said and Thompson decided to organize a joint punitive expedition.[62] Elphinstone consented to help Sayyid Said, endorsing the plan the sultan had elaborated with Thompson. Yet he asked that Thompson's troops remain confined to the littoral and not move into the interior of the sultanate.

Elphinstone's orders arrived too late, and on 1 November the joint expedition began to march across the desert toward the Ash Sharqiyah district.[63] Historians have tended to overlook Thompson's campaign against the Bani buʿAli, even though this venture can be viewed as tantamount to a third British anti-pirate expedition in the Gulf. Just like the two interventions against Ras al-Khaimah, this punitive expedition against the Bani buʿAli was conceived as a show of strength, intended to assert dominance in the Gulf region. The crime of killing the shaykh of Ras al Hadd, who had been acting as an envoy of the Company when he was shot, had to be punished. But this time, the joint operation, despite the military superiority of the alliance, ended in a fiasco, with an attack on 9 November leading to heavy losses on the British side.[64] Having ignored Elphinstone's instructions, Thompson would be dismissed from his role as political agent for the lower Gulf and be obliged to accept responsibility for this disaster before the Bombay Council, in addition to being court-martialled.[65] For Elphinstone and the Bombay Council, Thompson's failure gave the impression that the whole purpose of the expedition had been to restore Sayyid Said's authority over the Bani buʿAli. It looked as if the Company, which had been discredited by this military fiasco, had deliberately chosen to get involved in the relations between local polities in the sultanate.[66] The sole object of his mission should have remained "the extirpation of piracy."[67]

This overhasty and unsuccessful third anti-pirate operation illustrates how the Company's delegates in Bombay and the Gulf struggled to define the Company's degree of political involvement in the region. Was the sultan of Oman an ally whom the British ought to help when his territorial sovereignty was being contested? Or should the Company's role be confined to ensuring maritime peace for the sake of safeguarding British India's economic interests in the Gulf? Thompson had been told to cooperate with Sayyid Said, but for the sole purpose of suppressing Bani buʿAli piracy. He was censured for giving the impression that British forces had been employed to restore Said's authority in a region of the Sultanate of Oman.

The expedition against the Bani buʿAli was the Company's first defeat in the Gulf region. This blow to its military prestige obscured the successes of the 1809 and 1819 expeditions. Following this humiliation, Bombay planned a fourth anti-pirate expedition in January 1821. A substantive intervention force was mobilized. In January 1821 this expedition of around 3,000 British and sepoy troops cleared Bombay harbour under the command of Major General Lionel Smith of the Bombay army.[68] The Bani buʿAli engaged in fierce resistance for nearly three months before capitulating in March. Just as at Ras al-Khaimah in 1819, symbolic attention was paid to eradicating the traces of Bani buʿAli resistance to the Company's rule: their forts and most of their dwelling places would be razed, along with their palm date plantations in the Ash Sharqiyah.[69]

After the relative success of this fourth expedition, however, the Company's position in the Gulf was again damaged a year later, in the summer of 1822, when Elphinstone had to order the evacuation of the Qeshm garrison.[70] The troops' situation there had become untenable over the course of two years. In late 1820, Fathʿ Ali Shah had handed the British chargé d'affaires in Tehran, Henry Willock, a formal demand for the immediate withdrawal of British troops; this ultimatum may well have been precipitated by the news of Thompson's defeat.[71] In the spring of 1821, Elphinstone had then sent an envoy, Andrew Jukes, a Bombay army surgeon, who was familiar with Gulf affairs, to dissuade the Persian authorities from undertaking any hostile moves against the British garrison. But Jukes's mission failed, and the inevitable rupture between Britain and Persia came in the summer of 1822, with Willock's departure from Tehran.[72] Elphinstone's subsequent decision to remove the garrison from Qeshm, however, was essentially precipitated by what came to be seen as a strategic misstep by the resident, William Bruce.[73] In the summer of 1822, Bruce had accepted the invitation of the shah's son, Hosayn Aliʿ Mirza, the prince-governor of Fars, to visit him in Shiraz to discuss matters of mutual concern to their respective governments.[74] As soon as the news of Bruce's projected visit to Shiraz arrived in Bombay, orders were sent to him to remain at Bushire, since diplomatic relations had been suspended upon Willock's departure for England.[75] Yet the orders did not arrive in time, and in late August 1822 Bruce concluded a written agreement, sometimes referred to as the "Treaty of Shiraz," with the prince. Some articles were of little significance, but the second was not: it asserted Persia's right to Bahrain. Elphinstone condemned every aspect of the agreement, which violated all principles of British policy in the Gulf, and dismissed Bruce from his post.[76] The recognition of Persia's title to Bahrain prejudiced not only the independence of the Al Khalifa but also the claims to the island of the Company's ally, the Sultan of Oman. Whatever justification there might have been for Bruce's behaviour, the episode of the Shiraz agreement demonstrates the continued multiplicity of viewpoints held by the Company's delegates regarding its policy in the Gulf. Apart from anything else, Elphinstone felt, Bruce's initiative had made the British position on Qeshm untenable; thus, in January 1823 the garrison was withdrawn from the island.[77]

As of early 1823, after four expeditions in the Gulf since 1809, the challenges of maintaining peace on the seas and of implementing the new 1820 General Maritime Treaty remained unresolved. Nepean's project of transforming the Company's presence in the Gulf by creating a military station there had largely failed. Elphinstone and the Company's appointees in the Gulf were still struggling to define what Britain's degree of involvement in local politics should be. British authorities in India wanted prestige and success in the Gulf, but at a low cost, and their position was only partly restored by the hollow retaliatory victory against the Bani buʿAli. Furthermore, the Qeshm affair and Bruce's initiatives had undermined what scholarship on British diplomacy in the region has termed a vital "Persian connection," and did so just when Russian interests were gaining ground in Persia.[78]

In the aftermaths of these setbacks, British India's imperialism in the Gulf began to move incrementally in a new and ultimately more systematized direction. One aspect of this was that a series of measures were introduced to the existing system of maritime patrols. At the end of the Bani buʿAli campaign, General Smith had toured the ports of the lower Gulf. In the report he addressed to Elphinstone in the spring of 1821, Smith advised a reform of the existing Gulf Squadron, which had been created after 1819. As part of this, he advocated that a small, mobile, and well-equipped military detachment also be kept in the Gulf. In his opinion, this was essential for the suppression of piracy.[79] Elphinstone took up most of Smith's recommendations. In 1822, on Smith's suggestion, he appointed Henry Meriton, a senior officer in the East India Company's naval forces, the Bombay Marine, as commander of the Gulf Squadron.[80] Meriton quickly worked out a plan for the squadron's organization and operations. The plan, which became known as the "watch and cruise system," was based on the assumption that six cruisers would be available for service in the Gulf, with three of them patrolling exclusively in the waters off the "Pirate Coast."[81] The squadron's officers received precise instructions regarding their conduct toward Arab shipping: all vessels of suspicious appearance were to be visited and searched, and those found to belong to tribes signatory to the General Maritime Treaty would have their register and port clearance examined. Any *nakhoda* who could not produce these documents would be warned that if found at sea again without them, his boat would be detained.[82]

Also in 1822, Elphinstone introduced a further change, this time to the structure of the Company's system of political representation in the Gulf, which was felt to have become too costly. Elphinstone decided to combine the post of political agent for the lower Gulf with that of resident of Bushire, who henceforth would be called "Resident in the Persian Gulf."[83] The residency at Baghdad, which had been established during the wars with France, was rolled up, and that at Basra was henceforth to be called the "Residency for the Upper Gulf."[84] The reform of the residency system led to a redefinition of the role of the resident in Bushire. In the late eighteenth century, the residents in Bushire and their assistants had tended to have only limited political functions, being concerned instead mainly with managing the flow of letters between Bombay, Calcutta, and British diplomats in Persia. At the onset of Britain's wars with Napoleonic France, the residents in Bushire were still mostly engaged in administration connected to commercial activities. The early nineteenth century had been characterized by French activities in Persia during the Napoleonic Wars and by increased contact between the Wahhabis and the tribes of the Arabian coast, and the need to react to these dynamics had heightened the residency's political role. In the early 1820s, however, residents in Bushire were still struggling to define their position in the Gulf, as the Treaty of Shiraz episode had demonstrated. The instructions Elphinstone sent in October 1822 to Bruce's successor, John Macleod, illustrate the new role that residents were to play for the rest of the century. Macleod's main task was to watch over the implementation of the 1820 treaty. "The suppression of piracy" was the resident's top priority, and under no circumstances was he to become involved in the internal political affairs of Persia and the Arab states of the Gulf. His main duty remained the protection of trade between India and the Gulf.[85]

On arriving at Bushire in late 1822, Macleod supervised the retreat of the garrison from Qeshm; then, in January 1823, he departed on an information-gathering mission that saw him visit much of the coast from Ras al-Khaimah to Qatar.[86] The following month he would address a report to Bombay concerning his tour. In this important document, Macleod noted that the possibility of future warfare remained present, citing the size of the Qasimi fleet: at Sharjah, for instance, he counted thirty ships, each able to transport fifty to one hundred men. Macleod also pointed out problems in applying some of the restrictive provisions of the General Maritime Treaty, notably in connection with the issuing of registers. The slave trade raised similar difficulties: while this traffic had been condemned in one of the treaty's articles, Macleod's view was that this article's wording was somewhat cloudy and that blanket enforcement was in any case largely impracticable. In this and other respects, his report emphasized that some of the most interventionist provisions of the treaty were an unsatisfactory fit for the Gulf's political, societal, and economic environment. At the same time, Macleod pointed to possible larger policy directions that might prove efficacious in rendering the Gulf a place of greater security both for its inhabitants and for British interests. He concluded that "the Arab Chiefs have at present every disposition to respect their relations with us"; he also laid it down as a principle that "[w]e ought to encourage them as much as possible to embark in commerce, and endeavour to bring them to more peaceful habits, by affording them all the protection in our power; and at the same time asserting our right to maintain the peace of the Sea."[87]

Macleod's report may be said to have marked a turning point in the history of the Company's presence in the Gulf region. In some measure, its conclusions set out how, in effect, the situation in the Gulf might prove amenable to a kind of indirect rule arrangement — an approach that had proved efficacious in the administration of British India and that could be fruitfully reinvented for the terraqueous geopolitics of the Gulf. More specifically, Macleod's account illustrated the failures of the 1820 treaty but also some of the potentialities afforded by the prevailing situation, as well as the need for further changes in the Company's imperialism in order to realize them. These ambitions would bear fruit in the 1830s with the conclusion of a new type of agreement, namely the maritime truces undertaken between the British government and the tribes of the Arabian coast.

The Trucial System: Securing the Gulf as a Borderland for British India

Besides Macleod's report, a series of wider shifts in the political landscape of the Gulf and the Arabian Peninsula pointed to a need for further changes in the Company's policy in the region. In 1820, Turki ibn Abdullah, a grandson of the founder of the first Wahhabi state, established the second Wahhabi state.[88] Between that year and 1824,

Turki conquered Najd and expelled the Egyptians from Riyadh, which became the capital of the newly founded state. From Riyadh, this renewed Wahhabi power then expanded in 1830 to the east of the Arabian Peninsula, to the Hasa and its shores, and to the south of the Musandam Peninsula, to the oasis of Buraimi. The reverberations of the Wahhabi conquests were quickly felt by the Gulf powers.[89] From Buraimi, Wahhabi troops led by the governor of the Hasa, Umar ibn Ufaisan, began threatening Oman's stability with a series of violent raids into the sultanate.[90] Sayyid Said adopted a conciliatory attitude toward the Wahhabi. In 1833, he signed an agreement with Umar ibn Ufaisan by which the two parties agreed to respect the frontiers of each other's dominions. Sayyid Said also agreed to pay a tribute to Riyadh.[91] Sayyid Said's rapid surrender to the Wahhabi threat surprised Bushire and Bombay.[92] After the accord with the Wahhabi had been signed, the existence of Oman as an independent state seemed at stake. Bushire and Bombay quickly feared that Oman would become a dependency of Riyadh, with Wahhabi rule extending from the Hasa to Oman.[93]

However, over 1833–34 a more immediate threat to the maritime peace of the Gulf region came in the form of new explosions of violence occasioned by conflicts between the Qasimi of Ras al-Khaimah and the Bani Yas of Abu Dhabi. In September and November 1833, Sultan Bin Saqr, the chief of the Qasimi, led two attacks on Abu Dhabi. In June 1834, new conflicts at sea between the Qasimi and the Bani Yas disturbed the pearl harvest.[94] Further conflicts involving additional groups erupted elsewhere along the coast. Thus, in November, on the coast of Batinah, a region that was loosely under control of the ruler of Oman, the chief of Sohar attacked another small port city, Suwayq, taking advantage of the fact that Sayyid Said was away touring his dominions in eastern Africa. One of Sayyid Said's sons organized a punitive expedition against Sohar with the help of his father's allies at the time, namely the Qasimi shaykh, the shaykh of the Bani Yas, and the shaykh of Ajman.[95] At the end of that operation, in February 1835, the Bani Yas stationed themselves off the Quoin islands in the Strait of Hormuz. From this location, the Bani Yas started harassing boats entering the Gulf. Between February and April 1835, they attacked seventeen vessels, including two flying the British colours.[96] In April 1835 the commander of the Gulf Squadron would launch a successful attack on the Bani Yas.[97]

It was in this context of Wahhabi expansion and political unrest in the Gulf that the British assistant resident in the Gulf, Samuel Hennel, would arrange a meeting at the naval depot of Basidu on Qeshm Island in May 1835 with shaykh Sultan Bin Saqr of the Qasimi of Ras al-Khaimah and Sharjah and shaykh Shakhbut al-Nahyan of the Bani Yas of Abu Dhabi.[98] The immediate goal of this encounter was a relatively minor one, namely the recovery of property seized during the recent attacks launched from Abu Dhabi on boats from Sharjah. During the discussions, however, Hennel took an initiative that would prove, quite unexpectedly, to be the key to unlocking a new and lasting pattern of indirect-style rule for the British in the Gulf. Hennel offered the two shaykhs the opportunity to sign a truce that would ban maritime warfare from May to October of that year. Hennel's idea of an all-encompassing but time-limited truce was received favourably, probably because it was fundamentally different from the agreements the Gulf shaykhs had been signing since the late eighteenth century. Notably, unlike the previous agreement, the General Maritime Treaty of 1820, this truce did not aim to ban piracy permanently. Rather, it was intended to ensure that peace at sea would reign in the Gulf during the pearling season, which normally ran from May to October, and from which the Gulf populations derived most of their revenues. From this relatively modest agreement involving these two key Gulf powers, Hennel rapidly engineered a larger accord. Seeking to take advantage of the moment, he dispatched a cruiser to Dubai and Ajman to invite their respective rulers to come to Basidu to join in and expand the conference. It thus transpired that a few days later, Shaykh Sultan Bin Saqr and Shaykh Shakhbut al-Nahyan were joined in Basidu by the chiefs of Dubai and Ajman. On 21 May the four shaykhs signed the maritime truce drafted by Hennel. In doing so they promised to abstain from maritime warfare from May through October of 1835.[99] According to the terms of the accord designed by Hennel, the suspension of hostilities at sea would be enforced by the signatory shaykhs agreeing to pay compensation for any maritime aggression committed by their subjects upon one another and, rather than retaliate, to notify the resident of any breaches of the truce.[100]

In spring 1836 the truce was renewed for a further year. This new truce resembled the first, but it was to last for eight months and included the shaykh of Umm al-Quwain.[101] From 1836 until 1843, these temporary truces were renewed each year. To enforce the truces, boats of the Gulf Squadron patrolled the pearl banks at the height of the pearl fishing season. In 1841, Bombay, on the basis of the favourable reports sent by Bushire emphasizing the satisfactory working of the trucial system, announced that it was in favour of concluding a more permanent agreement.[102] Bombay's support of the enhancement of the emergent maritime truces system at this point accorded with the broader geopolitical demands of the time.[103] In the late 1830s, two distinct geopolitical crises were coming to a head that, while not unfolding directly in the space of the Gulf itself, had nevertheless fostered a sense among policy-makers both in London and in British India that strengthening the Company's position in West Asia as a whole was a pressing imperative.

The first of these crises had developed in the 1830s against the backdrop of the growing power of the Pasha of Egypt, Mehmed Ali. In 1831, Mehmed Ali had turned against the Porte and invaded Ottoman Syria, thereby starting a war against the Ottoman sultan. Following this, he led successful campaigns in Yemen, but also in the Arabian Peninsula against the second Wahhabi state. By the late 1830s, Mehmed Ali's power stretched from Alexandria, on the Mediterranean, to the Red Sea, and from Sudan to Syria. Egyptian expansion was destabilizing the balance of power in the Orient; in particular, it threatened to overshadow the Ottoman Empire, so bringing a new urgency for European powers to address the "Eastern Question" and the region's future. These conjunctures were of vital importance to British India, whose security on its westward flank had long been predicated on the relative quiescence and stability of the Ottoman Empire.[104]

The second crisis centred on conflicts in Herat in Afghanistan that were coming to a head at around the same time, thus threatening British India's defensive framework from another front. In the summer of 1837, Muhammad Shah of Persia had marched from Tehran toward Herat, in Afghanistan, which controlled strategic land routes leading to India. Since 1828 and the signing of the Treaty of Turkmanchai, Persia and Russia had been allies. Persia's conquest of Herat would therefore provide Russia with an advance post from which to intrigue at the borders of British India.[105] The siege of Herat, which began in November 1837, accordingly alarmed both the Indian presidencies and

Whitehall. In this context, Robert Grant, the Governor of Bombay, received orders from London to dispatch a contingent of troops to the Gulf. In May 1838 more than 500 sepoys and three Royal Navy ships set sail from Bombay for the Gulf.[106] That September, the shah lifted the siege on Herat.[107]

In 1839, while government officials in London were working on a settlement with Persia and Russia, the situation in the Ottoman Empire reached a crisis point. That year, Khorshid Pasha, the commander of Egyptian troops in Najd, won a series of decisive victories against the Wahhabis and gained control of the Hasa. Khorshid Pasha then established contacts with the shaykh of Bahrain, who in June 1839 submitted to Egyptian authority.[108] Still in 1839, Ottoman Sultan Mahmud II died and was replaced by his sixteen-year-old son. With Mahmud's death, the last rampart against Mehmed Ali's ambitions in West Asia seemed to crumble. A climate of panic took hold among the Company's officials in Bushire and India, and in London the Foreign Secretary, Palmerston, also became concerned. How much of a threat did Egyptian imperialism represent to British interests in the Gulf? Was this fear justified? Probably not, for the Egyptian army did not exceed four to five thousand men, and it included in its ranks a fair proportion of irregular Bedouin fighters. An Egyptian advance in the Gulf toward British possessions in India was therefore unlikely to have been realistic around 1839.[109] However, as had been the case with French imperialism after Bonaparte's expedition in Egypt, the rumour-fuelled spectre of an Egyptian threat to the Gulf – and thus to India – seemed plausible enough to concern the Indian presidencies and the government in London.

At this juncture, concrete steps began to be taken toward reinforcing the network of territories protecting the western flank of the British colonies in India; most notably, a force was sent to occupy Aden in 1839.[110] At the same time, Palmerston began advocating for the establishment of a protectorate over Bahrain as a means to shore up Britain's position in the Gulf. In 1840, he sent an order to Bombay for an inquiry into the island's resources and regarding the possibility of an occupation by British troops. Palmerston also considered setting up a naval and military station in the Gulf. Hennel, who by this point had succeeded to the position of resident at Bushire, and Lord Auckland,

Governor General of India since 1836, disagreed with Palmerston on how to respond to the threat to British interests embodied by Mehmed Ali. In 1840 a military campaign in the Gulf was something Auckland wished to avoid, for the Company's military resources were already strained by the First Anglo-Afghan War (1839–42). Also, forces were about to be deployed from India to the Far East, on account of developments around the outbreak of the First Opium War (1839–42). Ultimately, Palmerston would abandon his idea of establishing a protectorate in Bahrain.[111] The crisis between Egypt and the Ottoman Empire finally came to an end in late 1840, after Mehmed Ali suffered a series of defeats against a coalition of British, Ottoman, Austrian, and French troops. In late 1840 he agreed to withdraw from Syria, the Hijaz, Palestine, and southern Anatolia and to reduce the size of his army and naval forces, provided that he and his descendants were assured thereafter of hereditary rule over Egypt and the Sudan.[112]

In 1843, three years after the system built by the British in the Gulf had seemed to be at Mehmed Ali's mercy, Hennel dispatched his assistant, Lieutenant Arnold B. Kemball of the British army, for discussions with the shaykhs regarding their willingness to sign a ten-year maritime truce.[113] On 1 June 1843, four signatories – Sultan Bin Saqr, shaykh of the Qasimi, Khalifa bin Shakhbut, shaykh of Abu Dhabi, Abdullah bin Rashid, shaykh of Umm al-Quwain, and Abdul Aziz bin Rashid, shaykh of Ajman – agreed to observe peace at sea for ten years. Each shaykh undertook to afford full redress for any aggressions committed by his subjects at sea upon any other party to the truce and to refrain from retaliating. He would seek redress only from the British resident, who thus acted as the proximate guarantor of the truce. Article 4 of the treaty envisaged, for the future, the principle of signing a longer-term truce if this ten-year one were to prove successful.[114]

The duration of the ten-year truce coincided with the re-establishment of Wahhabi power in central and eastern Arabia after Mehmed Ali's withdrawal in 1840. The former Wahhabi ruler, Faysal, was released from captivity in Cairo and quickly reinstated his sovereignty over Najd. Oman was again exposed to Wahhabi raids, organized from Buraimi, as early as 1845. Tensions between the British and the Wahhabi peaked in April 1851 when Hennel was informed that Faysal had asked the Al Khalifah of Bahrain to pay him tribute or face the consequences.

The Gulf Squadron blockaded the Wahhabi port of Qatif throughout July to prevent any invasion of Bahrain. In late August, Faysal announced that he had decided to abandon his project to invade Bahrain.

In this context of renewed Wahhabi expansionism in the Gulf, in March 1853 Hennel's successor, Kemball, negotiated a new truce with the shaykhs, this one more permanent.[115] Between 4 and 9 May the five shaykhs of Sharjah and Ras al-Khaimah, Umm al-Quwain, Ajman, Dubai, and Abu Dhabi signed the Perpetual Maritime Truce (also known as the Treaty of Maritime Peace in Perpetuity), thus binding themselves, their heirs, and their successors to observe "a lasting and inviolable peace from this time forth in perpetuity."[116] According to the terms used by the British, the "Pirate Coast" had thus become the "Trucial Coast." The new treaty was not very different from the 1843 truce. The only notable change was in the utopian element of the rhetoric adopted by the British. According to the vision adumbrated by the treaty, the British Empire was to be regarded as immortal, with the Perpetual Maritime Truce declared valid not just for the generation of the signatory chiefs and their immediate descendants but for eternity: "That from this date, viz. Rujjub 1269, 4th May 1853, and hereafter, there shall be a complete cessation of hostilities at sea between our respective subjects and dependents, and a perfect maritime truce shall endure between ourselves and between our successors, respectively, for evermore."

In addition to announcing this symbolically laden vision of open-ended British power in the Gulf, the Perpetual Maritime Truce took further practical steps toward enforcing the Company's authority there. Maintaining peace at sea was entrusted to the Company's representatives, the resident, and the senior naval officer commanding the Gulf Squadron, to whom any aggressions that might occur were to be reported. These men were recognized as the regulatory authorities, responsible for maintaining maritime peace. The treaty laid out in precise terms the transformation of the terraqueous lower Gulf region into a borderland of sand and water protecting British India's western flank. After decades of inconsistency, indecision, and failure in the Gulf, the signing of the successive agreements that together formed the trucial system was a great boon for the British; this new policy framework would soon lead to a dramatic shift in fortunes. Adapting methods of indirect rule to the Gulf context meant co-opting the shaykhs and promoting their economic interests under British oversight; it was also a relatively low-cost way of fostering peace in a region whose ructions had previously occasioned costly and hazardous military interventions launched from British India.

But had the shaykhs agreed freely to this framework, or had they been pressured by the British? The historian James Onley has drawn on anthropological studies in hypothesizing why the shaykhs accepted, through the truces, British "domination." Onley contends that the relationship between the British and the shaykhs in the nineteenth century was characterized by a protector/protected dynamic, and on this basis he questions the idea that the British imposed themselves on the Lower Gulf.[117] Onley's analysis involves a reconstruction of how the region's societies and economies functioned. Until the discovery of oil in the mid-twentieth century, the Gulf shaykhs' authority rested, among other things, on the size of their revenue, which rested partly on agriculture but largely on pearl fishing and trade. Social prestige – measured by the number of tribes or tribal subgroups who placed themselves under a given shaykh's protection – was another important dimension. Family power also played a role, as did military might.[118] Moreover, well into the nineteenth century the various tribal groups of the Arabian Peninsula were often at war; the rise of the Wahhabis in the late eighteenth century had also deeply transformed the political landscape. Given the scarcity of resources, an economy based on predation and raids was also of paramount importance. Violence in various forms had an essential regulatory function in these tribal societies. However, many of the tribal chiefs did not have sufficient means to protect the individuals under their authority from the recurring conflicts and the constant violence. For this reason, some shaykhs chose to place themselves under the rule of another shaykh, one who was more powerful and thus able to ensure protection. In exchange for this service, the "protected" shaykh paid a tax to the "protector" after swearing allegiance to him. The tribes of the Arabian Peninsula and Gulf region thus had their own system of relationships of "protector" and "protected."

According to Onley, if British domination was not imposed but rather was accepted by the shaykhs, it was because the British offered an alternative protector figure. In the context of Wahhabi expansion in the Arabian Peninsula, and because of the power vacuum created by the withdrawal from the Gulf region of the Qajar and Ottoman governments, the shaykhs would have seen the British as an authority capable of defending them and ensuring the peace. It is in this context, accordingly, that the multiple calls by the Gulf shaykhs and the Sultan of Oman for protection or intervention in their feuds during the nineteenth century may be situated.

Onley's theory offers a fruitful basis for discussion, and one that may perhaps be further extended.[119] In installing the trucial system, the British were seeking, after a fashion, to wipe out violence as a regulatory authority and to replace it with mediation, with that mediation being dispensed under their auspices. More precisely, British mediation substituted the existing violence among Gulf societies with another form of violence, one that the British exerted in multiple ways. The trucial system confronts the historian with a process of deculturation and transformation as much as one of integration or accommodation. In this analysis, one can say that the British aimed progressively to subvert the culture of the peoples of the Gulf region, a culture that was, within the framework of societies organized around honour and vengeance, self-regulating, with its own symbolic codes and rituals.[120]

Why then did the shaykhs accept this loss of identity, which was disguised as a transition from violence to mediation? The following suggestions do not minimize the violence of British imperialism in the Gulf, which is transparently visible in the expeditions against Ras al-Khaimah, as well as in the force that lay behind the truces. Rather, they are an attempt to expand on Onley's suggestions. Did British protection seem to the Gulf shaykhs to be a lesser threat to their authority, in the face of so much political uncertainty in the region? Perhaps the Gulf shaykhs were turning to an external power, the British, who at the time seemed less dangerous to the shaykhs' own continued regional status, to the extent that British dominance still afforded them a privileged role and enabled them to preserve their political power. Admittedly, as has been shown in this chapter, the initiative for the truces came from the Company's representatives in the Gulf, such as the residents Hennel and Kemball. But were the shaykhs not demonstrating great political pragmatism in the face of the volatile alliances in the Gulf and the weakness of the Ottoman and Persian empires? The truces signed with Britain retained and even increased the shaykhs' prestige; they also helped strengthen their authority at a time when they were regularly confronted with intertribal challenges to their rule.

Scholarship from anthropology may also be usefully cited in understanding the emergence of the trucial system in the Gulf, notably the work of Clifford Geertz, who examined "culture" as an "interworked systems of construable signs" and as "a context" within which "social events, behaviors, institutions, or processes" may be intelligibly described.[121] In the hierarchy of tribal values in the Gulf, the concept of honour played a key role. One hypothesis is that the trucial system redistributed an honour, which was then reinforced by the treaties and shared by all those who adhered to the truces. In light of this hypothesis, both the British and their regional interlocutors in the nineteenth-century Gulf may be said to have been engaged in complex strategies and to have sought to advance specific ambitions. As Onley has argued, the imposition of a "Pax Britannica" in the Gulf cannot be explained solely by the British will to install it. Perhaps, then, we might envisage interaction between the actors not only in a vertical protector/protected sense, but also in terms of a horizontal process of mutual instrumentalization. Put another way, the trucial system brought the shaykhs some "social capital", or rather some "socio-symbolic capital," and thus an increased political and symbolic status.[122] In this sense, as Onley has highlighted, the trucial system was not simply imposed, but was constructed by all signing parties, each of whom could obtain significant practical and symbolic benefits from it.

3

Maps and Surveys

The Geographical Invention of the British Gulf

IN 1828, GEORGE B. KEMPTHORNE, an officer in the East India Company's naval forces, known as the Bombay Marine, undertook a survey of the eastern coasts of the Gulf. In his account of this work, subsequently published in the *Journal of the Royal Geographical Society*, he described scorched landscapes, inhospitable islands stripped bare of vegetation, and the treacherous deep waters of the Strait of Hormuz. He interspersed his narrative with literary and historical references. Indeed, he seemed to regard his journey as a voyage into a mythical space-time. When navigating the Strait of Hormuz, Kempthorne felt he could hear the Sirens of Odysseus. Upon reaching the island of Hormuz, he was amazed to see what a desert it had become, as he recalled its glorious past under Portuguese and earlier rulers and the cargo ships of gold, silk, and spices that had once been unloaded at its ports.[1] Kempthorne's observations demonstrate how behind the official agenda of a scientific mission, nineteenth-century surveying and mapping exercises reveal the historical imaginaries, cultural representations, and imperial ideologies that informed the British vision of the region that would ultimately be called the "Middle East".[2]

The links between geography and British imperialism have been the objects of an extensive and long-standing historiography.[3] From Africa to Australia, from West to Southeast Asia, British imperialism was accompanied by hugely ambitious surveying and mapmaking expeditions.[4] Maps and nautical charts located resources, opportunities, and potential trade routes. Exploratory missions and survey campaigns that led to the production of various forms of geographical knowledge, such as maps, charts, and sketches, were all instruments of British efforts to classify the world and thereby control it. In the words of one scholar, Matthew Edney, maps and surveys "allowed Europeans to conceptualize the world and to think that they could dominate the world itself."[5] They were tools that helped legitimize and reinforce British rule in territories under their formal and informal influence.

More recent scholarship has suggested further interpretative perspectives for investigating maps and similar forms of spatial representation.[6] One of the most fertile aspects of this work has been the insistence that we need to move away from the idea that spatial representations are forms of knowledge reproducing reality in total and uniform ways.[7] Maps, charts, surveys, and explorers' accounts are imperfect and contestable projections of the real; indeed, they also stand as performances and "narratives of socially constructed meanings."[8] Spatial representations shape reality more than they reproduce it.

Building on these analyses, this chapter explores the British geographical construction of the Gulf as this took shape over the nineteenth century. It contends that through survey campaigns and the production of various forms of spatial representation, the British invented a new geographical entity, the "British" Gulf.[9] Maps, charts, and survey reports helped define the contours of this terraqueous region, which extended from the Strait of Hormuz to the marshes of Lower Mesopotamia, encompassing the Arabian and Persian shores. The better fathoming and measuring of this arena and its topography became a vital concern for the British because it would play a crucial role in the safeguarding of their interests in India. This chapter begins by tracing the three successive survey campaigns that unfolded in the Gulf and Mesopotamia between 1820 and 1914; it then investigates how these surveys were carried out in practice, so as to reconstruct what the making of this geographical knowledge involved; the final part, through a series of examples of maps, sketches, and charts, analyzes the resultant production of the notion of the "British" Gulf.

Three Major Survey Campaigns

At the end of the eighteenth century, the Gulf was almost uncharted territory for the British. The East India Company sorely lacked information, notwithstanding that other Europeans – particularly the

Portuguese and the Dutch – had been sailing in Gulf waters since the beginning of the modern period, and that the Company itself had maintained trading posts on the Persian shores since the seventeenth century. Geographical knowledge about the Gulf was negligible and relied heavily on travel narratives and on nautical charts compiled from documents published in England, France, and the Netherlands, dating as far back as the sixteenth century. Since the seventeenth century, Company vessels had proceeded with great caution in the Gulf when en route to Bandar Abbas, Bushire, Kharg, and Basra. No adequate chart of the Gulf was yet available: the best existing one had been published by the Danish explorer and cartographer Carsten Niebuhr, who had sailed the Gulf in around 1760, but that one left much to be desired.[10] To European interlopers, at least, the Gulf was a blank space on the world map.[11]

The inaccuracies of such charts and maps of the Gulf as were available caught the Company's attention, and in the late eighteenth century the Bombay Presidency ordered a few small-scale surveys. In 1784–85, Lieutenant John McCluer of the Bombay Marine was instructed to conduct a survey of the Persian coast. He also explored the passage from the entrance of the Gulf to Basra. However, McCluer spent little time sailing the Arabian coast; his work here was confined to furnishing a number of corrections to Niebuhr's map. In 1788 the Company's hydrographer, Alexander Dalrymple, published a nautical chart of the Gulf based on the information collected by McCluer, titled "A Corrected Chart of Part of the Persian Gulph."[12] Further to this, in 1806 he published a version of McCluer's *Account of Navigation between India and the Gulf of Persia*, augmented with a selection of charts, maps, and views.[13] This work, which contained most of the geographical knowledge of the Gulf available at the time, formed the historical basis for the work of the Bombay Marine surveyors who followed McCluer in the Gulf in the early 1820s.[14]

In 1813, four years after the first expedition against Ras al-Khaimah, William Bruce, the resident at Bushire, pointed out in a letter addressed to the Bombay Presidency the problems that the lack of basic geographical data on the Gulf was causing the Company in its attempt to curb "piracy" in this terraqueous region – or, put in other terms, to secure and advance its own position there. Since the available maps and the existing information were highly inadequate, Bruce advocated undertaking a large-scale survey: "Nothing could more facilitate this than the Hon'ble Board's ordering a Survey to be made of the western side of the Gulph as at present it is but very little known to British navigators and considered very dangerous."[15] It was thus at Bruce's initiative that the Bombay Presidency ordered the Bombay Marine to conduct a survey of a portion of the Arabian coast of the Gulf. However, operations only began in 1820, since the Company's board of governors did not agree to Bombay's resolution until 1819, and the second intervention against Ras al-Khaimah and other Gulf "pirate" ports that autumn delayed the possibility of undertaking survey work. In 1820 the Bombay Marine's survey ship the *Margaret and Francis* came into port at Bombay after a long mission along China's coasts and was renamed *Discovery*. Later that year, Captain Philip Maughan and Lieutenant John M. Guy, both of the Bombay Marine, set sail for the Musandam Peninsula on board the *Discovery* and the *Psyche*, and the first survey campaign of the Gulf began. It would not end until 1829.[16]

Between October 1820 and June 1821, Maughan and Guy surveyed the shores of the Musandam Peninsula and the coast between Ras al-Khaimah and Jazirat al-Hamra.[17] In June 1821, owing to ill health, Maughan was forced to give up the survey, and Guy succeeded to the command of the mission. Upon his return to Bombay, Maughan advised against carrying out a general trigonometric survey of the entire Arabian coast. Instead, he recommended that the Bombay Marine officers focus for a few years on key zones, for example, certain coastal sections and some of the ports, so as to produce detailed maps of these. A cursory survey would, he felt, be enough to cover the rest of the coast. The Bombay Council accepted Maughan's suggestions. In the autumn of 1821, Captain George Brucks, who had been appointed commander of the Gulf survey, and Lieutenant Robert Cogan, acting assistant supervisor, set off for the Gulf with Guy on the *Discovery* and the *Psyche*.[18] Maughan's observations formed the basis of Bombay's instructions to Guy, Cogan, and Brucks, who began the Gulf survey afresh.

In 1822, Guy, Brucks, and Cogan conducted operations along the "Pirate Coast," continuing the work undertaken in 1820–21. These explorations resulted in maps of the "pirate" ports that had been targets of the 1819 intervention led by General Keir: Ras al-Khaimah, Jazirat al-Hamra, Umm al-Quwain, Ajman, Sharjah, Abu Dhabi, and Dubai.[19] In early 1823 the three surveyors also explored and mapped some islands, including Dalma Island, off the coast between Abu Dhabi and Qatar. In late 1823, three charts covering the coast from the Musandam Peninsula to Ras Rakan, the northernmost point on the Qatar Peninsula, were sent to Bombay.[20]

Between late 1824 and the spring of 1825, the *Psyche* and the *Discovery* ventured into the Gulf's more northerly zones. Cogan, Guy, and Brucks focused their efforts on the coastline stretching from Qatar to Kuwait. They surveyed Kuwait, Qatif, and Bahrain between November 1824 and May 1825.[21] By late 1825 the whole of the Gulf's western coast had been surveyed.[22] The three surveyors returned to Bombay in the summer of 1825, and the *Psyche* was sold.[23]

More than a year later, in February 1826, Bombay ordered Brucks to return to the Gulf on the *Discovery* without Cogan or Guy. In March he surveyed the harbour of Bushire and the islands of Kharg and Kharku. In September 1826, Brucks, with his new assistant, Stafford Bettesworth Haines, also of the Bombay Marine, was then ordered to survey the waters between Bushire and Basidu on Qeshm Island, a mission that lasted until 1827.[24] More operations followed in 1828: in January and February of that year, Clarence Strait, which separates Qeshm from the Iranian mainland, was mapped.[25] Brucks then carried out a reconnaissance mission on the *Discovery* along the coast of the Sultanate of Oman north of Muscat. Among other sites, he explored Dibba, Khor Fakkan, and Khor Kalba. In April 1828, Muttrah and Muscat were also surveyed.[26] Finally, Brucks set sail for Qeshm, continuing on to the coast of Makran between Jask and Karachi for small mapping missions. The first survey campaign came to an end in May 1829.[27]

What conclusions may be drawn from this first major survey and mapmaking enterprise in the Gulf? Around fifteen maps and charts and a memoir were produced, allowing geographical knowledge of the Gulf to progress. Despite the efforts made by Brucks and his men, however, only a small part of the Gulf had been mapped by 1829.[28] There remained a significant amount of work to be done. In the 1830s a few small-scale surveys were conducted.[29] However, after 1835 the Indian presidencies would focus their efforts on Mesopotamia, a vital segment of the overland route between Britain and India, and a region under Ottoman rule, where the Company was seeking to extend its influence.

British surveying and mapmaking efforts in Mesopotamia began with Francis Rawdon Chesney's mission. Chesney, then a lieutenant colonel in the Royal Artillery, was tasked with surveying the Euphrates and assessing its navigability for steamers. Parliament granted him the very large sum of £20,000. Two dismantled steamers, the *Euphrates* and the *Tigris*, designed for the complex Mesopotamian terrain, were transported in pieces to the region. Descending the Euphrates proved difficult, and one boat was lost.[30] Despite the problems encountered, Chesney's expedition paved the way for new surveys in the region. The Survey of India – the surveying and mapping arm of the East India Company – retained an abiding interest in Mesopotamia from the mid-1830s until the onset of the First World War.

In 1837, Henry Blosse Lynch of the Indian Navy (which had developed from the Bombay Marine), who had served as second in command of Chesney's Euphrates expedition, was appointed to lead what was named the Mesopotamian Survey. This involved, from 1837 to 1843, Lynch and his team surveying the Tigris on board three steam vessels, the *Nitocris*, the *Assyria*, and the *Nimrod*.[31] In 1843, after Lynch left the Mesopotamian Survey, James Felix Jones, who had been part of that survey since 1839, took command of the mission.[32] Jones carried out many expeditions until 1854, at which point he took up the position of political agent in Baghdad.[33] He explored the region between Baghdad and Mosul and the Old Nahwan Canal before, accompanied by the British consul in Baghdad, Henry C. Rawlinson, undertaking a long journey in 1844 to collect information about the frontier regions between Iraq and Persia.[34] In 1846, Jones compiled a general map of Mesopotamia, from Alexandretta (today's Iskenderun) on the Mediterranean to Basra on the Gulf.[35] In 1850 he surveyed the old bed of the Tigris and discovered the site of the ancient city of Opis. In 1852, Jones carried out a trigonometrical survey of the area between the Tigris and one of its affluents, the Great Zab River, including the ruins of Nineveh; that same year, he accompanied the British archaeologist Austen Henry Layard to map the site of Nineveh. In 1855, with the assistance of Lieutenant William Collingwood, another Indian Navy officer, Jones completed a large-scale map of Baghdad. Jones would write up a series of detailed memoirs and reports concerning a number of these undertakings.[36]

In 1855, William Beaumont Selby took the leadership of the Mesopotamian Survey. An experienced surveyor, he had explored the Karun and Dizful Rivers in southwestern Persia in 1842.[37] Under Selby's direction, the Mesopotamian Survey made significant progress. Selby and his men would make a trigonometrical survey, part of which has been lost, of a vast region west of the Euphrates, including the Najaf Sea and embracing the classical sites of Nimrud, Karbela, and Babylon.[38] In the late 1850s, Selby and Collingwood surveyed and drew maps of the Shatt al-ʿArab from Basra to Makil and of the course of the old Hindiyeh Canal.[39] By 1862, when Selby retired, only a few sections of the Euphrates and the Tigris had yet to be surveyed. These would be done after 1865.

In the late 1850s a third survey campaign began, over the course of which the Indian presidencies and the Government of India refocused their efforts on the terraqueous region of the Gulf. This work ended with the First World War. Beginning in 1856, and with the appointment of James Felix Jones as resident at Bushire, the officers of the Indian Navy undertook a revision of the old Persian Gulf surveys. On the *Euphrates* and the schooner *Mary*, from 1857 to 1860, Captain Charles G. Constable and Lieutenant Arthur W. Stiffe addressed the errors and omissions that had been discovered in the work of their predecessors.[40] The result of their labours was a general chart of the Persian Gulf in 1860 and a detailed guide for navigation, *The Persian Gulf Pilot*, which Constable, upon his return to London, wrote from 1860 to 1864, when it was published by the Admiralty.[41] Constable and Stiffe's work also greatly advanced knowledge about the Gulf in ways that went beyond hydrography and topography. For instance, during their explorations they collected geological specimens from various places along the shores and islands, which were then sent to London, where they were studied by the secretary of the Bombay branch of the Royal Asiatic Society, Henry John Carter, a distinguished naturalist.[42] Meanwhile, a survey of the harbour of Bahrain was made in 1859.[43]

No fresh surveys were then undertaken for more than ten years while, in the aftermath of the Indian Rebellion and the end of Company rule in India, the Indian Navy underwent significant structural changes.[44] In 1871, however, a new phase of this third survey campaign began, focusing primarily on the Upper Gulf and the Persian coast. Once again, the link between the timeline of the surveys and that of British political expansion in the wider Gulf region must be emphasized. Around the 1870s, the British faced a resurgence of Ottoman imperialism in Bahrain, Kuwait, and Qatar, and this stimulated Britain's own imperial endeavours in the upper Gulf. Indian Navy surveyors thus concentrated their efforts on correcting the information that had been collected by Brucks and Cogan in the 1820s along the northern portion of the Arabian coast. In 1871, the Bombay Presidency, at the suggestion of the resident at Bushire, Colonel Lewis Pelly, dispatched a mission to survey the waters off Bahrain and Qatar. In the 1890s, operations were conducted in the Shatt al-ʿArab and on the Bahmishir River. Following that, little was done until Curzon's viceregal tour in the Gulf in 1903 gave renewed impetus. Between that year and the eve of the First World War, various surveys were conducted, notably along the Persian coast and in Kuwait and Bahrain.[45]

The Making of Geographical Knowledge

What tools did the surveyors in the Gulf and Mesopotamia use in their work? How was geographical and topographical information gathered and recorded before its translation into maps and charts?

The reports by Brucks, Guy, and Cogan describe the various equipment problems they encountered, including difficulties with the boats themselves, which were not properly fitted out for this kind of work; they also reveal the mix of improvisation and scientific know-how that characterized these early survey expeditions in the Gulf. The work was hazardous. Surveys were frequently interrupted by unfavourable weather, forcing surveyors to either change their plans or take shelter in Basidu or Bushire. Both the *Discovery* and the *Psyche* seem to have been difficult to manoeuvre, and they were not equipped with the necessary instruments (notwithstanding the fact that the former ship had been used for surveying China's coasts around 1810).[46] The Indian Navy surveyors had to ask the surveyor general to remedy these problems.[47] After his appointment as commander of the Gulf survey in 1820, Maughan wrote to the Surveyor General of Calcutta in June, requesting surveying instruments for carrying out the mapping work: a theodolite, a compass, and a telescope. Additional technical instruments, such as sextants, telescopes, and chronometers, would also be necessary.[48] After these instruments were transferred to the *Discovery* in late 1820, Maughan began using them to carry out survey operations. In 1821 he requested a more comprehensive list of instruments, based on his experience over the preceding months.

Yet despite efforts by the Indian presidencies to equip the surveyors as well as possible, the quality of the tools seems often to have been less than satisfactory. The surveyors could not escape the limitations of nineteenth-century surveying instruments.[49] For instance, reports sent during the first survey campaign in the Gulf mention tools that frequently broke and that were unsuitable for a desert environment. The optical instruments used were not designed to handle refraction, which is particularly high in the Gulf and had the effect of making most of Brucks's measurements incorrect.[50] The precision and rationality of surveying and mapping practices were, in the final analysis, an illusion.[51]

In the late 1820s, just as the Company was intensifying its mapping and surveying efforts on the subcontinent, the Surveyors General of India became aware of the difficulties that Brucks and other officers tasked with surveys were facing with their equipment.[52] To address this, in the 1830s the Surveyor General of India, John A. Hodgson, built a workshop in Calcutta that specialized in repairing surveying equipment. This factory also made Barrow's theodolite, a precision optical instrument indispensable for trigonometric surveying.[53] In the 1860s, the portability, design, and precision of surveying instruments were all further improved. In addition, the position of Inspector of Scientific Equipment was created in British India in 1862, for the purpose of examining and enhancing the quality of the equipment used.[54]

These surveyors working to advance the Company's interests in the Gulf possessed yet another tool during their missions there: *A Treatise on Marine Surveying* by the Scottish hydrographer and cartographer Murdoch Mackenzie, edited and introduced by another Scottish surveyor, James Horsburgh.[55] This work provided a synthesis of contemporary knowledge regarding hydrographic surveying and charting, which had its specific requirements and logic. Following an introduction to the general geometric principles of hydrographic surveying, there were very detailed chapters dedicated to measuring space based on trigonometric rules, as well as to various problems that might be encountered. Other chapters dealt with surveying techniques for specific types of regions in terms of their physical geography – sandy coasts, ports, islands, archipelagos – and with the use of certain tools such as the sextant. The works of Charles-François Beautemps-Beaupré, a famous French hydrographer of the late eighteenth century, had been translated into English in the early nineteenth century and may also have been available to the surveying missions.[56] Another reference work for British hydrography was astronomer John Herschel's *A Manual of Scientific Enquiry*.[57] It described hydrographers' instruments, surveying techniques, and the information to collect; its chapters focused on bearings, meteorological observations, soundings, astronomical measurements, and various other dimensions of the hydrographer's craft.

Who were the Bombay Marine and Indian Navy officers who surveyed the Gulf waters and Mesopotamia during the long nineteenth century? They were men who, rather than having received specific training, gained most of their knowledge over the course of the surveying work itself. James Felix Jones's trajectory in West Asia exemplifies how Indian Navy surveyors developed expertise and multifarious skills while conducting their missions. He had what amounted to a kind of apprenticeship through working as a subordinate in the 1830s to an important figure among the Company's surveyors, Robert Moresby, during a broad campaign of reconnaissance missions in the Red Sea.[58] Under Moresby's guidance, Jones learned to master all the different steps of the cartographic process, from survey data collection to drawing. He was then able to negotiate the complex geographical and political terrain while in command of the Mesopotamian Survey.

Jones offers a case in point of the Indian Navy surveyors' adaptability to local circumstances. The flat, marshy plains of Mesopotamia could prove difficult to survey, given their topography, but also because of the limitations of survey instruments discussed above. Surveyors needed to be on high ground to take their measurements. Thus, Jones encountered difficulties when surveying the swampy region around Mosul.

But thanks to a good command of Arabic, Jones secured the protection of an imam in Mosul, who allowed him to enter the Great Mosque.[59] This helped him make progress in his measurements and surveys of Mosul and its hinterland. Unlike some metropolitan explorers, such as Layard, who became notorious for his abrasiveness, Jones seems to have been more effectively diplomatic in his engagements with local authorities and populations. The narrative of his survey in Baghdad is quite revealing in this respect. Ottoman authorities became weary of his activities and forbade him to explore the city. Jones asked his assistant, Collingwood, to take the measurements, which he recorded on the inside of his shirt to avoid being detected. Based on Collingwood's data, Jones created a very accurate map of Baghdad.[60]

How did the surveyors in the Gulf gather the names of places and other reference points, which they recorded as toponyms on their maps and in their reports? Brucks and his successors probably relied on older maps, especially eighteenth-century ones, to name many of the places and locales they surveyed. But Indian Navy surveyors also imposed a new toponymy on the Gulf as they sought to inscribe British imperial power on the space. Thus, on British maps of the Gulf, places such as "Elphinstone Inlet" and "Clarence Strait" appear. Admittedly, the British were not alone in wanting to commemorate imperial "explorers" or statesmen by (re)naming places after them, whether a strait, an island, or the source of a river, seeking in the process to take symbolic possession of these locales. This practice was common among European states in the age of global imperialism.[61] Nevertheless, it is possible to talk about a form of symbolic violence done to the Gulf region in the process of mapping and inventing a new, English-language toponymy, one that involved annihilating each place's identity and imposing a new one, which was then fixed and sanctioned through cartographical language. Certain places in the Gulf were from then on understood and identified through the lens of the conquering British advance and its written memorializing. The space lost its previous indeterminate nature, the semantic freedom that was part of its identity, and was thenceforth subject to rules and external norms that had been superimposed on existing reality. Indigenous toponomy that was based on usage, customs, memorizations, and native systems of representation was replaced by another that precisely orchestrated the process of semiotic appropriation that was part and parcel of imperial advancement.

But maps and surveys were never unilateral constructions. Indian Navy officers and surveyors benefited from local sources of information as they identified, learned about, and came to understand each geographical feature during their missions. Survey work was greatly assisted by encounters and collaborations between native populations and surveyors. This crucial local input and the hybrid nature of the making of geographical knowledge are, however, effectively invisible on the maps themselves, which reflect the imperial gaze of European military officers.[62] In the Gulf and in Mesopotamia, full acknowledgment must therefore be given to the region's inhabitants, as well as to the intermediaries who facilitated contacts among the different parties, for example the interpreters who accompanied Chesney in Mesopotamia.[63] The various cartographic expeditions began by making essential contacts on the ground — not always without resistance; then started a slow process of information-gathering. Local knowledge pervaded the British geographical creation of a "British" Gulf. Maps of the Gulf region were, in varying degrees, a compromise between new and indigenous names. They must be read as palimpsests where, underneath the lines drawn by British surveyors and topographers, there existed a framework of the space as understood by its inhabitants. From this perspective, the colonial map is a collection of various spatialities from which the imperial territory emerges as an attempt to encompass diverse realities.[64]

That surveyors and local populations encountered one another should not hide the fact that in some cases the presence of Indian Navy surveyors involved conflict. For instance, when surveying the Mesopotamian marshes in the late 1850s, Selby and Collingwood faced the growing discontent of local tribes and their chiefs.[65] Also, a shaykh or local ruler who proved to be too helpful to an explorer might invite the distrust of his subjects.[66]

How was the information that had been collected subsequently managed? How were the maps made and distributed? Information and geographical data collected in the Gulf and in Mesopotamia were sent first to Bombay, which then sent them to Calcutta, where they were sorted and categorized. Before 1814, the marine superintendent of the Bombay Marine was an important link in this chain, but after that year his role was removed and it was left to the Surveyor General of Calcutta and his staff to examine the results of each mission carried out in Britain's Indian empire, basing their decisions as to whether the goals had been reached on the quality of the information collected. Then London intervened: the various types of documents came into the hands of the East India Company and, from 1858, India Office employees as well as, among others, the Admiralty; these various organizations then reproduced the maps, had them printed, and oversaw their distribution. From the 1870s onward, offices in India assumed more of the printing duties. By this time, printing costs had fallen and presses had improved. Colour printing became more affordable and allowed experimentation.[67] Parallel organizations, the Royal Geographical Society in particular, were associated with this process of spreading the geographical knowledge thereby gathered.[68] They published accounts from surveyors and topographers and organized conferences aimed at a variety of audiences.

This chain of transmission was, however, far from being as smooth as might first appear. A great deal of information was lost, incorrectly classified, or even destroyed — and sometimes this happened on the shores of the Gulf or in the Mesopotamian marshes before findings ever had a chance to reach India. Furthermore, not all of the documents that were sent to Calcutta and London were published. Some of the Mesopotamian survey reports were destroyed.[69] Economic concerns also controlled the decisions, so that hydrographers and topographers were required to rework the maps drawn and the documents produced by surveyors on the ground before sending them for printing. The costs of publishing these different kinds of maps were clearly not insignificant. Sometimes the documents were simply archived. At other times the surveys were only partly conserved, to be incorporated later into other types of publications. However, when the usefulness of these geographical products was obvious, they could be published very quickly.

But what was the actual contribution of these surveys and maps? Was their function simply the transparent communication of information? Or did they contribute to the creation of a space, the British Gulf, consolidating a geographically and politically diverse region into a single entity via the compasses and pencil lines of engineers, topographers, and surveyors?

Imaginary Geographies: The Creation of the British Gulf

With the maps and charts of the Gulf they produced from the late 1820s onward, the British did more than just provide East India Company traders with tools for navigating the rugged coasts and shoals of this inland sea. Geographical documents also helped shape a sense of a geographical and imperial reality, a Gulf of British invention, just as they would ultimately invent the vast region of the "Middle East." Spatial representations recoded this terraqueous region so as to render it legible in geographical terms. But this was not a mere matter of recording order on spaces thereby delineated; it also meant creating and imposing that order. With maps and charts, the British delineated the borders of "their" Gulf on the world map. Spatial representations also contributed to defining British imperial ideas in the Gulf. The examples that follow evoke the accretion and thickening of representations and imaginaries of the British Gulf in the making over the course of the nineteenth century.

A 1874 document relating to the island of Hormuz offers a particularly rich case in point, revealing as it does multiple layers of representations regarding British imperial ideas in the Gulf. Composed as a kind of visual collage of views of the island, with a series of representations printed on a single large fold-out sheet, this document was produced to illustrate an article by Arthur W. Stiffe on "The Island of Hormúz (Ormuz)," published in a London periodical, *Geographical Magazine*, in April 1874. The imagery used here had been gathered by the author from a wide range of sources.[70] As discussed earlier, Stiffe had surveyed the Strait of Hormuz around the late 1850s, and he reused portions of those official surveys to illustrate his 1874 article. He had visited Hormuz again the year prior to his article's publication, drawing maps (Figure 3.1) and taking sketches and tracing historical inscriptions, which were also reproduced as elements of this illustrative ensemble.

Stiffe's text and his set of illustrations paid particular attention to the remains of the Portuguese presence on the island. Hormuz was

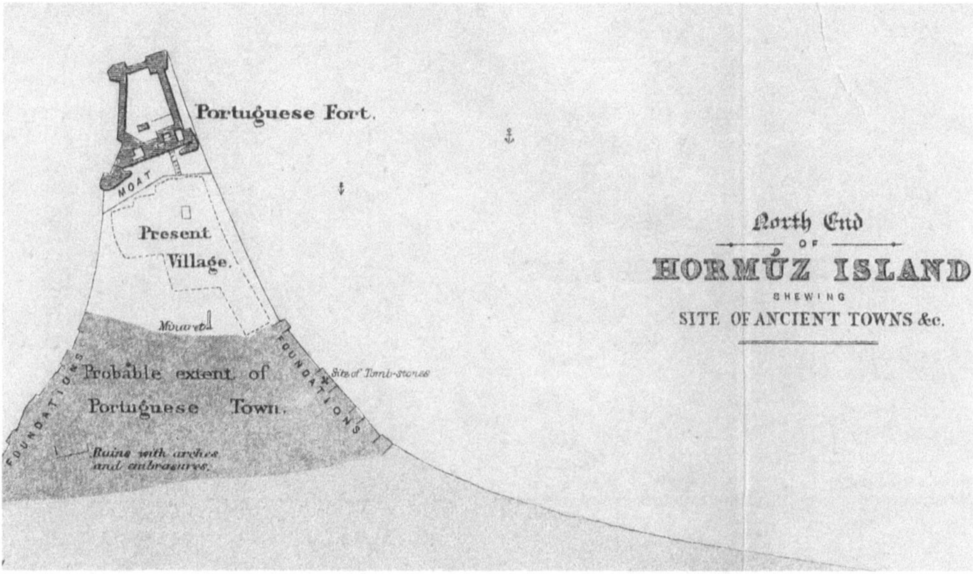

Figure 3.1 Detail from "North End of Hormuz Island shewing Site of Ancient Towns &c.," part of a compilation illustration for A.W. Stiffe's article "The Island of Hormúz (Ormuz)," *Geographical Magazine*, April 1874.

part of the Portuguese Empire from the early sixteenth century and, until captured in 1622 by Persian forces with assistance from the East India Company, it had played a key role in the trading networks of that empire, linking Africa and India.[71] On Stiffe's small map on the top left corner of the sheet, the vestiges of the "old Portuguese town" are depicted, with the fort and ruined chapels located alongside the "present village." The fort is also represented in the small lithograph, alongside a minaret, which is described in Stiffe's account as "the most important ruin" of the "Arab city" of the flourishing kingdom of Hormuz, which predated the Portuguese occupation. Stiffe's reconstruction of the history of Hormuz described its once-flourishing trading and political position, its subsequent decline under Portuguese auspices, and its near-total destruction around the events of 1622. Strikingly, Stiffe's illustrations sheet also included, as another of its component parts, a reworking of a historical "quaint little map or picture" of the island (Figure 3.2), the original version of which had been published in London in the eighteenth century as an engraving in a well-known

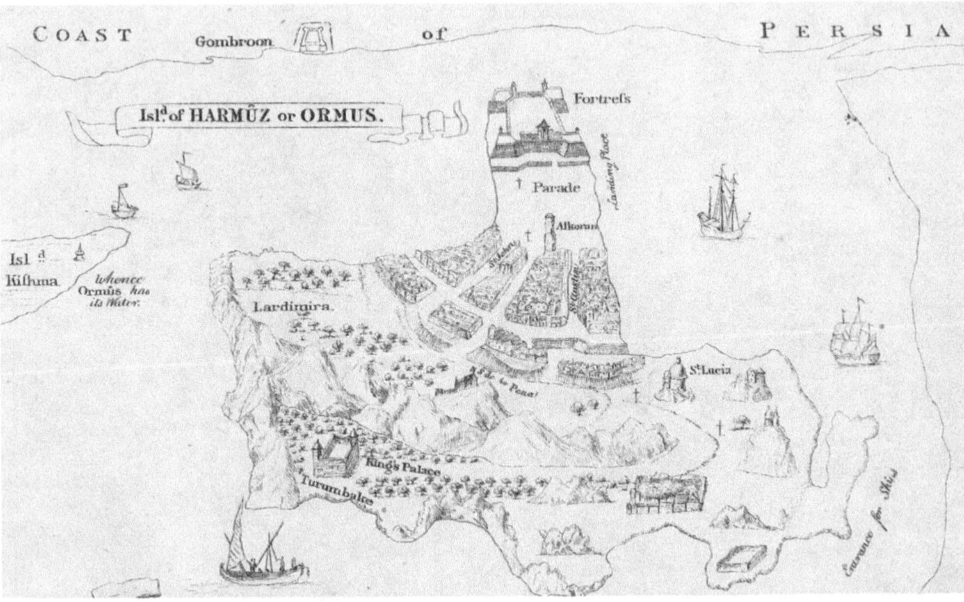

Figure 3.2 "Bird's-Eye View of Hormúz from 'Astley's' Collection," part of a compilation illustration for A.W. Stiffe's article "The Island of Hormúz (Ormuz)," *Geographical Magazine*, April 1874.

travel compendium, *A New General Collection of Voyages and Travels* (Figure 3.3). When published in 1745, that engraving had served to evoke Hormuz around the time of the Portuguese conquest, and Stiffe himself estimated that the scene represented in the image itself dated to around the early seventeenth century.[72] Interestingly, the engraver of this earlier map had wanted to reference, but in some ways also to supersede, the Portuguese history, which may be read in the very topography of this long-contested fortified site. Thus, the map features for example one point labelled "Santa Lucia" and a street named "N.S. de la Pena"; at the same time, though, English remains the framing language, and is used also to designate places such as "the King's palace" or to identify "St John" and "St Custin" Streets.

Stiffe's 1874 collage of representations of Hormuz may thus be said to have drawn eclectically on various representations encompassing his own recent travels to the island, his decades-earlier surveying career, and much earlier historical engravings. He was offering a kind of visual

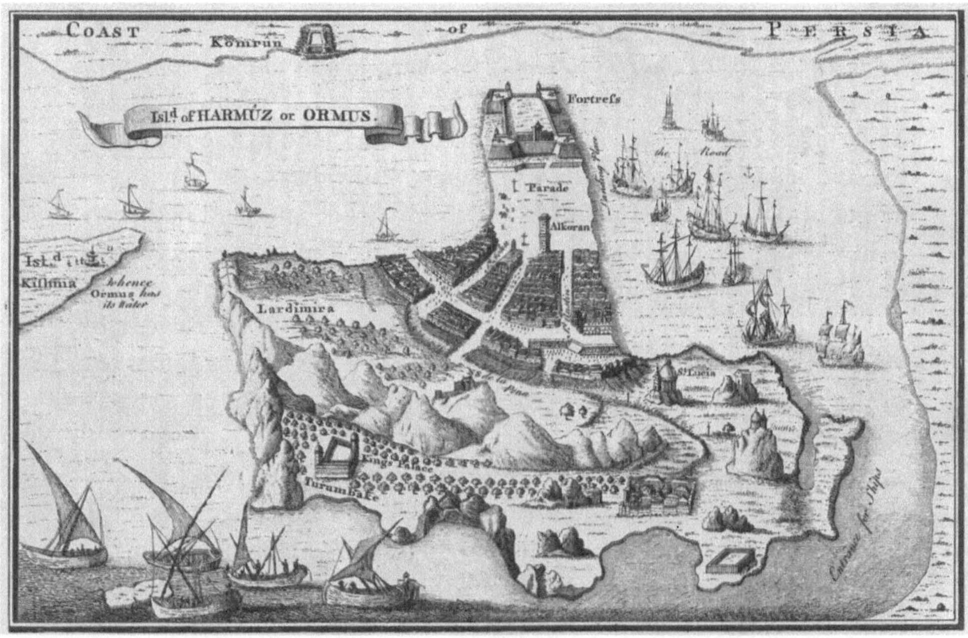

Figure 3.3 "A Prospect of the Island of Ormus," in *A New General Collection of Voyages and Travels: Consisting of the Most Esteemed Relations, Which Have Been Hitherto Published in Any Language*, 1745–47.

genealogy of British depictions of the island, and indeed of the gradual ascendancy of British interests in the wider Gulf. While Stiffe's text in fact condemned elements of the 1622 attack involving the East India Company on Hormuz, which effectively ended the island's role as a trading centre, his account was nevertheless written from the vantage point of the late nineteenth-century British primacy in the Gulf, which such historical episodes had helped foster. As well as being disseminated to the wider public through the commercial world of print, a copy of Stiffe's illustrations would find its way into the collections of the India Office, highlighting how this material was of official interest in embodying bureaucratic knowledge about imperial geographies but also in encapsulating a kind of retrospective representational narrative for the historical creation of a British Gulf.[73]

While Stiffe's 1874 set of images is thus a particularly rich example, it can be situated among a wide range of other instances of British mapping and visual recording efforts. Another case in point is furnished by a series of six drawings of Kharg Island dating from 1839 made by a field engineer, Lieutenant C. Walker.[74] The drawings were undertaken during the brief occupation of the island by the British in the summer of that year. In these drawings Walker has focused particular attention on the island's little Dutch fort. This landmark had been built when the Dutch East India Company decided to open a factory on Kharg in the mid-eighteenth century to boost its trade with Persia.[75] Abandoned irrigation canals and gardens are also represented. In Walker's sketches, Kharg Island accordingly appears as a place marked by the history of empires, where the British may be said to have superseded the Dutch.

Other maps evoke more recent history: notably, British victories and the slow emergence of the British Gulf are denoted. For instance, a British officer, John Hill, would make a sketch to commemorate the capitulation of Bushire in December 1856 after a short British naval bombardment during the brief Anglo-Persian War (1856–57). Hill's depiction, titled "Rough Sketch of the Peninsula on which Bushire is situated Shewing the Landing Place and Different Positions of the Force. From the 7th to the 10th Dec. 1856, when the Place Surrendered," would be printed as a lithograph by the Surveyor General's Office in Calcutta a decade later (Figure 3.3).[76] On this sheet, the sequential advance of the British fleet into the bay of Bushire over a period of days is represented in detail.

The custom of including references to British military actions as part of maps of locales in the Gulf was an old one. In a comparable earlier case, the British victory over Ras al-Khaimah had been highlighted in a depiction showing that port city made by Brucks in around 1822. In Brucks's image, titled "A Plan of the Backwater of Rassulkyma with the Soundings off the Entrance," the "ruins of Rassulkyma," bombed and burned by Keir in 1829, are clearly represented.[77]

In these various spatial representations of the Gulf composed by Stiffe and by a series of other officials and military figures, Britain may be said to be situated as the natural successor both to European empires and to local potentates, whose various histories are still visible in the ruins. By the same token, these surveys and images in aggregate serve as projections of the idea of the Gulf as a British "lake." By the early

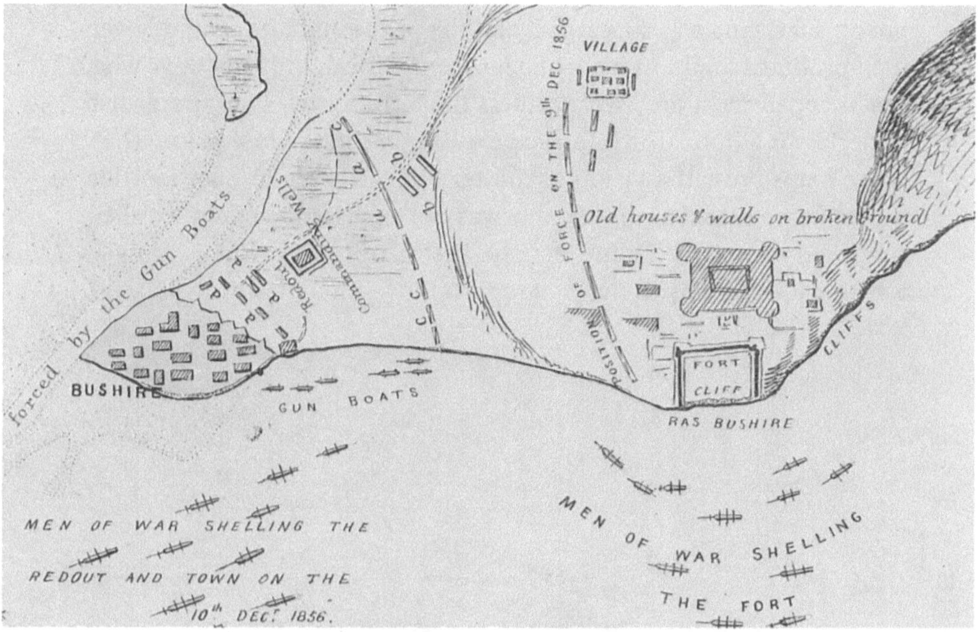

3.4 Detail taken from John Hill, "Rough Sketch of the Peninsula on which Bushire is Situated Shewing the Landing Place and Different Positions of the Force, from the 7th to the 10th Dec. 1856. When the Place Surrendered," 1857.

twentieth century, accordingly, as far as the British were concerned, the Gulf was no longer a blank on the world map. Survey campaigns, charts, and maps formed a crucial juncture in the sub-imperialism in the Gulf conducted under the auspices of British India. This terraqueous region, which had been considered dangerous for sailors and merchants of the East India Company in the late eighteenth century, was gradually territorialized, in the sense of becoming cartographically known. But it also thereby became more susceptible to control.

All of these efforts, moreover, were conducted within an ideological framework that inflected these understandings with a teleological narrative of British technical expertise and imperial achievement. The presence of surveyors and mapmakers in the region signified a new level of British interest and investment in the region, and the cartographical products of their labours were a catalyst for the further consolidation of these dynamics. While, as has been seen in this chapter, not all surveying was successful, and the purported precision of given map products might in reality be far from perfect, in many ways what was mapped most precisely was less the terrain itself than the British imperial ambitions that informed the exercise in the first place. Thus, if the maps present a vision of mastery of the space in question that was to some extent a mirage, this was not necessarily a flaw, for their supposed success or failure may be best gauged in cultural terms as forming a testimony to the geographical invention of a "British" Gulf.

4

The Globalization of the Gulf Economy

EARLY NINETEENTH-CENTURY military interventions in the Gulf led by the British administration in India, and the latter's expanding role in the region thereafter, had been based in part on rhetoric about defending trading freedoms and the liberty of the seas. As has been seen, however, such discourses cannot be separated from the larger expansionist agenda of the East India Company on the subcontinent and of the Government of India that succeeded it in the late 1850s. Previous chapters in this book have explored how by this juncture British India was increasingly inserting itself into the Gulf, which had by this time had become one of its most significant peripheral regions. While bloody military interventions conducted in the name of combating piracy were an early element of this role for British India in the Gulf, the longer-term form of that role involved frameworks of indirect rule or "informal" empire. Through these techniques of imperialism, the British were able to seek maximum advantage for the overlapping interests of the government in London and the administration in British India while keeping the associated costs to a minimum. This style of arm's-length oversight, backed if necessary by coercive force, also relied on the co-opting of local rulers. The centrepiece of all this was the trucial system, which had established and now enforced a maritime peace in the Gulf under British surveillance, having been crafted during the mid-nineteenth century through a series of agreements with the region's micropowers. Besides securing and pacifying this terraqueous region in line with their own interests, the administration of

British India appropriated the region in technical and symbolic ways through surveying and mapping campaigns. In doing so it may be said to have invented a new geographical entity, the "British" Gulf.

This chapter extends the analysis by examining the economic transformations that occurred in the context of these geopolitical frameworks. As an extensive recent historiography has underscored, characteristic of European political economy in colonial contexts around this period was a growing emphasis on internal "development" (or at least on ventures construed as such), one feature of this being the establishment of a monopoly over the use of violence in order to provide a context for policies geared toward enhancing agriculture, production, and trade.[1] A variation on this model had been put into operation in the terraqueous context of the Gulf. The trucial system – together with British maritime patrols, the residency network, and various treaties – amounted to a sustained program of oversight of the Gulf from British India. Here the immediate gain was not in revenue extraction as such – which was largely left to local rulers; rather it was strategic, in the sense that a Gulf political economy reshaped in line with the imperial interests of British India promised to bring the latter an immense advantage in the form of security in what had formerly been a threatened border zone.

What, then, was the nature of the Gulf economy thus fostered and transformed under the regional political system established by British India over the course of the nineteenth century? By some measures, the development of trade in Gulf commodities succeeded beyond all expectations. This chapter examines three elements in turn. First, a booming global commerce would develop over the late nineteenth and early twentieth centuries in two major Gulf products, one drawn from the sea and the other from the land. Pearls (and mother-of-pearl, extracted from the inner layer of oyster shells) and palm dates, the two products involved, had both long been extensively traded at the inter-regional level. But during this period the global demand for both would soar, especially in the rapidly expanding consumer markets of Europe and North America.[2] Gulf pearls and mother-of-pearl were sought after for jewellery and other luxury objects for the expanding ranks of the wealthy in the West. Palm dates also became globalized: a booming international market emerged for this foodstuff, which was used, especially in the United States, as a "trendy" and nutritious ingredient in both sweet and savoury dishes. Changing consumption patterns in global markets thus had a powerful impact on the Gulf's pearl and date trades. It can be said, then, that Western consumers underwrote the costs of anchoring the security of the Gulf under the auspices of British India.[3]

Ultimately, however, as this chapter's second section explores, the pearl and date booms were powered to a significant degree by another traffic, namely the slave trade, especially between the Gulf and Africa. The immediate profits of that trade were small compared to those reaped from commodities such as pearls and dates; but as the historian Matthew S. Hopper has recently argued, the boom in the two latter businesses, and the large profits they enabled, were crucially sustained by slave labour. The slave trade also strengthened connections between the Gulf and the Indian Ocean, the Arabian Peninsula, and the Red Sea. However, traffic in slaves had been condemned in formal terms by the government in London in the early nineteenth century; moreover, in the Gulf region this traffic had been loosely equated with piracy by the terms of the General Maritime Treaty of 1820. Measures would be taken to combat the slave trade in the region – measures that may themselves be seen as a further element in this space's globalization – yet initial efforts in this respect by London and British India were notable mainly for their half-heartedness. Even when stronger efforts were made in the later decades of the nineteenth century, these were apparently insufficient to destroy the Gulf slave trade.

Indirect rule in the Gulf allowed the British to adopt a convenient double standard around the slave trade. They could congratulate themselves for such anti-slaving actions as they did take even while retaining an alibi for their broader systematic failure to crush that trade – one that propped up the Gulf economy and, it follows, regional security for British India. However, a final element of commerce in the Gulf, examined in this chapter's third section, highlights some of the limitations of an informal imperial framework from a British perspective. In the last decades of the nineteenth century, yet another trade, the trafficking of arms and ammunition, was energizing ports and creating further links between the Gulf, Persia, Afghanistan, and British India's North-West Frontier. Yet this trade, often conducted via smuggling, undermined the British empire in West Asia, in that many of these shipments were destined precisely to supply rebellions on the North-West Frontier, beginning in the late 1880s.

Historians today are increasingly raising the notion that given commodities and objects of commerce exercise so much power in making and reshaping world markets that it makes sense to talk about their possessing a kind of agency and forging commodity "empires." Examples include the notions of a world "empire of cotton," of "opium regimes," and of "how tea shaped the modern world."[4] This chapter reviews the extent to which Gulf commodities could be considered under such rubrics and how the several trades that coalesced around the Gulf might both be channelled to buttress — but could also perhaps undermine — a territorial empire such as the one constructed by British imperialism in India.

Golden Harvests: The Globalization of Gulf Commodities

Praised since antiquity for their beauty and quality, pearls sourced from the Gulf were to some extent already gaining far-flung markets during the early modern period.[5] In Europe in the seventeenth and eighteenth centuries, Gulf pearls were sought to adorn dresses, jewellery, hair, and precious and religious objects; they were also used as a pharmaceutical ingredient.[6] In the nineteenth century, pearls enjoyed a golden age as a "pearl fever" swept through the flourishing middle classes of the West.[7] This increased consumption, which made pearls a global commodity, was made possible by increased harvesting in the world's pearl fisheries, in Australia, the Pacific islands, and Venezuela, but particularly in the Gulf. The rising consumption of pearls – and of objects made from mother-of-pearl, or nacre, found in the lining of pearl oyster shells – as luxury and fashion objects had major repercussions for the Gulf's pearl fisheries, in that the prices for both commodities increased notably over the century. By the early twentieth century, the Gulf had become the centre of a global empire of pearls – one that encompassed Paris, London, and Bombay – supplying the markets of Europe, the United States, the Ottoman Empire, and India.[8]

Why were pearls found in the Gulf, particularly along the Arabian coast? How were they fished before they were exported to adorn the ears, necks, and wrists of global consumers? Pearl oysters grow in "banks" in certain marine environments, particularly in warm, clear, shallow waters with rocky, sandy seabeds.[9] In the Gulf, the great majority of oyster banks were between three and ten nautical miles off the Arabian coast, between Qatar and the Musandam Peninsula. The most productive pearl banks were found between the Qatar Peninsula and Abu Dhabi.[10]

A significant proportion of the Gulf region's inhabitants lived according to the rhythms of the annual pearl cycle, from growth to harvest to trade. For five or six months of the year, their lives were governed by this "golden harvest," the description coined by Captain Edward L. Durand, a British official in the region, in 1877.[11] This harvest comprised three periods spread over 130 to 150 fishing days. The first period, *ghaus al-barid*, began around mid-April and lasted one month. Then came the main fishing season, *ghaus al-kabir*, which began in June and lasted until September or October. Finally, fishing, but at a more moderate pace, continued until October or November. Throughout this cycle, time was marked by a daily rhythm. Fishing days began very early in the morning, around five o'clock, and ended when the sun set, with a break for the fishermen during the hottest hours of the day. Dhow crews were small, comprising fifteen to thirty men (no women).[12] The *nakhoda*, or captain, was in charge of the divers and rope-pullers as well as various other crew members.[13] The pearl divers used heavy stones as ballast to enable them to swim down to the depths. Diving dozens of times per day and armed only with rudimentary equipment such as knives, nose clips, and sometimes gloves, these divers gathered oysters on the sandbanks and collected them in baskets attached to their waists. Meanwhile, a second group, the rope-pullers, stayed on the boat's deck, monitoring the divers and using ropes to help them back up to the surface.[14] A series of illustrations representing these various stages would be published under the title "The Pearl Fishery in the Persian Gulf" in the London magazine *The Graphic* in 1881 (Figure 4.1). These fishing techniques had barely changed since the time of writing of *The Epic of Gilgamesh* in the third century BC.[15] Each morning, the deck crew opened the oysters to check for precious pearls, which the *nakhoda* set aside to be sorted by size and sold.[16]

1. "Sidi-Arab" Diver with "Pince Nez."—2. The "Mosquito Fleet" at Anchor.—3. The Divers at Work Below.—4. Apparatus used by the Divers.

Figure 4.1 "The Pearl Fishery in the Persian Gulf," from *The Graphic*, 1 October 1881.

During the months of the golden harvest, the Gulf waters were dotted with pearling dhows and their inhabitants lived almost entirely on the water.[17] Much of the Gulf population was involved in the pearl cycle; this harvest and trade constituted the region's main economic activity and source of revenue.[18] By the time the pearl boom reached its peak around 1905, more than 74,000 men – a significant proportion of the total Gulf population – were employed in the pearl harvest. Over the course of the nineteenth century, between 50 and 70 percent of the male population in Umm al-Quwain, Sharjah, and Kuwait made a living from pearl fishing. Another sign of the importance of the pearl economy was the size of the pearling fleets in small ports along the Arabian coast. For instance, Dubai's flotilla experienced a great increase, from 90 boats in 1844 to 335 in 1907.[19]

After the fishing season ended each year, it was time for pearl trading.[20] Pearls were exported to many markets, and many of the initial transactions were carried out in Arabian or Persian ports. Muscat was the heart of the pearl trade early on but was somewhat overtaken by Manama in Bahrain in the final decades of the nineteenth century. From the early twentieth century, Dubai also supplanted Muscat. Some of the pearl harvest was exported to regional markets. Around 1800, pearls from Bahrain were being exported to Surat, Calcutta, Mocha, and especially Bombay.[21] Until around 1907, when a stock market crash in the United States brought about an economic recession, Bombay was the capital of a global pearl empire and the centre of re-export to regional markets.[22] The various regional markets did not all buy the same kinds of pearls. Buyers in Baghdad seemed to prefer smaller, whiter pearls. Larger pearls were exported to India. In the Ottoman Empire, the preference was for small, irregular pearls, which were widely used to decorate clothing, furniture, and other objects. Mother-of-pearl was also popular.[23]

Demand from regional markets, namely Persia, the Ottoman Empire, and India, remained stable during the nineteenth century.[24] However, this was supplemented by increased global demand, especially in Europe and North America. There had always been a widespread desire for pearls, but during the nineteenth century this global market's growth was transformational. The globalization of Gulf pearls took on a new dimension: pearls became an indispensable and abiding fashion accessory not just for the social elite but also for a burgeoning middle class that had been created by the Industrial Revolution. In Britain the fashion was in some measure sustained and boosted by Queen Victoria, a pearl aficionado. In France, Empress Eugénie almost always wore pearls, including a tiara of fine pearls given to her by Napoleon III. Various celebrities, including actresses such as Sarah Bernhardt, were also notable for their pearl adornments, thereby both drawing on and renewing pearls' cultural cachet. For men, pearl-decorated tie pins became the vogue. In the United States, financial and industrial magnates caught on to the pearl trend, and in the 1870s they began buying pearls that were ever bigger and more beautiful as symbols of their newly acquired wealth. One particularly notable instance of conspicuous consumption saw the New York millionaire William K. Vanderbilt purchase a necklace for his first wife made up of five hundred pearls that had belonged to Catherine de' Medici. [25]

In Europe the fashion for mother-of-pearl buttons, associated with the clothing style of the Romantics, opened up a major new market for pearls. As small factories for manufacturing these buttons proliferated, the demand for mother-of-pearl increased. Such factories were developed in the English Midlands around the 1820s and then in Méru in northern France around mid-century. The Méru industrial cluster specializing in marquetry and button-making demonstrates both the extent of the Gulf pearl trade and the widely dispersed ramifications of the globalized pearl empire. The countryside around Méru and the nearby town of Andeville, a region that had specialized in fine marquetry since the late seventeenth century, would become industrialized as a result of the opening up of new markets.[26] Méru's mother-of-pearl button industry grew to meet the increasing demand. What had begun as a small cluster of country craftsmen working with bone, ivory, wood, and mother-of-pearl morphed into a highly specialized button-making nexus. The mother-of-pearl buttons made in Méru and Andeville supplied markets all over the world. The town of Méru would come to be known as one of the world capitals of the pearl button industry and as a destination for pearl shell deliveries from ports all over Europe.[27]

With the growing demand from world markets, pearl exports from the Gulf grew at a notable rate after the 1830s. An increase in the price of pearls was also discernible during this period. Over the space of seventy years, the value of Gulf pearl exports would grow nearly fivefold. By 1833, total exports were already £300,000; by 1866 they were £400,000; and between 1873 and 1905 they doubled, reaching £1,434,399.[28] Two main phases in the growth of pearl exports can be identified. After some early signs of growth between 1830 and 1850, the first surge began in the late 1860s. A second period of growth would then reach its peak in the first decade of the twentieth century.[29] It is estimated that between 1860 and 1914, the Gulf provided more than half the pearls sold on the global market and almost 80 percent of finer, high-value pearls. In 1906, the Gulf accounted for 49 percent of global pearl production; Ceylon, 15 percent; Australia, 6 percent; and Southeast Asia, 5 percent.[30] But it was the years 1902 to 1905 that were truly the "golden age" of Gulf pearls. Export values at that time reached record highs of around 1,400,000 rupees for the entire Gulf region. The same conclusions can be drawn from the fluctuations in the mother-of-pearl market.[31]

One consequence of pearl fever was that more and more traders, jewellers, pearl brokers, and foreign adventurers travelled to the Gulf to purchase pearls. Until that time, Indian merchants had controlled almost all trade in pearls.[32] Europeans conducted two distinct types of business in the Gulf: some simply wanted to buy large quantities of pearls, while others set out to establish themselves on a longer-term basis with the aim of introducing modern intensive pearl fishing methods. Attempts by Europeans to penetrate the Gulf pearl market date from around the 1860s; by the early twentieth century these traders were entering the pearl market in increasing numbers. During the stock market panic of 1907, British creditors, who until that point had extended substantial credit to the Indian traders controlling part of the Gulf pearl harvest to furnish the Bombay market, called in their debts. This caused long-lasting disruption to the various procurement mechanisms related to pearls.[33] Amid these upheavals, a figure who would gain a leading role in the pearl trade, Leonard Rosenthal, seized his chance. Originally from Russia, Rosenthal in the 1890s formed a Paris-based company, Rosenthal & Frères, in partnership with his brothers Victor and Adolphe, specializing in precious stones and pearls.[34] In 1906, Victor Rosenthal visited Bahrain and purchased 187,000 rupees' worth of pearls (a considerable sum at the time).[35] In 1907, when the stock market panic began, the company was not in the best of health. The Paris market for precious stones suffered deeply. However, the withdrawal of British credit from the pearl market created favourable conditions for newcomers. The Rosenthals took advantage of this crisis, and within a few years Rosenthal & Frères had become the most successful pearl trading company in the world.

According to a British official posted at Bahrain, Francis B. Prideaux, Victor Rosenthal stayed there for thirteen weeks in 1907, buying up almost the entire stock of the island's pearls, having convinced a prominent French banker to lend his firm substantial funds.[36] Each year, Victor Rosenthal would return to Bahrain, purchasing great quantities of pearls.[37] In 1911, Rosenthal & Frères shipped pearl cargoes valued at 6,400,000 rupees to Paris for resale.[38] As a direct consequence of the stock market crisis and the withdrawal of Indian traders from the pearl business, and following the arrival of the Rosenthal brothers in the Gulf, Paris replaced Bombay as the centre of pearl brokering.[39] Leonard Rosenthal, kingpin of the pearl empire, built an impressive fortune from the Gulf pearl trade. On the eve of the First World War it was estimated at around 450 million francs.[40]

Many other traders, brokers, and employees of European and American jewellers made comparable efforts to source Gulf pearls. For instance, in 1917 Rehavia Moussaieff, the Russian owner of Moussaieff Frères, a prominent Parisian jewellery shop, arrived in Bahrain.[41] Germans would also be among the most conspicuous interlopers in the pearl market in the early twentieth century, as revealed by the *Times of India* headline "Germans Buying Up Pearls" (19 June 1918).[42] Sources emphasized the flourishing trade in the Gulf of one German company in particular, Wönckhaus, which had been established in Bushire since 1897. Wönckhaus specialized in pearls and had quickly opened branches in all the Gulf's major ports.[43] Operating under the name Perlen Compagnie Wönckhaus GmbH, the company employed local agents in its offices based in Bandar Abbas, Dubai, and Sharjah. Before the end of the pearl fishing season, these agents travelled to the Gulf's ports seeking to obtain the most beautiful pearls. Wönckhaus's economic activities were complemented after 1906 by a new shipping line run by the Hamburg-Amerikanische Packetfahrt Actien-Gesellschaft.[44] This steamer line linked Hamburg, Germany, with the Persian Gulf, with stops at Antwerp, Marseille, Port Sudan, Djibouti, Aden, Muscat, Bandar Abbas, Bandar Lengeh, Bahrain, Bushire, and Muhammara, and facilitated exports of Gulf pearls to Germany.[45] There was some traffic in the other direction as well: pearl dealers from the Gulf might spend a couple of months in Paris and London selling their stocks.[46]

During the run-up to the First World War, the British were concerned about the presence of European interlopers in the Gulf, especially when Wönckhaus began seeking to supply pearl fishermen with modern diving equipment.[47] In 1912 there were attempts along similar lines to introduce modern fishing techniques to the Gulf's fisheries, particularly in Bahrain, including one effort led by Abdul Wahab Musahri, a Bandar Lengeh pearl merchant.[48] Against this backdrop, at the instigation of the Government of India, legal opinions were prepared setting out the rights of the Gulf shaikhs on the coast to pearl beds, but also declaring that it was the responsibility of British India, as guarantor of those rights, to intervene to preserve the Gulf pearl banks from overexploitation by adventurers and merchants. Such measures were driven by the need to protect what was by far the Gulf region's most valuable natural resource in the world economy of the time, one that was so vital to the shaykhs and to the people of the Gulf. On the eve of the First World War, further agreements were forged with various shaikhs to put a check on the introduction of modern fishing techniques as well as on the concession of pearl banks to foreign companies or individuals.[49] Underscoring the need for such a policy was that, at the height of the pearl boom, the first signs were appearing that the pearl banks were being depleted. In 1905 the British began taking measures to combat overfishing and to prevent fishermen from being forced into debt.[50] This was meant to protect the Gulf's economy and, beyond that, the political system that British India had built around pearls. Pearls, which over the nineteenth century had become one of the most fashionable commodities, were also guarantees of peace and security in one of India's most strategic border zones.

Despite these efforts to preserve the pearl trade, the British could not prevent the consequences of the arrival of cultured pearls. These had been created in 1894 by the Japanese entrepreneur Kokichi Mikimoto.[51] By 1908, Mikimoto's pearls were appearing in Paris, London, New York, and Antwerp jewellery shops, where they sold for around one quarter of the price of natural Gulf pearls.[52] The Japanese and Southeast Asian fisheries where these pearls were cultivated became new centres of the global pearl empire, with Mikimoto as the dominant figure in this transformed commerce. Demand for natural Gulf pearls collapsed, and prices plunged. Serious social unrest arose in major Gulf pearl centres, especially on the island of Bahrain in 1925 and 1927.[53] In January 1927, two hundred divers sacked Manama's bazaar. Others attacked a moneylender's house, destroying his account books and pillaging his rice stockpile.[54] In May 1932 a new cycle of riots began in Bahrain, even more violent than those of the 1920s, which spoke to the gravity of the crisis.[55] One German newspaper described these events as the "swan song" of Bahraini pearl fishermen. They may be posited as the symbolic end of the "golden harvest" in the Gulf.[56]

Pearls were not the only commodity from the Gulf to be globalized during the nineteenth century. The same period saw a fad for palm dates take hold in Europe and, especially, the United States. Although dates and alcohol from fermented date palms had fascinated the European explorer Marco Polo as far back as the thirteenth century, it was only around in the mid-1800s that the fruit gained substantial markets in the West. Dates were a more affordable commodity and thus less profitable than pearls, but they also reached wider social groups than those who could afford to buy pearls.

Like pearls, date palms grow only in very specific environments. They bloom in desert areas of the intertropical zone, except for a few species that flourish in Mediterranean climates.[57] The first accurate estimates of the number of date palms in the Gulf region were compiled in the early twentieth century. These indicate that around that time, out of a total of 90 million date palms in the world, more than half were in the Gulf, where there were two major production areas, the Sultanate of Oman and the Shatt al-ʿArab.[58] Around 1905, the Ottoman province of Iraq had more than 30 million date palms, 15 million of them in the Shatt al-ʿArab region.[59] The number of date palms in Oman was over 4 million, three quarters of them growing on the Batinah coast in the north of the sultanate.[60]

Although a large portion of the dates harvested in the Gulf were consumed locally, dates — like pearls — were also a primary export.[61] The Gulf was the centre of a far-flung regional date market that at the beginning of the nineteenth century extended from South Asia to the Red Sea. Between 1899 and 1906, the date harvest in Oman, most of which at this point was exported from Muscat to India, totalled around £81,000 per year.[62] Ottoman Syria and Iraq also imported palm dates, principally from Bahrain, the third-largest date-exporting port after Muscat and Basra.[63] Dates were exported to Red Sea ports as well. Boats loaded with dates sailed to India and returned with rice, which became a staple food among Gulf populations, and to the Red Sea, returning with coffee.

While these regional markets remained important, in the second half of the nineteenth century the Gulf's date exports began to be shipped to more distant destinations as well, again demonstrating the Gulf's integration into the expanding world economy. Regional exports remained significant, but the Gulf's date trade would be transformed and globalized by new markets. Transformational, in particular, was the growing demand for dates in Europe and especially the United States. The demand for dates remained steady until the interwar period. For global consumers, dates, like pearls, would become a signature commodity associated with the emergent "Middle East."[64] To some extent, just as it is possible to evoke a "pearl fever" around this period, the same may be said of the vogue for dates that swept through parts of American society.

Prized for their nutritious qualities, dates would become a key ingredient in American cooking.[65] They could be eaten unprocessed or used in various stuffing and cake recipes. The Hills Brothers Company, a prominent American firm in this business in the Gulf, produced a series of cookbooks for American audiences in which date products featured conspicuously, such as the *Dromedary Cook Book* (1912) and *One Hundred Delights* (1923); these books offered recipes for stuffed dates, date custard pie, date cornbread, date and nut bread, date and corn muffins, date and celery salad, date soufflé with custard sauce, date sponge cake with lemon sauce, date cream pie, Old English date pie, and date cream filling. Dates were especially sought after for Thanksgiving, where diners might find on the table "date marmalade," "Newport date ice cream," and little "bacon and date sandwiches" as appetizers.[66]

How was this globalized date trade organized in the Gulf region? From 1870 onwards, Basra primarily served the American market, with Muscat having a more mixed trade in which regional demand, particularly from India, played an important role.[67] Global date exports from Basra increased from £67,000 in 1859 to £126,000 in 1869.[68] Growth continued at a spectacular rate thereafter, spurred by the opening of the Suez Canal. Gulf date exports to the United States peaked in the 1920s, and by 1929, on the eve of the Great Depression, more than 83 percent of all dates consumed there were from Iraq. Dates from Muscat long retained popularity in the United States and were priced at a premium over Iraqi dates.[69] In Los Angeles in 1895, *fardh* dates from Oman were worth 15 cents a pound, while "golden dates" from Iraq cost 10 cents a pound. Ultimately, the Basra trade came to dominate, given the scale of the transatlantic demand, though the Muscat trade continued to have an American dimension.[70]

Until the 1860s, American companies used Indian merchants as intermediaries in the date trade. While the fad for dates was in full swing around 1890, American companies introduced significant changes to the date industry. First, some companies gradually replaced the Indian brokers with their own representatives. Notably, this was done by the Hills Brothers Company, which dominated the American trade in Iraqi dates from 1880 to 1930. Founded in 1871 by John Hills, this Brooklyn-based firm specialized in dried fruit importing.[71] At the beginning of the twentieth century, the Hills business was apparently well-established in Basra. Its agent, H.P. Chalk, was also the US consul there, and the firm's offices were housed in a building called Beit Hills, or "Hills's House." The company's main intermediary in Basra, Haji Abdullah Negem, was entrusted with $10,000 in gold pieces every year to make purchases from farmers on behalf of the company.[72] American companies also changed how dates were packaged. In the early 1880s they started sending unassembled wooden crates from Scandinavia to the Gulf. These arrived several months before the date harvest and were then assembled in the Gulf before the fruit was packed.[73]

The marketing of Gulf dates was transformed under American auspices. Taking advantage of the birth of advertising agencies in the United States, Hills Brothers played on orientalist images in both their packaging and their marketing: the fruit imported by Hills was sold in boxes stamped with the picture of an Arabian camel or the slogan "A Gift from the Orient."[74] The date export boom finally came to an end during the 1920s, when the US Department of Agriculture developed date palm cultivation in California.[75] As with the history of the Gulf pearl, the date was a commodity whose very scale of success had enticed far-flung competitors to undercut the market.

The Slave Trade in the Northern Indian Ocean and the Gulf

In a 1931 work that drew on his reporting from the east coast of Africa, the Red Sea, and the Persian Gulf, Albert Londres, a leading French journalist of the day, described the pearl "harvest" at Bahrain, a place that had long been a central node of the Gulf region's pearl industry. The misery of the pearl divers was at the heart of Londres's book. The photographs and text portrayed the divers, who, physically exhausted by months of diving, were exploited by boat captains, boat owners, and Indian traders. These divers were the poorest of the poor, even though pearls commanded high prices on the global markets in the first decades of the twentieth century. The sheen and glamour of the pearls that were sold in Europe and the United States had long masked the suffering of the pearl fishermen, many of whom were slaves from East Africa.[76]

While the generalized industry crisis in Gulf pearling at this point may have made the picture of distress drawn by Londres all the more extreme, the human misery of those involved in the labour of harvesting pearls was by then of long duration. Slave labour in the Gulf would take on a new scale amid the nineteenth-century booms in global demand for Gulf commodities: not only the pearl trade but also that that in dates came to rely to a significant degree on slave labour. Slaves were employed as divers in the pearl fisheries and as workers on the date palm plantations. The globalization of the Gulf, the existence of an economic cycle based on two global commodities, and the slave trade in the northern Indian Ocean would be closely linked throughout the nineteenth and early twentieth centuries.

How did this slave trade supply the Gulf with the necessary labour force as the date and pearl harvests grew ever larger? Where did these pearl divers and date plantation workers come from? Most of the enslaved workers who arrived in the Gulf beginning in the 1820s came through Zanzibar, the hub of the slave trade in the northern Indian Ocean.[77] The island served as a way station for the slave trade between the Swahili Coast, Africa's Great Lakes, and the south coast of the Sultanate of Oman.[78] Beginning in the 1820s, there was a quantifiable increase in the slave trade from the African coast to Zanzibar, corresponding to the growth of the pearl and date sectors.[79] From Zanzibar, slaves were brought to Oman, notably to Muscat and Sohar; some of them were then sent onward to Persia, particularly to Bandar Abbas, Qeshm, Bandar Lengeh, and Bandar Kangan, but also to ports on the Arabian coast such as Ras al-Khaimah, Dubai, and Bahrain.[80] These ports of the lower Gulf brought in between 3,000 and 8,000 captives from Oman in 1860. Around the same time, between 3,000 and 5,000 enslaved people were sent from Oman to the Upper Gulf, particularly to Basra and the date palm plantations.

What functions did these enslaved workers carry out? Throughout the nineteenth century, a number of the captives, especially women, were employed in household-based labour such as cooking, cleaning, sewing, child care, and gardening. Men could also be used in domestic labour.[81] However, the development of the slave trade after the late 1820s seems to have corresponded especially to the growing needs of the pearl and palm date sectors. The proportion of divers working on pearling dhows who were enslaved was often very high; as late as 1904, African slaves made up more than half the crews of pearl dhows sailing out of Ras al-Khaimah.[82] Date growing was highly labour intensive, especially in Oman's Batinah region, where the date plantations' complex irrigation systems required constant maintenance.[83]

This demand for labour and the globalization of dates and pearls had a major impact on the Gulf's demographics. At the beginning of the twentieth century, enslaved people represented a significant proportion of the population in every port along the Arabian coast. Around 1830, slaves accounted for more than half the population of Bahrain, the centre of the pearl empire. In 1903 slaves represented 11 percent of the population of Kuwait and Bahrain, 28 percent of the Trucial Coast population, and 25 percent of the population of Muscat and Muttrah.[84] The date trade fostered similar demographics: as one recent study has noted, around 1900 Batinah was "widely known as the home of the largest concentration of Africans in the Gulf."[85]

The response from Britain and India to the slave trade in the northern Indian Ocean and the Gulf was quite paradoxical, seemingly hedged between toleration and suppression from the 1820s onward.[86] In the late eighteenth and early nineteenth centuries, the East India Company had taken various measures against the slave trade in India, but these were limited in scope and did not directly affect the Gulf and the northern Indian Ocean.[87] In 1820 the General Maritime Treaty, the agreement between the British and various Arab shaikhs orchestrated by General Keir in the wake of the second expedition against Ras al-Khaimah, had equated slave trading with piracy and proscribed it as such. Around the same time, Robert Farquhar, the governor of Mauritius after the British had taken it from France in 1810, actively sought to eradicate the slave trade as far as this related to his jurisdiction; indeed, he was obligated to do so, in line with a ban on slave trading by British subjects that had passed through Parliament in London in 1807.

Farquhar's effort gradually succeeded in shrinking the main slave trading route, from Madagascar; but a notable clandestine traffic then developed with Zanzibar, which was part of the domains of the Sultanate of Oman. Farquhar accordingly suggested that the administration in British India take action at a regional level.[88] Notably, in 1821, he wrote to Governor General Hastings about the extent of slave trading in the northern Indian Ocean, suggesting that the logical next step for ending the traffic in slaves to Mauritius was to request that the Sultan of Oman, Sayyid Said, order the blocking of the sale of slaves at his ports. In London, meanwhile, the East India Company's Court of Directors was directing that the sultan be approached about abolishing the slave trade in his dominions. But it soon became clear that the sultan would never agree to this request without heavy financial compensation.[89] Nevertheless, a limited agreement was made in September 1822 when Captain Fairfax Moresby of the Royal Navy was tasked with a negotiating mission to Muscat.[90] This treaty saw the sultan agree to a series of measures limiting the slave trade as it related to Mauritius and other European possessions. Yet the series of restrictions agreed to did not block the crucial axis of the slave trade from Zanzibar to the Gulf itself. It thus had only a limited impact on the slave-trading network linking the northern Indian Ocean and the Gulf.

A broader policy appraisal around the question of how far Britain should seek to police the slave trade in the Gulf was undertaken by John Macleod in 1823 as part of a report he wrote as incoming British resident at Bushire.[91] Macleod began by highlighting problems in the General Maritime Treaty's provisions as they related to the slave trade. He noted how, despite the treaty's strictures, traffic in slaves "continues to a considerable degree," pointing out that "there is an open slave market both at Muscat and Bahrain, and also I believe in the Persian ports."[92] At the same time, he underscored that the wording of the relevant treaty article admitted of doubt concerning the precise aspect of the maritime slave trade thereby ostensibly proscribed; and that "even the most extended acceptation" of the treaty's wording could not "be construed into forbidding the purchase of slaves, and the transport of them overland."[93]

In any case, Macleod was not sanguine that any anti-slave-trade regime that was fundamentally coercive, and that did not encompass crucial actors in the slave trade such as the Sultanate of Oman, would be efficacious:

> We may perhaps put a stop to the carrying off of slaves, but their purchase and transport we never can prevent; the slaves will be disguised and concealed in a Thousand ways, so that it will be impossible for us to detect them.... With all our efforts we shall find it impracticable to put a stop to a traffic, which is sanctioned by their religion and by immemorial custom, unless it were relinquished by the common consent of the whole of the Chiefs of the Gulf.

Macleod also argued that any active British policy of "stopping boats and searching them for slaves" would also "risk a renewal of hostilities" with the Gulf tribes. Overall, he concluded, the article of the treaty concerning the slave trade was incapable of curtailing the traffic and would produce "danger" if the British attempted "to carry it into effect." Accordingly, he declared himself "compelled with much reluctance to recommend that it should not be enforced except in very glaring cases."

To some extent, Macleod's recommendations that policing of the slave trade be undertaken at only a minimal level may be placed in the context of the broader agenda he proposed for British policy in the Gulf. There was scant appetite in British India at this juncture for a sustained interventionist commitment to the region, without which confronting the slave trade was hardly feasible. Macleod, then, suggested that British efforts be restricted to targeting piracy and that the panacea be economic: "We ought to encourage them as much as possible to embark in commerce, and endeavour to bring them to more peaceful habits." Pushing for the uncoupling of the slave trade from piracy, thereby disavowing the association between these two phenomena that had been implied by the terms of the General Maritime Treaty, moved the slave trade tacitly from the realm of policing to that of mere commerce.[94] Put another way, the slave trade was, in Macleod's pragmatic vision, to some extent part of the price of maintaining a peace cheaply in the region – cheaply, that is, in the limited sense that the costs would be borne by the slaves themselves; the alternative would be an onerous policing bill for British India. The General Maritime Treaty of 1820 had hinted at a more interventionist approach; Macleod's stance constituted a return to earlier practice, when, in the words of one scholar, not only "had the British authorities in India no desire to interfere with the Arab slave trade, but they took pains to avoid giving the impression of wishing to do so."[95]

Given all this, British India's nominal anti-slave-trading policy in the Indian Ocean achieved decidedly modest results around this juncture. The government in London, however, had a more expansive notion – at least on paper – of what actions Britain should take against the slave trade. In 1838 the Foreign Secretary, Lord Palmerston, proposed that a commercial agreement be signed with Sayyid Said, the Sultan of Oman. This would reinforce the links between Britain and Oman; more importantly, it would also reinforce the British position in the Gulf at a time when the larger region's geopolitics were at a critical juncture on account of the rising power of the Pasha of Egypt, Mehmed Ali.[96] The treaty designed by Palmerston had fourteen articles, three of which addressed the slave trade in Oman. Article 6 in particular went much further than Moresby's treaty by declaring that "His Highness further engages to prohibit and to prevent the transport of Slaves between his Dominions and other Countries, whatever be the dominant religion of those countries; and in particular to the countries of India, those lying upon the Red Sea, and those lying upon the Persian Gulph."[97] Article 17 stated that all boats flying the Omani flag could be searched by Royal Navy ships if they were suspected of having slaves on board.[98] The Company's representatives then negotiated the fine print of the treaty with Sayyid Said. The result was a heavily amended version of the document that had been prepared under Palmerston's auspices. Signed in May 1839, along with a trade agreement, it included only one article mentioning the slave trade, and that article was merely a reminder of the clauses in the Moresby treaty that extended the right of search to the Indian Navy.[99] Far from being the head-on attack on slave trading that Palmerston had sought, this treaty was faithful to British India's policy of accommodating its oldest ally in the Gulf, the Sultan of Oman, for whom slave trading was an important source of revenue.

Other efforts around the same juncture were similarly characterized by only limited efforts against the slave trade, with priority instead accorded to safeguarding and reinforcing the system of local alliances in the Gulf developed over previous decades. In this vein, Samuel Hennel, the British resident at Bushire, concluded a treaty with a number of shaykhs of the "Pirate Coast" in July 1839. The chiefs agreed to stop slave-trading activities to the west of a line between Cape Guadel on the Makran coast and a point two degrees east of Socotra. The Indian Navy was authorized to search ships belonging to subjects of the signatory shaykhs east of this line.[100]

In summary, by the end of the 1830s, little concrete action had been taken to combat slave trading in the Gulf. For the East India Company's representatives in India and in the Gulf, humanitarian values remained secondary to its main priorities, which were conciliating the Arab shaykhs and the Sultan of Oman and strengthening the Company's interests in the Gulf region. During the 1840s, however, the Indian presidencies began to initiate somewhat stronger measures. In 1845, Sayyid Said and the Company's agent in the Sultanate of Oman, Atkins Hamerton, signed a new treaty that was far more rigorous than the previous agreements. This one committed Sayyid Said to banning the export of slaves from his African dominions to Muscat. It also gave East India Company and Royal Navy ships the right to search and seize any boat belonging to his subjects suspected of slave trading.[101] This measure was followed by an agreement made in 1848 by which the shaykhs of Bahrain, Ras al-Khaimah, Sharjah, Dubai, Ajman, Umm al-Quwain, and Abu Dhabi forbade the importation of slaves on any vessel that belonged to either them or their subjects.[102] In May 1849, the governor of Sohar, the second-biggest slave-importing port in the Sultanate of Oman, signed an agreement with Hennel banning his subjects from importing any slaves from Africa into his territories.[103] Finally, in 1853, by signing the Perpetual Maritime Truce, the shaykhs of the erstwhile "Pirate Coast" (later recast as the "Trucial Coast") undertook to ban imports of slaves into ports under their authority.

After the limited progress of the 1840s and 1850s came a critical period between 1868 and 1873 during which efforts were focused on the two slave-trading hubs of Zanzibar and Oman. This was not without tension between London and the Government of India. The thorny problem on which the India Office and the British Foreign Office struggled to agree was a follow-up to the separation in 1861 of Oman and Zanzibar, which resulted in the creation of two distinct sultanates.[104] Given the economic repercussions for Oman of this scission, the new Sultan of Zanzibar, Sayyid Majid bin Said, agreed in 1861 to pay the Sultan of Oman, Sayyid Thuwaini (successor to Sayyid Said), an annual tax fixed at 40,000 crowns; this undertaking, made at the behest of the Viceroy of India, Charles Canning, would be referred to as the Canning Award.[105] Thereafter, however, one of the arguments Sayyid Majid put forward for not signing anti-slave-trading treaties was that he was obliged to continue allowing the slave trade in Zanzibar in order to gather enough revenue to pay the Canning Award. In the 1860s the Foreign Office favoured cancelling the Canning Award, but the India Office did not.[106]

In this complicated context, negotiations began in the early 1870s between the Government of India and the Sultan of Zanzibar over a treaty that would ban the slave trade between Zanzibar and eastern Africa, which would have a determining effect on the Gulf markets. In January 1872, Henry Bartle Frere, a former Governor of Bombay, arrived in Zanzibar accompanied by the resident at Bushire, Lewis Pelly.[107] The discussions with Barghash bin Said, Sayyid Majid's successor, culminated with an agreement formalized in 1873 by which the Sultan of Zanzibar consented to close the slave markets in his dominions, protect freed slaves, and ban slave trading between Zanzibar and Africa. The Omani sultan Sayyid Thuwaini signed a similar agreement. Further conventions concluded over the following decade with the Ottoman Empire and Persia consolidated British leeway to combat the slave trade in the Red Sea and the Persian Gulf. This brought about a relative heyday of maritime operations to that end, which would extend into the early twentieth century.[108]

Even at this point, however, the scale of these operations should not be exaggerated. It has been estimated that, all told, captures by British ships tasked with stopping the slave trade with Arabia did not exceed 12,000 slaves.[109] As Hopper has argued, the nub of the British difficulty in finding a coherent strategy in this respect was that "the aims of liberal politics clashed with the aims of liberal economics." Despite pressure from an antislavery movement in Britain itself, a perceived need for slave labour in the Gulf pearl and date trade militated against truly transformative action under British auspices. Ultimately, according to this argument, the Gulf should be understood not as a reliable "British lake," but rather as a "contested imperial space" – one where turning a blind eye to the slave trade was seen as the price of attaining "bigger imperial goals in the Indian Ocean."[110] The British did not want to jeopardize what they viewed as the fragile socio-economic balance of these territories – upon which their own fortunes in the region were based – and therefore took only timid measures against the slave trade.

"An Embarrassing Trade": Arms and Munitions Trafficking and Smuggling

In the 1880s, another kind of trafficking – in arms and munitions – was on the increase in the Gulf. Around this period, the Gulf would become an integral part of a global arms trade that has recently been described as a global "empire of guns."[111] But unlike commerce in pearls and dates, or the slave trade, this "empire of guns" would directly threaten the stability of the regional systems that had been under construction under the auspices of British India since the early nineteenth century.

How and to what end were these arms imported into the Gulf? How was this global market organized on a regional and local scale? In the late nineteenth century the British found themselves confronted with a surge in arms trafficking in the Gulf region, and those smuggled armaments were feeding a number of rebellions, including an uprising on British India's North-West Frontier that had begun in the 1880s. This network of arms trafficking now linked two borderlands of British India, the Gulf and the North-West Frontier, posing a major challenge for British authorities in India. In the cracks created as a result of the political fragmentation of these borderland regions, a transnational territory of arms smuggling emerged, involving ships and caravans that transported arms and ammunition from Europe to the Gulf ports. These munitions were products of the Industrial Revolution and symbols of British imperial expansion. Yet by the end of the nineteenth century they had become tools for opposing Britain's imperial order not only on the Indian subcontinent but also in West Asia more widely.

At this time, the importing of European and American weaponry to the Middle East was not a new phenomenon: Persia and the Ottoman

Empire had been importing European-made swords, sabres, revolvers, and long guns since the fifteenth century. These imports increased around the 1850s, partly because of the Crimean War (1853–56) and partly because the reputation of firearms made in Europe and the United States had grown. They were lighter and more technologically sophisticated, so they were increasingly sought.[112] Between 1869 and 1879, the Ottoman Empire imported more than 1 million American and English firearms. British Martini-Henry rifles – which at this point were being mass-produced and adopted by the British army – met with early success in both Egypt and Persia. Qajar Persia, the Ottoman Empire, and Egypt purchased mainly magazine rifles and machine guns in the 1860s, as well as pistols and revolvers manufactured by Colt and Adam.[113] In the Persian Gulf region around the 1870s, buyers were almost exclusively seeking breech-loading rifles.[114] As a result of these purchases, the terrain that would soon be dubbed the "Middle East" was well on the way to becoming a prominent part of the global "empire of guns": Persia, the Ottoman Empire, and the Gulf served as major outlets for British, Russian, American, and French arms manufacturers. By the end of the century, the Gulf would be one of the key centres of this empire.[115]

Around this time, Africa was another primary market for European arms manufacturers and merchants. Second-hand weapons were exported to the African continent in greater numbers than new weapons; these came from manufacturers' surpluses and the arsenals of European states.[116] Markets varied. During the First Boer War (1880–81), the Zulus and Boers fighting the British were armed with European rifles.[117] In the early 1890s, the French exported significant numbers of weapons to Ethiopia to arm the forces of Menelik II, which were resisting the establishment in Ethiopia of an Italian protectorate.[118] This trade and the trafficking associated with it had a considerable impact on the region. Anticolonial revolts and outbursts of violence grew more and more frequent, leading to the implementation of a naval blockade by British, German, and Italian forces along the eastern African coast at the end of the 1890s.[119] Local measures were taken to curb trafficking in the zones under German and British influence. Signatories at the international Brussels Conference of 1890, another colonial conference geared toward Africa, envisaged the reduction of arms exports to eastern and tropical Africa as one of their main objectives. In the final act of the conference, it was formally forbidden to export firearms, gunpowder, and cartridges to all of tropical Africa and the territories extending from the Atlantic Ocean to the Indian Ocean between the 20th northern parallel and the 22nd southern parallel. [120] However, this convention, which had been agreed upon for a twelve-year period, would have very little impact.

Meanwhile, in the Gulf region Muscat was becoming an arms entrepôt. That port in the Sultanate of Oman was outside the surveillance zone that had been defined in the last act of the Brussels Conference of 1890, and the shift occurred just as Oman saw a decline in its trade in dates, which had been the source of most of its wealth until then. Thus, Oman would serve from the early 1890s as the primary hub of arms trading and trafficking for a region extending from the Arabian Sea to the Shatt al-ʿArab and the Arabian side of the Gulf, Afghanistan, and India's North-West Frontier. The 1890s saw an explosion in this smuggling in line with the rising tensions along India's North-West Frontier. Between April 1890 and June 1892, more than 11,500 firearms were imported from Europe to Muscat.[121] The increase was particularly impressive in 1895 and 1896. In 1895, Oman imported 4,350 rifles and 604,000 cartridges. In 1896, the number of imported rifles more than quadrupled, reaching 20,000.[122] This led the French vice-consul in Oman, Paul Ottavi, to declare that Muscat had become "a major entrepot for arms."[123] In 1900 imports reached 25,000 rifles and 2.25 million cartridges. Weapons continued to flow in increasing numbers after the end of the Second Boer War in 1902, with surplus munitions arriving from Africa and Europe: in 1906, 45,000 rifles and 1 million cartridges passed through Muscat. Even after this trade began to decline in 1908, owing to British measures, it still represented 43 percent of all imports to the city.[124]

Where did these products come from? British industry was heavily represented, owing to a preference for Lee-Metford, Martini-Henry, and Snider-Enfield rifles in the Gulf, Persia, and Afghanistan.[125] Manufacturers, brokers, and shippers from numerous British companies, based notably in London, Birmingham, and Manchester, had a role in the trade. The companies that dominated the cartridge market, for example, were G. Kynoch & Co. of Birmingham and Eley Brothers Ltd. of London. Exports from Birmingham to the Gulf multiplied over the course of the 1890s: they were worth £4,750 in 1889, £37,678 in 1894, and £105,000 in 1897.[126] One British official would comment on the "the paradox of empire" that had produced such a situation: "Government maintains warships in the Gulf to preserve the peace, and the Birmingham manufacturers and London exporters ship out whole cargoes of rifles and cartridges which can only destroy peace."[127] Some British industrialists and capitalists found that, in this instance at least, their interests were more aligned with a transnational "empire of guns" than with the British imperial state.

In an attempt to reduce the risk of seizure, such cargoes were often not shipped from London but from Cardiff, Liverpool, and Manchester. Manufacturers worked with numerous intermediaries, especially shipping companies. The Anglo-Arabian and Persian Steam Navigation Company was indirectly involved in this development, along with the British and Colonial Steam Navigation Company. Crates of arms and ammunition were loaded onto these companies' steamers. Anglo-Arabian's ships alone transported more than 4,847 rifles from European ports to Oman in 1902.[128] The commodity chain of arms trafficking that linked Europe and the Gulf relied on networks established and controlled by Europeans. These included steamer lines, ports in Europe, and European manufacturing, shipping, and brokering companies. Arms were transported from Europe on imperial maritime routes extending across the English Channel, the Mediterranean, the Red Sea, and the Arabian Sea. They left the docks of the largest European ports, passed through the Suez Canal, and stopped in Port Said before reaching Djibouti, Aden, and Muscat.

How did the trafficking bypass port authorities? Exporting companies used a number of tricks, such as declaring other kinds of goods instead, or secreting arms and ammunition among other kinds of cargo, such as sugar, or even dry limes and halvah.[129] An example of the subterfuge techniques involved in these shipments, and the confrontations that exposure might occasion, is provided by the *Baluchistan* affair in 1897, which was notable for revealing the dominance of Birmingham-based companies in the Gulf market around this time and the role of steamer companies and other key intermediaries in this commodity chain.[130] The *Baluchistan*, a ship sailing the Persian flag, belonged to the prosperous Anglo-Persian firm Fracis, Times & Co., which was based in Bushire and heavily involved in arms trafficking between Europe and the Gulf. In December 1897 the *Baluchistan* left the Manchester Ship Canal for Marseille and then Bushire, via the Suez Canal. Aboard were 306 crates of cartridges and 280 crates of rifles, mostly produced by Birmingham's leading manufacturers, such as Isaac Hollis & Sons. The cargo was listed simply as "hardware." On the crates was written "Bahrain via Bushire. Optional: Muscat."

While the *Baluchistan* was sailing through the Mediterranean to Marseille, the captain learned that Fracis, Times & Co. had been subject to major seizures at its Bushire warehouse. The British authorities were beginning to step up their efforts against arms smuggling, in cooperation with the regional powers. In December 1897, Mozaffar-al-Din Shah had authorized Britain to intercept and search ships flying the Persian flag in the Qajar empire's territorial waters. It also appears that the British resident in the Gulf, Malcolm Meade, had warned Fracis, Times & Co.'s agents that the cargo sailing from Marseille to the Gulf was likely to be intercepted and confiscated. Nonetheless, in December 1897, in Marseille, the *Baluchistan* loaded up with 272 additional crates of weapons, these ones made in Russia, which were supposedly destined for Ethiopia via Djibouti. At Marseille, the captain carefully erased the name "Bushire" on all the crates and wrote "Muscat" instead. In January 1898, off the coast of the Sultanate of Oman, HMS *Lapwing* intercepted the *Baluchistan*. Its crew confiscated the entire cargo, which was then sent to the custody of British officials at Muscat. In total, more than 400 crates of smuggled arms and ammunition fell into the hands of the British: 7,856 rifles and 700,000 cartridges. The *Baluchistan* affair did not end there: arms manufacturers in Birmingham vigorously protested. For Fracis, Times & Co., the seizing of the *Baluchistan*'s cargo was disastrous, causing losses of between £30,000 and £40,000.

The turn of the century saw a significant shift in the flow of arms and ammunition to the Gulf. In 1897, imports of such commodities to the area were valued at $900,000 coming from Britain and $100,000 coming from France. By 1900, however, imports of French arms had grown, directly competing with those from Britain. Ottavi observed that most of the arms smuggled into Oman came from Marseille.[131] Every month since 1898, a large quantity of cargo consisting of arms had been sent from the Mediterranean port, primarily bound for Oman. In

October 1900 alone, two shipments were sent. According to Ottavi, in 1900–1, weapons were sometimes shipped as often as three times per month. In 1902 and 1903, trafficking between Marseille, Boulogne, and Muscat continued to increase. In 1903, French Minister of Foreign Affairs Théophile Delcassé informed Ottavi's successor in Muscat, Lucien Laronce, that consignments including 85,000 Martini cartridges had been shipped from France that April for Oman.[132] In 1899–1900, 25 percent of all imported arms in Muscat were from France, and by 1905 this proportion had increased to 40 percent. That year, the French controlled 49 percent of the arms trade in Oman; the Omanis themselves, 27 percent; and the British, 24 percent. The French share in this traffic continued to grow between 1900 and 1908, from 14 percent of the total traffic in 1900 to 49 percent in 1908.[133] Arms made in Liège by the Fabrique nationale Herstal were found in shipments from Marseille. But much of the munitions sourced via France, as well as some of the firearms, were produced by the Société Française de Munitions de Chasse de Tir et de Guerre, based in Paris and Issy-les-Moulineaux. Exports of German-manufactured arms to the Gulf also grew noticeably from 1907 to 1909, bringing further competition for British-based manufacturers. Among these German arms were those made by the Hamburg-based company Geco, founded in 1887 by Gustav Genschow, and by Meffert, a manufacturer based in Suhl in Thuringia.

It was a mark of the growth and globalization of this Gulf trade in arms that several of the international companies involved began seeking to trade directly at the local level of the commodity chain. Initially, in the 1880s, some opened branches in Persian ports. But in the following decade, many transferred their businesses to Oman and other ports on the Arabian side of the Gulf to meet the stronger market developing there. This was the case for the Armenian-Persian importing business A. & T.J. Malcolm & Co. The Anglo-Persian firm Fracis, Times & Co., operating in Bushire since 1886, opened agencies in Bahrain in 1895 and Muscat the following year.[134] Representatives for the German firms O'Swald and Hansing could also be found in Muscat early in the twentieth century.[135] By 1900, Dresse, Laloux & Co., based in Liège, also had an agent in Muscat.[136] Additionally, a few Russian companies were involved in trafficking in Muscat through Keverkoff & Co. from Odessa.[137] Baijeot & Co., based in Djibouti, was said to have had several men with French passports based in Muscat.[138]

It seems that the kingpin of the arms traffic in Muscat around 1900 was a Frenchman named Antonin Goguyer.[139] His career can only be imperfectly reconstructed. In 1899 he supposedly settled in Muscat, after having lived in Tunis, and following a brief stay in the Horn of Africa, where he was involved in arms trafficking. While he displayed an interest in pearl trading, he quickly focused on the arms traffic as his primary activity, setting up his own trading house in 1900, named the Bazar Français.[140] All of his business dealings were with the Société Française de Munitions de Chasse de Tir et de Guerre, and he worked with numerous local intermediaries. Goguyer's relationships with the British and with representatives of France in Oman were contentious, and he reportedly left Muscat for Basra around 1903. He resurfaced in Kuwait, an important trafficking emporium at the beginning of the twentieth century, several months later.[141] Goguyer managed to become the main foreign arms smuggler in Kuwait after 1904, bringing in arms from Muscat. In 1905 he controlled 60 percent of the French arms traffic there. By the time he died in 1909, Goguyer had amassed a fortune of more than £40,000. How did Goguyer and his main associate, his nephew Ibrahim Elbaz, who took over the business in 1909, manage to bypass British surveillance? They appear to have relied on a network of dhows flying the French flag. Accordingly, the vessels were not subject to British inspection, which enabled Goguyer and his associate to transport arms and ammunition from Djibouti to Muscat, and from there to other Gulf ports.

If Muscat was the main hub of the "empire of guns" in this region, how were arms and ammunition redistributed from there? What were the networks and territories of trafficking? As with the infrastructure and networks that sustained slave trading in the Gulf, arms smuggling in the region was characterized by multiple small centres, either temporary or semi-permanent, linked by the routes of traders and smugglers. In this regard, the high degree of spatial integration of the Arabian and Persian sides of the Gulf is worth noting, as well as the fragmentation of arms and ammunition smuggling into small regional networks. The Persian coast of the Gulf was dotted with outlets for munitions. In the 1890s, smuggling was a major activity in Bushire. In 1897, for example, more than 30,000 rifles were received at that port.[142] Shiraz and Bandar Abbas were also involved in this network after 1890.

Farther south, ports along the coast of Makran were also involved in trafficking with Muscat for two decades, beginning around 1890.[143] For instance, Gwadar was the main hub for most of the caravans originating in Afghanistan and the tribal zones in the northwest of the Indian subcontinent. In the winter of 1908–9, more than 30,000 rifles were imported to Gwadar from Muscat. The Afghans took various routes to Makran. Around 1890, they would leave Quetta in Baluchistan and traverse Kurdistan to reach the coast of Makran. After 1900, most caravans used a route that passed through Khorasan and Mashhad before descending toward Sistan, a desert region on the border between Iran and Afghanistan. Sources describe caravans of around 80 men and 300 camels transporting 1,500 guns and more than 200,000 rounds of ammunition. Arms trafficking peaked in the Gulf in 1905 as the tribal uprising on the North-West Frontier unfolded; around that time, more than 3,000 rifles were imported into Persia and on the Makran coast.[144] Mohmands, Afridis, Waziris, Mahsuds, and other Pashtun tribes in the North-West Frontier purchased these arms and ammunition. Some information regarding prices survives: around 1899 a rifle sourced from Britain could reportedly be obtained for 40–50 rupees in Muscat, but with prices significantly higher, perhaps 300 rupees, in the frontier lands joining Afghanistan and British India.[145]

On the Arabian coast, Bahrain was one of the major outlets. By 1894–95, people were travelling there to buy weapons from the Persian coast, but also from the Najd and the Hasa. One of the agents for Fracis, Times & Co., Muhammad Rahim, made considerable profits in Bahrain.[146] Between 1895 and 1897, he sold around 6,000 rifles and more than 1 million cartridges to merchants from the regions mentioned above, to the value of £40,000. Arms imports from Bahrain continued to grow after 1900, and the port became the secondary hub of the Gulf arms empire, just behind Muscat. By the beginning of the twentieth century, Kuwait had become a smuggling hub for the northern Gulf, and by 1904 smuggling was in full swing, with the complicity of Shaykh Mubarak, who earned revenues of more than $50,000 per year.[147]

The British apparently did not realize until around 1896 that a large portion of the arms consignments being exported to the Gulf was being re-exported to the North-West Frontier. Representatives of British

India in the Gulf would become increasingly alarmed by the situation, echoing growing fears expressed by those posted in the North-West Frontier itself. Facing pressure from London, which viewed this traffic as a matter of imperial security, the Government of India assembled evidence that would help it adopt an effective policy and monitor the flow of arms. William Lee Warner, from the India Office, who had previously served as the government's political secretary in Bombay, was the first to put forward the notion that the porousness of the borders between Persia, Afghanistan, and India had allowed arms and ammunition to circulate. Lord Elgin, the Viceroy of India at the time, accused him of "hunting a shadow."[148] But there were other warning signs. In October 1897, London asked the British consul in Kerman, Percy M. Sykes, to gather information about arms trafficking in this region of Persia.[149] In his report, Sykes described Afghan caravans with hundreds of men and camels coming to Bandar Abbas to purchase rifles and ammunition.[150] Troops fighting the tribal uprising in the North-West Frontier added further data to the evidence that had already been assembled. In the territories held by the Afridis, they found Belgian-made cartridges.[151] In November 1898, a man from the Ghilzai tribe was captured carrying a Martini-Henry rifle inscribed "Fracis, Times & Company, 27 Leadenhall Street, London."[152] He claimed that, like many Ghilzais, he had bought his gun from Afghani merchants.[153] In early 1902 a revolver bearing the inscription "Made for Fracis, Times & Company, London" was found on the corpse of the son of a tribal chief in Waziristan.[154]

What measures did the British take to try to end arms smuggling between the Gulf and India's North-West Frontier? While military campaigns were progressing in the North-West Frontier, the British sought to strengthen their control over the Gulf's maritime space, specifically to curb the trafficking of European-made arms and ammunition. Just as with piracy and the slave trade, arms smuggling to some extent allowed the British to reinforce the framework of treaties signed between the Government of India and local powers, thereby to some extent bolstering indirect rule in region. In the case of Persia, in 1897, Mozaffar al-Din Shah signed an accord allowing the British to search any merchant vessel flying the Persian flag that was suspected of carrying arms.[155] The British also targeted the outlet markets on the

Arabian side of the Gulf: Muscat and various smaller ports in Oman in 1897, and Bahrain in 1898. In 1900, a treaty identical to the one signed with the Shaykh of Bahrain two years earlier would be concluded with Shaykh Mubarak al-Sabah of Kuwait.[156] In November 1902 the shaykhs from the Trucial Coast signed an accord banning the import and export of arms in their respective territories.[157]

Did these measures have any effect? Over the protests of British arms manufacturers and shipowners, British authorities continued their attempts to halt this regional traffic. In 1900 the Exportation of Arms Act was passed into law by the British Parliament. It allowed the government to ban the export of arms to a country where they could be used against British troops.[158] Nothing, however, was done to block the flow of arms to the Gulf. Under rules set out by the Admiralty, British warships did not have any right to intercept ships flying the British flag in international waters. While ships owned by the Sultan of Oman or the Shah of Persia were frequently inspected by the Royal Navy, those flying the British flag were treated very differently. In 1907, the Government of India's representatives in the Gulf highlighted the ineffectiveness of such measures. In Muscat, European arms continued to be freely imported and re-exported to Afghanistan and the North-West Frontier. Nothing seemed to have changed.[159] In 1908 a second international conference on arms traffic was held in Brussels, assembling the same powers that had met at the end of the nineteenth century. The conference proved a failure, notably owing to the lack of cooperation between France and Britain.[160]

Another strategy was adopted following these setbacks. Instead of targeting international emporia, a new policy sought to block the import of arms on a regional scale, at the level of the Makran coast, a transit point where most of the arms were bound for the North-West Frontier. Indeed, Makran had become an Achilles' heel of the British Empire, threatening the stability of Britain's Indian colonies. In 1910 the Government of India established the Persian Gulf naval blockade.[161] Headed by Edmund Slade, commander-in-chief of the East Indies Squadron, the blockade was quickly reinforced by land troops, the Makran Field Force. In 1910–11, Slade had more than 1,000 troops under his command. The blockade had an immediate effect. The troops' first interventions took place between Chabahar and Jask, near the very centre of the arms traffic along the coast of Makran. After 1910, smuggling between Muscat and the Makran coast seemed to decrease. In June 1912 a final measure was taken to strictly curb the arms traffic in the Gulf. The Sultan of Muscat agreed that all arms imported to Muscat would be stocked in a specific building so as to control their resale and re-exportation.[162] After this date, only buyers with a permit granted by the sultan could purchase arms from this site, and arms trafficking in Muscat declined quite rapidly.

The global economic flows in relation to the boom and collapse of the pearl and date trades buffeted the Gulf in ways which, insofar as they fostered a decades-long interlude of peace and profit, may be said to have served the interests of British India in the region. Additionally, the pearl and date commodity trades enjoyed an exploitative economic advantage as a result of the slave trade, which provided a large proportion of their labour. Interventionist suppression of the traffic in slaves was becoming pantheonized around just this juncture as a central and self-flattering narrative about Britain's imperial role as a moral force for good in the world. Anti-slave-trade efforts in the Gulf were thus vital in reputational terms; revealingly, however, the scale of the effort made would never match the scale of the challenge, and a more thoroughgoing intervention might have damaged the interests of local rulers whose co-option was central to sustaining British indirect rule in the region. But in the final analysis it is arguably the arms trade that does most to reveal the nature of that indirect rule in the Gulf, and also its limits. Traffic in arms highlights how the Gulf was an arena in which trades could develop that were highly inimical to the interests of British India, and how this could happen notwithstanding the frameworks of arm's-length rule in the region and indeed the relative flourishing of the Gulf economy. Informal empire could thus be undercut by an informal economy. Put another way, a territorial empire – here present in a salient border zone – also existed in relation to figurative empires of commodities; and what one scholar has called the "caprice of global markets" as these played out in the Gulf could in their ramifications disrupt the interests of the British India.[163] Notwithstanding the existence of a multilayered British presence and power in the Gulf, this region to some extent remained one of abidingly unruly waters.[164]

5

Passages to India

Mesopotamia and the Gulf in British Imperial Imaginaries

IN THE EARLY 1860s, Lieutenant J.B. Bewsher of the Royal Navy was sent from India to survey parts of the Tigris River and its environs. Bewsher's survey was part of a larger effort conducted under the auspices of the Survey of India, the surveying and mapping arm of the East India Company administration, which had a decades-long interest in gathering topographical information about the waterways and interior spaces of Mesopotamia. With his work completed, Bewsher presented a paper, which included the map produced by his survey, to the Royal Geographical Society in London. His paper, later published in the society's journal, provided much more than bare topographical data and descriptions of the landscape.[1] He also narrated the water routes criss-crossing the map as a kind of voyage into the region's past, or rather its multiple pasts. In his description, the Tigris and its surroundings, and the material traces that could still be seen there of ancient and medieval empires, added up to a kind of vivid palimpsest. This brought home to his London audience a potent vision of the history of Mesopotamia – a land feted as the cradle of civilization – as it had unfolded through a succession of great conquerors, from the ancient past down to more recent centuries. For example, Bewsher evoked, near the town of Kathemain, the ruins of the tomb of Zobeida, the favourite wife of Haroun al-Rasheed, a caliph of the Abbasid empire, and "a name familiar to all readers of the *Arabian Nights*."[2] He also alluded to ancient history, citing Xenophon's account and recent British classical scholarship to evoke Cyrus the Younger's attempt to seize control of the Persian Empire and the passage of his army through Mesopotamia.[3] Bewsher's account ended with a meditation on the rise and fall of the ancient cities of Seleucia and Ctesiphon.[4] The region's then-current status within the Ottoman province of Iraq was presented obliquely as an unacknowledged symptom of its economic and geopolitical decline.

Bewsher was one of several significant figures involved in the Survey of India's work in Mesopotamia. A principal aim of these efforts was to optimize transport connections between Britain and India. The possibility of developing a steamship route along the rivers of Mesopotamia captivated officials in both India and London. At the time, the mainstay of existing transportation networks, the "Cape Road" around the Cape of Good Hope, meant a long, hard, and expensive journey for people and goods. These obvious drawbacks amounted to a standing invitation for British officials, and others, to develop alternative routes. Two main possibilities came to dominate such discussions and exploratory efforts. The first of these was the "overland" route, hinging on Egypt – overland in the sense that it involved unloading ships and transporting goods and people by land across the desert from the Mediterranean to the Red Sea (the Suez Canal was still only an unrealized dream). The second was the "direct" route, whose anticipated fulcrum would be the Tigris and Euphrates rivers. By this route, ships would again cross the Mediterranean, then unload on the Syrian coast; people and goods would then transit Ottoman desert lands, to connect with river steamers that would take them down to Basra, about 100 kilometres from the Gulf. The information-gathering efforts of Bewsher and his contemporaries in Mesopotamia fit in with this dynamic.

Insofar as this history has been studied to date, emphasis has tended to be placed on the overland route, given that it would ultimately win out, thanks to the transformative possibilities of the Suez Canal, which opened in 1869.[5] The present chapter focuses instead on the "direct" route and the Gulf region. Certainly, this eventually proved to be a dead end among the rival schemes for more efficacious links between Britain and India. Indeed, it would lose ground discursively to the rival overland route even before the Suez Canal became a plausible proposition. Nevertheless, it is argued here, the debates, projects, and fantasies the direct route fostered amounted to the first flowering of a vision of a British role in the redevelopment of the Gulf and its hinterlands. As hinted by Bewsher's account cited earlier, British officials regarded Mesopotamia as a land of ruins – but also one fit for rehabilitation through British technological prowess and its attendant economic benefits, centring on the revival of its waterways linking the Gulf to the interior.

Bewsher's account is also ideologically representative of those of his contemporaries who were engaged with this frontier of British imperialism, in that it is saturated with a vision of the region as one of successive great empires and civilizations, stretching back millennia. This powerful narrative of place, through the very processes of surveying, mapping, and commentary by individuals such as Bewsher, was framed so as to tacitly position Britain as the heir to this imperial mantle of oversight and interventionism. Significantly, as will be seen here, these decades also witnessed a surge in Assyrian archaeology – a major effort spearheaded by British excavators, many of whose trophies would end up ornamenting the British Museum.

Later, at the end of the nineteenth century, commentators such as Valentine Chirol and Alfred Mahan would designate the larger space encompassing the Gulf and its backwaters and landward territories such as Mesopotamia under the new rubric of "Middle East," viewing the region as a vital bridge securing links between Britain and the Indian subcontinent. But, as is explored in the present chapter, a much earlier array of British officials and ideologues had already gone some way toward envisioning, and even achieving, a British proto-imperial role in the region.

The chapter begins by tracing the debates between Britain and India over the rival overland and direct routes, with particular reference to the experiments regarding the viability of the direct route and their ultimate failure in practical terms. It then sets this in larger contexts by turning to the archaeological explorations that were being conducted in the region at around the same time. Finally, it examines, at a slightly later chronological juncture, how around the 1860s a kind of second wind produced a renewal of interest in a direct route through Mesopotamia, this time built around railways rather than waterways.

Mesopotamian Waterways and the Route to India

By 1815 it had become increasingly clear to officials in London and in India that the sailing routes between Britain and the subcontinent via the Cape of Good Hope could barely satisfy the existing needs of commercial and passenger traffic. As such, they could not reliably underpin larger British economic and political ambitions in South Asia and the Indian Ocean world. For the East India Company, which was intent on expansion, improved transportation connections had become of first importance.[6]

Steam navigation was rapidly expanding and promised to transform existing communication networks. The idea of opening a steamship line linking Britain and India began to take shape, and various projects were developed in India starting around the 1820s.[7] These early endeavours favoured the overland route via Egypt and the Red Sea. In 1822, James H. Johnston, a Royal Navy officer, tried, with a view to profiting from public and business interest in steam shipping, to launch a steamship company linking Calcutta and Suez.[8] This attempt eventually failed, despite the support of the Society for the Encouragement of Steam Navigation between Great Britain and India, a group created in Calcutta around this time, and that of the Governor General of India, William Pitt Amherst.[9] Meanwhile, other entrepreneurs and visionaries were working toward the same goal. Johnston's imitators included another Royal Navy officer, Thomas Waghorn, who called for a monthly postal steam service between Britain and Calcutta, also via the overland route.[10] Though it drew interest in both India and Britain, Waghorn's postal service was never established.[11]

Other initiatives were launched by the successive governors of Bombay, Mountstuart Elphinstone and John Malcolm, who lobbied the East India Company's directors in the late 1820s for a regular steamship service between Bombay and Suez.[12] With that project in mind, both governors would send surveys and expeditions to map the coasts of southern Arabia and the Red Sea. During 1828–29, at Bombay's direction, naval coal depots were established in Mocha, Aden, Jeddah, and Suez.[13] In 1830, Malcolm ordered a small steamship, the *Hugh Lindsay*, to sail from Bombay to Suez to determine whether the new coaling stations made steam travel from India to the Red Sea feasible.[14]

The *Hugh Lindsay* reached Suez just one month later.[15] This first leg of the journey had gone smoothly; it proved more complicated, however, to transport goods and mail from Suez to Britain. From Suez, ship cargoes were carried by camel to Cairo, where they were loaded onto barges and sailed down the Nile to Alexandria. From there, mail and goods were shipped to Malta and, finally, to Britain.[16] However slow this trial journey had been, Malcolm remained enthusiastic about opening a steamship line between Bombay and Suez. When he left his governorship in late 1830, he sent the Company's directors a report in which he recommended a monthly steamship service between Bombay and London via Suez. That service would run for only nine months of the year, for the monsoon winds from the southwest would force suspension of the route for four months.[17]

In 1830, Bombay and Calcutta became involved in a bitter competition, with each presidency seeking to establish a steamship connection with the Red Sea. By mid-1833 the *Hugh Lindsay* had made four voyages from Bombay to Suez, with each proving faster and more encouraging than the last. Dedicated steam committees and funds were set up in both Bombay and Calcutta in the 1830s. Those committees became vocal lobby groups that, with a view to establishing permanent steamship lines between London and the subcontinent via Suez, and against the backdrop of new trial voyages, would shower petitions on the Company's directors, the House of Commons, and various British government departments.[18]

Bombay's and Calcutta's initiatives caught the attention of the Company's directors. However, it was also at just this point, when the overland route seemed to be gaining increased traction, that the direct route, structured around Mesopotamia and the Gulf, also began to be seriously broached as an alternative both in London and on the subcontinent.

In 1798, during the French occupation of Egypt, the direct route had been used to carry mail between Britain and India.[19] In the late 1820s, as speculation began to grow about a potential Russian threat to the British colonies on the subcontinent, that route began to attract renewed interest.[20] Russia and Persia signed the Treaty of Turkmanchai in 1828, marking a major step in the growth of Russian political influence in the Qajar empire and seeming to place the British colonies on the subcontinent under threat of Russian invasion.[21] For London and for the Indian presidencies, it therefore seemed necessary to reinforce British influence on India's western flank and to find a route for despatching troops to the subcontinent in the event of a Russian invasion. Recent steam navigation experiments via Suez had not yet brought sufficiently satisfactory results. Thomas Love Peacock, a Company official based in London who had studied all aspects of steam navigation to India and had become the Company's in-house expert on that topic, wrote in 1829 that the Russians "have now steam boats on the Volga and the Caspian Sea" and that they "will soon have them on the Sea of Aral and on the Oxus and in all probability on the Euphrates and Tigris." He warned that "they will do everything in Asia that is worth the doing, and that we leave undone."[22] From this point on, a series of efforts were made to explore the possibilities of the direct steamship route.

The first attempt was undertaken in 1830 by Robert Taylor, the East India Company political agent in Baghdad, and his brother James Taylor.[23] The latter had long been intrigued by the idea of steamship lines connecting London with India. Between 1825 and 1829, he had invested in several trial voyages in the Red Sea. But these efforts ultimately convinced him that the Indian Ocean monsoon was an insuperable obstacle to the opening of the Red Sea to steam navigation. He therefore changed tack and became a strong advocate for the direct route. The Taylor brothers developed good relations with the Ottoman governor of Iraq, Daud Pasha, and in the summer of 1830, they were granted a concession to run a steamship service on the Tigris and Euphrates rivers. This project was, however, abandoned after James Taylor's death in August 1830.[24]

A second attempt was made by a Royal Artillery officer named Francis Rawdon Chesney. In 1829 the East India Company's administration in London had sent Robert Gordon, British ambassador to the Porte, a long list of queries regarding the relative advantages of the overland and direct routes.[25] Chesney had come to Constantinople at about this time and was casting around for employment. With Gordon's encouragement, he undertook a comparative examination of both possible routes to India.[26] Chesney began his mission in 1830 by surveying the Isthmus of Suez. This led him to propose a canal system that would

Figure 5.1 "Capt. Chesney's Raft, in 1830. Descending the Euphrates Towards Hadisah." Lithograph by A. Picken, 1868.

cross the isthmus.[27] In late 1830 he travelled to Syria to begin the more hazardous part of his mission. In Damascus, Chesney met with the consul general in Syria, Robert Farren, who advised him to report on Syrian harbours, on roads between the Syrian coast and the Euphrates, and on the possibility of British commerce in the region.[28] After visiting Baalbek, Jerash, and Palmyra, Chesney began his descent of the Euphrates in January 1831 on a raft, starting at Anah in Ottoman Iraq.[29] Chesney was accompanied by an Arabian guide named Getgood, a dragoman named Halil, a slave, and two Arabian boatmen who handled the raft. The raft was fourteen feet long and supported by inflated goatskins (Figure 5.1). Chesney's journey is described in a detailed account he drafted of his enterprise, in which he also provides sidelights on the activities of the local populations, their farming systems, and their irrigation techniques. Four months after leaving Anah, Chesney arrived in Baghdad in spring 1831. Next, he travelled to Basra, 500 kilometres south of Baghdad, to map the lower Euphrates. He returned to Britain via Tabriz in Persia. Back in London in 1832, Chesney wrote a series of reports that concluded that the Euphrates was navigable for steamers, and he became an apostle for the direct route for British steamers. He published his account of his journey, together with a range of related documents, in *Reports on the Navigation of the Euphrates* (1833).[30]

In the wake of Chesney's well-publicized venture, several influential figures lobbied Charles Grant, the president of the India Board – the arm of government overseeing British affairs in India – for a more extensive survey to be conducted in Syria and Iraq on the feasibility of the direct route.[31] Among these men was Sir Stratford Canning, former ambassador to the Porte and a strong advocate for the reinforcement of Britain's position in the Arabian provinces of the Ottoman Empire.[32] This lobbying effort was seconded by the consul general in Syria, Farren, and by the chargé d'affaires in Tehran, John N. Campbell.[33] Meanwhile, developments during the Oriental Crisis of 1832–33 had convinced Grant British influence in Iraq and Syria needed to be strengthened.[34] In the wake of Mehmed Ali Pasha's advance in the Arabian provinces of the Ottoman Empire, Sultan Mahmud II had requested military assistance from France and Britain to preserve his sultanate, but had ultimately found that help was more readily forthcoming from Russia. In July 1833, Tsar Nicholas I and Sultan Mahmud II signed the Treaty of Unkiar Skelessi, which was basically a defensive alliance between the two powers.[35] Mehmed Ali's advance was perceived by the British as threatening Russian domination over the Ottoman territories, which might then threaten India's western flank.

In this context, in June 1834 the House of Commons appointed a Select Committee on Steam Navigation to India, presided over by Grant. In June and July 1834, Grant and his thirty-six-strong committee summoned the various protagonists, who by this point had been pressing for well over a decade for a steamship line to India. The committee gathered information about a series of issues: the political situation in Iraq and in Persia, Russia's encroachments and ambitions in the East, and the respective advantages and pitfalls of the overland and direct routes.[36] Among the men interviewed by the committee was Thomas Love Peacock, the key Company expert on the steam navigation question.[37] Peacock had become an apostle for the direct route. The committee also heard from two other partisans of the direct route, namely

Chesney, who recounted his voyage, and Robert Taylor Jr, son of the Company's influential resident in Baghdad.[38]

Supporters of the overland route were also called upon. Sir Pulteney Malcolm, commander-in-chief of the Mediterranean fleet, advocated for a steamship line between Suez and India, reminding the committee of the efforts made in the 1820s by his brothers – John Malcolm, the Governor of Bombay, and Charles Malcolm, the Superintendent of the Bombay Marine – to develop steam navigation along this route.[39] The committee also collected evidence from individuals who had taken part in trial voyages in the Red Sea. For technological advice on steamships, it also turned to Macgregor Laird, the son of the iron-founder and shipbuilder William Laird.[40] Macgregor Laird, describing the advantages of iron-hulled river steamers for exploration, presented radically new ideas to the committee, which took them on board.[41]

At the end of the hearings, the committee published a report underscoring that "regular and expeditious communication with India by steam vessels is of great importance both to Great Britain and to India."[42] It recommended that the overland and the direct routes both be developed, viewing them as complementing each other.[43] When the monsoon impaired navigation for steamships in the Red and Arabian Seas during four or more months of the year, the direct route could be used as an alternative for transporting troops, goods, and mail to India. The same report noted that the Euphrates's low-water season might pose a risk to steam navigation. However, the dry season in Mesopotamia ran from November to February, during which period the Arabian and Red Seas were not affected by monsoon winds (as occurred between June and September). Thus, it might be that the overland route was practicable when the seaward route via Suez was not, and vice versa. Regarding the direct route, however, the report concluded that not enough was known about the overland part of the journey through Syria and Mesopotamia and its riverine continuation down the Euphrates to the Gulf. The Euphrates's potential thus required further exploration, and to that end, a budget of £20,000 was approved to finance a detailed survey. Chesney was appointed to lead this venture, dubbed the Mesopotamian Survey, which would involve a team of around sixty men. An official decree, or *firman*, from the

Ottoman sultan was negotiated in Constantinople by the British ambassador, John Ponsonby.[44]

For this second expedition led by Chesney in Mesopotamia, two small flat-bottomed steamers, the *Euphrates* and the *Tigris*, were built in England. They left the country in February 1835 on board the *George Canning*, having been disassembled and packed for shipping, and arrived in April in Antioch, near the Syrian coast. From Antioch, the two disassembled steamboats were hauled on a 120-mile journey across Syrian deserts and mountains. The two steamers were finally launched near Bir (today's Birecik), a town on the Euphrates, and in the spring of 1836 the expedition began its journey down the river.[45] The *Tigris* preceded the heavier, more powerful *Euphrates*. Chesney had estimated that two months would be necessary to complete the descent to Basra, a distance of around 1,100 miles. During the first hundred miles, from Bir to Beles, navigation was difficult. Several stops were made to resupply wood, water, and food. Chesney envisaged his journey as a kind of exploration of a mythical past. From the deck of the *Euphrates*, he was able to view the ruins of ancient historical and biblical sites, such as Karkemish, Calmeh, and Halabi, as well as the summer palace of Zenobia, queen of the Palmyrene Empire.[46]

The second leg of the journey, from Beles to Anah, a distance of more than four hundred miles, was travelled without too much difficulty. But five hundred miles from their starting point, an unexpected disaster struck the expedition. On 21 May 1836, both ships were struck by a violent hurricane just as they were sailing through a narrow gorge.[47] The raging winds blew the *Euphrates* into the *Tigris*, and the latter was thrown roughly against the shore and sank rapidly. Twenty members of the expedition died.[48] Chesney reported the incident to the India Board, which gave its approval for the expedition to continue. The *Euphrates* therefore continued the trip alone, from Anah to Baghdad, the same itinerary Chesney had experimented with five years earlier. For the rest of the trip, the expedition continued to confront various hindrances. Strong opposition from tribesmen delayed the mission. Stops were made, notably at Hit (built on the site of the ancient Mesopotamian city of Is), and then at Babylon, where Chesney noted that the ruins of the city had been pillaged since his first voyage.[49] On 19 June 1836, Chesney's group arrived in Basra. A boat had brought some mail from India bound for Britain, which Chesney was supposed to take on board for a subsequent ascent of the Euphrates. But the remaining steamer, the *Euphrates*, had suffered too much damage during the descent of the river and had to be towed to Bushire for repairs.

In September, with the *Euphrates* repaired, Chesney decided, in total disregard of the India Board's orders, to sail up to Baghdad on the Tigris, conveying some newly arrived mail. From Baghdad, where he arrived in late September, Chesney continued his ascent of the Tigris to Kurnah (today's Al-Qurnah).[50] At Kurnah, the confluence of the Euphrates and the Tigris, Chesney began his journey up the Euphrates. The expedition progressed well, but technical problems with the *Euphrates*'s engines forced Chesney to put an early end to the attempt and to turn back. It thus transpired that the first Indian mail that Chesney was supposed to deliver to Britain ended up being sent by the overland route rather than the direct route, as had been anticipated.[51] In December 1836, Chesney and his party arrived in Bombay. The *Euphrates* was then turned over to an army officer, John Estcourt, with instructions to complete surveys of the Karun and Tigris Rivers.[52]

While in Bombay, Chesney was able to meet with the governor, Robert Grant. He also managed to bring Bombay's trading community around to his cause. Meetings with the Bombay Steam Fund were organized. In Chesney's mind, at least, his mission had proven that the Euphrates was navigable for steamers. He proposed to develop both the direct and the overland routes over a period of twelve to eighteen months in order to determine the most expedient route to India. Chesney arrived back in London in August 1837 but did not enjoy any great acclaim there. The opponents of the direct route – for example, Thomas Waghorn – were quick to criticize Chesney for wasteful and ineffective leadership and for delaying the opening of the overland route to steam navigation. Far from being filled with stories of success, Chesney's reports showed a high number of casualties, the complete loss of one vessel, and a financial expenditure of £43,000 instead of the expected £13,000. The expedition had provided a substantial amount of historical and geographic information about Mesopotamia; however, both the British government and the Company's directors judged that the direct route was not reliably navigable for steamers and therefore that priority should be accorded to the overland alternative.[53]

Despite the relative failure of Chesney's venture, the project of strengthening the British role in Iraq through the opening of a steamship line was not completely abandoned. New projects were developed; for instance, in 1837 mail service between India and Constantinople via Baghdad was inaugurated. Small steamboats carried despatches every fortnight between Basra and Baghdad, where the mail was then loaded onto dromedaries to be taken to Constantinople.[54]

Also in 1837, the president of the India Board, John Cam Hobhouse, ordered that a new survey of the Tigris be conducted, under the command of Henry Blosse Lynch.[55] Lynch's reports of the survey operations arrived in London in the summer of 1838, just as the British government was caught up in two major diplomatic crises, one concerning Herat and the other the Near East.[56] Hobhouse and Peacock took advantage of the political situation to present to the Company's directors the idea of a flotilla of steamboats on the Tigris.[57] In September 1838 the directors gave the go-ahead for this. Three small steamers – the *Nitocris*, the *Nimrod*, and the *Assyria* – were built in England and then transported disassembled via the Cape of Good Hope to Basra. By the spring of 1840 the small fleet was navigating on the Tigris and the Euphrates and in the Shatt al-ʿArab.[58] However, this little flotilla did not encounter the success it had expected. In 1842 only one steamer remained, the *Nitocris*, and in 1843 the Bombay Presidency requested that this steamship line be abandoned.[59] Nevertheless, with Lord Palmerston's return to government in 1846 as Foreign Secretary, and with the lobbying of Taylor's successor in Baghdad, Henry Rawlinson, the decision was made to keep the small Mesopotamian fleet.[60]

Ultimately, this steamer line established by London in Iraq in the 1840s to strengthen British influence in the region did not bring about faster connections between London and India.[61] In the 1860s, however, a private enterprise developed this service. In 1861, Lynch and his two younger brothers, Thomas and Stephen, founded the Euphrates and Tigris Steam Navigation Company, establishing regular service on the Tigris between Basra and Baghdad. The Lynch brothers' endeavours in Mesopotamia created new political, economic, and spatial dynamics, in that they integrated Mesopotamia into the networks of a steam empire extending to the Gulf and the Indian Ocean.[62] The company was endowed with initial capital of £15,000, which by 1914 had been progressively increased to £100,000. In 1862 the company commissioned its first steamer, and its second followed in 1865 – a sign of good results.[63]

The Euphrates and Tigris Steam Navigation Company carried passengers, goods, and mail, for which it received a small amount of financial support from the Government of India. By the end of the nineteenth century there were seven steamers on the Tigris, including three run by the Lynch company – the *Blosse Lynch*, the *Calipha*, and the *Mejidieh*.[64] The other four, the *Mosul*, the *Frat*, the *Resafa*, and the *Bagdadi*, belonged to the Ottoman company Seniye Steamers.[65] In 1907 the Lynch business's capital was increased as a result of an association with another British company, the British India Steam Navigation Company.[66] This involved the latter company transporting goods and despatches to Basra, where they were then handled by Lynch. Thanks to this partnership, the Lynch company's old steamers were progressively replaced by larger, more powerful ones.[67] Around 1907 the service established by the Lynch brothers could make the journey from Baghdad to Basra in two to three days, compared to five to eight days for sailing ships.[68] The journey in the opposite direction took four days for steamers but around fifty days at full sail. Despite the competition of the Ottoman steamship line, the Lynch brothers were in a strong position on the Tigris. From 1908 to 1912, the Lynch operation represented 52 percent of the traffic, compared to 48 percent for the Ottoman company.[69]

The hopes and dreams of Chesney and other apostles of the direct route were thus only partly fulfilled. The steamboats travelled only between Baghdad and Basra, and the project of the direct route remained a chimera. Nevertheless, these various steam projects contributed to the expansion of Britain's influence in Iraq. The outer frontier of the Indian empire may be said to have expanded to the northern part of the Gulf, to the region centred around Baghdad and Basra. British interests were represented by the influential residents in Baghdad, by the Lynch company, and by the men who surveyed what they considered to be the most compelling water route to India, the Euphrates. Despite the relative failure of Chesney's vision and, from the late 1840s, the growing importance of the overland route, the project to build a passage to India through Mesopotamia and the Gulf was not totally abandoned. Beginning in the 1840s, new endeavours around steam were conducted. Meanwhile, British archaeological campaigns carried out around the same period were beginning to reveal Mesopotamia and its history to the British public, in quite spectacular ways.

Excavating Empires: British Archaeology in Mesopotamia

Mesopotamia held a special place in the Victorian imagination. Soldiers and surveyors sailing down the Euphrates in the 1830s felt that they were in familiar territory, in an epic world of celebrated biblical and historical cities and empires. Travelling in Mesopotamia was thus a voyage into a remote but also known past, one that the region rendered physically tangible. A series of symbolic landmarks, ancient cities, and archaeological remains rose from a landscape that was sometimes desert, sometimes verdant and agricultural, and these sites served as markers to guide travellers. Among the waterways and irrigation canals, the British surveyors and military men at this frontier of their contemporary empire noted the ancient vestiges of palaces built by the Babylonian king Nebuchadnezzar and the Roman emperor Trajan. Babylon and Nineveh, capitals of the ancient Assyrian Empire, were nodal points on this mental map.[70] However, the spectacle of Mesopotamia inspired complex feelings. The ruins of Babylon and the irrigation canals fallen into disrepair symbolized, to the imperially minded observer, the possible horizon of approaching apocalypse. Babylon had fallen, along with its palaces, prosperous marketplaces, and religious buildings. Of the splendour of its hanging gardens, and of the farming and trading that had made its fortune, all that remained was dust and stones. The fall of Babylon demonstrated the mortality of empires – a fate to which all empires, including the British Empire, appeared ultimately doomed.[71] Babylon, Nineveh, Nimrud, and Khorsabad became overarching symbols of human and civilizational cycles.[72] Archaeology played a central role in the construction of a multilayered Victorian imaginary of Mesopotamia, revealing the past splendour of these long-fallen empires and cities while offering scope for reflection on Britain's imperial present.[73]

British archaeological adventuring in Mesopotamia began under the aegis of Claudius Rich, Robert Taylor's predecessor as British resident

Figure 5.2 William Radclyffe after Joseph Mallord William Turner, "Nineveh, Moussul on the Tigris," 1836.

in Baghdad. In particular, Rich directed a notable first set of excavations in Babylon in 1811.[74] He went on to assemble a major collection of artifacts, which after his death in 1821 would be acquired by the British Museum.[75] In this context a hint of the public interest and imaginative appeal that Mesopotamia's ancient sites were beginning to garner around this period may be noted in a drawing made by J.M.W. Turner based on a sketch by Rich, showing "Nineveh, Moussul on the Tigris," published in 1835 in London as an engraving (Figure 5.2). After Rich's lifetime, Mesopotamia would indeed become a hotbed of archaeological rivalry.[76] In 1840, with the appointment of Paul-Emile Botta as French consul in Mosul, the French began taking an active part in archaeological competition in the region; they soon appeared to have gained an edge over their British peers.[77]

Then a major newcomer, Austen Henry Layard (1817–1894), arrived on the scene.[78] Since 1839, Layard had been engaged in extensive travels in Persia and the Ottoman lands, and he had become captivated by the ancient ruins of Mesopotamia. In Constantinople in 1842, he gained the patronage of the British ambassador, Stratford Canning, who went on to support Layard's exploratory excavation projects in the mid-1840s at Assyrian ruins near Mosul.[79] Layard would subsequently gain further support and funds from the British Museum and from Henry Rawlinson, the East India Company representative in the region who had gone on (like Taylor, whom he had replaced in office) to hold in tandem the position of British consul in Baghdad. On this basis Layard would ultimately lead two long excavation campaigns in Mesopotamia.[80] First, from 1845 to 1847, he concentrated his energy on the site of the Assyrian city of Nimrud, with the help of his assistant, Hormuzd Rassam.[81] Among other spectacular finds, in 1845 Layard and Rassam uncovered the colossal brick wall of the palace of the Assyrian king Ashurbanipal.[82] After a short stay in Britain between 1847 and 1849, Layard began a second excavation campaign in Mesopotamia in 1849, which continued for around eighteen months. This time, his efforts focused on a site that, it was eventually ascertained, was that of ancient Nineveh. His new effort focused on the palace of Sennacherib and unearthed many extraordinary ancient objects, as well as a large number of cuneiform tablets from which much about Assyrian and Babylonian culture and history was eventually learned.[83] Layard also made soundings at Babylon during this period.

In 1853 the British Museum opened the Nineveh Gallery, where many objects from Layard's excavations were exhibited, bearing witness to the success of the program of digs he had directed.[84] Rawlinson could not prevent Victor Place, appointed French consul in Mosul in 1852, from reopening a French archaeological mission in Khorsabad that Botta had abandoned a few years earlier.[85] Place directed the Khorsabad excavation site during 1852–53.[86] Then began what amounted to an archaeological war, which ended in 1855 with a sort of agreement between Place and Rawlinson. A line separating the different archaeological sites was drawn, with the British and the French each allocated their designated area to excavate: Khorsabad fell to the French, and Nineveh became the exclusive domain of the British.[87]

What assessment can be made of these decades of archaeological explorations and Franco-British rivalries in Mesopotamia? Layard's

Figure 5.3 "Assyrian Rock Sculpture," from Austen Henry Layard, *A Second Series of the Monuments of Nineveh*, 1853.

Figure 5.4 After James Fergusson, "The Palaces of Nimroud Restored," from Layard, *A Second Series of the Monuments of Nineveh*, 1853.

excavations, and those of his competitors, allowed Europe's great museums to amass collections of Assyrian and Babylonian artifacts that amazed visitors throughout the latter half of the nineteenth century. Layard published a series of accounts of his archaeological adventures, lavishly illustrated with large-format colour plates (Figure 5.3), which achieved considerable success with the public.[88] In Britain, archaeology would acquire an important role in the development of a new imperial discourse on Mesopotamia. Standing in front of the ruins of what had once been prosperous, flourishing empires, the British to some extent took it as their role, envisaged variously as duty and as destiny, to re-create Babylon's and Nineveh's past splendours and to refashion a region of prosperity around Mesopotamia and the Gulf. Layard's publications achieved this visually through retrospective illustrations of an imagined ancient past (Figure 5.4). Steam power and British capital promised to help restore the ancient prosperity of biblical and ancient lands in the present day. British investments in Mesopotamia might reverse the fate of this once fertile and prosperous region, which had become barren and poor.[89] In this context, new projects, relying once again on the power of steam, were imagined and justified by discourses emphasizing the decline of the lands of the Bible and of the Assyrian kings, and feting a British informal-imperialist role there as a kind of benign blessing that in its wake would bring regional renewal under the aegis of modernity and progress.

Railways of Empire: New Steam for a British Role in Mesopotamia

New projects related to the Mesopotamia–Gulf axis developed in the context of the Crimean and Anglo-Persian wars. The Crimean War, which began in 1853 and plunged the Ottoman Empire into chaos, was a culminating explosion of the longer-term frictions that had been building between Russian expansionism in the Orient and a countervailing Franco-British sense of regional primacy. Until the end of the war in 1856, the British feared that the Ottoman Empire would entirely collapse.[90] Meanwhile, in early 1856, the Shah of Persia, Naser al-Din, marched toward Afghanistan and besieged Herat.[91] Unlike his predecessor, Muhammad Shah, whose siege of the city in 1838 had failed, Naser al-Din succeeded, with Herat surrendering in October 1856.[92] The fall of Herat was a severe blow to the system of buffer states protecting British India. The Crimean War, and the Anglo-Persian War even more so, had revealed the need to consolidate the defence apparatus protecting British India in West Asia. The Russian threat to British colonies on the subcontinent now stimulated the development of a new project, a railway in the Euphrates valley, which would strengthen Britain's military and political position west of India.

In the mid-nineteenth century, railways inspired just as much excitement as steam-powered ships, and they came to be seen as the future of transportation and communication.[93] With vast distances being bridged by railways in Europe at this time, consideration was now given to a railway line that would link Europe to India by way of Mesopotamia and the Gulf. In 1857, Chesney wrote a short essay supporting the construction of a railway in the Euphrates valley. In it, he described the political and economic advantages that Britain might accrue from an increased presence in Mesopotamia under the auspices of such a project. The arguments Chesney proposed were similar to those he had advanced in his reports on the opening of the Euphrates to steam navigation in earlier decades. With the Euphrates Valley Railway, British and Indian products would find a new market and prosperity would come to the region. Mesopotamia would renew its long-lost agricultural heritage. The arrival of steam power would notably stimulate cultures of "cotton, silk and grain." But more importantly, such a railway would strengthen the system protecting British India on its western flank. It would enable the transportation of "troops and warlike stores" from "England to India (Kurrachee) [today's Karachi] in the space of 15 or 16 days." It would form a defensive infrastructure at the borders of the Caucasus and northern Persia, regions where Russian influence predominated.[94]

In the late 1850s the Euphrates project found a new advocate in William Andrew, a railway baron and engineer. Andrew had founded the Scinde Railway Company in 1855, having been contracted by British authorities in India to build a railway line in the northwest of the country, running along the Indus River between Karachi and Kotri. That line opened in 1858 and was later extended to Hyderabad. The Scinde Railway worked in tandem with the Indus Steam Flotilla, a freight and passenger steamship company that operated on the Indus from Kotri to Multan, south of Lahore. It was envisaged already in the late 1850s that this "ill-adapted" steamship line would be replaced by an extended railway along the Indus from Multan to Lahore. Eventually, the railway system would be extended to connect the Sindh with the Punjab, with a stop at Amritsar.[95]

A strong supporter of steam railways, which for him were paragons of modernity, Andrew wrote numerous essays on the Euphrates railway project. He dreamed of linking the envisaged Euphrates Valley Railway to the Scinde Railway and from there to the larger steam transport network in northwestern India.[96] In this project he was influenced not only by Chesney and his 1857 proposals for a railway along the Euphrates but also by another railway engineer, Rowland Stephenson, who since the mid-1840s had been the managing director of the East India Railway Company. In the early 1850s, Stephenson had pictured constructing what he called the "world's highway," an international railway line that would connect the European lines with those of India at Bombay, by a route running through Turkey, Iraq, and the Gulf. While this project did not garner much support in Britain, it inspired later grandiose railway schemes such as the German–Ottoman project for a Baghdadbahn (see next chapter).[97]

In his essays and pamphlets, and particularly in his *Euphrates Valley Route to India* and *The Scinde Railway and Its Relations to the Euphrates Valley*, Andrew relied on sources such as Chesney's reports on his two expeditions in Mesopotamia to argue against the overland route. That route, he concluded, had many disadvantages, and it left an opening for his own project. The Gulf was at the very centre of Andrew's overall scheme: it was there that the meeting point of two rail networks, and indeed of two fertile and prosperous regions, Mesopotamia and the Indus valley, would be found. Unlike the Red Sea, the Gulf presented "such facilities for steam navigation" that "an almost daily communication could be established without incurring overwhelming expenses."[98]

The Euphrates Valley Railway would start at "the ancient port of Seleucia" on the shores of the Mediterranean, pass through Antioch and Aleppo in Syria, and then follow the Euphrates, with potential stops at Jaʿbar Castle, Hit, Baghdad, Kurnah, and Basra. From Basra, steamers would take passengers and merchandise to India. This railway line would revolutionize transportation, enabling passengers to travel from London to Karachi via Trieste, Seleucia, Jaʿbar Castle, and Basra in just over two weeks. The journey would be eight days shorter than via the overland route. From London to Bombay would take only seventeen and a half days.[99] Like Chesney, Andrew saw the Euphrates Valley Railway as an important geopolitical tool, securing "the quiet possession of British India" and blocking a Russian imperial advance behind the "icy barrier of the Caucasus." The recent Persian attack on Herat and the Anglo-Persian War had demonstrated that the frontier system protecting British India needed to be strengthened. The construction of the railway would amount to a demonstration of strength against Russia, enabling Britain and its ally, the Ottoman Empire, to regain some of the prestige they had lost during the Crimean War, when Russia had advanced into Asiatic Turkey. A British presence in Ottoman Iraq arising from the railway scheme would block any plans for a Russian invasion of India.[100] Furthermore, with this railway line three regions bordering British India would be linked: the Gulf, the Sindh, and the Punjab.[101] Through this railway, the system protecting India in West Asia and on the subcontinent would be strengthened.

Andrew also advanced economic arguments in favour of building the Euphrates Valley Railway. Britain would gain access to two vast granaries: one already producing huge quantities of wheat, the Sindh, and one that had once been extremely fertile, "the rich and forgotten plains of the Euphrates and Tigris."[102] Like many of his contemporaries, Andrew argued that steam and British capital would make ancient Mesopotamia fertile again. Modern technology would stimulate the region's once prosperous irrigated agriculture. Andrew rhapsodized that as locomotives loaded with passengers and goods travelled through Mesopotamia, the newly restored canals would allow the irrigation of lands where cotton and wheat would then grow in large quantities. The ancient prosperous cities of Babylon, Nineveh, Ctesiphon, and Baghdad would rise from their ashes in a "resuscitation in a modern shape."[103]

Andrew's writings also discussed a railway down the Euphrates from a historical perspective. He argued that such a line would mark the final step in a long historical process. The British would succeed the Babylonians, the Assyrians, and the Romans in this region centred around the Euphrates. Empires had succeeded one another in Mesopotamia, but they had also perished there, as demonstrated by the ruins of Babylon and Nineveh. In Andrew's account the great historical conquerors – Nebuchadnezzar, Darius, Alexander, Trajan, and Napoleon – had all taken advantage of the Euphrates route to conquer and dominate the Orient.[104] Mesopotamia was the cradle not only of humanity but of all of history's great empires. Controlling this region would thus allow Britain to return to the very source of the imperial idea. With the occupation of Mesopotamia enabled by Britain's command of technology and science, history would reach an end point. The world's first cities and imperial capitals, Babylon and Nineveh, bathed by the waters of the Tigris and the Euphrates, would thenceforth come to be integrated into the only empire that was destined to see its dominion endure – namely, the British Empire.

Andrew's scheme had many supporters, including Justin Sheil, former British envoy to Persia, and representatives of commercial and shipping interests such as J.C. Ewart, a co-founder of the Peninsular and Oriental Steam Navigation Company. The Association for the Promotion of the Euphrates Valley was formed to lobby for the project.[105]

That association's activities and Andrew's lobbying bore fruit, and in 1856 the Euphrates Valley Railway Company was founded with the aim of connecting "the Mediterranean and the Persian Gulf by a railway from the ancient port of Seleucia," from which point communications "by steamers" were to be "established with all parts of India."[106] Raising the necessary capital proved straightforward, and Andrew became chairman of the board of directors.[107] The project received support from the Foreign Office. In Constantinople, Canning lobbied Sultan Abdulmejid I, who in 1857 officially authorized the construction of the railway line in Iraq and Syria. Chesney would be involved in this project, leading some preliminary surveys in Syria in 1856 and 1857.[108]

In early 1857, however, the political and strategic context was transformed when reports reached London that a mutiny had broken out in India. To meet this crisis in British rule in India, Britain sent military reinforcements to the subcontinent to crush the revolt; all of them would be transported by ship via the Cape of Good Hope. The Indian Mutiny demonstrated once again the need for a steam route to India. In this context, Palmerston ultimately decided not to support the projected railway in the Euphrates River valley. The decision was taken to shelve the direct route and to invest instead in strengthening steam communications with India via the overland route.[109] The British government would make only one significant investment in Iraq in the years after 1857 – the construction of telegraph lines between London and India.[110]

Neither the direct route nor the Euphrates Valley Railway that sought to revive it in a new guise would ever come to fruition. Yet the spatial set of reference points – traced in person and imagined on paper by figures such as Chesney and Andrew – would survive and prove to be of enduring importance. While existing scholarship has tended to retell the history of these ventures as a recitation of fanciful but failed attempts to bridge Europe and India by steam technology, their larger importance may arguably be situated in the realm of imperial ideology. As this chapter has suggested, it is noteworthy that these efforts geared around waterways and railways were made over the same decades, and on the same Mesopotamian terrain, as major archaeological efforts to excavate ancient Assyrian sites – Britain took a lead role in all of these endeavours. It is productive to bring these two parallel phenomena together, for "modernity" imported via technology, capital furnished by imperial Britain, and archaeology uncovering fabled but failed empires of the past overlapped in Victorian imperial imaginaries. To some extent, they may even be considered two sides of the same coin: technological sophistication both underpinned and justified a British role in the region while also ensuring that its imperial mission would not only replace the great fallen empires of the past but also succeed far better than they had – that they would be more deserving of longevity and more destined to achieve it.

India and London's technological imperialism tended toward the creation of a region between Europe and the East, a region that in the early twentieth century Alfred T. Mahan and Valentine I. Chirol would perceive as an intermediary space, the "Middle East." In this emerging "Middle East," the Gulf region would play a crucial role as the aquatic "seam" that would allow Europe to connect to South Asia, in addition to providing the British Empire with some kind of cohesion by linking imperial possessions together. But before Chirol and Mahan, Chesney and Andrew had imagined a prosperous region west of India where British imperialism would be able to revive an idyllic biblical and mythical-historical time. The British would bring about the return of a time that had seen the reigns of Nebuchadnezzar, Alexander the Great, and Trajan and the glory of the cities of Babylon and Nineveh. In Mesopotamia, where, in the biblical *imaginaire* of the time, the original site of the Garden of Eden could be found, there would spring forth in this way a promise of eternal peace, associated in the Victorian mind with Pax Britannica. This "Middle East" as sketched out by Andrew and Chesney, albeit without being named "Middle East," was not a region with clearly defined boundaries, but a vast buffer zone demarcated by railway and steamship lines. It was also a kind of pioneer front that would allow "civilization" to take hold, along with trade, agriculture, and even industry.

The Gulf region, which was initially understood as a borderland or as a thoroughfare on the edge of the British empire in India, slowly emerged as a centre.

6

The Gulf in the Age of New Imperialism

IN 1896 A FRENCH OFFICIAL POSTED IN OMAN, Paul Ottavi, wrote to his superiors in Paris giving a panoramic survey of the imperial competition that had rapidly heightened across the Gulf region in the preceding years. He noted that France was not the only power seeking to gain a firm foothold in a space that had long been dominated by Britain: French efforts had to some extent been overtaken by Ottoman, Russian, and German projects with this same aim. These rival bids were a serious challenge to British authority: "England realizes that she is no longer the only country holding Neptune's trident and the sceptre of the world." In this evaluation, the Gulf was certainly "one of the most important seas in Asia." But it was no longer "a British Caspian" in the way that the British had long imagined it to be.[1]

The case Ottavi made was in many ways a strong one. Since around the 1870s, the Gulf had indeed become a place of progressively sharp contention between Britain and these four other imperial powers. For France and the Ottoman Empire, this dynamic constituted something of a revival, for both had to differing extents enjoyed greater influence in the Gulf region in the past. Germany and Russia were, by contrast, essentially new arrivals on the scene. This surge in geopolitical tensions was by no means restricted to the Gulf region, but rather reflected larger global trends. At this juncture, imperial rivalries involving both European and non-European powers was were rapidly intensifying, with relations becoming strained over the control of numerous territories in Africa, South and Southeast Asia, China, and the Pacific.

Almost all the powers involved would dub this an age of "new imperialism," a phenomenon that would involve European countries such as France, Britain, Italy, and Germany, but also polities whose interests were more oriented around Asia (such as Russia, the Ottoman Empire, and the semiautonomous British empire in India), and even the Pacific (in the case of Japan).

This "new imperialism" has been the subject of extensive scholarship, with historians proposing a wide range of explanations for the surge in imperial projects and clashes. Some accounts have emphasized the importance of economic considerations, while others have pointed to contingent factors such as the "men on the spot," or to crises on the "periphery," as precipitating more thoroughgoing territorial implantation of structures of colonial government. One valuable recent overview of the phenomenon has been put forward by Christopher A. Bayly, who notes that there may not be "one overarching explanation" for such a diverse phenomenon, even if its common features of "velocity and ferocity" may be observed across a range of different places and time periods.[2] More specifically, Bayly argues that the new imperialism may also have been underpinned by shared preconditions and that these revolved less around economic factors than political ones, above all nationalism. In this view the critical element in the new imperialism was the concurrence of a "new phase of imperial expansion with the full emergence of the European, American and Japanese nation-state and the rise of extra-European national movements."[3] In this context, it may also be highlighted that recent historiography has revised away any notion that the Ottoman Empire was uninvolved in the late nineteenth-century global movement of imperial expansion.[4]

Following along the lines of analysis suggested by Bayly, this chapter explores the overlapping imperial intrusions of France, Germany, Russia, and the Ottoman Empire into the late nineteenth-century Gulf, arguing that these dynamics may be explained less by economic necessity than by strategic and nationalist considerations. The same may be said of the series of British countermeasures taken in response to these manoeuvres by rival powers, with a sense among policy-makers in London and in India that their primacy in the Gulf was being encroached upon and that this maritime space's strategic sinecure as a kind of "British Caspian" was indeed coming under unprecedented threat after nearly a century of British dominance. Pressure exerted by Britain's imperial competitors would set the stage for correspondingly assertive British ripostes, with the net result being both a reinforcement of Britain's role in the lower Gulf and an extension of its authority more explicitly into the upper Gulf, notably through the signing of treaties with Bahrain and Kuwait.

This chapter identifies three successive phases of how the "new imperialism" unfolded in the Gulf during this crowded period of imperial rivalries and frictions. It first analyzes France's imperialism in the region, centring on Oman, which became a kind of miniature theatre of a wider shift in Franco-British relations at this time. The second part examines Ottoman, German, and Russian encroachments in the Gulf region, as well as British responses to them. The final part describes Curzon's major tour of the Gulf in 1903, which came as these imperial threats were still being felt. That tour was simultaneously a celebration of the role of British India in this terraqueous region during the previous century and an affirmation of the ongoing central role of the Gulf for the empire of the Raj, in ways that in some measure went well beyond treating it as merely a periphery guarding the empire on its western flank. Instead, the boosted British presence in the Gulf and the extension to the region of practices of imperial government associated with British rule in India itself provided the specific context in which this space would gain a new toponym: the "Middle East." The greater press of encroaching threats from rival powers centred on the Gulf region may be said to have led to British efforts to anchor this space ever more firmly and directly in imperial frameworks connected to, and protective of, the Indian subcontinent.

French Bids for Influence in Oman and the Gulf

The diplomatic perch representing French interests in Muscat from which Ottavi wrote in 1896 was of recent vintage. It had been established just two years earlier, on the decision of France's foreign minister, Gabriel Hanotaux, as part of a larger effort to strengthen the country's diplomatic presence in the region. Ottavi, a brilliant diplomat and Arabist who had previously been posted to Zanzibar, became the first holder of France's new vice-consulship in Oman.[5]

At the same time, however, French efforts to construct a relationship with Oman were not wholly novel, for they also reconnected with a much earlier history. In the mid-eighteenth century, France had already sought diplomatic relations with Ahmad bin Said, the founder of the Al Bu Said dynasty and a significant political player in the Indian Ocean.[6] He granted France permission to establish a trading post at Muscat in 1775; a decade later his successor, Sultan Said Bin Ahmad, authorized the appointment of a French representative there.[7] The French Revolution, however, interrupted progress in diplomatic relations with Oman.[8] France's ambitions in the region were renewed in the early 1800s, with Oman regaining importance in the eyes of the government in Paris as part of Napoleon's drive to restore French influence in the Indian Ocean and the Orient. In 1803 a consul appointed to Oman by Napoleon arrived in Muscat, only to find himself at the centre of a diplomatic tussle in which the regent, Badr bin Sayf, constrained by agreements signed by his predecessors with Britain, refused to allow him to disembark.[9] A further effort in 1807 was more auspicious: the governor of the Île-de-France (Mauritius), Charles-Mathieu-Isidore Decaen, signed a convention with the new sultan, Sayyid Said, and as part of these overtures a representative named Dallous was appointed to Oman to advance French interests. Ultimately, though, in the context of continuing war with Britain in the Indian Ocean, Napoleon's strategic hopes in Oman proved unattainable: military and naval setbacks in the Indian Ocean suffered by France forced Dallous to quit Muscat in 1810. This left the British in the favourable position of being able to engage with Oman without any third-party rival.[10]

Nevertheless, in the decades that followed, even as Oman essentially fell under the sway of the East India Company (and then its successor entity, the Government of India), the French gained an unexpected windfall. Beginning in the late 1830s, Sayyid Said signed numerous commercial agreements and treaties of friendship with various Western powers. France became a beneficiary of this new policy, gaining a treaty of friendship and commerce with Oman in 1844. This allowed trade to flourish not only between France and Oman but also between Oman's African dominions and French possessions in the Indian Ocean.[11] At this point the French king, Louis-Philippe, also established a consulate in Zanzibar.[12]

What was the rationale behind the French decision in 1894 to renew diplomatic representation in Oman, after an interval of eighty-four years? Hanotaux's decision to establish a French vice-consulate in Muscat should, according to one interpretation, be viewed against the backdrop of the Franco-Russian alliance concluded that same year. This military and political pact constituted one of the fundamental European alignments of the pre-First World War era, and the Persian Gulf was a region where these two newly minted allies might cooperate to advance their overlapping imperial ambitions.[13] In particular, an enhanced French presence in Oman would be consonant with Russian interests, given that the latter had already achieved a strong footing in Persia over preceding decades and was now seeking to further extend its influence into the Indian Ocean.

Seen from another perspective, however, it might equally be argued that the moment was ripe, even without regard to the Russian alliance, for France to enhance its position in the region. In the broader context of France's Indian Ocean policies, its diplomatic implantation in Oman in 1894 may be understood as part of a larger global strategy.[14] French colonization along the Somali coast had been developing apace over the previous decade: the town of Obock had been acquired much earlier, during Napoleon III's reign in 1863, but only in the 1880s had its use for state purposes been actively pursued.[15] Meanwhile, a French colony in Djibouti had been founded in 1888, so as to provide a counterweight to the influence that had long been wielded by Britain over the Strait of Bab el-Mandeb, connecting the Red Sea to the Indian Ocean. (The British authorities in India had successively occupied Aden in 1839, the island of Perim in 1857, Zeila and Berbera in 1884, and the island of Socotra in 1886.)[16] By around 1890, therefore, France was in possession of limited terrain along the Bab el-Mandeb. This toehold offered little room for expansion, however, being boxed in by neighbouring areas under domination by Britain and, to a lesser extent, Italy.[17] With Oman, therefore, France may be said to have been seeking a new point of influence, and perhaps ultimately a strategic staging post for its larger commercial and military ambitions; such a nexus would, in particular, allow France to influence the coasts around another crucial maritime nexus, the Strait of Hormuz, and would also open up access to the Gulf and to wider stretches of the Indian Ocean.

France's moves to establish a diplomatic presence in Oman may also be interpreted as an attempt to counter the Government of India's dominance there, which was otherwise effectively unchallenged. Notably, in 1888, after Turki bin Said's death, Calcutta had intervened in the process of the sultan's succession, favouring his second son, Faisal ibn Turki, who would go on to reign until 1913.[18] Then, in 1891, Calcutta convinced the newly installed Faisal to sign a treaty by which he agreed not to "cede, sell, mortgage, or otherwise give for occupation" any portion of his territory to any power other than Britain.[19] This agreement, valid for fifty years, transformed Oman into a British protectorate.

France's imperial endeavours in Oman soon became a source of significant tensions between Paris, London, and India. The newly appointed Ottavi rapidly developed cordial relations with Faisal, much to the dismay of the British. In 1896 the sultan even offered Ottavi a mansion in the heart of Muscat as a gift; it became the official residence of the French consuls, known as the *beit firansa*, the "French House."[20] Two notable Franco-British diplomatic conflicts centring around Oman developed during this period. One slow-burning controversy revolved around Arab dhows flying the French flag, which were viewed with suspicion by the British; another more pointed dispute centred on a coaling depot in Oman granted by Faisal to France. The latter quarrel erupted just months after the Fashoda Incident of 1898, an episode of Franco-British imperial competition in what is now South Sudan that dramatically heightened tensions between the two countries.[21] These issues unfolding around Oman meant that for several years this periphery of the British empire in India would be a hotspot of diplomatic tussles between London, Calcutta, and Paris, conducted against the backdrop of a long process of diplomatic rapprochement between Britain and France following the low point represented by Fashoda.

The coaling depot affair began in November 1898, when a few lines published in a French newspaper, the *Journal des Débats*, made public Faisal's grant of a concession for France to build a coaling station at Bandar Jissah, five miles south of Muscat.[22] Two weeks later, Théophile Delcassé, Hanotaux's successor as France's foreign minister, sent the British ambassador a letter in which he denied any knowledge of the project.[23] Rumours spread despite this denial, ratcheting up tensions between France and Britain.

The project did indeed exist. In 1885, during France's war in Tonkin (in today's Vietnam), Britain had barred French ships from coaling in Aden.[24] French navy ships therefore stopped at Obock during the war to re-coal, but faced delays and problems as the French struggled to maintain coal stocks in the colony.[25] Paris therefore felt the need to obtain a foothold in the northern Indian Ocean that might serve as a coaling station on the maritime route to East Asia. For Whitehall and the Government of India, however, allowing the French to gain any more ground in Oman was out of the question.

In January 1899, George Nathaniel Curzon was appointed Viceroy of India and took personal charge of the coaling depot affair, having been given a free hand on the matter by the Secretary of State for India. He quickly delegated the Government of India's representatives in the region, namely the resident in Bushire, Malcolm Meade, and the agent in Oman, Christopher G.B. Fagan, to make inquiries concerning the grant made to France. But in late January, Fagan informed Bushire and Calcutta that, while waiting for Meade's arrival in Muscat, he had ordered a gunboat, HMS *Sphinx*, to Bandar Jissah with "instructions to hoist the British Flag" in the event of any French naval ships appearing at that harbour.[26] Fagan was responsible for this show of force, which he had orchestrated without higher approval. The initiative violated the terms of a treaty signed by France and Britain in 1862, in the aftermath of the separation of Oman and Zanzibar, whereby the two European powers had agreed to respect the independence of the sultans of Oman and of Zanzibar.[27] As the situation seemed to be spinning out of control, the Foreign Office, concerned about how the French might react, began corresponding with Curzon in an attempt to find a solution. London was aware of the dangers inherent in Fagan's forceful gesture aimed against the French.[28] After discussing the matter, Whitehall and the Government of India agreed that the viceroy would inform Faisal, through Meade, that the Government of India would seek to block any attempt by Faisal to gain financial support as long as this issue of a potential territorial concession to France remained unsettled. But it was also decided that further acts of hostility against France were to be avoided.

The next stage of the coaling depot affair illustrates the latitude Curzon allowed himself in settling the crisis. In effect it was the viceroy who set the conditions for resolving the issue, ignoring London's directives. In the winter of 1899, London recommended moderation and insisted that Faisal clarify whether he had granted the concession to the French government or to a French citizen residing in Oman. Indeed, under the Franco-Omani treaty of 1844, French citizens had the right to acquire properties in Oman. If the plot of land in Bandar Jissah had been conceded to a Frenchman rather than to France, the Government of India's argument would become weaker. Curzon, however, gave short shrift to such legal niceties and adopted a much harsher line, circumventing Whitehall's caution. Through Meade and Fagan, he quickly began to exert strong pressure on Faisal, with a series of demands centred around the public cancellation of the concession.[29]

The crisis reached a peak in mid-February 1899, with Curzon having ordered the commander-in-chief of the Royal Navy's East Indies Station, Archibald L. Douglas, to sail to Muscat aboard the cruiser HMS *Eclipse* to provide a show of force. On 14 February the cruiser hove into sight of Muscat, where it was joined by other British ships stationed in the Gulf, forming a squadron. On 15 February, Meade concerted with Douglas on how to ensure that this "show of strength" served to "bring the Sultan to his senses" and to "compel him to do" what had been required of him; given Ottavi's attempt, representing France, to outface British influence in Oman, this matter was also taken to be one that had established a narrative that "has been damaging to our prestige all over the Persian Gulf" and that required explicit remedy.[30] Events then appear to have moved quickly, with Douglas summoning Faisal to meet him on the *Eclipse* and publicizing a threat to bombard the sultan's palace and forts in the event of non-compliance. On 16 February, Faisal wrote to Douglas that the concession to France had been cancelled, but without responding to the summons to come aboard the *Eclipse*. Douglas then sent a new ultimatum to the sultan: either he would come to see him before two o'clock that afternoon, or the commander of the *Eclipse* would find himself forced to execute the orders he had received. Faisal sent his brother to Douglas, who refused to allow him on board. Finally, at 1:45 p.m., fifteen minutes before the expiry of the ultimatum, Faisal presented himself to Douglas and yielded to all the demands made by the Government of India. Faisal would publicly announce the cancellation of the grant to France of a coaling station.

The decision would also be posted on the gates and customs houses of Muscat and Muttrah.[31] It may be said that at this point the French, almost a century after Napoleon's project in the Indian Ocean, had lost a second battle for Oman. Whether France would have been prepared to back up its ambitions in Oman is unclear: its stance may have been built more on bluff. In any case, it did not express much support for Faisal throughout the critical period of January and February when Curzon was dramatically increasing pressure on the sultan.

The affair was concluded to Britain's great satisfaction. For France, however, the issue was less favourable. Meetings took place in London in February and March between Prime Minister Salisbury and the French ambassador, Paul Cambon, to discuss the concession's cancellation, amid praise in the British press for Curzon's handling of the affair. Cambon made it clear that while France was willing to renounce the concession in Bandar Jissah, Paris still desired a coaling station somewhere in Oman. After Fashoda, London was keen to show consideration to Paris. Therefore, in March 1899 the Foreign Office informed Curzon that the 1862 treaty entitled Paris to obtain "coaling facilities" in Muscat.[32] But Curzon was not yet ready to surrender. He replied that he would of course submit to the India Office's orders, but in private the viceroy expressed exasperation. "Coaling-shed today, it will be something else tomorrow," he would write, declaring that the French "are not likely to seek another Fashoda at Muscat." As he saw it, the crucial factor was less France than the sultan, for whom he expressed a racialized contempt, but who he felt could readily be brought back into line: "We are dealing with a vain, stupid, negroid princelet, whose head has been turned by French promises and intrigue."[33]

A somewhat imprudent declaration from Delcassé turned events in Curzon's favour. Delcassé had issued no press release about the February 1899 episode in Oman. Yet on 7 March of that year he discussed the affair in the French Chamber of Deputies. On this occasion he gained applause for issuing a statement that "'Her Majesty's Government has expressed her profound regret,' for the actions of her agents, 'as incorrect as spontaneous.'" On learning of this, Curzon immediately telegraphed the Secretary of State for India, declaring that the Reuters despatch of Delcassé's statement "renders Meade's position untenable, and seriously comprises mine, and will be greatly resented in India."[34]

Nor was London prepared to accept Delcassé's interpretation of the affair.[35] In a near-instantaneous rebuttal, a Foreign Office minister stated in the House of Commons that "we expressed no disapproval of the action of our Agent, which, indeed, was taken under our instructions"; a few days later, the Secretary of State for India telegraphed Curzon that the government "will continue to support and defend course taken; promptitude of measures adopted has prevented a possible repetition of Fashoda."[36]

To some extent the tensions created by the concession of a coaling station to France illustrate the different attitudes regarding Oman held by the Government of India and the "Home Government" (as it was then called) in London. The affair allowed the newly appointed Curzon to demonstrate his intention of making safeguarding British interests in the Gulf region a priority of his viceroyalty. Ultimately, however, these battles were mainly symbolic, and a willingness to compromise would eventually win out, with France permitted to have a coaling station in Oman the following year.

Beyond this search for a coaling station, Paris had long sought to develop other means to exert its influence in Oman and the Indian Ocean. This was notably done through permitting Arab dhows to fly the French flag. The French had been granting this right to dhow owners based in Oman and other ports of the Indian Ocean since the late 1840s. According to British officials based in the Gulf and the Indian Ocean, these French-flagged boats became more numerous after 1880.

On what basis did the British judge there to have been a sudden abundance of dhows flying the French tricolour in the Indian Ocean at the end of the nineteenth century? Long-standing French policies in the Indian Ocean had set up conditions whereby the French flag could be flown by relatively sizable groups, extending the protections it afforded to them while also potentially extending French influence. Such policies can be found formalized as early as 1846, with a regulation promulgated by the governor of the island of Mayotte, near Madagascar, which set out two conditions for flying the French flag. The first was that the dhow be owned or part-owned by "individuals under French domination"; the second was that half the crew had to be French subjects. Who could be encompassed under these designations? Arguably, what is most striking here was the looseness of the criteria for gaining what was called a *patente de francisation*, a licence to fly the French flag. A wide range of individuals could claim to be "under French domination" or argue that in some respect they might be considered French subjects.[37] The Mayotte regulations of 1846 were subsequently extended to other territories under French domination in the Indian Ocean, notably Madagascar and islands of the Comoros archipelago but also Obock and Djibouti. It appears that similar procedures came to be applied in Oman for allowing dhows there to fly the tricolour.

The trading communities of the Indian Ocean had, since the early nineteenth century, benefited from the existence of different legal regimes in this maritime world. It was not unusual for ship captains to choose to fly the flag of one country instead of another so as to navigate more freely, escape inspections, or avoid attack.[38] It was this legal patchwork that the British would increasingly try to reform away over the latter years of the nineteenth century, since dhows flying the French flag might be suspected of engaging in various illicit activities, such as gold smuggling, gun-running, piracy, and especially slave trading. As steam navigation developed in the Indian Ocean with the opening of the Suez Canal, the dhow trade began to symbolize for the British an alternative, retrograde, and illegal regional economy.[39]

The "Suris," dhow owners from Sur, in Oman, quickly became the target of these accusations around 1880. Sur, one hundred miles from the capital, had around twelve thousand inhabitants at this point. For the British, Sur was synonymous with the slave trade, and Royal Navy ships had been chasing Suri dhows since the 1850s. How had Suri dhow owners based in Oman, a British protectorate, come to be in possession of *patentes de francisation*? The treaty signed between France and Oman in 1844 had created two categories of "French protected subjects" in the sultanate. France offered its protection and a certain number of privileges not only to French subjects in Oman but also to people merely working for the French.[40] Moreover, according to the treaty's terms, the property of subjects under French protection was under the sole authority of France and could be subjected to search only with French authorization.[41] Thus, a major consequence of this agreement was that dhows owned by French protected subjects were exempt from Royal Navy ships' right to search.[42] The French flag was thus a valuable flag of convenience in this part of the Indian Ocean.[43]

In the 1890s the French-flagged dhows affair began causing tensions between France and Britain. The British gathered evidence that Suris and other Arab dhow owners were using their right to fly the French flag to engage in the slave trade. In September 1898 the commander of HMS *Sphinx* stopped two French-flagged ships in the waters off Muscat that had more than seventy-five slaves on board.[44] Around 1900, according to the Royal Navy, around one thousand slaves were being shipped every year to the Gulf region via Sur on dhows flying the tricolour.[45] In an October 1898 letter addressed to Delcassé, Salisbury described considerable slave traffic off the coast of Africa conducted by dhows from Oman flying the French flag.[46] Recent research has underscored that the British appear to have overestimated both the numbers of Arab dhows flying the tricolour in the Indian Ocean and their role in the slave trade. For instance, in 1904 only fifty-six Suri dhow owners held a *patente de francisation*.[47] From the point of view of the French authorities, it may also be noted, the value of having the Suris flying the tricolour was not related to thwarting the British crusade against the slave trade as such. Instead, the Suris constituted a means to resist Calcutta's aggressive policy in Oman and, in Ottavi's words, to increase "our influence as opposed to that of the English."[48]

In 1899, Faisal, under pressure from the Government of India, began taking steps to push dhow owners based in Oman to stop flying the French flag. Fagan's successor as agent at Muscat, Percy Cox, accorded the question priority.[49] In June he travelled with Faisal to Sur. Faisal publicly declared that henceforth he would "neither recognize nor permit that any subject of mine, no matter who he may be, should take so-called protection papers and flags from the French Government."[50] During their visit, Cox and Faisal received pledges from forty-five dhow owners to stop flying the tricolour. These papers were forwarded to Ottavi, who protested that the procedure was "contrary to usage."[51]

The reactions on the British side were rather different. Curzon was delighted by Faisal's intervention. In his view the sultan had, quite unknowingly, served to advance the interests of British India in its own dispute about tactics with the government in London: "I am delighted that the Sultan is forcing the hand of the Foreign Office."[52] In London there was much less amusement about the Sur episode, which was thought likely to create new tensions with France. Nonetheless, Curzon continued his offensive against the *patentes de francisation*. In April 1901, Cox put forward the idea that Faisal should be encouraged to officially declare that from a given date all Omanis would be forbidden to fly foreign flags in the sultanate's waters without the sultan's authorization.[53] The plan did not meet with the expected approval in London, and the Foreign Office recommended a more measured approach, which bore fruit in the summer of 1901. In August, Cambon informed London that Paris had given orders not to renew any *patente de francisation* granted to Omanis without further careful examination.[54] It seems that after Cambon's intervention, France had decided to adopt a much more flexible policy regarding the French-flagged dhows in Oman. This shift may be traced to a new French vice-consul in Oman and, more importantly, to larger shifts in Franco-British relations.[55] Ottavi would be replaced in 1902 by Lucien Laronce, who was less of an Anglophobe than his predecessor. In addition, Britain and France were beginning a diplomatic rapprochement, which would lead to the signing in April 1904 of a series of bilateral accords known as the Entente Cordiale.[56] Thus, all the conditions seemed to have been met for France and Britain to achieve détente on the subject of Omani dhows flying the tricolour.

However, negotiations between London and Paris continued between 1902 and 1904, without success. Curzon urged London to include Oman in the discussions of the Entente Cordiale. The viceroy wanted France to formally recognize British predominance in Oman, just as Britain had recognized that of France in Madagascar.[57] Arab dhows flying the French flag thus became the centre of a *mésentente cordiale* between Paris and London. Because of this diplomatic impasse, in 1904 the two parties chose to refer the issue for resolution through the recently formed Permanent Court of Arbitration at The Hague (which provided a mechanism for nations to resolve disputes via arbitration conducted by independent jurists).[58] France and Britain both submitted their cases and documents to that court; these were reviewed by the court's panel of experts and arbiters in the summer of 1905.[59] The ruling was handed down on 8 August of that year.[60]

The British case was constructed around the argument that the granting of *patentes de francisation* to Omani subjects constituted a fundamental infringement of Oman's independence, which both France and Britain had committed to respecting when they signed the 1862 treaty.[61] The court rejected this argument, citing the fundamental right of any state to give permission for its flag to be flown.[62] However, the court decision emphasized that France had committed infractions against a number of treaties and thus had to be sanctioned. France had notably contravened a series of texts that regulated the legal status of French protected subjects in Oman.[63] The court demanded that France in the future recognize as protected subjects only individuals who were either inhabitants of French protectorates or susceptible to designation as protected subjects by the terms of the 1844 treaty. The court also highlighted that France, by conceding the *patentes de francisation* that facilitated the slave trade, was not respecting the international agreement made at the Brussels Conference of 1890, which committed the signing powers, including France (and Britain), to work to suppress the slave trade in Africa.[64] The court decided that the subjects of the Sultan of Oman who had obtained a *patente* to fly French colours before 1890 could keep it. But the ruling stated that from 1905, France could only grant the right to fly the tricolour to Omanis who could be recognized as French protected subjects according to the criteria it outlined.[65]

The British case also raised the question of whether dhows granted the right to fly the tricolour before 1890 could be searched by British ships. Recalling the extraterritoriality that French protected subjects enjoyed, the arbiters made it clear that French-flagged dhows from Oman were thereby immune from the Royal Navy's right to search.[66]

Between the relative failure of the coaling station project and the fact that the Permanent Court of Arbitration's decision had brought a halt to the granting of the *patentes de francisation*, France's surreptitious imperialism in and around Oman may be said to have fizzled out. But the story did not stop there. An enigmatic figure named Antonin Goguyer would take centre stage in an outlandish but striking coda to the history just explored. Having arrived in Oman in the 1890s, Goguyer came to personify the dream of French ascendancy there. Ultimately, his sense of himself as a man of destiny would prove false, for in seeking to harm British interests in Oman and the Gulf region, Goguyer grew increasingly out of step with the priorities of the French Third Republic.

Who was Antonin Goguyer (Figure 6.1)? Crossing multiple categories, Goguyer remains almost undefinable: an adventurer, a distinguished Arabist, a pearl trader and arms dealer, the owner of a trading company based in Oman, and a journalist and essayist. He also benefited from significant support from the most prominent French colonialist lobby, the "colonial party" (*parti colonial*). A blatant Anglophobe, Goguyer had a vision for an enhanced French role in Oman. For the British, Goguyer came to symbolize the surreptitious imperialism that had been developed by Paris in Oman and the wider Indian Ocean since the 1880s. An element of myth swirled around Goguyer, created partly by himself and partly by the representatives of the Government of India in Oman. The latter saw Goguyer as more than just an agent of French imperialism in the Gulf, occasionally suspecting that he might, in the wake of the 1894 Franco-Russian Alliance, be seeking to advance a Russian expansionist agenda in the region as well.[67] Set against the complex and contradictory body of representations that grew up around Goguyer, archival sources – notably the records of the French vice-consulate in Oman – provide a somewhat more solid basis for separating myth from reality.[68]

Goguyer settled in Muscat in March 1899, having previously based himself for a few years in Tunisia, where he worked for the French colonial administration, and, more briefly, in the Horn of Africa, where he dealt arms. Shortly after arriving in Oman, he contacted Ottavi, to whom he confided a project for Oman that was both economic and political. Goguyer envisaged developing the sultanate's northern coast through the granting of a concession by the Sultan of Oman. His main objective was to obtain exclusive rights for a company that he proposed to establish with a Parisian jeweller, Sigismond N. Ettinghausen, to exploit mines, quarries, forests, and pearl fisheries along coast between Sib (near Muscat) and Khor Fakkan (close to the Musandam Peninsula).[69] But Goguyer's dream could only materialize if the French

Figure 6.1 Antonin Goguyer, 1890

government invested in his project – more specifically, if it supported the construction of a railway line along this coast, as well as the establishment of a steamer line for coastal shipping, to enable the export of goods.[70] The central node of this projected grand economic system was to be Dibba, a small port on the east coast of the Musandam Peninsula, from where minerals and other goods would be shipped. Goguyer claimed that the investment would be profitable: "Deba" (as it was termed in French accounts) would become the most important port in Oman. Muscat would lose its central position in trading networks, and British interests would be weakened by this new French stronghold in the sultanate.

Goguyer's plan also had heady political aims. He dreamed of creating a vast kingdom encompassing the Arabian Peninsula and the Gulf region, which would be under French tutelage. In his correspondence with Ottavi from March 1899, Goguyer urged the vice-consul to convince Paris to contact the son of the founder of the second Saudi state, Abd al-Rahman. Politically speaking, the kingdom envisaged by Goguyer would have been a kind of federal monarchy, where Abd al-Rahman would ally himself, through treaties and military interventions, with the shaykhs of "El Catif, El Hasa, El Bahreïn, El Qatar and the Nedj."[71] And Goguyer's scheme went even further. Abd al-Rahman and the French would reign over the Arabian Peninsula and the Gulf, and Russia would reinforce its position in Persia; British influence west of India would correspondingly wane. These projects dreamed up by Goguyer, imagining a grand role for France (and for himself) in the Gulf region in association with local Arab rulers, might seem to make him a kind of French prefiguration of Lawrence of Arabia. Yet they remained fanciful and unfulfilled, receiving no support from the French government.

Around 1899, Goguyer began smuggling arms, as demand for contraband arms and munitions exploded in the Gulf region. According to Ottavi, Goguyer worked for a prominent French arms manufacturer, Société Française des Munitions de Chasse, de Tir et de Guerre.[72] He owned a Muscat-based trading house called the "Bazar français," where arms and munitions imported from France were stored.[73] Around 1900, Goguyer became the leading arms dealer in the Gulf.[74] In this way he waged a minor war with the British empire by fuelling, with his commerce in arms and munitions, the insurgency against the Government of India on the northwest frontier. He grew rich in the process: by the time of his death in 1909, his personal fortune amounted to £40,000.[75]

In 1903, however, while he was flourishing as an arms dealer, Goguyer came into conflict with the French representative in Oman, owing to several episodes that placed vice-consul Laronce in a delicate position with regard to not only Faisal but also the British. The year 1903 therefore marks a break in the course of Goguyer's brief but fervid career in the Gulf, and the beginning of a long "twilight" in the adventurer's life and business. According to Laronce, Goguyer sought a passport at the French vice-consulate for travel to Asiatic Turkey and left Muscat in September 1903 because of a conflict with a local trader.[76] After a brief stay in Basra, Goguyer settled in Kuwait between September 1903 and January 1904. Around this time, he had reportedly become the main arms smuggler in Kuwait, while still controlling more than 60 percent of arms trafficking in Oman.[77]

As Goguyer approached the height of his career as an arms smuggler, a series of events precipitated his fall. He returned to Muscat in 1904 but left in 1908. How did this ending play out, with Oman as a backdrop? It seems that in 1900, Goguyer had led a defamatory press campaign against not just Faisal but also Britain.[78] While living in Oman in 1900, Goguyer, who had a history as a pamphleteer and polemicist in not only Tunisia but also the Horn of Africa, began publishing articles in a satirical journal, the *Fath-al-Basiar*, published as a monthly and distributed from Beirut. Notably, one of this publication's sallies had involved revisiting the coaling station affair and, particularly, the moment of Douglas's threat to bombard Muscat and the sultan's humiliation. Copies of *Fath-al-Basiar* were addressed to the Gulf shaykhs. It seems that Goguyer developed further his activities as a pamphleteer, especially between 1902 and 1904, publishing more articles in the *Fath-al-Basiar*, which changed its name in 1902 to *Murshid-al-Albad*. According to the Government of India, the sole aim of this journal was to "inflame Muhammadan feelings everywhere against Britain, whose policy was presented in an odious light."[79] In 1904, Faisal demanded, no doubt under pressure from Cox, that Goguyer be expelled from Oman. As the tension continued to mount between vice-consul Laronce and Faisal in 1904, Paris took control of what had by this point been dubbed the "Goguyer affair." Thanks to Delcassé's intervention and to the support of the French colonial party, Goguyer escaped sanction by Faisal. However, a year later the Frenchman targeted Britain again, in a series of articles. During 1905 and 1906 he published several articles in a journal called *Les Pyramides* criticizing the relations between the Gulf shaykhs and the British and targeting France's inaction against Britain.[80] While these articles circulated in the Gulf, vice-consul Jean Beguin-Billecocq wrote several letters to the French government stressing the need to stop according Goguyer any support.[81]

By 1908, the support of the French vice-consul had dwindled and as British measures put a halt to arms contraband. Goguyer now left Muscat. What happened to him after 1908? A letter from Léon Michel de la Croix of the Carmelite Friars Convent in Baghdad, dated 24 October 1909, sheds some light on the end of this "swindler's" life. Goguyer arrived in Baghdad in July 1909, in a terrible state of health, after spending some time travelling. He spent nearly two months with the Carmelites. Then, in September, he was seen boarding a boat chartered for Basra and Muscat, where he died in October 1909 of heatstroke.[82]

Imperial Entanglements in the Upper Gulf

France's resurgence in Oman and the Indian Ocean, as it has emerged in the course of this chapter, would appear to be a story of much ado about nothing. By no serious measure can France be said to have constituted a real threat to British interests west of India. At the same time, however, looking beyond the French case, Britain in the late nineteenth century was certainly facing more serious dangers in the Gulf. Three powers, the Ottoman Empire, Russia, and Germany, were flexing their muscles to gain a foothold in the region. British responses to these imperial manoeuvres were piecemeal, but all of them tended in the same direction of extending British rule to the Upper Gulf, specifically to Bahrain and Kuwait.

The 1870s marked the Ottoman Empire's return to the Gulf, not its arrival. In the sixteenth century the Ottomans had conquered the Arabian coast of the Gulf from Basra to Bahrain, as well as Yemen and the Arabian Peninsula (the Hasa, Najd, and the Hijaz).[83] Although the Porte's authority had dwindled over the seventeenth and eighteenth centuries on the Arabian Peninsula, in the early nineteenth century Bahrain, Qatar, and Kuwait were still under Ottoman rule and governed from the *vilayet* (administrative division) of Baghdad.

Between the mid-1840s and 1908, the Ottoman Empire was reshaped by a vast program of renewal, first during the "Tanzimat" period of reforms, which lasted until 1876, and then continuing over three more decades during the long reign of Sultan Abdülhamid II.[84] These reforms profoundly transformed the Arabian provinces of the empire. In the Gulf region they led to the reassertion of the Porte's authority and to a sort of Ottoman renaissance on the shores of this inland sea.[85] Beginning in 1869, the chief proponent of this Ottoman reformism in the Gulf was the governor of the *vilayet* of Baghdad, Midhat Pasha.[86] In 1870, Midhat Pasha re-established Ottoman authority over Kuwait, granting the Shaykh of Kuwait the title of *kaymakam* (which translates as "status" or "position"). This local-level post was given to state administrators or rulers representing the Ottoman sultan, all of whom were appointed by the reigning sultan. In 1871, Midhat Pasha organized a series of relatively successful military campaigns on the Arabian Peninsula and along the coast of the Hasa. In 1872, Qatar became a *kaza* (subdistrict) of the *sanjak* (provincial district) of Najd, which made official this Ottoman comeback on the northern shores of the Gulf.[87]

These administrative and military successes in the upper Gulf marked a turning point in the history of the Ottoman Empire in the Gulf region. They also quickly became a source of concern for both the Government of India and London.[88] Outlandish rumours swirled about Midhat Pasha's real intentions. In the minds of the British, the Ottomans aimed to create a vast province extending from Baghdad to Oman and encompassing Aden and the Red Sea.[89] It was mainly as a response to this Ottoman renaissance in the Gulf that the British decided to strengthen their position in the upper Gulf and take control of Bahrain.

At this juncture, Bahrain was far from being *terra incognita* for the British. Since the 1820s the rulers of Bahrain had been signing a series of treaties with the British, notably the General Maritime Treaty of 1820 and agreements related to the slave trade in 1847 and 1856.[90] Moreover, in 1861, Bahrain had been obliged by the British to agree to the provisions of the trucial system.[91] At this point, then, the British already felt that Bahrain, as the then Secretary of State for India wrote, "should be regarded as independent and as subject neither to Turkey nor to Persia."[92] In 1879, tensions between Britain and the Porte rose when rumours spread that the Ottomans were planning to build a coaling station in Bahrain.[93] The reaction was not long in coming: in December 1880 the British signed a new treaty with the ruler of Bahrain, Isa ibn Ali al-Khalifa. The shaykh agreed to abstain from entering into negotiations or signing treaties of any sort with any foreign power without the agreement of the British government. Isa also bound himself to refrain from granting foreign powers permission to open diplomatic posts or build coaling stations.[94]

But things did not stop there. Between 1880 and the early 1890s, the Ottomans redoubled their efforts in the Hasa and Bahrain, notably deploying military forces and organizing naval patrols.[95] On 13 March 1892, Shaykh Isa and Adelbert C. Talbot, the resident at Bushire, signed an exclusive agreement. This treaty reiterated the shaykh's 1880 pledge not to enter into agreements or correspondence with foreign powers other than the British, or allow agents of other governments to reside on his territory without British permission. In 1892 Isa further undertook not to cede, sell, mortgage, or otherwise give up for occupation any part of his territory except to the British government.[96] This treaty complemented a further set of agreements, similar to the one concluded with Isa, that had been signed a few days earlier between Talbot and the shaykhs of the Trucial Coast on 8 March 1892.[97] Thus, 1892 marked the creation of a series of veiled British protectorates extending from Oman to Bahrain. Two spheres of jurisdiction may thus be said to have been emerging in the Gulf region at this point, one falling under the auspices of the Government of India in the lower Gulf, extending from Oman to Bahrain, and the other stretching from the Shatt al-ʿArab to Qatar, in the upper Gulf, under Ottoman authority.

However, from the late 1890s, German–Ottoman railway projects to the Gulf threatened to upend the region's existing geopolitics. The British responded by deepening their imprint on the upper Gulf. Since the late 1870s, Sultan Abdülhamid had been granting concessions to foreign powers, especially France, Britain, and Germany, to build railway lines in the Ottoman Empire. For the sultan these railways were part of a modernization effort; they were also intended to reinforce Constantinople's authority in distant regions. By 1890 the railway network had become relatively dense in Anatolia, and Abdülhamid now envisaged the extension of railway links to the empire's Arabian provinces. The sultan turned to Germany for capital to fund this new infrastructure.[98] In 1898, Kaiser Wilhelm of Germany met with Abdülhamid to discuss a project that would connect Istanbul with Baghdad.[99] This German–Ottoman diplomatic rapprochement was part of Wilhelm's *Weltpolitik*, a bid to enhance German power in the world and thereby achieve a place in the same colonial league as Britain and France.[100] The following year the Ottoman government granted Germany the concession to build an Istanbul–Baghdad railway, which soon became dubbed the Baghdadbahn.[101] That same year, as work on this 2,800 kilometre railway was just starting, new extensions were being envisaged that would see it connected to additional hubs such as Aleppo, Mosul, and Kuwait. For the British, this railway project, with Kuwait as an anticipated terminus that would provide Germany with access to the Indian Ocean, was a dangerous threat to their interests in West and South Asia.

Also in 1899, a fresh rumour about yet another foreign project, Russian this time, increased British panic even more. The Government of India caught wind that Vladimir Kapnist, a Russian subject, had been intriguing to obtain a concession from the Ottoman government to construct a railway line from Tripoli to Kuwait.[102] The British embassy in Constantinople then caught wind that the French were providing financial backing for this enterprise.

With the development of these Ottoman–German and Russian projects, Kuwait, which the British regarded as a backwater dependency of the Porte, rapidly became a flashpoint in Gulf geopolitics. The Government of India began establishing contacts with the ruler of Kuwait, with the ultimate goal of transforming this small state into a British protectorate. Thus, a "Kuwait question" may be said to have begun to seize the attention of the administrations in India and the government in London.[103] The British took advantage of a succession crisis that had been destabilizing the ruling dynasty of Kuwait since the late 1890s to approach Mubarak al-Sabah. Mubarak had gained paramountcy in Kuwait in 1896 after assassinating his brother Muhammad, ruler of Kuwait since 1892.[104] During the discussions between Mubarak and representatives of the Government of India, the shaykh, who was facing significant tribal opposition, expressed a desire to free Kuwait from Ottoman rule and to gain British protection.[105]

Curzon tasked Meade, the resident at Bushire, with conducting the negotiations with Mubarak.[106] This led, in January 1899, to Mubarak signing an agreement that established a British protectorate over Kuwait. Mubarak pledged not to receive foreign agents or representatives, as well as not to sell, lease, mortgage, or cede any part of the territory under his control to a foreign state without the prior consent of the British. In return the British were to grant the shaykh £1,000 per year and protect Kuwait against foreign aggression.[107]

The signing of the treaty was something of a triumph for Curzon, whose agent, Meade, had gone beyond the Foreign Office's recommendations. Officials in London had wished to forge a bond with the shaykh that would guard Kuwait from Russian and German territorial claims. From their perspective, however, the establishment of a British protectorate over Kuwait by a treaty modelled on those signed with the rulers of Bahrain and the Trucial Coast was something to be avoided. Salisbury was particularly concerned about avoiding the new commitments and costs that such a protectorate would entail.[108] Most officials in London shared the opinion of the senior official in the India Office, Arthur Godley: "We don't want Kowait, but we don't want anyone else to have it."[109] In January 1899, Curzon had been instructed to follow the example of the Muscat agreement of 1891 when signing a treaty with Mubarak.[110] However, given the multiplying rumours that German engineers were about to arrive in Kuwait, the government in London had no choice but to ratify, in March 1899, the treaty that Meade had negotiated.[111]

The signing of the 1899 agreement was a key moment in the history of British imperialism in the Gulf. The Government of India's authority now extended almost continuously from Muscat to Kuwait, with the exception of the Qatar Peninsula and the enclave of the Hasa coast. Yet Russian and German pressure on the system built by British India over the course of the previous century would continue beyond this point. In the spring of 1899 the Government of India received reports that the Shah of Persia, Mozaffar-al-Din Shah, had granted Russia permission to build a coaling station at Bandar Abbas.[112] In January 1900, while panic over this Russian move toward the Gulf was taking hold in London and India, a German team of engineers and surveyors led by Wilhelm von Stemrich, the German general consul in Constantinople, arrived in Kuwait with a view to pursuing the project for a railway extension that would terminate there. German diplomats based in Bushire and Baghdad assisted Stemrich's team during this mission.[113]

The Russian "coaling station affair" peaked in early 1900 when reports reached Calcutta that the captain of a Russian ship, the *Gilyak*, had made overtures to the governor at Bandar Abbas for a coaling station.[114] However, the resident at Bushire, Charles A. Kemball, soon ascertained that the rumour that the shah had allowed Russia to establish a coaling station there was incorrect: the Russians had been granted no such concession. The crisis now turned into a farce. The reality behind this geopolitical scare appears to have been that the consignment of coal that the captain of the *Gilyak* had brought from India was so large that he had decided to leave the surplus at Bandar Abbas: this was merely a mercantile matter rather than the thin edge of a Russian wedge.[115]

Then two other episodes renewed British paranoia about a Russian encroachment in the Gulf. In the spring of 1900, a Russian expedition, which included the secretary-general of the Russian legation in Persia and more than sixty Cossacks, led a survey in Persia with the aim of gathering information for the purpose of building a railway line that would connect the Caspian Sea to the Gulf.[116] That summer, two Russian intelligence officers surveyed the ports of Bandar Deylam and Bandar Lengeh and ventured to northern Persia, notably to the towns of Muhammara and Ahwaz. One of them also briefly visited Kuwait during this period and was granted an audience with Shaykh Mubarak. Upon their return to Russia, the two agents recommended the creation of a commercial steamship line between Odessa, on the Black Sea, and the Gulf, via the Suez Canal, with the aim of increasing Russia's economic presence in the Gulf region. In March 1901 the *Korniloff*, a steamer of the Russian Steam Navigation and Trading Company, made the first voyage between Odessa and the Gulf with more than one thousand tons of goods onboard, stopping at Muscat, Jask, Bushire, Bandar Abbas, Bandar Lengeh, Bushire, and Basra.[117] This line was a success, and by 1903 it was being expanded into a regular service of four sailings per year, transporting goods and passengers.[118] Furthermore, over these same years, Russian naval demonstrations in the Gulf continued, culminating in the winter of 1903 in a joint Franco-Russian show of strength.[119]

In this context of separate German and Russian threats, Curzon, the Viceroy of India, began planning a tour of the Gulf for himself and his administration. Preparations began in India and in the Gulf, which the French vice-consul in Oman, Charles Dorville, described in the following terms: "A great political demonstration is underway" that amounted to "the affirmation of the undisputed predominance of

England in the waters of the Gulf," indeed, of "a sort of Monroe Doctrine in this inland sea."[120]

A British Riposte: Curzon Tours the Gulf

Curzon had a long-standing interest in the defence of British colonies on the subcontinent. At the heart of his policy vision since he had become viceroy had been the reinforcement of British India's frontiers, notably on its western flank.[121] The Gulf region thus occupied a strategic place in Curzon's idea of a defence system built around British India. With these priorities in mind, in November and December 1903 Curzon undertook a three-week tour of the Gulf, which he had been planning since 1901.[122] The tour can be seen within a larger context of manoeuvres to reinforce British influence in the Gulf in the face of growing Russian and German interests in the region. Curzon and his party stopped at a series of port cities on both the Persian and the Arabian shores of the Gulf. The visit staged a range of diplomatic ceremonies and meetings with several local shaykhs. This viceregal voyage was intended to be, and would succeed in becoming, a symbolically powerful event in the Gulf, both for British representatives and for local and regional powers.

The tour began on 16 November 1903, when Curzon left Karachi for Muscat with an impressive naval escort. The viceroy and his wife travelled aboard the Royal Indian Marine Ship (RIMS) *Hardinge* (Figure 6.2), accompanied by four other warships and a large contingent of troops for ceremonial purposes (including a military band). It was the first time since the bombing of Ras al-Khaimah in 1809 that such a large military and civil party had visited the Gulf. On 18 November, Curzon's convoy arrived at Muscat; Kemball, the resident at Bushire, was already there. Sultan Faisal welcomed Curzon with an honorific thirty-one-gun salute.[123] In Oman – British India's oldest ally in the Gulf region, albeit one that by this point had in effect become a client state – the celebrations in honour of the viceroy's visit were resounding.

On the morning of his arrival, Curzon received a group of guests on the *Hardinge*: Faisal, his half-brother Saiyid Muhammad, and Saiyid Muhammad's son and heir, Saiyid Taimur. The latter two had met the viceroy a few months earlier in Delhi during the ceremonies organized around Edward VII's coronation.[124] Cox was also present, along

Figure 6.2 "Lord and Lady Curzon and Staff on the Tour," from "Photographs of Lord Curzon's Tour in the Persian Gulf," 1903.

with foreign diplomats, namely the French vice-consul Laronce and the American consul, who were also granted an audience.[125] After lunch at the British Agency, Curzon attended a ceremony organized in his honour at the sultan's palace, where he met seventy shaykhs representing the main tribes of the sultanate.[126] Finally, in the evening, after the arrival in Muscat of the British minister in Tehran, Arthur Hardinge, a banquet for more than seventy people was held on board the *Hardinge*, which culminated with a fireworks display.[127]

Celebrations continued the next day. A special ceremony, a *durbar*, was held aboard the RIMS *Argonaut*. In Mughal India, "durbar" was the term used to designate the meeting of a ruler's court or council. The British had appropriated it to refer to a ceremonial gathering held to demonstrate loyalty to the British Crown.[128] In the Gulf reinvention of this practice, as recounted in lavish detail several years later in John Gordon Lorimer's *Gazetteer of the Persian Gulf, Oman, and Central Arabia* (1908–15), the ship was turned into a *durbar* stage, with its quarterdeck "ablaze with rich hangings and gold-embroidered carpets and draped with the flags of all nations," and its stern equipped with a "splendid pavilion" and a raised dais on which Curzon was seated. On his right was Faisal, and on his left, George Atkinson-Willes, who headed the Royal Navy's East Indies Station; around them were Curzon's secretaries as well as officials from the Government of India. Facing the viceroy, on a platform lower than that on which the party around Curzon was seated, were Cox, Faisal's half-brother and son, and other members of the sultan's party. Both the sultan and Curzon gave speeches praising the good relations between Oman and Britain and highlighting the importance of the sultanate in the system built by British India in West Asia. Next, Curzon withdrew for a few moments before returning dressed in his ceremonial robes as Grand Master of the Order of the Indian Empire, an imperial honour system that had been established in 1878; he now gave the sultan the insignia denoting induction into membership of the Order. After this tightly choreographed ceremony, Curzon and the sultan had a final private meeting.[129]

How can we interpret the carefully staged ceremony that Curzon and his administration organized on board the *Argonaut* on 19 November? In a letter he wrote two days after his departure from Oman, Curzon compared Oman to a "Native State," a term used to designate India's semiautonomous princely states: "To all intents and appearances the State is as much a Native State of the Indian empire as Lus Beyla or Kelat, and far more so than Nepal or Afghanistan."[130] Characterizing Muscat as tantamount to a princely state was a potent rhetorical manoeuvre, a kind of speech act, demonstrating the extension of both the Raj's sphere of influence and the system of indirect rule.[131] The *durbar* system was a symbolic encapsulation of this kind of imperial authority and of the local rulers' consent under which it was implied as operating. Curzon often used the *durbar* as a political tool during his time as viceroy, the most important time being the great coronation *durbar* in Delhi in 1903. Furthermore, during the *durbar*, Faisal had been inducted into the Order of the Indian Empire, an honours system used by the Government of India, particularly by Curzon, as a tool to give its recipients a sense that their services and loyalty to the Raj were being acknowledged. Bestowing such titles on the indigenous elites of India and on British Indian officials was an attempt on the part of the Government of India to bond native elites to the colonial regime. On the list of members of the Order were numerous Indian princes, in particular the maharajahs of Benares and Mysore. By conferring on Faisal the title of commander, Curzon was treating him like one of the *nawabs* or *rajahs* of India's princely states and acknowledging Oman's distinctive status for the British empire in India.[132]

One final element demonstrated Oman's special position in the empire of the Raj. When the viceregal party entered the harbour at Muscat, the thirty-one-gun salute that resounded in honour of Curzon was succeeded by a twenty-one-gun reply in honour of Faisal from the ships escorting the viceroy. This was no mere chance. Every year, the India Office published a list titled *Table of Salutes Fired in India*, fixing the rules regarding gun salutes in the Raj and its empire.[133] According to this document, 101 shots were reserved for British monarchs, and three for the ruler of a small princely state. Being included on this list was a signal honour, one not accorded to all Indian princes. Bahrain, Kuwait, and Abu Dhabi were eligible for five-gun salutes, while the other Trucial States were eligible for three. According to the *Table of Salutes Fired in India*, only seven of the most important Indian princes, including the Nizam of Hyderabad, the Maharajah of Mysore, and the Shah of Persia, were granted twenty-one-gun salutes. By the turn of the century Oman and, to a lesser extent, the Trucial States, along with Kuwait and Bahrain, had thus stopped being mere peripheries protecting British India on its western flank. As here revealed by the viceroy's meticulous choreography, these territories had gained a central position in the empire of the Raj, as well as in a new region that was just beginning to be called the Middle East.[134]

After Muscat, the viceregal escort sailed into Sharjah on 21 November. The shaykhs of the Trucial Coast were invited on board the *Argonaut*, where another *durbar* was organized. Shaykh Zayed of Abu Dhabi was present with two of his sons, as well as the shaykhs of Sharjah and Dubai, each with a son accompanying. The Shaykh of Ajman was represented by his son Rashid.[135] During the *durbar*, Curzon gave a speech, which an interpreter translated into Arabic. The viceroy's address proposed a retrospective vision of Britain's role in the Persian Gulf, one that was also a manifesto for the future. History – or rather a form of history – was beginning to be written. Curzon depicted the

Gulf region, just as Hastings, Elphinstone, and Malcolm had done before him, as being populated at the end of the eighteenth century by tribes that were inclined to piracy and feuds:

> Chiefs, your fathers and grandfathers before you have doubtless told you of the history of the past. You know that a hundred years ago there were constant trouble and fighting in the Gulf; almost every man was a marauder or a pirate; kidnapping and slave-trading flourished; fighting and bloodshed went on without stint or respite; no ship could put to sea without fear of attack; the pearl fishery was a scene of annual conflict; and security of trade or peace there was none.[136]

Curzon went on to lay out a vision of how, after a century of British interventionism, the Gulf had become a prosperous, flourishing region. From chaos, order had emerged: "We found strife and we have created order." The legend of the Pirate Coast and the myth of British pacification were being established, a history that Lorimer and Jerome Saldanha were already beginning to write around these same years.[137]

Yet Curzon also claimed that these successes, obtained as a result of multiple sacrifices since the late eighteenth century, were entirely the work of British authorities in India. It was taken as axiomatic from this that the British could not let other Western powers gain a foothold in the Gulf:

> The Great Empire of India, which is our duty to defend, lies almost at your gates . . . We opened these seas to the ships of all nations, and enabled their flags to fly in peace. We have not seized or held your territory. We have not destroyed your independence but have preserved it. We are not going to throw away this century of costly and triumphant enterprise; we shall not wipe out the most unselfish page in history . . . The influence of the British Government must remain supreme.

After a ceremonial gift exchange, the viceregal escort left for Bandar Abbas and Bandar Lengeh, where Curzon and his party stopped before sailing to Bahrain on 26 November.

Figure 6.3 "Landing at Koweit," from "Photographs of Lord Curzon's Tour in the Persian Gulf," 1903.

In Bahrain, Curzon's visit provided an occasion to consolidate the alliance signed a decade earlier with Shaykh Isa bin Ali al-Khalifa. The formula of the visit to both the Trucial States and Bahrain was much the same as in Muscat, though briefer. During a *durbar* on the *Hardinge*, which was attended by Assistant Political Agent in Bahrain John Calcott Gaskin and members of Shaykh Isa's family, Curzon recognized Hamad, the ruler's eldest son, as his successor.[138] The next stop on the tour was Kuwait (Figure 6.3), where festivities were organized in honour of Curzon from 28 November onward. It was the longest single stop of the tour, signalling the importance of Kuwait for the Government of India in the context of the Russo-German threat. In addition to several meetings with Mubarak and his eldest son, Jabir, Curzon was treated to an equestrian display with hundreds of horsemen, camel drivers, and men at arms. After a brief stop at Bushire, the return journey to Karachi began on the evening of 3 December. Curzon's squadron reached Karachi on 7 December after a short stop in Pasni to meet the Baluchistani chiefs.[139]

Curzon's elaborate tour, written on the waters of the Gulf, had broadcast to the world that this space was now linked to British India.

CONCLUSION

This book has explored a century-long foundational conjuncture in the making of the modern Middle East. It has taken as one of its points of departure the existence of a growing scholarship over recent decades that has sought to rethink the Middle East's past by interrogating its assumed historical geography. One originator of this debate was the twentieth-century historian Roderic H. Davison, who asked, in a pointed critique, "Where is the Middle East?," and who noted that the "fact remains that no one knows where the Middle East is, although many claim to know."[1] One current scholar, Nile Green, has brought this debate up to the present by highlighting that one way of seeking to answer such questions is to rethink the Middle East's history over many centuries by reference to the "Oceanic Turn" in wider historiography. Most conventional accounts focus on specific territorial spaces, notably centred on the lands of the former Ottoman Empire, so that the region of the Middle East is often understood as being landlocked, and organized in particular around the deserts of the Arabian Peninsula, extending into the Levant and its hinterlands and onwards into the spaces of ancient Mesopotamia. Adopting a maritime perspective, by contrast, may prove more heuristically germane to advancing the task of rethinking the Middle East. In the formulation proposed by Green, the Middle East that emerges in the light of such an analysis may best be described as one of a series of overlapping "arenas," including a vast "Indian Ocean arena" defined by "social geographies" and "mobile societies" and in which the Gulf was a central component.[2] This book has adopted a congruent task but also a more specific one, namely that of exploring how the Gulf came to be the key locus of the emergent concept of a "Middle East" in anglophone commentary around the beginning of the twentieth century, and the genesis of this in turn amid a preceding era of imperial interventions in and around the Gulf region from the late 1700s onwards conducted under the aegis of an expansionist British India. It has argued that in the long-term history of this maritime Middle East, one that connected the waters of the Euphrates and the Tigris to those of the Indian Ocean, imperial geopolitics centring around British interests on the Indian subcontinent would ultimately give rise to a new nomenclature to describe the region centring on the Gulf and in the process see that region's transformation and to some extent its advancing globalization. These dramatic shifts took place in ways that were channelled by imperial dynamics, though without ever being totally subsumed by them.

The specific term "Middle East" first appeared in the decades around 1900 in the writings of strategists and commentators on British India and on the terraqueous spaces of the Gulf. These men included Thomas Gordon, Valentine Chirol, and Alfred T. Mahan. Gordon and Chirol defined the "Middle East" as an immense borderland extending from Egypt to Afghanistan and protecting British colonies in India on their western flank. Thus envisioned, the Middle East was composed of land and sea territories centred around a maritime space, the Gulf. Its frontiers transcended those of West Asia, North Africa, and Central Asia. Mahan, meanwhile, defined his "Middle East" in overlapping but distinctive terms, characterizing it as a strategically critical nexus of communications extending over land and water and as the site of growing geopolitical competition: in this Middle East, the lines of communication linking London to British India were increasingly threatened by competing powers such as Russia and Germany. As this cluster of intersecting attempts around the same date to name this space indicate, this historical juncture was certainly a semantically critical one. But as this book has shown, the "Middle East" as a space may be said to have been thought of and practised well before the moment of its ostensible naming as such. Indeed, it has been argued here that the region that would come to be described as Middle East was invented gradually as a function of the simultaneous territorial expansion of the British Empire in India after the late eighteenth century. In particular, the Gulf region would come to play a crucial role as an intermediate zone tying India and Europe together. It may be said that as British

India developed as a semiautonomous imperial polity over course of the nineteenth century, a "British" Gulf, a terraqueous expanse of seas and coasts and their hinterlands, substantially prefigured the space that would later be labelled the "Middle East." This frontier zone for British India centred on the Gulf became a pivotal space, with both a defensive function – that of blocking potential invasions of British territories in India – and a connecting dimension as a space of commerce and communication.

The threat that British colonies in India might be invaded was a determining factor in British imperialism around the Gulf region, which was simultaneously a barrier and a passage to the subcontinent. Whether it was the perception of a French threat, which reached its zenith under Napoleon, or in later decades a Russian one, or in the early twentieth century a German one, control of the waters and hinterlands leading to British India would drive a range of interventions. These began in the name of combatting piracy and proliferated until an informal empire took shape across much of the Gulf, which itself ultimately evolved into a degree of direct rule over a number of specific places in the region.[3] It seems that the perceived threat from European competitors, and fears that local or regional powers would become those competitors' allies or proxies in encroaching on British India, were powerfully felt by British imperial officials. Yet given the dynamics of British expansionism in India and its peripheries in the later 1700s and throughout the nineteenth century, some form of British encroachment into the Gulf was probably already overdetermined.

This book has spent much time examining the British presence in and around the Gulf and various facets of the invention of a "British" Gulf. Crucial to that development was an informal imperial system in the Gulf region that was constructed gradually with reference to British India and that was characterized by the importation of a system of indirect rule imported from the subcontinent. Treaties were signed with local rulers, especially those arrayed along the Arabian coast of the Gulf, and surveys and mapping campaigns were conducted so as to plant and grow British influence. These agreements and the production of geographical documents contributed to the inventing of a "British" Gulf in both material and ideological ways. A further element of imperial visions with respect to the Gulf was a sense that transformations might be effected that would nominally benefit the region even while advancing British interests there. Several schemes along these lines were advanced, which often focused on the Gulf's connecting function and the maritime aspects that underpinned it. From the late 1830s, notably, various projects geared around a belief in technology and the power of steam would seek to develop this connecting function of the region, with steam power envisaged as a means of enabling goods, troops, and people to travel between Europe and India via the Mediterranean, Mesopotamia, the Gulf, and the Indian Ocean. Such schemes may be said to have put notions of "Middle East" into practice even before the term itself was coined.

The history of the nineteenth-century Gulf goes well beyond its profile as a space invested with global strategic salience and meaning by European imperialism. Yet the invention during this period of a British "Gulf," or more specifically of a Gulf that sat as a crucial feature in imperial calculations between London on the one hand and British India on the other, proves to have gone far beyond its role in occasioning the specific "Middle East" nomenclature still deployed to describe the wider space: for the interventions conducted under British auspices during the 1800s would have profound ramifications both for the wider histories of the region and for its populations. To some extent, the wider British interventions in the Gulf also served to give a kind of enhanced discursive and even practical unity to a region that remained politically and geographically fragmented. Specific policy measures adopted by British officials might tend to some extent to merge different polities: the "Trucial States," brought together under the rubric of maritime peace arrangements under British oversight, was one notable example of this. More widely, as on the subcontinent, a key element in handling relations with local rulers was the system of "residents," these delegates being representatives of the East India Company and, after 1858, of the Government of India. The political role of the residents would be heightened amid the wars with France down to 1815, the emergence of the Wahhabi states, and growing Russian influence in the Gulf region from the late 1830s. They would ultimately become a linchpin of arm's-length British imperial oversight in the region. In the verdict of the French diplomat Paul Ottavi, writing in 1895, the scope and power of the British resident at Bushire was such as to render this role that of "the uncrowned king of the Gulf."[4] The resident at Bushire in turn liaised with other representatives of British India based in Oman and Bahrain, but also with representatives of the government in London, for instance the British consuls in Ottoman Iraq and in Qajar Persia. However, as this book has also shown, the system of indirect rule was adapted to the specific political and geographical environment of the Gulf region. British imperialism was geared, in particular, around a close monitoring of the seas in the region, and this seaward element in an imperial political economy for the Gulf would take centre stage throughout a decades-long effort to transform a region supposedly characterized by piracy into one of peaceful prosperity based on fishing and an increasingly globalized maritime commerce.

For all the strengths of this "informal" pattern of imperial oversight in the Gulf, there were also corresponding weaknesses. This arm's-length strategy aimed at meeting British priorities around the Gulf region in the nineteenth century was itself as much improvised, and elaborated on contingently over time, as it was born of long-term grand designs. Indeed, its construction was piecemeal and, especially in the early 1800s, notably haphazard and erratic. Some of the initial interventions made by British India in the Gulf, notably the punitive expeditions sent against Ras al-Khaimah, were marked by moments of great violence, and indeed by occasional military setbacks and even humiliations. There was also a significant degree of sclerosis among officials in British India over what their larger policy in the region should be. Ultimately, however, the system that was established would prove to offer, from the point of view of British India, a minimally burdensome way of maximizing effective influence in the management of a strategically critical geopolitical space. Informal empire formed a pathway whereby, at relatively little expense either to London or to British India, a political economy was established in the Gulf region that functioned as something of a virtuous circle for buttressing their interests while also suborning and instrumentalizing local rulers. Thus, the system of maritime truces brokered and administered under British auspices enabled a flourishing trade in regional commodities, notably pearls and dates, to develop over the course of the nineteenth century; this prospering economy ensured continued peace in Gulf waters while also propping up shaykhs whose interests were thus encompassed within a system that ensured their continued domestic power even as it effectively usurped their role in regional security.[5] If, from the point of view of British India, this pacified Gulf involved a modicum of expense, this paid for itself in that it helped ensure the security, and therefore the profitability, of the subcontinent itself. The true costs of the informal imperial arrangements at their mid-nineteenth century height may be said to have fallen on slaves, given that slave labour often significantly underpinned the pearl and date industries that propelled the Gulf's prosperity. British efforts to halt the slave trade to the Gulf would, in a way that is revealing of the true nature of imperial calculations in the region, tend to be mainly a matter of rhetoric rather than a cause for systematic intervention.

This informal empire was somewhat brittle. It functioned relatively seamlessly at its height, during the period of the British "imperial meridian" around the mid-nineteenth century.[6] But it also threatened to unravel rapidly should its preconditions for success begin to erode. In particular, given that the military and diplomatic infrastructure that Britain maintained in the Gulf was, despite occasional special shows of force, as a rule relatively minimal, this meant that much of the credibility of British claims to hegemony there was founded on prestige. Accommodations as well as alignments of interests with local power brokers were at risk of breaking down should that prestige begin to fray. To some extent, toward the close of the nineteenth century, an increasingly geopolitically crowded Gulf – awash with German railway projects, French gun-runners, and Russian trading networks – became a space where new interests might be activated for various local actors, and such interests might no longer be fully consonant with ongoing British regional priorities. At this juncture, some of the weaknesses of an informal imperial structure for sustaining British interests in the Gulf began to become apparent. Complex threats to British preeminence there emerged both through the growing encroachment into the region of other imperial powers, notably Germany, but also through challenges arising within the Gulf area itself, notably through the booming trade in smuggled arms. This latter trade was directly destabilizing to British imperial security, given that much of this military contraband was destined for armed conflicts and uprisings in British India's North-West Frontier.

British pre-eminence in the Gulf became ever more contested in the run-up to the First World War; however, it had far from dissipated, for there would also be opportune efforts on the part of British India and the government in London to refurbish and even extend British influence in this terraqueous space. Curzon's 1903 viceregal tour of the Gulf, and the establishment of a protectorate over Kuwait in 1914, were some of the higher-profile elements of this continued investment of resources in the region, and of the responses to global challenges the British were developing there. Finally, while the Middle East that emerged semantically at this juncture was a space that made sense in large measure in relation to British India, during the twentieth century a revised vision of the wider region became a central space of transformed British imperial designs in its own right.[7] With the so-called oil revolution of the early twentieth century, with the crucial role played by the region during the First World War, and with the territorial reshaping of the wider political map amid the dismemberment of the Ottoman Empire at the peace conferences in the aftermath of that conflict, a reconceived Middle East would become a centre for a second phase of British imperialism in the region.[8] This would be structured less around the maritime spaces of the Gulf than around a double landward-oriented geography: first, that of the political administrations issuing from the Mandates System of the League of Nations; and second, that of the region's oil resources and oilfields.[9] In the latter context, in particular, another form of informal imperialism may be traced, which in many ways would eclipse what had been built over the nineteenth century. This new conjuncture was one in which oil companies played a crucial role and where the agreements they signed with local powers, such as Persia, in order to access oilfields might attain huge geopolitical importance. Even if the region still in some measure remained under the informal imperial oversight of the Government of India, the role of London increased as a new nexus of capital and empire in the Middle East rapidly coalesced around oil agreements and oil infrastructure.[10] The informal empire constructed in the waters and sands of the Gulf region over the 1800s would prove to be the unexpected focal point for the reinvention of imperial and geopolitical priorities around oil.

NOTES

Preface

1 Christopher A. Bayly, *Imperial Meridian: The British Empire and the World, 1780–1830* (London: Longman, 1989).
2 Guillemette Crouzet, *Genèses du Moyen-Orient. Le Golfe Persique à l'âge des imperialismes (vers 1800–vers 1914)* (Ceyzérieu: Champ Vallon, 2015).
3 For one further important study, published just as the present book was going to press, see Jonathan Parry, *Promised Lands: The British and the Ottoman Middle East* (Princeton: Princeton University Press, 2022).

Introduction

1 Valentine Chirol, *The Middle Eastern Question; or, Some Political Problems of Indian Defence* (London: John Murray, 1903), vii.
2 Chirol, *The Middle Eastern Question*, 5.
3 Thomas E. Gordon, "The Problems of the Middle East," *Nineteenth Century* 37 (March 1900): 413–24 at 413.
4 Clayton R. Koppes, "Captain Mahan, General Gordon, and the Origins of the Term 'Middle East,'" *Middle Eastern Studies* 12, no. 1 (1976): 95–8.
5 On Gordon's career, see Thomas E. Gordon, *A Varied Life* (London: John Murray, 1906); and Thomas E. Gordon, *Persia Revisited* (London: E. Arnold, 1896).
6 Alfred Thayer Mahan, "The Persian Gulf and International Relations," *National Review* 40 (September 1902): 27–45 at 39.
7 Mahan, "The Persian Gulf," 39; Alfred T. Mahan, *The Influence of Sea Power upon History, 1660–1783* (London: Sampson Low, Marston, 1890).
8 British Library, London: IOR/L/PS/10/60, 1908. Frederick F. Hunter's map was produced to accompany Lorimer's *Gazetteer*. See Frederick F. Hunter, "Reminiscences of the Map of Arabia and the Persian Gulf,"

Geographical Journal 54, no. 6 (1919): 355–63. For a short analysis of this map published a few years after the map was produced, see Frederick F. Hunter, "A New Map of Arabia," *Bulletin of the American Geographical Society* 42, no. 5 (1910): 362–3. For a general perspective on mapping the Middle East, see Karen Culcasi, "Cartographic Constructions of the Middle East," *Imago Mundi* 60, no. 1 (2008): 120–1. See also John G. Lorimer, *Gazetteer of the Persian Gulf, Oman and Central Arabia*, 2 vols. (Calcutta: Superintendent Government Printing, India, 1908–15). On Lorimer's *Gazetteer*, see Nelida Fuccaro, "Knowledge at the Service of the British Empire: The Gazetteer of the Persian Gulf, Oman and Central Arabia," in *Borders and the Changing Boundaries of Knowledge*, ed. Inga Brandell, Marie Carlson, and Önver A. Çetrez, Transactions, vol. 22 (Stockholm: Svenska forskningsinstitutet i Istanbul, 2015), 17–34.

9 Hüseyin Yılmaz, "The Eastern Question and the Ottoman Empire: The Genesis of the Near and Middle East in the Nineteenth Century," in *Is There a Middle East? The Evolution of a Geopolitical Concept*, ed. Michael E. Bonine, Abbas Amanat, and Michael Ezekiel Gasper (Stanford: Stanford University Press, 2012), 11–35.

10 On metageography, see Martin W. Lewis and Kären Wigen, *The Myth of Continents: A Critique of Metageography* (Berkeley: University of California Press, 1997).

11 Reinhart Koselleck, *Future Pasts: On the Semantics of Historical Time* (Cambridge, MA: MIT Press, 1985), 87, 89.

12 Koselleck, *Future Pasts*, 91.

13 Koselleck, *Future Pasts*, 90.

14 Thomas Scheffler, "'Fertile Crescent,' 'Orient,' 'Middle East': The Changing Mental Maps of Southwest Asia," *European Review of History / Revue européenne d'histoire* 10, no. 2 (2003): 253–72.

15 Halford Mackinder, "The Geographical Pivot of History," *Geographical Journal* 23, no. 4 (1904): 421–37; Friedrich Naumann, *Mitteleuropa* (Berlin: Georg Reimer, 1915); Ewald Banse, "Der Orient – Ein geographischer Begriff?," *Deutsche Rundschau für Geographie und Statistik* 31, no. 1 (1908): 1–7. On Mackinder, see Sarah O'Hara and Michael Heffernan, "From Geo-Strategy to Geo-Economics: 'The Heartland' and British Imperialism before and after Mackinder," *Geopolitics* 11, no. 1 (2006): 54–73. On regional geographical constructs, see Anssi Paasi, "Place and Region: Looking through the Prism of Scale," *Progress in Human Geography* 28, no. 4 (2004): 536–46.

16 George N. Curzon, *Problems of the Far East* (London: Longmans, 1894).

17 Valentine I. Chirol, *The Far Eastern Question* (London: Macmillan, 1896).

18 Daniel Foliard, *Dislocating the Orient: British Maps and the Making of the Middle East, 1854–1921* (Chicago: University of Chicago Press, 2017).

19 Edward Gibbon, *The Decline and Fall of the Roman Empire*, 6 vols. (London: W. Strahan; T. Cadell, 1776–88). For a detailed study of links between ancient history, ideas of empire, and imperialism, see Christopher Hagerman, *Britain's Imperial Muse: The Classics, Imperialism, and the Indian Empire, 1784–1914* (London: Palgrave Macmillan, 2013).

20 For an overview of British travellers in the Orient, see, among a vast historiography, Geoffrey P. Nash, *From Empire to Orient: Travellers to the Middle East 1830–1926* (London: I.B. Tauris, 2005); and Paul and Janet Starkey, *Unfolding the Orient: Travellers in Egypt and the Near East* (Ithaca: Cornell University Press, 2001). On travels in Arabia, see Kathryn Tidrick, *Heart-Beguiling Araby: The English Romance with Arabia* (London: Tauris, 1989); and Robin Bidwell, *Travellers in Arabia* (London: Hamlyn, 1976). On female travellers, see, for example, Dea Birkett, *Off the Beaten Track: Three Centuries of Women Travellers* (London: National Portrait Gallery, 2004); Dea Birkett, *Spinsters Abroad: Victorian Lady Explorers* (Oxford: Basil Blackwell, 1989); and Reina Lewis, *Rethinking Orientalism: Women, Travel and the Oriental Harem* (London: I.B. Tauris, 2004).

21 See, for example, Foliard, *Dislocating the Orient*, 62–4; Eitan Bar-Yosef, *The Holy Land in English Culture 1799–1917: Palestine and the Question of Orientalism* (Oxford: Oxford University Press, 2005); and Edward Said, *Orientalism: Western Conceptions of the Orient* (New York: Pantheon Books, 1978). On the holy geography of the Middle East, see Daniel M. Varisco, "When Did the Holy Land Stop Being Holy? Surveying the Middle East as Sacred Geography," in Bonine, Amanat, and Gasper, eds., *Is There a Middle East?*, 119–38. For a superb study of the British imagination of Arabia in the late nineteenth and early twentieth centuries, see Priya Satia, *Spies in Arabia: The Great War and the Cultural Foundations of Britain's Covert Empire in the Middle East* (Oxford: Oxford University Press, 2009).

22 David G. Hogarth, *The Nearer East* (London: William Heinemann, 1902).

23 Hogarth, *The Nearer East*, 279–80.

24 John Fisher, "Lord Robert Cecil and the Formation of a Middle East Department of the Foreign Office," *Middle Eastern Studies* 42, no. 3 (2006): 365–80; Roger Adelson, *London and the Invention of the Middle East:*

Money, Power, and War, 1902–1922 (New Haven: Yale University Press, 1995).

25 Scheffler, "'Fertile Crescent,'" 265.

26 Arnold J. Toynbee, *The Western Question in Greece and Turkey: A Study in the Contact of Civilisations* (London: Constable, 1922), 20, 24.

27 Roderic H. Davison, "Where Is the Middle East?," *Foreign Affairs* 38, no. 4 (1960): 665–75; Gordon C. Smith, "The Emergence of the Middle East," *Journal of Contemporary History* 3, no. 3 (1968): 3–17.

28 Jillian Schwedler and Deborah J. Gerner, eds., *Understanding the Contemporary Middle East* (Boulder: Lynne Rienner, 2004), 9. On Orientalism in relation to Britain, see Lisa Lowe, *Critical Terrains: French and British Orientalisms* (Ithaca: Cornell University Press, 1994); Edward Zitter, *The Orient on the Victorian Stage* (Cambridge: Cambridge University Press, 2003); John MacKenzie, *Orientalism: History, Theory, and the Arts* (Manchester: Manchester University Press, 1995); Zachary Lockman, *Contending Visions of the Middle East: The History and Politics of Orientalism* (Cambridge: Cambridge University Press, 2010); Nigel Leask, *British Romantic Writers and the East: Anxieties of Empire* (Cambridge: Cambridge University Press, 2004); Nigel Leask, *Curiosity and the Aesthetics of Travel Writing, 1770–1840: "From an Antique Land"* (Oxford: Oxford University Press, 2002); Andrew C. Long, *Reading Arabia: British Orientalism in the Age of Mass Publication, 1880–1930* (Syracuse: Syracuse University Press, 2014); and Tony Ballantyne, *Orientalism and Race: Aryanism in the British Empire* (Basingstoke: Palgrave, 2002). For a twentieth-century perspective, see Ali Behdad, *Belated Travelers: Orientalism in the Age of Colonial Dissolution* (Durham: Duke University Press, 1994).

29 Karen Culcasi, "Mapping the Middle East from Within: (Counter-) Cartographies of an Imperialist Construction," *Antipode* 44, no. 4 (2012): 1099–1118 at 1106.

30 Davison, "Where Is the Middle East?," 666.

31 David Fromkin, "How the Modern Middle East Map Came to Be Drawn," *Smithsonian Magazine* 22, no. 2 (1991): 132–47; Nikki R. Keddie, "Is There a Middle East?," *International Journal of Middle East Studies* 4, no. 3 (1973): 255–71.

32 Adelson, *London and the Invention of the Middle East*; David Fromkin, *A Peace to End All Peace: Creating the Modern Middle East, 1914–1922* (London: Deutsch, 1989); John Fisher, *Curzon and British Imperialism in the Middle East, 1916–19* (London: Cass, 1999); John Darwin, *Britain, Egypt, and the Middle East: Imperial Policy in the Aftermath of War,*

1918–1922 (London: Macmillan, 1981); Uriel Dann, ed., *The Great Powers in the Middle East, 1919–1939* (New York: Holmes and Meier, 1988). Older works with a similar thesis include Reader Bullard, *Britain and the Middle East: From the Earliest Times to 1950* (London: Hutchinson, 1951); Elie Kedourie, *England and the Middle East: The Destruction of the Ottoman Empire, 1914–1921* (London: Bowes and Bowes, 1956); and Albert Hourani, *Europe and the Middle East* (Berkeley: University of California Press, 1980).

33 Karen Culcasi, "Constructing and Naturalizing the Middle East," *Geographical Review* 100, no. 4 (2010): 583–97 at 584.

34 For a history of the second British Empire centred in South and West Asia, see Christopher A. Bayly, *The Imperial Meridian, the British Empire, and the World, 1780–1830* (London: Longman, 1989).

35 Christopher A. Bayly, "India and West Asia, c. 1700–1830," *Asian Affairs* 19, no. 3 (1988): 3–19 at 3.

36 See, in particular, Bayly, *The Imperial Meridian*; and Christopher A. Bayly, *Indian Society and the Making of the British Empire* (Cambridge: Cambridge University Press, 1990). For an older but still relevant study, see Vincent T. Harlow, *The Founding of the Second British Empire, 1763–1793* (London: Longmans, 1952).

37 See, for example, Kirti N. Chaudhuri, *The English East India Company: The Study of an Early Joint-Stock Company 1600–1640* (London: Frank Cass, 1965); and Ashin Das Gupta, *Malabar in Asian Trade, 1740–1800* (Cambridge: Cambridge University Press, 1967).

38 Two books published in the 1960s, John B. Kelly, *Britain and the Persian Gulf, 1795–1880* (Oxford: Clarendon, 1968), and Briton C. Busch, *Britain and the Persian Gulf, 1894–1914* (Berkeley: University of California Press, 1967), and James Onley's study of the residency system, James Onley, *The Arabian Frontier of the Raj: Merchants, Rulers, and the British in the Nineteenth-Century Gulf* (Oxford: Oxford University Press, 2007), have examined certain aspects of British India's imperialism in the Gulf without ever drawing attention to the role of this space in the construction of the British Middle East. The lack of studies on the Gulf in the nineteenth century has been noted: Michael C. Low, "Introduction: The Indian Ocean and Other Middle Easts," *Comparative Studies of South Asia, Africa, and the Middle East* 34, no. 3 (2014): 539–55; and Sheila Carapico, "Arabia Incognita: An Invitation to Arabian Peninsula Studies," in *Counter-Narratives: History, Contemporary Society, and Politics in Saudi Arabia and Yemen*, ed. Madawi Al-Rasheed and Robert Vitalis (New York: Palgrave Macmillan, 2003), 11–34. Studies on the Gulf include

Ravinder Kumar, *India and the Persian Gulf Region, 1858–1907: A Study in British Imperial Policy* (Bombay: Asia Publishing House, 1965); Lawrence G. Potter, ed., *The Persian Gulf in Modern Times: People, Ports, and History* (New York: Palgrave Macmillan, 2014); Lawrence G. Potter, ed., *The Persian Gulf in History* (New York: Palgrave Macmillan, 2009); Nelida Fuccaro, *Histories of City and State in the Persian Gulf: Manama since 1800* (Cambridge: Cambridge University Press, 2009); and J.E. Peterson, ed., *The Emergence of the Gulf States: Studies in Modern History* (London: Bloomsbury, 2016).

39 Thomas Simpson, "Bordering and Frontier-Making in Nineteenth-Century British India," *Historical Journal* 58, no. 2 (2015): 513–42. On India's imperial domains, see, for example, Sujit Sivasundaram, *Islanded: Britain, Sri Lanka, and the Bounds of an Indian Ocean Colony* (Chicago: University of Chicago Press, 2013); Sunil Amrith, *Crossing the Bay of Bengal: The Furies of Nature and the Fortunes of Migrants* (Cambridge, MA: Harvard University Press, 2013); and Thant Myint U, *The Making of Modern Burma* (Cambridge: Cambridge University Press, 2001). On Iraq, see J.P. Parry, "Steam Power and British Influence in Baghdad, 1820–1860," *Historical Journal* 56, no. 1 (2013): 145–73; and John Slight, *The British Empire and the Hajj, 1865–1956* (Cambridge, MA: Harvard University Press, 2015).

40 Christopher A. Bayly, "Returning the British to South Asian History: The Limits of Colonial Hegemony," *South Asia: Journal of South Asian Studies* 17, no. 2 (1994): 1–25 at 13–15.

41 John M. Willis, "Making Yemen Indian: Rewriting the Boundaries of Imperial Arabia," *International Journal of Middle East Studies* 41, no. 1 (2009): 23–38.

42 Alison Bashford, "Terraqueous Histories," *Historical Journal* 60, no. 2 (2017): 253–72.

43 Sugata Bose, *A Hundred Horizons: The Indian Ocean in the Age of Global Empire* (Cambridge, MA: Harvard University Press, 2006); Thomas Metcalf, *Imperial Connections: India in the Indian Ocean Arena, 1860–1920* (Berkeley: University of California Press, 2007). On the Company's expansion in Bengal, see Robert Travers, *Ideology and Empire in Eighteenth-Century India: The British in Bengal* (Cambridge: Cambridge University Press, 2007); Nicholas B. Dirks, *The Scandal of Empire: India and the Creation of Imperial Britain* (Cambridge, MA: Harvard University Press, 2008); Jon Wilson, *The Domination of Strangers: Modern Governance in Eastern India, 1780–1835* (Basingstoke: Palgrave Macmillan,

2010); and Peter J. Marshall, *The Eighteenth Century in Indian History: Evolution or Revolution?* (Oxford: Oxford University Press, 2003).

44 Robert J. Blyth, *The Empire of the Raj: India, Eastern Africa, and the Middle East, 1858–1947* (Basingstoke: Palgrave Macmillan, 2003).

45 In no way does the present study seek to take a side in relation to contemporary ideological debates regarding the naming of the "Gulf" as "Persian Gulf," "Arabian Gulf," or "Arabo-Persian Gulf."

46 On global history as a methodology, see Sebastian Conrad, *What Is Global History?* (Princeton: Princeton University Press, 2016); Lynn Hunt, *Writing History in the Global Era* (New York: W.W. Norton, 2015); Maxine Berg, ed., *Writing the History of the Global: Challenges for the 21st Century* (Oxford: Oxford University Press, 2013); Jürgen Osterhammel, *The Transformation of the World: A Global History of the Nineteenth Century* (Princeton: Princeton University Press, 2014); and Emily S. Rosenberg, *A World Connecting, 1870–1945* (Cambridge, MA: Harvard University Press, 2012). On recent reflections on the connections between British imperial history and global history, see, for example, Tehila Sasson, James Vernon, Miles Ogborn, Priya Satia, and Catherine Hall, "Britain and the World: A New Field?," *Journal of British Studies* 57, no. 4 (2018): 677–708; and Simon J. Potter and Jonathan Saha, "Global History, Imperial History, and Connected Histories of Empire," *Journal of Colonialism and Colonial History* 16, no. 1 (2015), *Project MUSE*, https://doi.org/10.1353/cch.2015.0009.

47 On the "oceanic turn" and Middle East history, see Nile Green, "Rethinking the 'Middle East' after the Oceanic Turn," *Comparative Studies of South Asia, Africa, and the Middle East* 34, no. 3 (2014): 556–64; and Low, "Introduction: The Indian Ocean." On the "oceanic turn," among a vast historiography, see Kären Wigen, "Oceans of History: Introduction," *American Historical Review* 111, no. 3 (2006): 717–21; Jerry H. Bentley, "Sea and Ocean Basins as Frameworks of Historical Analysis," *Geographical Review* 89, no. 2 (1999): 215–24; Hester Blum, "Terraqueous Planet: The Case for Oceanic Studies," in *The Planetary Turn: Relationality and Geoaesthetics in the Twenty-First Century*, ed. Amy J. Elias and Christian Moraru (Evanston: Northwestern University Press, 2015), 25–36; and Sujit Sivasundaram, Alison Bashford, and David Armitage, "Introduction: Writing World Oceanic Histories," in *Oceanic Histories*, ed. Sujit Sivasundaram, Alison Bashford, and David Armitage (Cambridge: Cambridge University Press, 2018), 1–27. On the "oceanic turn" and the Indian Ocean, see, among others, Antoinette Burton, Madhavi

Kale, Isabel Hofmeyr, Clare Anderson, Christopher J. Lee, and Nile Green, "Sea Tracks and Trails: Indian Ocean Worlds as Method," *History Compass* 11, no. 7 (2013): 497–502; Marcus Vink, "Indian Ocean Studies and the 'New Thalassology,'" *Journal of Global History* 2, no. 1 (2007): 41–62; Isabel Hofmeyr, "The Complicating Sea: The Indian Ocean as Method," *Comparative Studies of South Asia, Africa, and the Middle East* 32, no. 3 (2012): 584–90; and Sebastian Prange, "Scholars and the Sea: A Historiography of the Indian Ocean," *History Compass* 6, no. 5 (2008): 1382–93.

48 Nile Green, "Rethinking the 'Middle East'"; and Nile Green, "The View from the Edge: The Indian Ocean's Middle East," *International Journal of Middle East Studies* 48, no. 4 (2016): 746–9.

49 On globalization and European imperialism in the Indian Ocean, see, among a vast literature, Michael N. Pearson, *The Indian Ocean* (London: Routledge, 2003); Pamila Gupta, Isabel Hofmeyr, and Michael N. Pearson, eds., *Eyes across the Water: Navigating the Indian Ocean* (Pretoria: UNISA Press, 2010); Edward Alpers, *The Indian Ocean in World History* (Oxford: Oxford University Press, 2014); Abdul Sheriff and Engseng Ho, eds., *The Indian Ocean: Oceanic Connections and the Creation of New Societies* (London: Hurst, 2014); and Himanshu Prabha Ray and Edward A. Alpers, *Cross Currents and Community Networks: The History of the Indian Ocean World* (Oxford: Oxford University Press, 2007).

50 Fernand Braudel, *The Mediterranean and the Mediterranean World in the Age of Philip II*, trans. Siân Reynolds, 2 vols. (London: Collins, 1972). On the legacy of this historical analysis model, see Leila T. Fawaz and Christopher A. Bayly, eds., *Modernity and Culture: From the Mediterranean to the Indian Ocean* (New York: Columbia University Press, 2002); and Nile Green, "Maritime Worlds and Global History: Comparing the Mediterranean and Indian Ocean through Barcelona and Bombay," *History Compass* 11, no. 7 (2013): 513–23. On the historiographical renewal concerning the Indian Ocean and new methodologies for studying maritime spaces, see Sivasundaram, Bashford, and Armitage, "Introduction: Writing World Oceanic Histories"; Burton et al., "Sea Tracks and Trails"; Vink, "Indian Ocean Studies and the 'New Thalassology'"; Hofmeyr, "The Complicating Sea"; and Prange, "Scholars and the Sea."

51 Kirti N. Chaudhuri, *Asia before Europe: Economy and Civilisation of the Indian Ocean from the Rise of Islam to 1750* (Cambridge: Cambridge University Press, 1990); and Kirti N. Chaudhuri, *Trade and Civilisation in the Indian Ocean: An Economic History from the Rise of Islam to 1750* (Cambridge: Cambridge University Press, 1985). See also Philippe

Beaujard, *Les Mondes de l'océan Indien*, 2 vols. (Paris: Armand Colin, 2012); and André Wink, *Al-Hind: The Making of the Indo-Islamic World*, 3 vols. (Leiden: Brill, 1996).

52 See, for example, Sunil Amrith, *Migration and Diaspora in Modern Asia* (Cambridge: Cambridge University Press, 2011); Clare Anderson, *Subaltern Lives: Biographies of Colonialism in the Indian Ocean World, 1790–1820* (Cambridge: Cambridge University Press, 2012); Nile Green, *Bombay Islam: The Religious Economy of the West Indian Ocean, 1840–1915* (Cambridge: Cambridge University Press, 2011); Engseng Ho, *The Graves of Tarim: Genealogy and Mobility across the Indian Ocean* (Berkeley: University of California Press, 2006); John Slight, *The British Empire and the Hajj*; and Gopalan Balchandran, *Globalizing Labour? Indian Seafarers and World Shipping, c. 1870–1945* (Oxford: Oxford University Press, 2012).

53 On this argument, see Engseng Ho, "Inter-Asian Concepts for Mobile Societies," *Journal of Asian Studies* 76, no. 4 (2017): 907–28.

54 This archival material is largely now held in the UK (notably in the British Library's India Office Records series). But some further relevant material is held in the Maharashtra State Archives in Bombay.

55 Rila Mukherjee, "Escape from Terracentrism: Writing a Water History," *Indian Historical Review* 41, no. 1 (2014): 87–101.

56 On the need for a "maritime history" of the Middle East, see Green, "Rethinking the 'Middle East'"; and Green, "The View from the Edge." On the perspectives offered by maritime history and for new historiographical approaches through this specific lens see, for example, Blum, "Terraqueous Planet"; Bashford, "Terraqueous Histories"; Mukherjee, "Escape from Terracentrism"; and Martin W. Lewis and Kären Wigen, "A Maritime Response to the Crisis in Area Studies," *Geographical Review* 89, no. 2 (1999): 161–8.

Chapter One

1 Christopher A. Bayly, *Imperial Meridian: The British Empire and the World, 1780–1830* (London: Longman, 1989).

2 *Bombay Gazette*, 30 September 1809.

3 *Caledonian Mercury*, 1 January 1810.

4 Roxani Eleni Margariti, "Mercantile Networks, Port Cities, and 'Pirate' States: Conflict and Competition in the Indian Ocean World of Trade before the Sixteenth Century," *Journal of the Economic and Social History of the Orient* 51, no. 4 (2008): 543–77.

5 Louise E. Sweet, "Pirates or Polities? Arab Societies of the Persian or Arabian Gulf, 18th Century," *Ethnohistory* 11, no. 3 (1964): 262–80.

6 Thabit Abdullah, *Merchants, Mamluks, and Murder: The Political Economy of Trade in Eighteenth-century Basra* (Albany: SUNY Press, 2001), 67–8.

7 On the Qasimi, see, for example, Charles E. Davies, The *Blood-Red Arab Flag: An Investigation into Qasimi Piracy* (Exeter: University of Exeter Press, 1997); Hideaki Suzuki, "The Making of the 'Joasmee' Pirates: A Relativist Reconsideration of the Qawāsimi Piracy in the Persian Gulf," in *In the Name of the Battle against Piracy: Ideas and Practices in State Monopoly of Maritime Violence in Europe and Asia in the Period of Transition*, edited by Ota Atsushi (Leiden: Brill, 2018), 69–96; Frauke Heard-Bey, *From Trucial States to United Arab Emirates: A Society in Transition* (London: Longman, 1982), 60–83.

8 Mubarak Al-Otabi, "The Qawasim and British Control of the Arabian Gulf," unpublished PhD diss., University of Salford, 1989, 25–30; Arnold T. Wilson, *The Persian Gulf: A Historical Sketch from the Earliest Times to the Beginning of the Twentieth Century* (Oxford: Clarendon Press, 1928), 199–201.

9 Davies, *Blood-Red Arab Flag*, 82–3.

10 University of Exeter, Arab World Documentation Unit of the Centre for Gulf Studies, photocopied selections from Maharastra State Archives (Mumbai): Bombay Diaries, Diary 253, Bruce to Duncan, 18 April 1808.

11 Sweet, "Pirates or Polities?," 271.

12 Davies, *Blood-Red Arab Flag*, 58.

13 Sweet, "Pirates or Polities?," 272; Al-Otabi, "The Qawasim and British Control of the Arabian Gulf," 10–15.

14 British Library, London, IOR/R/15/1/8 [16v] (40/475), Bruce to Duncan, 12 March 1806.

15 Bombay Diaries, 215/13005–6, Minutes of the Bombay Council, 11 November 1808, cited in Davies, *Blood-Red Arab Flag*, 137. A more extensive quotation from this source is given in Suzuki, "The Making of the 'Joasmee' Pirates," 92.

16 On Wahhabi expansionism in the Gulf, see, for example, Davies, *Blood-Red Arab Flag*, 37–44; John B. Kelly, *Britain and the Persian Gulf, 1795–1880* (Oxford: Clarendon, 1968), 99–110; Ravinder Kumar, *India and the Persian Gulf Region: A Study in British Imperial Policy* (London: Asia Publishing House, 1966), 35–9; Jeremy Jones and Nicholas Ridout, *Oman, Culture and Diplomacy* (Edinburgh: Edinburgh University Press, 2012), 91–101.

17 Jones and Ridout, *Oman: Culture and Diplomacy*, 93–5.

18 Donald Hawley, *The Trucial States* (London: Allen and Unwin, 1970), 97.

19 Davies, *Blood-Red Arab Flag*, 91–7, 100–3.

20 For these incidents, see John G. Lorimer, *Gazetteer of the Persian Gulf, Oman and Central Arabia*, 2 vols. (Calcutta: Superintendent Government Printing, India, 1908–15), 1:634; Kelly, *Britain and the Persian Gulf*, 106; Wilson, *The Persian Gulf*, 200–2; Jerome A. Saldanha, ed., *Précis of Correspondence Regarding the Affairs of the Persian Gulf, 1801–1853* (Calcutta: Office of the Superintendent of Government Printing, India, 1906), 33.

21 Bombay Diaries, 122, Jones to Duncan, 7 May 1802; Bombay Diaries, 167, Bruce to Duncan, 21 March 1805.

22 The *Shannon* and the *Trimmer* belonged to Samuel Manesty, Resident of the East India Company in Basra from 1784. On Manesty see Denis Wright, "Samuel Manesty and his Unauthorised Embassy to the Court of Fath' li Shah," *Iran: Journal of the British Institute of Persian Studies* 24 (1986): 153–60; and Malcolm E. Yapp, "The Establishment of the East India Company Residency at Baghdad, 1798–1806," *Bulletin of the School of Oriental and African Studies* 30, no. 2 (1967): 323–36.

23 Lorimer, *Gazetteer*, 1:637–42; Charles R. Low, *History of the Indian Navy (1613–1863)*, 2 vols. (London: R. Bentley and Son, 1877), 1:319–23.

24 Bombay Diaries, 119, Seton to Duncan, 22 October 1802.

25 Bombay Diaries, 113, Seton to Duncan, 1 June 1801.

26 Francis Warden, "Historical Sketch of the Joasmee Tribe of Arabs; from the Year 1747 to the Year 1819" (1819), in *Selections from the Records of the Bombay Government*, n.s. 24, edited by R. Hughes Thomas (Bombay: Bombay Education Society Press, 1856; Cambridge: Oleander Press, 1985), 361–72; Arnold B. Kemball, "Chronological Table of Events Connected with the Government of Muskat from the Year 1765 to 1843; with the Joasmee Tribe of Arabs, from the Year 1765 to 1843 [...]" (1844), in *Selections from the Records of the Bombay Government*, ed. Thomas, 121–65.

27 Gwyn Campbell, "Piracy in the Indian Ocean World," *International Journal of Postcolonial Studies* 16, no. 6 (2014): 775–94.

28 Patricia Risso, "Cross-Cultural Perceptions of Piracy: Maritime Violence in the Western Indian Ocean and Persian Gulf Region during a Long Eighteenth Century," *Journal of World History* 12, no. 2 (2001): 293–319 at 318–19.

29 See also Christopher A. Bayly, *Recovering Liberties: Indian Thought in the Age of Liberalism and Empire* (Cambridge: Cambridge University Press, 2011).

30 Simon Layton, "The 'Moghul's Admiral': Angrian 'Piracy' and the Rise of British Bombay," *Journal of Early Modern History* 17, no. 1 (2013): 75–93 at 78–9.

31 Studies of the Indian Ocean have emphasized that piracy may have been one economic activity among others for the populations of this vast maritime region over many centuries. See, for example, Sebastian R. Prange, "The Contested Sea: Regimes of Maritime Violence in the Pre-Modern Indian Ocean," *Journal of Early Modern History* 17, no. 1 (2013): 9–33; Prange, "A Trade of No Dishonor: Piracy, Commerce, and Community in the Western Indian Ocean, Twelfth to Sixteenth Century," *American Historical Review* 116, no. 5 (2011): 1269–93; Gwyn Campbell, "Piracy in the Indian Ocean World," *International Journal of Postcolonial Studies* 16, no. 6 (2014): 775–94 at 780–4; and Margariti, "Mercantile Networks, Port Cities, and 'Pirate' States."

32 Jatin Dua, "A Sea of Trade and a Sea of Fish: Piracy and Protection in the Western Indian Ocean," *Journal of Eastern African Studies* 7, no. 2 (2013): 353–70; and Dua, *Captured at Sea: Piracy and Protection in the Indian Ocean* (Berkeley: University of California Press, 2019).

33 Louise E. Sweet, "Camel Raiding of North Arabian Bedouin: A Mechanism of Ecological Adaptation," *American Anthropologist* 67, no. 5, pt 1 (1965): 1132–50.

34 Quoted in Penelope Tuson, "Writing the General Treaty: Anne Thompson and the British Expedition to the Gulf, 1819–1821," *Liwa: Journal of the National Center for Documentation and Research* 5, no. 10 (2013): 25–39.

35 Alexander Mikaberidze, *The Napoleonic Wars: A Global History* (New York: Oxford Unviersity Press, 2020).

36 For the chronology of the Egyptian expedition, see Jacques-Olivier Boudon, *La Campagne d'Egypte* (Paris: Belin, 2018); Henry Laurens, ed., *L'Expédition d'Egypte. Bonaparte et l'Islam. Le choc des cultures* (Paris: Armand Colin, 1982); Irene Bierman, *Napoleon in Egypt* (Los Angeles: Gustave E. von Grunebaum Center for Near Eastern Studies, 2003); and Paul Strathern, *Napoleon in Egypt* (New York: Bantam Books, 2008). On the intellectual context and legacy of the expedition, see Henry Laurens, *Les Origines intellectuelles de l'expédition d'Egypte (1698–1798)* (Paris and Istanbul: Isis, 1985); and Laurens, *Orientales I. Autour de l'expédition d'Egypte* (Paris: CNRS Editions, 2004).

37 On the revolutionary age outside of Europe and particularly in the Indian Ocean, see Sujit Sivansundaram, *Waves Across the South: A New History of Revolution and Empire* (London: HarperCollins, 2020).

38 Cited in Al-Otabi, "The Qawasim and British Control of the Arabian Gulf," 65.

39 On earlier French projects in the Red Sea and Persian Gulf, see Holden Furber, *John Company at Work: A Study of European Expansion in India in the Late Eighteenth Century* (Cambridge, MA: Harvard University Press, 1948), 32–77.

40 Cited in Beatrice Niccolini, *Makran, Oman, and Zanzibar: Three-Terminal Cultural Corridor in the Western Indian Ocean (1799–1856)*, translated by Penelope-Jane Watson (Leiden: Brill, 2004), 90.

41 On contacts established by the French with the Sharif of Mecca, see, for example, Husâm Muhammad 'Abd al-Mu'tî, "Le sharîf de La Mecque et les Français durant l'expédition d'Égypte," *Égypte/Monde arabe* 1 (1999): 151–60; and M. Abir, "The 'Arab Rebellion' of Amir Ghālib of Mecca (1788–1813)," *Middle Eastern Studies* 7, no. 2 (1971): 191–3.

42 Qtd in Beatrice Nicolini, "Little Known Aspects of the History of Muscat and Zanzibar during the First Half of the Nineteenth Century," *Proceedings of the Seminar for Arabian Studies* 27 (1997), 193–8. See also Napoléon Bonaparte, *Correspondance générale*, II: *La Campagne d'Egypte et l'avènement, 1798–1799* ([Paris]: Fayard, 2005), 816–17.

43 "Lettre du Directoire exécutif du 23 germinal an 6 (12 avril 1798)," in *Correspondance inédite officielle et confidentielle de Napoléon Bonaparte avec les cours étrangères, les princes, les ministres et les généraux français et étrangers, en Italie, en Allemagne et en Egypte*, 5 vols. (Paris: C.L.F. Panckoucke, 1819), 1:17.

44 Bonaparte, *Correspondance générale*, 2:729 (17 December 1798).

45 Jonathan Duncan (1756–1811) was governor of the Bombay Presidency from 1795 until his death. On Mahdi Ali Khan Bahadur, see James Onley, *The Arabian Frontier of the British Raj: Merchants, Rulers, and the British in the Nineteenth Century Gulf* (Oxford: Oxford University Press, 2007), 87–91.

46 Duncan, "Instructions to Mirza Mehedi Ali Khan for guidance as Resident at Bushire," 3 September 1798, in Jerome A. Saldanha, ed., *Selections from State Papers, Bombay, regarding the East India Company's Connections with the Persian Gulf, with a Summary of Events, 1600–1800* (Calcutta: Superintendent Government Printing, 1908), 342. For a translation of the agreement, see Patricia Risso, *Oman and Muscat: An Early Modern History* (London: Croom Helm, 1986), 218–20.

47 These alliances involved amity but also power plays and threats. When, a few years later, the sultan seemed poised to renege on his agreements with Britain by welcoming a French envoy, the governor of the Bombay Presidency warned him pointedly that "if the French obtain a footing at Muscat on any terms or in any situation, all communications between Muscat and India must cease." Qtd in Mikaberidze, *Napoleonic Wars*, 492.

48 On this agreement, see Mikaberidze, *Napoleonic Wars*, 96–7.

49 On the expedition to Perim, see Edward Ingram, "The Geopolitics of the First British Expedition to Egypt, III: The Red Sea Campaign, 1800–1," *Middle Eastern Studies* 31, no. 1 (1995): 158; and Ingram, "A Preview to the Great Game in Asia, I: The British Occupation of Perim and Aden in 1799," *Middle Eastern Studies* 9, no. 1 (1973): 3–18.

50 Mikaberidze, *Napoleonic Wars*, 87.

51 Ingram, "The Geopolitics," 147.

52 *Official Documents Relative to the Negotiations Carried on by Tippoo Sultaun, with the French Nation, and Other Foreign States, for Purposes Hostile to the British Nation; to Which is Added, Proceedings of a Jacobin Club, Formed at Seringapatam, by the French Soldiers in the Corps Commanded by M. Dompart: With a Translation* (Calcutta: "Printed at the Honorable Company's Press," 1799). For some of the relevant original documentation, see IOR Mss Eur D99, "Proceedings of a Jacobin club at Seringapatam," 5 May–4 June 1797. See also Jean Boutier, "Les "lettres de créances" du corsaire Ripaud. Un 'club jacobin' à Srirangapatnam (inde), mai–juin 1797," in *Le monde créole. Peuplement, sociétés et condition humaine XVIIᵉ–XXᵉ siècles. Mélanges offerts à Hubert Gerbeau*, edited by Jacques Weber (Paris: Les Indes savantes, 2005), 31–43.

53 John William Kaye, *The Life and Correspondence of Major-General Sir John Malcolm, G.C.B., Late Envoy to Persia, and Governor of Bombay*, 2 vols. (London: Smith, Elder & Co., 1856), 1:89–90.

54 On Malcolm's life, see Kaye, *The Life and Correspondence of Major-General Sir John Malcolm*; and Jack Harrington, *Sir John Malcolm and the Creation of British India* (London: Palgrave Macmillan, 2010). Malcolm's literary works include *Sketch of the Political History of India from the Introduction of Mr. Pitt's Bill, A.D. 1784, to the Present Date* (London: William Miller, 1811); *The Political History of India, from 1784 to 1823*, 2 vols. (London: John Murray, 1826); and *The History of Persia* (London: John Murray, 1815). On the latter, see Ann K.S. Lambton, "Major-General Sir John Malcolm (1769–1833) and *The History of Persia*," *Iran* 33, no. 1 (1995): 97–109.

55 On this visit, see Kaye, *The Life and Correspondence of Major-General Sir John Malcolm*, 1:111–16. On the commercial and political treaties signed, see C.U. Aitchison, *A Collection of Treaties, Engagements, and Sunnuds relating to India and Neighbouring Countries*, 8 vols. (Calcutta: Savielle and Cranenburgh; *then* O.T. Cuttee, Military Orphan Press), 7:112–17.

56 *The Argus, or London Review'd in Paris*, 22 January 1803.

57 On Malcolm's visit in Muscat, see Lorimer, *Gazetteer*, 1:429. The agent sent to Oman, Archibald Hamilton Bogle, would remain in post at Muscat between 1800 and 1802. On Bogle, see Niccolini, *Makran, Oman, and Zanzibar*, 90–1.

58 John Malcolm, *Sketches of Persia, from the Journals of a Traveller in the East* (London: John Murray, 1828), 6–8. On the treaty signed, see IOR/F/4/72/1595, "Treaty between Captain John Malcolm and Sayyid Sultan, Imam of Muscat," January 1800.

59 Muhammad al-Qasimi, ed., *John Malcolm and the British Commercial Base in the Gulf, 1800* (United Arab Emirates: Al-Sariqah, 1994).

60 For Napoleon's initial military successes against Ottomans, see Napoléon Bonaparte, *Campagnes d'Egypte et de Syrie*, edited by Henry Laurens (Paris: Imprimerie Nationale, 1988); and Boudon, *Campagne d'Egypte*, 135–64.

61 Montgomery Martin, ed., *The Despatches, Minutes, and Correspondence, of the Marquess Wellesley, K.G. during his Administration in India*, 5 vols. (London: John Murray; *then* W.H. Allen, 1836–37), 5:151.

62 Bombay Diaries, Diary 114, Manesty to Duncan, 8 September 1801.

63 On the 1801 Franco-Russian expedition, see Oleg Sokolov, *Le Combat de deux Empires: La Russie d'Alexandre Ier contre la France de Napoléon, 1805–1812*, translated by Michèle Kahn ([Paris]: Fayard, 2012); and J.L. Scheidman, "The Proposed Invasion of India by Russia and France in 1801," *Journal of Indian History* 35, no. 3 (1957): 167–75.

64 Signed in March 1802, the Peace of Amiens ended hostilities between France and Britain until it broke down in May 1803. By the treaty, Britain gave up its most recent conquests and France evacuated Naples and Egypt. Britain kept Ceylon and Trinidad. See John D. Grainger, *The Amiens Truce: Britain and Bonaparte, 1801–1803* (Rochester: Boydell Press, 2004).

65 *Gazette nationale ou le Moniteur universel*, 30 January 1803.

66 Mikaberidze, *Napoleonic Wars*, 153–4. See also André Auzoux, "La mission de Sebastiani à Tripoli en l'an X (1802)," *Revue des études Napoléoniennes* 16 (1919): 225–36.

67 This English translation of the Sebastiani report appeared spread over three successive issues of the newspaper: *The Argus, or London Review'd in Paris*, 31 January and 2 and 5 February 1803. By far the fullest surviving collection of copies of the *Argus* is that held at the BnF (shelfmark GR FOL-LC2-1026).

68 Edward Ingram, "The Geopolitics of the First British Expedition to Egypt, IV: Occupation and Withdrawal, 1801–3," *Middle Eastern Studies* 31, no. 2 (1995): 336–8.

69 C. Northcote Parkinson, *War in the Eastern Seas, 1793–1815* (London: George Allen and Unwin, 1954), 196–9.

70 On Linois's activities directed against British commerce, see Parkinson, *War in the Eastern Seas*, 236–77. On French privateers, see Henri Prentout, *L'Île de France sous Decaen, 1803–1810. Essai sur la politique coloniale du premier empire* (Paris: Hachette, 1901), 504–6.

71 Bombay Diaries, Diary 161, Wood to Manesty, 16 November 1804.

72 Davies, *Blood-Red Arab Flag*, 258–9; Sultan Muhammad Al-Qasimi, *Les relations entre Oman et la France, 1715–1905* (Paris: L'Harmattan, 1995), 87–8.

73 Bombay Diaries, Diary 172, Bruce to Duncan, 1 October 1805. See also Al-Qasimi, *Relations entre Oman et la France*, 88–91.

74 Prentout, *L'Île de France sous Decaen*, 16–31. See also Jacques Sandeau, *Le Général Decaen à l'Île de France* (Paris: Éditions de l'Amalthée, 2007).

75 On Cavaignac, see Robert Oddos, "Deux siècles de relations franco-omanaises (1735–1920); Aperçu historique," *Revue historique* 599 (1996): 96–8; André Auzoux, "La France et Mascate aux dix-huitième et dix-neuvième siècles," *Revue d'histoire diplomatique* 24 (1910): 234–65.

76 Bombay Diaries, Diary 140, Duncan to Sultan Bin Ahmad of Oman, 21 October 1803.

77 Bombay Diaries, Diary 183, April 1805; Diary 187, 1806.

78 Prentout, *L'Île de France sous Decaen*, 340–3.

79 Oddos, "Deux siècles de relations franco-omanaises," 98–9.

80 Rose L. Greaves, "Iranian Relations with Great Britain and British India, 1798–1821," in *Cambridge History of Iran*, edited by Peter Avery, 7 vols. (Cambridge: Cambridge University Press, 1991–2008), 7:375–9; Edward Ingram, *Britain's Persia Connection, 1798–1828: Prelude to the Great Game* (Oxford: Clarendon Press, 1992). On Fathʿ Ali Shah's strategy of alliance with France, see Iradj Amini, *Napoleon and Persia: Franco-Persian Relations under the First Empire* (Richmond: Curzon, 1999), 111–15.

81 Mikaberidgze, *Napoleonic Wars*, 90.

82 Mikaberidgze, *Napoleonic Wars*, 430; Irène Natchkebia, "Unrealized Project: Rousseau's Plan of Franco-Persian Trade in the Context of the Indian Expedition (1807)," in *Studies on Iran and the Caucasus*, edited by Uwe Bläsing, Victoria Arakelova, and Matthia Weinreich (Leiden: Brill, 2015), 115–29.

83 Mikaberidgze, *Napoleonic Wars*, 431.

84 On Romieu, see Nicole Gotteri, "Antoine-Alexandre Romieu, 1764–1805, général et diplomate," *Revue dromoise* 88, no. 468 (1993): 411–56; and 88, no. 469 (1993): 500–35. On these negotiations, see Amini, *Napoleon and Persia*, 76–89.

85 Roger M. Savory, "British and French Diplomacy in Persia, 1800–1810," *Iran: Journal of the British Institute of Persian Studies* 10 (1972): 31–44; Amini, *Napoleon and Persia*, 120–2; Napoleon Bonaparte, *Correspondance générale*, VII: *Tilsit, l'Apogée de l'Empire 1807* ([Paris]: Fayard 2010), 903.

86 On the treaty, see Amini, *Napoleon and Persia*, 205–8; and Édouard Driault, *La politique orientale de Napoléon: Sébastiani et Gardane, 1806–1808* (Paris: Alcan, 1904), 124–34.

87 Edward Ingram, *In Defence of British India: Great Britain in the Middle East, 1775–1842* (London: Frank Cass, 1984), 97.

88 Charles de Voogd, "Les Français en Perse (1805–1809)," *Studia Iranica* 10, no. 2 (1981): 247–68.

89 For Gardane's instructions, see Florence Hellot-Bellier, *France–Iran: quatre cents ans de dialogue* (Paris: Association pour l'avancement des études iraniennes, 2007), 796. On Gardane's mission, see Alfred de Gardane, *La mission du Général Gardane en Perse sous le Premier Empire* (Paris: A. Lainé, 1865); Paul-Ange-Louis de Gardane, *Journal d'un voyage dans la Turquie d'Asie et la Perse, fait en 1807 et 1808 et retour en France* (Paris: Le Normant; Marseille: Jean Mossy, 1809); Driault, *Politique orientale de Napoléon*, 309–42; and Amini, *Napoleon and Persia*, 118–26.

90 J.-E. Driault, "La mission Gardane en Perse (1807–1809), d'après les Archives nationales et les Archives du ministère des affaires étrangères," *Revue d'histoire moderne et contemporaine* 2, no. 2 (1900): 121–55.

91 Bombay Diaries, Diary 212, Seton to Duncan, 25 September 1807.

92 Bombay Diaries, Diary 220, Smith to Duncan, 8 November 1808.

93 Gardane, *La mission du général Gardane en Perse*, 106–9.

94 See Stephanie Cronin, "Importing Modernity: European Military Missions to Qajar Iran," *Comparative Studies in Society and History* 50, no. 1 (2008): 197–226; and Uzi Rabi and Nugzar Ter-Qganov, "The Military of

Qajar Iran: The Features of an Irregular Army from the Eighteenth to the Early Twentieth Century," *Iranian Studies* 45, no. 3 (2012): 333–54.

95 In addition, archaeological surveys were conducted during Gardane's mission: see Claire Barat, "Voyageurs et perception des vestiges archéologiques à Sinope au temps de la représentation diplomatique française, sous le Consulat et l'Empire," *Anabases* 2 (2005): 163–75; and David Vinson, "Napoléon en Perse: genèse, perspectives culturelles et littéraires de la mission Gardane (1807–1809)," *Revue d'histoire littéraire de la France* 109, no. 4 (2009): 871–97.

96 Bombay Diaries, Diary 212, 25 September 1807.

97 Minto to Colonel Barry Close, 11 October 1807, qtd in [Mary Elliot-Murray-Kynynmound] *Lord Minto in India: Life and Letters of Gilbert Elliot, First Earl of Minto, from 1807 to 1814, while Governor-General of India*, edited by countess of Minto (London: Longmans, Green & Co., 1880), 51.

98 Cited in Ingram, *In Defence of British India*, 124.

99 Qtd in [Elliot-Murray-Kynynmound], ed., *Lord Minto in India*, 100.

100 Bombay Diaries, Diary 220, Smith to Duncan, 8 November 1808.

101 Mountstuart Elphinstone, *An Account of the Kingdom of Caubul, and its Dependencies in Persia, Tartary, and India* (London: Longman, 1815), 1.

102 See Ingram, *In Defence of British India*, 125–6.

103 Savory, "British and French Diplomacy in Persia," 31–2.

104 Adrien Dupré, *Voyage en Perse fait dans les années 1807, 1808, 1809, en traversant l'Anatolie et la Mésopotamie*, 2 vols. (Paris: J.G. Dentu, 1819).

105 Born in 1847, Harford Jones-Brydges was "extraordinary envoy" and "minister plenipotentiary" to the Persian court from 1807 to 1811. On his mission in Tehran, see Harford Jones-Brydges, *An Account of His Majesty's Mission to the Court of Persia in the Years 1807–11* (London: James Bohn, 1834); and Malcolm E. Yapp, *Strategies of British India: Britain, Iran and Afghanistan, 1798–1850* (Oxford: Clarendon Press 1980).

106 On the Nigaristan paintings, see Layla S. Diba, "Invested with Life: Wall Painting and Imagery before the Qajars," *Iranian Studies* 34, nos. 1–4 (2001): 5–16; and Layla S. Diba and Mariam Ekhtiar, eds., *Royal Persian Paintings: The Qajar Epoch, 1785–1925* (London: I.B. Tauris Publishers in association with Brooklyn Museum of Art, 1998).

107 See Minto's instructions to Malcolm in Minto, *Lord Minto in India*, 110–11.

108 Minto, *Lord Minto in India*, 123.

109 Percy Sikes, *A History of Persia*, 2 vols. (London: Macmillan and co., 1915), 2:307–8.

110 For this treaty, see Aitchison, *A Collection of Treaties*, 7:117–20.

111 Qtd in Martin Bayly, *Taming the Imperial Imagination: Colonial Knowledge, International Relations, and the Anglo-Afghan Encounter, 1808–1878* (Cambridge: Cambridge University Press, 2016), 76.

112 Denis Wright, *The English amongst the Persians during the Qajar Period, 1787–1921* (London: Heinemann, 1977), 8–10; Ingram, *In Defence of British India*, 181; Savory, "British and French Diplomacy in Persia," 34–40.

113 Minto, *Lord Minto in India*, 137.

114 Morier published a famous romanced account of his time at the Persian Court: James J. Morier, *The Adventures of Hajji Baba of Ispahan*, 2 vols. (London: John Murray, 1824). This text had a fundamental impact on the perception of Qajar Iran in nineteenth-century Britain. On Mirza Abul Hasan, see Naghmeh Sohrabi, "Looking behind Hajji Baba of Ispahan: The Case of Mirza Abul Hasan Khan Ilchi Shirazi," in *Untold Histories of the Middle East: Recovering Voices from the 19th and 20th Centuries*, edited by Amy Singer, Christoph Neumann, and Selcuk Aksin Somel (London: Routledge, 2010), 171–88; Henry McKenzie Johnston, "Hajji Baba and Mirza Abul Hasan Khan: A Conundrum," *Iran* 33, no. 1 (1995), 93–6.

115 *Morning Post*, 21 December 1809.

116 Bombay Diaries, Diary 254, 1808, 1332.

117 Bombay Diaries, Diary 254, Duncan to Malcolm, 12 December 1808.

118 Minto, *Lord Minto in India*, 128.

119 Cited in Al-Otabi, "The Qawasim and British Control of the Arabian Gulf," 119 (Minto to Duncan, 3 April 1809).

120 Leonard Montreath Thompson, *A History of South Africa* (New Haven: Yale University Press, 1990).

121 Auguste Toussaint, *Histoire de l'Océan Indien* (Paris: Presses universitaires de France, 1980), 182.

122 Minto, *Lord Minto in India*, 142.

123 For an account of the mission, see Elphinstone, *An Account of the Kingdom of Caubul*. On this mission and on Afghanistan around 1800, see Bayly, *Taming the Imperial Imagination*, 52–5; Robert D. Crews, *Afghan Modern: The History of a Global Nation* (Cambridge, MA: Harvard University Press, 2015), 26–7; and Benjamin D. Hopkins, *The Making of Modern Afghanistan* (Basingstoke: Palgrave Macmillan, 2008), 12–17. I disagree with Martin Bayly's argument that by 1808 a French threat was no longer a reality and that the idea of a Russian threat served as a "post-facto rationalization" for Elphinstone's expedition (Bayly, *Taming the Imperial Imagination*, 76).

124 Shah Shuja Durrani succeeded his brother Zaman Shah in October 1801. *Lord Minto in India*, 160.

125 Elphinstone to Minto, 14 December 1808, qtd in *Lord Minto in India*, 163.

126 On the legacy of this mission, see: Shah Mahmoud Hanifi, ed., *Mountstuart Elphinstone in South Asia: Pioneer of British Colonial Rule* (Oxford: Oxford University Press, 2019).

127 See the account of this mission: Minto, *Lord Minto in India*, 141–58; and Amita Das, *Defending British India against Napoleon: The Foreign Policy of Governor-General Lord Minto 1807–13* (Woodbridge: Boydell, 2016), 106–8.

128 Das, *Defending British India*, 130–2.

129 Henry Pottinger, *Travels in Beloochistan and Sinde* (London: Longman, 1816).

130 On these military operations against French possessions in the Indian Ocean, see Toussaint, *Histoire de l'Océan Indien*, 71; Parkinson, *War in the Eastern Seas*, 397–410; Prentout, *L'Ile de France sous Decaen*, 592–614.

131 Romain Bertrand, *État colonial, noblesse et nationalisme à Java: la tradition parfaite* (Paris: Karthala, 2005), 186; Parkinson, *War in the Eastern Seas*, 414–17.

132 Christopher A. Bayly, *Indian Society and the Making of the British Empire* (Cambridge: Cambridge University Press, 1988).

Chapter Two

1 On indirect rule in the Gulf, see John B. Kelly, *Britain and the Persian Gulf, 1795–1880* (Oxford: Clarendon, 1968); and James Onley, *The Arabian Frontier of the British Raj: Merchants, Rulers, and the British in the Nineteenth-Century Gulf* (Oxford: Oxford University Press, 2007). On indirect rule in British India, see the landmark study by Michael H. Fisher, *Indirect Rule in India: Residents and the Residency System, 1764–1858* (Delhi: Oxford University Press, 1991).

2 British Library, London: IOR/R/15/1/14, f.16v, William Bruce to Francis Warden, 20 May 1813.

3 As above, f.19, Bruce to Warden, 10 June 1813. On Bin Akil, see also Mabel V. Jackson, *European Powers and South-East Africa: A Study of International Relations on the South-East Coast of Africa, 1796–1856*, rev. 2nd ed. (New York: Praeger, 1967), 129–30; Samuel B. Miles, *The Countries and Tribes of the Persian Gulf*, 2 vols. (London: Harrison and Sons, 1919), 2:512–13; and Dionisius A. Agius, *The Life of the Red Sea Dhow: A Cultural History of Seaborne Exploration in the Islamic World* (London: I.B.

Tauris, 2019), 125. Before Bin Akil, there were other comparable figures playing a complex game of alliances, most famously Rahmah bin Jabr: see Sugata Bose, *A Hundred Horizons: The Indian Ocean in the Age of Global Empire* (Cambridge, MA: Harvard University Press, 2006), 46–7; and Rosemarie Said Zahlan, *The Creation of Qatar* (London: Routledge, 2016), 31–2.

4 Charles Davies, *The Blood-Red Arab Flag: An Investigation into Qasimi Piracy, 1797–1820* (Exeter: University of Exeter Press, 1997), 82–4.

5 IOR/R/15/1/17, ff.39–44, Bruce to Warden, 11 August 1815.

6 Donald Hawley, *The Trucial States* (London: Allen and Unwin, 1970), 106–7.

7 IOR/R/15/1/18, ff.67v–78v, Bruce to Warden, 8 September 1816.

8 IOR/R/15/1/15, f.31r, Smith to Bruce, November 1813; IOR/R/15/1/15, ff.31v–32v, Warden to Bruce, November 1813.

9 Kelly, *Britain and the Persian Gulf*, 132.

10 Arnold T. Wilson, *The Persian Gulf: An Historical Sketch from the Earliest Times to the Beginning of the Twentieth Century* (Oxford: Clarendon, 1928), 206; Hubert Moyse-Bartlett, *The Pirates of Trucial Oman* (London: Macdonald, 1966), 108; Davies, *Blood-Red Arab Flag*, 107–25.

11 IOR/R/15/1/17, ff.43–4, Warden to Carinac, 3 January 1815.

12 Kelly, *Britain and the Persian Gulf*, 134–5.

13 Christopher A. Bayly, *Indian Society and the Making of the British Empire* (Cambridge: Cambridge University Press, 1990), 102–3.

14 Ctd in Kelly, *Britain and the Persian Gulf*, 140.

15 Kelly, *Britain and the Persian Gulf*, 140.

16 On Mehmed Ali, see, for example, Khaled Fahmy, *All the Pasha's Men: Mehmed Ali, His Army, and the Making of Modern Egypt* (Cambridge: Cambridge University Press, 1997); Fahmy, *From Ottoman Governor to Ruler of Egypt* (Oxford: Oneworld, 2009); and Madawi Al-Rasheed, *A History of Saudi Arabia* (New York: Cambridge University Press, 2002), 22–3.

17 Kelly, *Britain and the Persian Gulf*, 140.

18 University of Exeter, Arab World Documentation Unit of the Centre for Gulf Studies, photocopied selections from Maharastra State Archives (Mumbai, India): Bombay Diaries, Diary 311, Hastings to Ibrahim Pacha, 2 January 1819, 722–3.

19 Kelly, *Britain and the Persian Gulf*, 140.

20 Kelly, *Britain and the Persian Gulf*, 140–2. At the beginning of the nineteenth century, Qeshm Island was leased by the shah of Persia to the sultan of Oman: Gerald S. Graham, *Great Britain in the Indian Ocean:*

A Study of Maritime Enterprise 1810–1850 (Oxford: Clarendon, 1968), 252–8.

21 Kelly, *Britain and the Persian Gulf*, 141–2. On Persia's claim to Bahrain, see John B. Kelly, "The Persian Claim to Bahrain," *International Affairs* 33, no. 1 (1957): 51–70.

22 Ctd in Kelly, *Britain and the Persian Gulf*, 142.

23 Kelly, *Britain and the Persian Gulf*, 142–3.

24 Sadleir's instructions are reproduced in George F. Sadleir, *Diary of a Journey across Arabia (1819)* (Bombay: "Printed at the Education Society's Press, Byculla," 1866), 129–32.

25 On Ouseley's time in Persia, see the account by the British envoy in Tehran, James J. Morier: James J. Morier, *A Second Journey through Persia, Armenia, and Asia Minor, to Constantinople, between the Years 1810 and 1816* (London: Longman, 1818); and Nile Green, *The Love of Strangers: What Six Muslim Students Learned in Jane Austen's London* (Princeton: Princeton University Press, 2016). On Sadleir, see F.M. Edwards, "George Forster Sadleir (1789–1859) of the 47th Regt. The First European to Cross Arabia," *Journal of the Royal Central Asian Society* 44, no. 1 (1957), 38–49; and Denis Wright, *The English amongst the Persians during the Qajar Period* (London: Heinemann, 1977), 50.

26 Sadleir, *Diary of a Journey across Arabia*, 7–14.

27 IOR/R/15/1/19, ff.106v–107, Sadleir to Nepean, 16 June 1819.

28 One of the first British maps of the Arabian Peninsula was drawn around 1821, based on the information collected by Sadleir: IOR/X/3215, Route across Arabia from Elkatif in the Persian Gulf to Yambo in the Red Sea.

29 Sadleir, *Diary of a Journey across Arabia*, 81–7.

30 Kelly, *Britain and the Persian Gulf*, 145.

31 IOR/P/SEC/BOM/41, Bombay Secret Proceedings, vol. 41, minutes of the Bombay Council from 12 to 21 July 1819.

32 Kelly, *Britain and the Persian Gulf*, 145–9.

33 Francis Warden's memoranda are reproduced in R. Hughes Thomas, ed., *Selections from the Records of the Bombay Government*, no. 24, new series (Bombay: Printed for Govt at the Bombay Education Society's Press, 1856). See the following, from Warden's memoranda, found in Thomas, *Selections*: "Extracts from Brief Notes Containing Historical and Other Information Connected with the Province of Oman," 1–40; "Brief Notes Related to the Province of Oman," 41–4; "Extracts from Brief Notes Relative to the Rise and Progress of the Arab Tribes of the Persian Gulf, Prepared, in August 1819," 55–60; "Historical Sketch of the Rise and Progress of the Government of Muskat," 167–234; "Historical Sketch of

the Uttoobee Tribe of Arabs (Bahrein), from the Year 1716 to the Year 1817," 361–425; and "Historical Sketch of the Wahabee Tribe of Arabs, from the Year 1795 to the year 1818," 427–60.

34 Warden, "Historical Sketch of the Rise and Progress of the Government of Muskat." Sultan Bin Ahmad reigned from 1792 to 1804. On Ahmad's imperialism in the Gulf, see Jeremy Jones and Nicholas Ridout, *A History of Modern Oman* (Cambridge: Cambridge University Press, 2015), 39–46.

35 Ctd in Kelly, *Britain and the Persian Gulf*, 148.

36 Kelly, *Britain and the Persian Gulf*, 149.

37 IOR/R/15/1/19, ff.126–127, Keir to Bruce, 14 November 1819; IOR/R/15/1/19, ff.128–133, Newnham to Bruce, 9 October 1819.

38 IOR/R/15/1/19, ff.129–130, copy of a letter from Nepean to Sayyid Said, 9 October 1819; IOR/R/15/1/19, f.134, Jukes to Bruce, 3 November 1819.

39 Edward Ingram, *Britain's Persian Connection, 1798–1828: Prelude to the Great Game in Asia* (Oxford: Clarendon, 1992), 229.

40 John G. Lorimer, *Gazetteer of the Persian Gulf, Oman and Central Arabia*, 2 vols. (Calcutta: Superintendent Government Printing, India, 1908–15), 1:666.

41 Kelly, *Britain and the Persian Gulf*, 153.

42 IOR/R/15/1/19, f.142, Keir to Bruce, 18 December 1819.

43 Lorimer, *Gazetteer*, 1:668.

44 IOR/R/15/1/21, f.16, Keir to Bruce, 16 January 1820.

45 IOR/R/15/1/21, f.4, Keir to Bruce, 16 January 1820. Hasan bin-Rahmah had been in power since 1814.

46 IOR/R/15/1/21, ff.4–12, Keir to Bruce, 16 January 1820; IOR/R/15/1/21, ff.21–26, Keir to Bruce, 21 March 1820.

47 Copies of the preliminary treaties are enclosed in a letter addressed by Keir to Bruce on 16 January 1820, IOR/R/15/1/21, ff.9–12.

48 IOR/R/15/1/21, ff.37–43, Willock to Dow, 11 May 1820.

49 Leonard G. Johnson, *General T. Perronet Thompson, 1783–1869: His Military, Literary, and Political Campaigns* (London: G. Allen and Unwin, 1957); Nick Mansfield, *Soldiers as Citizens: Popular Politics and the Nineteenth-Century British Military* (Liverpool: Liverpool University Press, 2019), 108; Bose, *A Hundred Horizons*, 47–8.

50 For the articles of the treaty, as discussed in this and the following paragraph, see IOR/R/15/1/21, ff.6–9.

51 On Elphinstone, see Thomas E. Colebrooke, *Life of the Honourable Mountstuart Elphinstone*, 2 vols. (London: John Murray, 1884).

52 Kelly, *Britain and the Persian Gulf*, 157–9.

53 Patricia Risso, "Qasimi Piracy and the General Treaty of Peace (1820)," *Arabian Studies* 4 (1978): 47–57.
54 Kelly, *Britain and the Persian Gulf*, 163–6.
55 R/15/1/23, ff.26–28, Warden to Thompson, 1 May 1820. On the creation of this post, see Onley, *The Arabian Frontier of the British Raj*, 91–3; and Kelly, *Britain and the Persian Gulf*, 166, 175–9, 197–9.
56 On the Bani bu'Ali, see Jeremy Jones, *Oman, Culture and Diplomacy* (Edinburgh: Edinburgh University Press, 2012), 104–8; and J.E. Peterson, *Oman in the Twentieth Century: Political Foundations of an Emerging State* (London: Croom Helm, 1978), 127–30.
57 IOR/R/15/1/23, ff.76–78, Thompson to Warden, 3 December 1820.
58 IOR/R/15/1/23, f.41, Warden to Thompson, 8 June 1820.
59 On this episode, see Kelly, *Britain and the Persian Gulf*, 172.
60 IOR/R/15/1/23, f.67v, Translation of a letter from Sayyid bin Sultan to Elphinstone, 19 November 1820.
61 Kelly, *Britain and the Persian Gulf*, 172.
62 IOR/R/15/1/23, ff.42–6, Thompson to Warden, 13 October 1820; IOR Mss Eur F88/421, f.35, Warden on Thompson's proceedings, 1820.
63 Kelly, *Britain and the Persian Gulf*, 172.
64 IOR/R/15/1/23, ff.48–63, Thompson to Warden, 18 November 1820. See also Kelly, *Britain and the Persian Gulf*, 173–4.
65 IOR/R/15/1/23, ff.69–71, Warden to Thompson, 10 January 1821; IOR/R/15/1/23, ff.83–90, Thompson to Warden, 12 February 1821.
66 Ctd in Kelly, *Britain and the Persian Gulf*, 181.
67 IOR Mss Eur F88/421, f.21, 1821.
68 IOR/R/15/1/23, ff.91–2, Smith to Colville, 2 March 1821; IOR/R/15/1/23, ff.93–6, Smith to Warden, 15 March 1821.
69 Miles, *The Countries and Tribes of the Persian Gulf*, 2:326–7; Lorimer, *Gazetteer*, 1:464–6; Ingram, *Britain's Persian Connection*, 232–4; J.E. Peterson, *Oman's Insurgencies: The Sultanate's Struggle for Supremacy* (London: Saqi, 2007), 39–40.
70 IOR/R/15/1/23, ff.112–114, Warden to Jukes, 12 May 1821.
71 On this argument, see Kelly, *Britain and the Persian Gulf*, 181–92. Willock had held the post since 1815.
72 Kelly, *Britain and the Persian Gulf*, 187. Jukes was accompanied by a Scottish lieutenant of the Company, James B. Fraser, who left an account of the mission: James B. Fraser, *Narrative of a Journey into Khorasan* (London: Longman, Hurst, Rees, Orme, Brown, and Green, 1825).
73 Bruce was acting resident several times between 1804 and 1822.
74 IOR/R/15/1/25, f.43, Bruce to Warden, 8 June 1822.

75 Kelly, *Britain and the Persian Gulf*, 188.

76 IOR/R/15/1/25, ff.52–3, Bruce to Warden, 6 August 1822; ff.56–8, Bruce to Elphinstone, 3 September 1822; IOR/R/15/1/26, ff.39–40, Farish to Bruce, 1 November 1822.

77 IOR/R/15/1/27, ff.2v–3, Macleod to Taylor, 24 December 1822.

78 Ingram, *Britain's Persian Connection*.

79 IOR/R/15/1/23, ff.97–107, Smith to Warden, 23 April 1821; IOR/R/15/1/23, ff.91–92v, Smith to Colville, 3 March 1821; IOR/R/15/1/23, ff.93–96v, Smith to Warden, 15 March 1821.

80 Charles R. Low, *History of the Indian Navy (1613–1863)*, 2 vols. (London: R. Bentley and Son, 1877), 1:536–41; Edward Ingram, "A Scare of Seaborne Invasion: The Royal Navy at the Strait of Hormuz, 1807–1808," *Military Affairs* 46, no. 2 (1982): 64–8.

81 IOR/R/15/1/24, ff.6–10, Bombay Castle to Dow, 9 June 1821.

82 Kelly, *Britain and the Persian Gulf*, 196.

83 Onley, *The Arabian Frontier of the British Raj*, 45, 65–8.

84 Kelly, *Britain and the Persian Gulf*, 198–9. On the history of the residency in Baghdad, see Malcolm Yapp, "The Establishment of the East India Company Residency at Baghdad, 1798–1806," *Bulletin of the School of Oriental and African Studies* 30, no. 2 (1967): 323–36.

85 Kelly, *Britain and the Persian Gulf*, 200.

86 IOR/R/15/1/28, ff.123–127, Farish to Macleod, 20 November 1822.

87 IOR/R/15/1/30, ff.12–30v, Macleod to Willock, 27 February 1823.

88 Al-Rasheed, *A History of Saudi Arabia*, 22–4; George Rentz, "Wahhabism and Saudi Arabia," in *The Arabian Peninsula: Society and Politics*, ed. Derek Hopwood (Totowa: Rowman and Littlefield, 1972), 54–66; Joas Wagemakers, "The Enduring Legacy of the Second Saudi State: Quietist and Radical Wahhabi Contestations of al-walāʾ wa-l-barāʾ," *International Journal of Middle East Studies* 44, no. 1 (2012): 93–110.

89 IOR/R/15/1/63, ff.1v–2, Blane to Norris, 22 April 1833.

90 Hawley, *The Trucial States*, 150–5; John B. Kelly, "The Buraimi Oasis Dispute," *International Affairs* 32, no. 3 (1956): 321–4.

91 Kelly, *Britain and the Persian Gulf*, 231.

92 IOR/R/15/1/63, ff.12–13, Blane to Norris, 7 October 1833.

93 IOR/R/15/1/63, ff.6–7, Blane to Norris, 4 June 1833; IOR/R/15/1/63, ff.4v–5, Blane to Norris, 31 May 1833.

94 IOR/R/15/1/64, ff.1v–2v, Blane to Norris, 14 January 1834.

95 On this episode, see Salîl-Ibn-Razîk, *History of the Imams and Seyyids of 'Oman by Salil-ibn-Razik, from A.D. 661–1856*, trans. Percy Badger (London: Printed for the Hakluyt Society, 1871), 349–54.

96 IOR/R/15/1/67, f.48, Hennel to Brucks, 21 May 1835. See also Lorimer, *Gazetteer*, 1:454.

97 Kelly, *Britain and the Persian Gulf*, 354–5.

98 James Onley, *Britain and the Gulf Shaikhdoms, 1820–1971: The Politics of Protection*, Occasional Paper no. 4 (Doha: Center for International and Regional Studies, School of Foreign Service, Georgetown University School of Foreign Service in Qatar, 2009), 6–7.

99 IOR/R/15/1/67, ff.51v–52, 21 May 1835; Onley, *Britain and the Gulf Shaikhdoms*, 6–7.

100 Guillemette Crouzet, "The British Empire in India, the Gulf Pearl and the Making of the Middle East," *Middle Eastern Studies* 55, no. 6 (2019): 864–78.

101 Kelly, *Britain and the Persian Gulf*, 359.

102 IOR/R/15/1/92, ff.14–15, Hennel to Brucks, 13 February 1841.

103 Kelly, *Britain and the Persian Gulf*, 365.

104 Fahmy, *All the Pasha's Men*, 38–76.

105 Two treaties had led to the expansion of Russian influence in Persia. With the Treaty of Gulistan, signed in 1813, Persia lost all its territories north of the Aras River to Russia. Russia was also granted exclusive rights to station its military fleet in the Caspian Sea. With the Treaty of Turkmanchai, signed in 1828, Persia lost more of its northern territories to Russia. Muriel Atkin, *Russia and Iran, 1780–1828* (Minneapolis: University of Minnesota Press, 1980), 143–4, 152; Mansoureh Ettehadieh Nezam-Mafi, "Qajar Iran (1795–1921)," in *The Oxford Handbook of Iranian History*, ed. Touraj Daryaee (Oxford: Oxford University Press, 2012), 7–8.

106 IOR/R/15/1/77, ff.3–7, Willoughby to Hennel, 21 May 1838.

107 Benjamin D. Hopkins, *The Making of Modern Afghanistan* (London: Palgrave Macmillan, 2008), 62–4.

108 Kelly, *Britain and the Persian Gulf*, 290–353; Ibrahim Khalil Ahmed, "The Role of Bahrain in Mohammad Ali's Attempts to Establish a Unified Arab Nation," in *Bahrain through the Ages: The History*, ed. Shaikh Abdullah bin Khalid Al-Katif and Michael Rice (London: Kegan Paul International, 1993), 10–11.

109 John B. Kelly, "Mehemet 'Ali's Expedition to the Persian Gulf 1837–1840, Part II," *Middle Eastern Studies* 2, no. 1 (1965): 63.

110 Robert J. Blyth, *The Empire of the Raj: India, Eastern Africa, and the Middle East, 1858–1947* (Basingstoke: Palgrave Macmillan, 2003), 2; Robert J. Gavin, *Aden under British Rule* (London: Hurst, 1975)

111 Kelly, *Britain and the Persian Gulf*, 337–8.

112 Kelly, "Mehemet 'Ali's Expedition," 51–2.

113 IOR/R/15/1/99, ff.29–30r, Kemball to Lowe, 20 April 1843; ff.36–38v, Kemball to Willoughby, 19 May 1843. Kemball would himself be appointed to the position of resident later that year.

114 Charles U. Aitchison, *A Collection* of *Treaties, Engagements, and Sanads Relating to India and Neighbouring Countries*, 12 vols. (Calcutta: Superintendent Government Printing, India, 1909), 12:134–5.

115 IOR/R/15/1/130, f.73, Hennel to Malet, 9 February 1853.

116 Aitchison, *A Collection of Treaties*, 12:135–6.

117 Onley, *Britain and the Gulf Shaikhdoms*, 32–3.

118 James Onley and Sulayman Khalaf, "Shaikhly Authority in the Pre-oil Gulf: An Historical–Anthropological Study," *History and Anthropology* 17, no. 3 (2006): 189–208.

119 On the criticism received by Onley on this theory, see James Onley, "Imperial History and Political Correctness," *British Scholar* 2, no. 2 (2010): 339–47.

120 For a comparative study, see Hassan Rachik, *Le Sultan des autres. Rituel et politique dans le Haut-Atlas* ([Casablanca]: Afrique Orient, 1992).

121 Clifford Geertz, *The Interpretation of Cultures* (New York: Basic Books, 1973), 14.

122 Pierre Bourdieu, *Outline of a Theory of Practice*, trans., Richard Nice (Cambridge: Cambridge University Press, 1977); Pierre Bourdieu, *Pascalian Meditations*, trans. Richard Nice (Stanford: Stanford University Press, 2000), 187.

Chapter Three

1 George B. Kempthorne, "Notes Made on a Survey along the Eastern Shores of the Persian Gulf in 1828," *Journal of the Royal Geographical Society of London* 5 (1835): 263–85.

2 On this argument, see Daniel Foliard, *Dislocating the Orient: British Maps and the Making of the Middle East, 1854–1921* (Chicago: University of Chicago Press, 2017), 1–12. On the idea of "the heterogeneity of geographical knowledges" situated between reality and imagination, see Felix Driver, "Geography's Empire: Histories of Geographical Knowledge," *Environment and Planning D: Society and Space* 10, no. 1 (1992): 23–40.

3 See, for example, Anne Godlewska and Neil Smith, eds., *Geography and Empire* (Oxford: Blackwell, 1994); Felix Driver, *Geography Militant: Cultures of Exploration and Empire* (Oxford: Blackwell, 2000); Morag Bell,

Robin Butlin, and Michael Heffernan, eds., *Geography and Imperialism 1820–1940* (Manchester: Manchester University Press, 1995); and Pierre Singaravélou, ed., *L'Empire des géographes. Géographie, Exploration et Colonisation (XIXe–XXe siècles)* (Paris: Belin, 2008).

4 Dane Kennedy, *The Last Blank Spaces: Exploring Africa and Australia* (Cambridge, MA: Harvard University Press, 2013); Paul Carter, *The Road to Botany Bay: An Exploration of Landscape and History* (London: Faber and Faber, 1987); Timothy Mitchell, *Colonizing Egypt* (Berkeley: University of California Press, 1988); Marie de Rugy, *Aux Confins des Empires. Cartes et constructions territoriales dans le nord de la péninsule Indochinoise (1885–1914)* (Paris: Editions de la Sorbonne, 2018); D. Graham Burnett, *Masters of All They Surveyed: Exploration, Geography, and a British El Dorado* (Chicago: University of Chicago Press, 2000); Haim Goren, *Dead Sea Level: Science, Exploration and Imperial Interests in the Near East* (London: I.B. Tauris, 2010).

5 Matthew Edney, *Mapping an Empire: The Geographical Construction of British India, 1765–1843* (Chicago: University of Chicago Press, 1997), 78.

6 In particular, scholarship has moved away from John B. Harley's work, notably his *The New Nature of Maps: Essays in the History of Cartography* (Baltimore: Johns Hopkins University Press, 2001) and "Deconstructing the Map," *Cartographica* 26, no. 2 (1989): 1–20. For revisionist accounts, see Reuben Rose-Redwood, ed., "Deconstructing the Map: 25 Years On," special issue, *Cartographica* 50, no. 1 (2015); and Martin Dodge, Rob Kitchin, and Chris R. Perkins, *Rethinking Maps: New Frontiers in Cartographic Theory* (London: Routledge, 2009).

7 On this argument, see Thomas Simpson, *The Frontier in British India: Space, Science, and Power in the Nineteenth Century* (Cambridge: Cambridge University Press, 2021), 70–115.

8 Foliard, *Dislocating the Orient*, 4.

9 These analyses of the idea of the "production" of a space/region draw on Henri Lefebvre, *La Production de l'Espace* (Paris: Éditions Anthropos, 1974); Vincent Veschambres, "Appropriation et marquage de l'espace: quelques éléments de réflexion," ESO *Travaux et documents*, no. 21 (March 2004): 73–7; Pierre Bourdieu, "Effet de lieu," in *La Misère du monde*, ed. Pierre Bourdieu (Paris: Le Seuil, 1993), 249–62; and Claude Raffestin, "Ecogénèse territoriale et territorialité," in *Espaces, jeux et enjeux*, ed. Frank Auriac and Roger Brunet (Paris: Fayard, 1986), 175–85.

10 Andrew S. Cook, ed., *Survey of the Shores and Islands of the Persian Gulf 1820–1829*, 5 vols. (Gerrards Cross: Archive Editions, 1990), 1:xiv. Niebuhr left an account of his travels in the Gulf and Arabia: Carsten

Niebuhr, *Travels through Arabia, and Other Countries in the East*, trans. Robert Heron, 2 vols. (Edinburgh, 1792).

11 On this idea of "blanks" in maps, see Isabelle Laboulais-Lesage, ed., *Combler les blancs de la carte. Modalités et enjeux de la construction des savoirs géographiques (XVIe–XXe siècles)* (Strasbourg: Presses Universitaires de Strasbourg, 2004).

12 For this nautical chart, see British Library, London: IOR/X/14692/119.

13 Cook, *Survey of the Shores and Islands*, 1:xvi.

14 McCluer's wider career is also indicative of how the Gulf was part of a larger interest on the part of the Company in advancing its understanding of the subcontinent's peripheries: having joined the Bombay Marine in 1777, McCluer would ultimately carry out three major surveys: one of the Gulf, one of the Bay of Bombay, and one of the South Pacific and New Guinea. For McCluer's Gulf surveys, see Charles R. Low, *History of the Indian Navy (1613–1863)*, 2 vols. (London: R. Bentley and Son, 1877), 1:189–91.

15 Qtd in Cook, *Survey of the Shores and Islands*, 1:xii.

16 Cook, *Survey of the Shores and Islands*, 1:xiii, xviii. On the timeline of the Gulf surveys, see Clements R. Markham, *A Memoir on the Indian Surveys* (London: W.H. Allen & Co., 1871), 10–12, 33–4; Low, *History of the Indian Navy*, 2:402, 407–14; and Arnold T. Wilson, *The Persian Gulf: An Historical Sketch from the Earliest Times to the Beginning of the Twentieth Century* (Oxford: Clarendon, 1928), 262–3, 277–8.

17 For the surveys, plans, and charts of these sites located in the Ras Musandam and between Ras al-Khaimah and Jazirat al-Hamra and done under the auspices of Guy and Cogan over 1820–21, see IOR/F/4/676/18677; IOR/X/3682; and IOR/X/3681.

18 Cook, *Survey of the Shores and Islands*, 1:xviii, xix.

19 For the trigonometrical plans and charts of Ras al-Khaimah, Jazirat al-Hamra, Umm al-Quwain, Ajman, Sharjah, Abu Dhabi, and Dubai, and done under the auspices of Guy, Cogan, and Brucks in 1822, see IOR/X/3688, 1822; IOR/X/3685, 1822; IOR/X/3686, 1822; IOR/X/3689, 1822; and IOR/X/3690, 1822.

20 Cook, *Survey of the Shores and Islands*, 1:xix.

21 For the trigonometrical plans of Kuwait, Qatif, and Bahrain done in 1825, see IOR/X/3630/23, 1828; IOR/X/3630/20/3, 1828; and IOR/X/3630/21, 1828.

22 BL Add. MS 14383, Account of the Survey of the Persian Gulph, in 1821–35, by Capt. G. Brucks.

23 Cook, *Survey of the Shores and Islands*, 1:xx.

24 Haines served as Brucks's assistant surveyor, beginning in 1826. In 1833 he was instructed to survey the island of Socotra. He later convinced the Bombay government of the utility of seizing Aden, and he was involved in its ensuing capture in 1839. Haines was then political agent in Aden from 1839 to 1854. On Haines's surveys in the Red Sea, see Low, *History of the Indian Navy*, 2:73–4, 80; and Foliard, *Dislocating the Orient*, 24, 36–9.

25 For the trigonometrical survey of Clarence's Strait done in 1828 by Brucks and Haines, see IOR/X/3630/28/2, 1831.

26 For this survey, see IOR/X/3630/15, 1831.

27 A compilation of data gathered in the preceding years by the trigonometrical surveys allowed the following general chart of the Gulf to be produced: BL MS Eur F126/96, 1832. See also Brucks's account of his time in the Gulf survey: IOR/V/23/217, no. 24Y, Memoir descriptive of the navigation of the Gulf of Persia, 1856.

28 Daniel Foliard notes that at this time the mapping of the Gulf was nonetheless progressing faster than the mapping of the Red Sea: Foliard, *Dislocating the Orient*, 24.

29 These 1830–35 surveys notably focused on the entrance to the Gulf (Clarence Strait and Kishm Island): IOR/Z/E/4/43/C444; and IOR/Z/E/4/43/C928, 1830–35.

30 Chesney's activities in Mesopotamia are studied in detail in Chapter 5 below. On Chesney's survey see, for instance, Francis R. Chesney, *The Expedition for the Survey of the Rivers Euphrates and Tigris, Carried on by Order of the British Government, in the Years 1835, 1836, and 1837*, 2 vols. (London: Longman, Brown, Green and Longmans, 1850); and Goren, *Dead Sea Level*, 59–115.

31 On Lynch's work on the Mesopotamian survey, see Markham, *A Memoir on the Indian Surveys*, 27–8.

32 As analyzed in chapter 5, Lynch and his brother went on to create one of the most successful British trading companies in the region.

33 After serving briefly as political agent at Baghdad and consul general in Turkish Arabia, Jones was appointed Resident at Bushire in 1855. On Jones's time with the Mesopotamian survey, see Markham, *A Memoir on the Indian Surveys*, 28–37.

34 For more on Rawlinson's contribution to this expedition, see Markham, *A Memoir on the Indian Surveys*, 29. Jones left an account of this expedition to the Iraqi–Persian border: James Felix Jones, *Narrative of a Journey through Parts of Persia and Kurdistan* (n.p.: "Printed for the use of Government," n.d. [1847 or later]).

35 Markham, *A Memoir on the Indian Surveys*, 29; IOR/X/3140, Map of the countries between the Mediterranean Sea and the Gulf of Persia, 1847.

36 A number of these may be found in IOR/V/23/225 as part of the *Selections from the Records of the Bombay Government* series, including, for example (no. 43, new series), Jones's *Notes on the Topography of Nineveh and the Other Cities of Assyria: And on the General Geography of the Country between the Tigris and the Upper Zab* (Bombay: Bombay Education Society's Press, 1857). See also, for a recent reprint of six reports, James Felix Jones, *Memoirs of Baghdad, Kurdistan and Turkish Arabia, 1857: Selections from the Records of the Bombay Government, No. XLIII. – New Series* (Slough: Archive Editions, 1998).

37 On Selby, see Llewellyn S. Dawson, *Memoirs of Hydrography Including Brief Biographies of the Principal Officers Who Have Served in H.M. Naval Surveying Service between 1750 and 1885*, 2 vols. (Eastbourne: H.W. Keay, 1883–85), 2:114–32.

38 James Felix Jones, *Surveys of Ancient Babylon and the Surrounding Ruins with Part of the Rivers Tigris and Euphrates the Hindiyeh Canal the Sea of Nejf & the Shat Atshar* (London: W.H. Allen & Co., 1885).

39 On Collingwood, see Low, *History of the Indian Navy*, 2:416.

40 Markham, *A Memoir on the Indian Surveys*, 32–4.

41 Charles G. Constable and Arthur W. Stiffe, *The Persian Gulf Pilot* (London: Hydrographic Office, 1864); Low, *History of the Indian Navy*, 2:407; Wilson, *The Persian Gulf*, 282.

42 Low, *History of the Indian Navy*, 2:407.

43 Wilson, *The Persian Gulf*, 282.

44 On this see, for instance, Low, *History of the Indian Navy*, 2:540–50.

45 Wilson, *The Persian Gulf*, 263.

46 Cook, *Survey of the Shores and Islands*, 1:xx–xxi.

47 On the creation of the post of surveyor general of British India in 1814, see Edney, *Mapping an Empire*, 199–206. Before 1814, there were separate provincial surveyors in charge of the missions led by the Calcutta, Madras, and Bombay Presidencies.

48 Cook, *Survey of the Shores and Islands*, 1:xxi.

49 Foliard, *Dislocating the Orient*, 31–3. For a detailed study of survey instruments in the nineteenth century, see Fraser MacDonald and Charles W.J. Withers, eds., *Geography, Technology and Instruments of Exploration* (Farnham: Ashgate, 2015); and Marie-Noëlle Bourguet, Christian Licoppe, and H. Otto Sibum, eds., *Instruments, Travel and Science: Itineraries of Precision from the Seventeenth to the Twentieth Century* (London: Routledge, 2002).

50 Cook, *Survey of the Shores and Islands*, 1:xxi.
51 On this argument, see, for instance, M. Norton Wise, ed., *The Values of Precision* (Princeton: Princeton University Press, 1995); and Simon Schaffer, "Late Victorian Metrology and Its Instrumentation: A Manufactory of Ohms," in *The Science Studies Reader*, ed. Mario Biagioli (London: Routledge, 1999), 457–78.
52 On the chronology of surveys in India, see Edney, *Mapping an Empire*, 199–235.
53 Markham, *A Memoir on the Indian Surveys*, 139–40.
54 Foliard, *Dislocating the Orient*, 113–14.
55 Murdoch Mackenzie, *Treatise on Marine Surveying in Two Parts by Murdoch Mackenzie; Corrected and Republished, with a Supplement by James Horsburgh* (London: "Printed for the editor," 1819). The treatise had first been published in 1774. On Horsburgh, see, for instance, Andrew S. Cook, "Establishing the Sea Routes to India and China: Stages in the Development of Hydrographical Knowledge," in *The Worlds of the East India Company*, ed. H.V. Bowen, Margarette Lincoln, and Nigel Rigby (Woodbridge: Boydell, 2002), 119–36.
56 Charles F. Beautemps-Beaupré, Alexander Dalrymple, and Matthew Flinders, *An Introduction to the Practice of Nautical Surveying and the Construction of Sea-Charts* (London: R.H. Laurie, 1823). On the books at the disposal of surveyors in the Orient, see Foliard, *Dislocating the Orient*, 36.
57 John F.W. Herschel, *A Manual of Scientific Enquiry: Prepared for the Use of Her Majesty's Navy: And Adapted for Travellers in General* (London: J. Murray, 1849).
58 On Moresby's surveys of the Red Sea, see, for instance, Markham, *A Memoir on the Indian Surveys*, 13–16.
59 On Jones's time in Mesopotamia, see Foliard, *Dislocating the Orient*, 37–40.
60 See Low, *History of the Indian Navy*, 2:409–10.
61 On these arguments, see, for instance, Hélène Blais and Isabelle Laboulais, *Les sciences géographiques au moment de l'émergence des sciences humaines (1750–1850)* (Paris: L'Harmattan, 2006); and Singaravélou, *L'Empire des géographes*.
62 For the importance of go-betweens and local populations during survey and mapmaking expeditions, see Kapil Raj, "Circulation and the Emergence of Modern Mapping: Great Britain and Early Colonial India, 1764–1820," in *Society and Circulation: Mobile People and Itinerant Cultures*

in South Asia, 1750–1950, ed. Claude Markovits, Jacques Pouchepadass, and Sanjay Subrahmanyam (London: Anthem, 2006), 23–53; and Hélène Blais, "Les enquêtes des cartographes en Algérie, ou les ambiguïtés de l'usage des savoirs vernaculaires en situation coloniale," *Revue d'histoire moderne et contemporaine* 54, no. 4 (2007): 70–85.

63 On the interpreters who accompanied Chesney during his first mission in Mesopotamia in 1830, see John S. Guest, *The Euphrates Expedition* (London: Kegan Paul International, 1992).

64 On these arguments, see Hélène Blais, Florence Deprest, and Pierre Singaravélou, *Territoires impériaux. Une histoire spatiale du fait colonial* (Paris: Publications de la Sorbonne, 2011), 13.

65 Low, *History of the Indian Navy*, 2:415–16.

66 Foliard, *Dislocating the Orient*, 41. For a comparative perspective on tensions created by the presence of surveyors, see David Lambert, *Mastering the Niger: James MacQueen's African Geography and the Struggle over Atlantic Slavery* (Chicago: University of Chicago Press, 2013), 89–118.

67 On the development of colour printing, see Foliard, *Dislocating the Orient*, 71.

68 For the Royal Geographical Society's contribution to imperial geography, see Peter Collier and Rob Inkpen, "The Royal Geographical Society and the Development of Surveying, 1870–1914," *Journal of Historical Geography* 29, no. 1 (2003): 93–108; and Foliard, *Dislocating the Orient*, 159–62.

69 Foliard, *Dislocating the Orient*, 50.

70 A.W. Stiffe, "The Island of Hormúz (Ormuz)," *The Geographical Magazine* (April 1874), 12–17.

71 On the Portuguese presence in Hormuz, see for instance, Dejanirah Couto and Rui Manuel Loureiro, eds., *Revisiting Hormuz: Portuguese Interactions in the Persian Gulf Region in the Early Modern Period* (Wiesbaden: Harrassowitz Verlag, 2008); and Charles R. Boxer, "Anglo-Portuguese Rivalry in the Persian Gulf, 1615–1635," in *Portuguese Conquest and Commerce in Southern Asia, 1500–1750*, ed. Boxer (London: Variorum Reprints, 1985), 46–129. On the Portuguese presence in the Gulf, see, for instance, Rudolph P. Matthee and Jorge Flores, eds., *Portugal, the Persian Gulf and Safavid Persia* (Leuven: Peeters, 2011).

72 "A Prospect of the Island of Ormus," in *A New General Collection of Voyages and Travels: Consisting of the Most Esteemed Relations, Which Have Been Hitherto Published in Any Language*, 4 vols. (London: Thomas Astley, 1745–47), 1, plate xi (inserted following page 74).

73 IOR/X/3127.

74 IOR/X/3128, series of six drawings by C. Walker, 1839.

75 On the history of the Dutch presence on Kharg, see Wilhelm Floor, "The Dutch on Khark Island: A Commercial Mishap," *International Journal of Middle East Studies* 24, no. 3 (1992): 441–60. On the history of the Dutch East India Company (Vereenigde Oostindische Compagnie, VOC) in the Gulf, see Wilhelm Floor, "Dutch Relations with the Persian Gulf," in *The Persian Gulf in History,* ed. Lawrence G. Potter (New York: Palgrave Macmillan, 2009), 235–59.

76 IOR/X/3113, 1867.

77 IOR/X/3684, c. 1822.

Chapter Four

1 James Lees, "Retrenchment, Reform, and the Practice of Military-Fiscalism in the Early East India Company State," in *The Political Economy of Empire in the Early Modern World*, ed. Sophus A. Reinert and Pernille Røge (Basingstoke: Palgrave Macmillan, 2013), 186–7.

2 On the globalization of these two commodities, see Matthew S. Hopper, *Slaves of One Master: Globalization and Slavery in the Age of Empire* (New Haven: Yale University Press, 2015), 51–104. For a study of the globalization of the Gulf in the nineteenth century, see Johan Mathew, *Margins of the Market: Trafficking and Capitalism across the Arabian Sea* (Berkeley: University of California Press, 2016). On nineteenth-century globalization in general, see, for example, Anthony G. Hopkins, ed., *Globalization in World History* (London: Pimlico, 2002); and Christopher A. Bayly, *The Birth of the Modern World, 1780–1914: Global Connections and Comparisons* (Malden: Blackwell, 2004).

3 Guillemette Crouzet, "The British Empire in India, the Gulf Pearl, and the Making of the Middle East," *Middle Eastern Studies* 55, no. 6 (2019): 864–78. From the late eighteenth century, the British East India Company and then the Government of India introduced legislation to control the pearl fisheries of the Gulf of Mannar – the shallow body of water between present-day India and Sri Lanka – which was one of the largest sources of natural pearls in the world for at least two millennia. This legislation deeply reshaped the political, social, and economic foundations of the pearl industry in the Gulf of Mannar. On this, see Samuel Miles Ostroff, "The Beds of Empire: Power and Profit at the Pearl Fisheries of South India and Sri Lanka, c. 1770–1840" (PhD diss., University of Pennsylvania, 2016) and Tamara Fernando, "Seeing Like the Sea: A

Multispecies History of the Ceylon Pearl Fishery 1800–1925," *Past and Present* 254, no. 1 (2022): 127–60.

4 See, for example, Sven Beckert, *Empire of Cotton: A Global History* (New York: Alfred A. Knopf, 2015); Giorgio Riello, *Cotton: The Fabric that Made the Modern World* (Cambridge: Cambridge University Press, 2012); Erika Rappaport, *A Thirst for Empire: How Tea Shaped the Modern World* (Princeton: Princeton University Press, 2017); Timothy Brook and Bob Tadashi Wakabayashi, eds., *Opium Regimes: China, Britain, and Japan, 1839–1952* (Berkeley: University of California Press, 2000); and William G. Clarence-Smith and S. Topik, eds., *The Global Coffee Economy in Africa, Asia and Latin America, 1500–1989* (Cambridge: Cambridge University Press, 2003). On the links between globalization, global commodities, and changing patterns of consumption, see for example, Frank Trentmann, *Empire of Things: How We Became a World of Consumers, from the Fifteenth Century to the Twenty-First* (London: Allen Lane, 2016).

5 On the globalization of Gulf pearls over the very *longue durée*, see Robert Carter, "The History and Prehistory of Pearling in the Persian Gulf," *Journal of the Economic and Social History of the Orient* 48, no. 2 (2005): 139–208; Robert Carter, *Sea of Pearls: Seven Thousand Years of the Industry that Shaped the Gulf* (London: Arabian, 2012); and Xavier Beguin-Billecocq, *Les Emirats ou la fabuleuse histoire de la Côte des Perles* (Paris: Relations Internationales and Culture, 1995). On the wider history of pearls, see, for example, Robin Donkin, *Beyond Price: Pearls and Pearl-Fishing: Origins to the Age of Discoveries* (Philadelphia: American Philosophical Society, 1998); Alexander E. Farn, *Pearls: Natural, Cultured and Imitation* (Oxford: Butterworths, 1991); Silvia Malaguzzi, *The Pearl* (New York: Rizzoli, 2001); and Molly A. Warsh, *American Baroque: Pearls and the Nature of Empire, 1492–1700* (Chapel Hill: University of North Carolina Press, 2018).

6 George F. Kunz and Charles H. Stevenson, *The Book of the Pearl: The History, Art, Science, and Industry of the Queen of Gems* (London: Macmillan & Co, 1908), 55.

7 Hopper, *Slaves of One Master*, 96–100.

8 William G. Clarence-Smith, "The Pearl Commodity Chain, Early Nineteenth Century to the End of the Second World War: Trade, Processing and Consumption," in *Pearls, People, and Power: Pearling and Indian Ocean Worlds*, ed. Pedro Machado, Steve Mullins, and Joseph Christensen (Athens: Ohio University Press, 2020), 32–3; John G. Lorimer,

Gazetteer of the Persian Gulf, Oman and Central Arabia, 2 vols. (Calcutta: Superintendent Government Printing, India, 1908–15), 1:2252.

9 On the ecology and formation of pearl oysters, see Donkin, *Beyond Price*, 23–41.

10 British Library, London, IOR/L/PS/18/B134, "The Pearl Fisheries of the Persian Gulf. H.A. Haines," 17 March 1899.

11 Anita L.P. Burdett, ed., *Records of the Persian Gulf Pearl Fisheries 1857–1962*, 4 vols. (Slough: Cambridge Archive Editions, 1992), 1:72.

12 Hopper, *Slaves of One Master*, 82–3; Lorimer, *Gazetteer*, 1:2228–30.

13 On how pearl fishing was financed and on the role of the *nakhoda*, see Victoria Penziner Hightower, "Pearling and Political Power in the Trucial States, 1850–1930: Debts, Taxes, and Politics," *Journal of Arabian Studies* 3, no. 2 (2016): 220–2; and Chhaya Goswami, *Globalization before Its Time: The Gujarati Merchants from Kachchh* (Gurgaon: Portfolio-Penguin, 2016), 72–115.

14 Lorimer, *Gazetteer*, 1:2229–30.

15 *The Epic of Gilgamesh* is a tale from ancient Mesopotamia that mentions the beauty of Bahraini pearls.

16 Hopper, *Slaves of One Master*, 83.

17 On the different types of pearl fishing boats, see Lorimer, *Gazetteer*, 1:2228.

18 On the economic importance of the pearl sector for the Gulf economy, see Bernard Haykel, Clive Holes, Fahad Bishara, James Onley, and Steffen Hertog, "The Economic Transformation of the Gulf," in *The Emergence of the Gulf States: Studies in Modern History*, ed. J.E. Peterson (London: Bloomsbury Academic, 2016), 187–222.

19 On this see Lorimer, *Gazetteer*, 1:2262.

20 The price of pearls was determined by size and colour: Carter, *Sea of Pearls*. On the complex division of profits between the crew, the *nakhoda*, and the merchants, see Hightower, "Pearling and Political Power," 216–18.

21 Lorimer, *Gazetteer*, 1:2236; Hopper, *Slaves of One Master*, 82–3.

22 Kunz and Stevenson, *The Book of the Pearl*, 98–9; Jerzy Zdanowski, *Speaking with Their Own Voices: The Stories of Slaves in the Persian Gulf in the 20th Century* (Newcastle upon Tyne: Cambridge Scholars, 2014), 71–2.

23 Lorimer, *Gazetteer*, 1:2239–40.

24 On the demands of the markets, see Lewis Pelly, "Remarks on the Pearl Oyster Beds in the Persian Gulf," *Transactions of the Bombay Geographical Society* 17 (1867): 35–6.

25 Hopper, *Slaves of One Master*, 96–8.

26 On marquetry in this region see François Keen, "La tabletterie sous l'Ancien Régime, entre Paris et Méru," *Artefact: Techniques, Histoire et Sciences Humaines* 4 (2016): 319–24.

27 Laurence Bonnet, *La nacre: la tabletterie, le bouton, l'éventail* (n.p.: Edition District des Sablons, 1998). For a comparative perspective, see the following study of the pearl button industry in Muscatine, Iowa, which became the pearl button capital of the United States at the end of the nineteenth century: Melanie K. Alexander, *Muscatine's Pearl Button Industry* (Charleston: Arcadia, 2007).

28 Carter, "The History and Prehistory of Pearling," 160–1.

29 Lorimer, *Gazetteer*, 1:2252.

30 Hopper, *Slaves of One Master*, 100. On the pearl fisheries of Ceylon, see, for instance, Sanjay Subrahmanyam, "Noble Harvest from the Sea: Managing the Pearl Fishery of Mannar, 1500–1825," in *Institutions and Economic Change in South Asia*, ed. Burton Stein and Sanjay Subrahmanyam (New Delhi: Oxford University Press, 1996), 134–72; and Ostroff, "The Beds of Empire."

31 Lorimer, *Gazetteer*, 1:2252–4.

32 On this see, for instance, Clarence-Smith, "The Pearl Commodity Chain," 35–9.

33 For a discussion of the consequences of the 1907 crisis, see Clarence-Smith, "The Pearl Commodity Chain," 41.

34 See Rosenthal's memoirs: Léonard Rosenthal, *The Pearl Hunter, An Autobiography* (New York: H. Schuman, 1952), 21–60. On the importance of Paris for the global trade in precious stones and jewellery in the nineteenth century, see Jacqueline Viruega, *La bijouterie parisienne: 1860–1914. Du Second Empire à la Première Guerre Mondiale* (Paris: L'Harmattan, 2004).

35 IOR/R/15/1/710, f.92r, 1906.

36 Hopper, *Slaves of One Master*, 94.

37 IOR/R/15/1/710, f.203r, 1908.

38 Penelope Tuson, ed., *Persian Gulf Trade Reports, 1905–1940*, 8 vols. (Gerrards Cross: Archive Editions, 1987), 5:3.

39 Clarence-Smith, "The Pearl Commodity Chain," 33.

40 An estimate of Rosenthal's fortune is given in his daughter's autobiography: Rachel Rosenthal and Una Chaudhuri, eds., *Rachel's Brain and Other Storms: The Performance Scripts of Rachel Rosenthal* (New York: Continuum, 2001).

41 Rehavia Moussaieff, who was born in Jerusalem to a family of Jewish traders from Bukhara in Uzbekistan, eventually settled in Paris. IOR/R/15/2/14, f.23r, May 1907.

42 IOR/R/15/2/3 f.30, 19 June 1918.

43 On the history of Wönckhaus in the Gulf, see Eugene Staley, "Business and Politics in the Persian Gulf: The Story of the Wönckhaus Firm," *Political Science Quarterly* 48, no. 3 (1933): 367–85; William O. Henderson, "German Economic Penetration in the Middle East, 1870–1914," *Economic History Review* 18, nos. 1–2 (1948): 54–64; and Briton Cooper Busch, *Britain and the Persian Gulf, 1894–1914* (Berkeley: University of California Press, 1967), 353, 369.

44 Burdett, *Records of the Persian Gulf Pearl Fisheries*, 2:11–17.

45 Karen Jones, Giacomo Macola, and David Welch, eds., *A Cultural History of Firearms in the Age of Empire* (Farnham: Ashgate, 2013), 180–1.

46 On this see Clarence-Smith, "Pearl Commodity Chain," 42–3. The following account gives interesting details about the lives of these Arab pearl dealers between the Gulf and the West: Saif Marzooq al-Shamlan, *Pearling in the Arabian Gulf: A Kuwaiti Memoir*, trans. Peter Clark (London: London Centre of Arabic Studies, 2000).

47 IOR/R/15/2/3, f.27, Secretary of the Wolverine Motor Works to Robert Wonckhaus, 3 February 1915.

48 Burdett, *Records of the Persian Gulf Pearl Fisheries*, 2:199.

49 Crouzet, "British Empire in India," 869–73.

50 Matthew S. Hopper, "Debt and Slavery among Arabian Gulf Pearl Divers," in *Bonded Labour and Debt in the Indian Ocean World*, ed. Gwyn Campbell and Alessandro Stanziani (London: Pickering and Chatto, 2013), 103–18. On the specific measures taken against indebtedness, see Hightower, "Pearling and Political Power," 225–8. For a discussion about the awareness among British officials of the environmental consequences of overfishing Gulf pearls, see Victoria Penziner Hightower, "Pearls and the Southern Persian/Arabian Gulf: A Lesson in Sustainability," *Environmental History* 18, no. 1 (2013): 44–59.

51 On Mikimoto, see Robert Eunson, *The Pearl King: The Story of the Fabulous Mikimoto* (Tokyo: Charles E. Tuttle, 1963). On the arrival on the markets of these pearls, see Clarence-Smith, "The Pearl Commodity Chain," 43–4.

52 On the invention and distribution of cultured pearls and the surrounding polemics, see Micheline Cariño, "The Cultured Pearl Polemic," *World Aquaculture* 27, no. 1 (1996): 42–4; Farn, *Pearls*, 60–5; and Clarence-Smith, "The Pearl Commodity Chain," 43–4.

53 Nelida Fuccaro, *Histories of City and State in the Persian Gulf: Manama Since 1800* (Cambridge: Cambridge University Press, 2009), 160.
54 IOR/R/15/2/132, ff.149–152, Barrett to Horner, January 1927.
55 IOR/R/15/2/848, ff.4–10, "Report Addressed by the Political Agent in Bahrain, Captain Charles G. Prior to the Resident in the Gulf, Hugh V. Biscoe," May 1932.
56 See the translation of H.J. Von Bassewitz's article, titled "Swan Song on the Pearl Divers," IOR/R/15/2/848, f.30, 1932.
57 For a general history of dates in the world, see, for instance, A. Manickavasagan, M. Mohamed Essa, and E. Sukumar, eds., *Dates: Production, Processing, Food, and Medicinal Values* (Boca Raton: CRC Press, 2012).
58 Lorimer, *Gazetteer*, 1:2294–305; Paul Popenoe, "The Distribution of the Date Palm," *Geographical Review* 16, no. 1 (1926): 117–21. The most comprehensive work of reference on dates in the first half of the twentieth century is Popenoe, *Date Growing in the Old World and the New* (Altadena: West India Gardens, 1913).
59 V.H.W. Dowson, "Dates and Date Cultivation of the Iraq, Parts I and II," IOR Mss Eur F235/13, 1921.
60 On the Batinah date palms, see IOR/R/15/2/347, ff.12–22, 1927, "Report by Mr. Downson, American Manager of the Iraq Date Company Following a Visit to the Batinah in 1927." See also Dowson's reports on date palms in the Sultanate of Oman: IOR/R/15/1/460, 1927–31.
61 National Archives, London, FO 368/15/36, ff.129–138, "Date Trade in the Persian Gulf," August 1906. On Gulf local consumption of dates, see W.J. Donaldson, "A Note on the Tarkabah and the Omani Boiled Date Trade," *New Arabian Studies* 2 (1994): 68–74.
62 Lorimer, *Gazetteer*, 2:2296.
63 IOR/R/15/2/347, f.4, Dowson to Murphy, 9 October 1928.
64 On the globalization of some Middle East products, see Roger Owen, *Cotton and the Egyptian Economy, 1820–1914: A Study in Trade and Development* (Oxford: Clarendon, 1969); Roger Owen, *The Middle East in the World Economy* (London: Methuen, 1981), 83–91; Charles Issawi, "Middle East Economic Development, 1815–1914: The General and the Specific," in *The Modern Middle East*, ed. Albert Hourany, Philip S. Khoury, and Mary C. Wilson (Berkeley: University of California Press, 1993), 177–94; and Victoria Bernal, "Cotton and Colonial Order in Sudan: A Social History, with Emphasis on the Gezira Scheme," in *Cotton, Colonialism, and Social History in Sub-Saharan Africa*, ed. Allen Isaacman and Richard Roberts (Portsmouth: Heinemann, 1995), 96–118.
65 Hopper, *Slaves of One Master*, 58.

66 *Dromedary Cook Book* (New York: The Hills Brothers Company, 1923); *One Hundred Delights* (New York: The Hills Brothers Company, 1923).
67 Lorimer, *Gazetteer*, 1: 2299, 2306. See also, Hopper, *Slaves of One Master*, 72–3.
68 Hopper, *Slaves of One Master*, 71.
69 On varieties of palm dates, see Paul Popenoe, "The Home of the Fardh Date," *Monthly Bulletin of the California State Commission of Horticulture* 3, no. 1 (1914): 12.
70 Hopper, *Slaves of One Master*, 59–60, 71.
71 On the history of Hills Brothers, see Hopper, *Slaves of One Master*, 72–7, 187–9.
72 David G. Fairchild, *The World Was My Garden: Travels of a Plant Explorer* (New York: Charles Scribner's Sons, 1938), 236.
73 Popenoe, "The Home of the Fardh Date," 11.
74 Valentine H.W. Dowson, *Dates and Date Cultivation of the Iraq*. Part I. *The Cultivation of the Date Palm on the Shat Al' Arab* (Cambridge: Agricultural Directorate of Mesopotamia, 1921), 43–57; Valentine H.W. Dowson and Albert Aten, *Dates: Handling, Processing, and Packing* (Rome: UN Food and Agricultural Organization, 1962). On the marketing of dates, see Hopper, *Slaves of One Master*, 76–8.
75 David G. Fairchild, *Persian Gulf Dates and Their Introduction into America*, USDA Bureau of Plant Industry, Bulletin 54 (Washington: Government Printing Office, 1903), 24–30.
76 Albert Londres, *Pêcheurs de perles* (Paris: Albin Michel, 1931): 183–268.
77 On the slave trade in the north Indian Ocean, see, for instance, William G. Clarence-Smith, ed., *The Economics of the Indian Ocean Slave Trade in the Nineteenth Century* (London: Frank Cass, 1989); Robert Harms, Bernard K. Freamon, and David W. Blight, eds., *Indian Ocean Slavery in the Age of Abolition* (New Haven: Yale University Press, 2013); Erik Gilbert, *Dhows and the Colonial Economy in Zanzibar, 1860–1970* (Athens: Ohio University Press, 2004); Abdul Sheriff and Engseng Ho, eds., *The Indian Ocean: Oceanic Connections and the Creation of New Societies* (London: Hurst, 2014); and Gwyn Campbell, "Slavery in the Indian Ocean World," in *The Routledge History of Slavery*, ed. Gad Heuman and Trevor Burnard (London: Routledge, 2010), 52–63.
78 Ralph Austen, "The 19th Century Islamic Slave Trade from East Africa (Swahili and Red Sea Coasts): A Tentative Census," in *The Economics of the Indian Ocean Slave Trade*, ed. Clarence-Smith, 21–44. On the importance of the slave trade for Zanzibar's economy, see Frederick Cooper,

From Slaves to Squatters: Plantation Labor and Agriculture in Zanzibar and Coastal Kenya, 1890–1925 (New Haven: Yale University Press, 1980).

79 Historians' estimates on this slave traffic vary, as emphasized by Thomas M. Ricks, "Slaves and Slave Traders in the Persian Gulf, 18th and 19th Centuries: An Assessment," in *The Economics of the Indian Ocean Slave Trade*, ed. Clarence-Smith, 60–70. William G. Clarence-Smith gives the figure of 500,000 slaves over the whole course of the nineteenth century, which would mean almost 5,000 exported to the Gulf every year (Clarence-Smith, "The Economics of the Indian Ocean and Red Sea Slave Trades in the 19th Century: An Overview," in *The Economics of the Indian Ocean Slave Trade*, 5). Henri Médard estimates 1,500 to 3,000 per year between 1872 and 1902: Henri Médard, "La plus ancienne et la plus récente des traites: panorama de la traite et de l'esclavage en Afrique orientale et dans l'océan Indien," in *Traites et esclavages en Afrique orientale et dans l'océan Indien*, ed. Henri Médard, Marie-Laure Derat, Thomas Vernet, and Marie-Pierre Ballarin (Paris: Karthala, 2013), 65–118. Abdul Sheriff estimates that 3,000 slaves were exported every year from Zanzibar to Oman: Abdul Sheriff, *Slaves, Spices, and Ivory in Zanzibar: Integration of an East African Commercial Empire into the World Economy, 1770–1873* (Athens: Ohio University Press, 1987).

80 Anita L.P. Burdett, ed., *The Slave Trade into Arabia*, 9 vols. (Slough: Archive Editions, 2006), 1:316–20. On slavery in Iran and slaves imported from the Persian Gulf to Persian ports, see, for instance, Behnaz A. Mirzai, *A History of Slavery and Emancipation in Iran, 1800–1929* (Austin: University of Texas Press, 2017), 53–73.

81 Burdett, *The Slave Trade into Arabia*, 1:323–4. On slavery in the Ottoman Gulf, see Ehud Toledano, *The Ottoman Slave Trade and Its Suppression, 1840–1890* (Princeton: Princeton University Press, 1982), 60.

82 Lorimer, *Gazetteer*, 1:2228.

83 On this see, for instance, Matthew S. Hopper, "The Globalization of Dried Fruit: Transformation of the Eastern Arabian Economy, 1860s–1920s," in *Global Muslims in the Age of Steam and Print*, ed. James L. Gelvin and Nile Green (Berkeley: University of California Press, 2014), 170–1.

84 Matthew S. Hopper, "The African Presence in Eastern Arabia," in *The Persian Gulf in Modern Times: People, Ports, and History*, ed. Lawrence G. Potter (New York: Palgrave Macmillan, 2014), 327–50; Hopper, "Was Nineteenth-Century Eastern Arabia a Slave Society?," in *What Is a Slave Society? The Practice of Slavery in Global Perspective*, ed. Catherine M. Cameron and Noel Lenski (Cambridge: Cambridge University Press, 2019), 317.

85 Hopper, *Slaves of One Master*, 19.

86 Recent studies have relativized the zeal of the British crusade against the slave trade in the Gulf, the Indian Ocean, and the Red Sea in the nineteenth century. See, for instance, Matthew S. Hopper, "Imperialism and the Dilemma of Slavery in Eastern Arabia and the Gulf," *Itinerario* 30, no. 3 (2006): 76–94; Suzanne Miers, "The Anti-Slavery Game: Britain and the Suppression of Slavery in Africa and Arabia, 1890–1975," in *Slavery, Diplomacy, and Empire: Britain and the Suppression of the Slave Trade, 1807–1975*, ed. Keith Hamilton and Patrick Salmon (Brighton: Sussex Academic Press, 2009), 196–214; and Benjamin J. Reilly, "A Well-Intentioned Failure: British Anti-Slavery Measures and the Arabian Peninsula, 1820–1940," *Journal of Arabian Studies* 5, no. 2 (2015): 91–115. Jerzy Zdanowski has argued, on the contrary, that British measures were strong and efficient in these regions from the 1820s onward: Jerzy Zdanowski, *Slavery and Manumission: British Policy in the Red Sea and the Persian Gulf in the First Half of the 20th Century* (Reading: Ithaca Press, 2013).

87 On these early attempts of the East India Company to act against the slave trade, see Richard B. Allen, "Suppressing a Nefarious Traffic: Britain and the Abolition of Slave Trading in India and the Western Indian Ocean, 1770–1830," *William and Mary Quarterly* 66, no. 4 (2009): 873–94; and Andrea Major, *Slavery, Abolitionism, and Empire in India, 1772–1843* (Liverpool: Liverpool University Press, 2012), 170–1.

88 One of the major problems that explains the persistence of the slave trade in the Indian Ocean lies in the French islands' need for a labour force. This need continued throughout the 1830s and 1840s, as the sugar plantation economy of Réunion required a large slave labour force. On this see, for instance, Richard B. Allen, "The Constant Demand of the French: The Mascarene Slave Trade and the Worlds of the Indian Ocean and Atlantic during the Eighteenth and Nineteenth Centuries," *Journal of African History* 49, no. 1 (2008): 43–72; Richard B. Allen, "The Mascarene Slave-Trade and Labour Migration in the Indian Ocean during the Eighteenth and Nineteenth Centuries," *Slavery and Abolition* 24, no. 2 (2003): 33–50; and Meghan Vaughan, *Creating the Creole Island: Slavery in Eighteenth Century Mauritius* (Durham: Duke University Press, 2005), 252–70.

89 John B. Kelly, *Britain and the Persian Gulf, 1795–1880* (Oxford: Clarendon, 1968), 421–5.

90 IOR/F/4/746/20306, "Papers Regarding the Slave Trade at Zanzibar, Mauritius. Treaty Concluded between Captain Fairfax Moresby and the

Imam of Muscat Forbidding European Nations to Engage in the Zanzibar Slave Trade, etc.," 1822. See Jeremy Jones and Nicholas Ridout, *A History of Modern Oman* (Cambridge: Cambridge University Press, 2015), 58–61.

91 IOR/R/15/1/30, ff.25v–27v, Macleod to Willock, 27 February 1823.

92 For accounts from the 1820s describing "sizable populations of enslaved Africans in Gulf port cities," see Hopper, *Slaves of One Master*, 9.

93 "The words [of the relevant article of the treaty] are 'the carrying off of slaves, men, women, & children, from the coasts of Africa or elsewhere, and the transporting of them in vessels, is plunder & piracy, and the friendly Arabs shall do nothing of this nature.' Now it strikes me, that this sentence may be understood to forbid only the carrying off of men, women and children as slaves, and the transporting them in vessels when so carried off; although the words will also bear the more comprehensive sense of forbidding the carrying off of slaves, and the transporting of slaves, however, procured, in vessels."

94 For comparable rhetoric from other officials, see Kelly, *Britain and the Persian Gulf*, 412.

95 Kelly, *Britain and the Persian Gulf*, 420.

96 On Palmerston's fear of an alliance between Egypt and Russia threatening British interests in the Orient, see Khaled Fahmy, *All the Pasha's Men: Mehmed Ali, His Army, and the Making of Modern Egypt* (Cambridge: Cambridge University Press, 1997), 288–301.

97 Kelly, *Britain and the Persian Gulf*, 435.

98 Penelope Tuson and Emma Quick, *Arabian Treaties, 1600–1900*, 4 vols. ([Slough]: Archive Editions, 1992), 3:41.

99 IOR/R/15/1/88, ff.18–22, April 1840; Tuson and Quick, *Arabian Treaties*, 3:53–4.

100 Hughes Thomas, ed., *Selections from the Records of the Bombay Government*, no. 24, new series (Bombay: Printed for Government at the Bombay Education Society's Press, 1856), 669–70.

101 For the treaty, see Charles U. Aitchison, *A Collection of Treaties, Engagements, and Sanads Relating to India and Neighbouring Countries*, 12 vols. (Calcutta: Superintendent Government Printing, India, 1909), 12:170–3. On the treaty's negotiations and consequences, see Kelly, *Britain and the Persian Gulf*, 592–4; John E. Peterson, *Oman in the Twentieth Century: Political Foundations of an Emerging State* (London: Croom Helm, 1978), 139–41; and Hopper, *Slaves of One Master*, 150–1.

102 IOR/R/15/1/115, ff.207–210, Hennel to Malet, 28 September 1848; Aitchison, *A Collection of Treaties*, 7:256–7.

103 IOR/R/15/1/113, ff.79–81, 22 May 1849.
104 On the creation of the Sultanate of Zanzibar see, for instance, Beatrice Nicolini, *The First Sultan of Zanzibar: Scrambling for Power and Trade in the 19th Century Indian Ocean* (Princeton: Markus Wiener, 2012).
105 On the Canning Agreement see, for example, Jeremy Jones, *Oman, Culture and Diplomacy* (Edinburgh: Edinburgh University Press, 2012), 147–8; and Mohamed Reda Bhacker, "Family Strife and Foreign Intervention: Causes in the Separation of Zanzibar from Oman: A Reappraisal," *Bulletin of the School of Oriental and African Studies* 54, no. 2 (1991): 269–80.
106 R.J. Gavin, "The Bartle Frere Mission to Zanzibar, 1873," *Historical Journal* 5, no. 2 (1962): 122–48.
107 FO 84/1426, "Papers Relating to the Interpretation of the Treaty with Zanzibar of 5 June, 1873"; Lorimer, *Gazetteer*, 1:2500–2. See also Robert G. Landen, *Oman Since 1856: Disruptive Modernization in a Traditional Arab Society* (Princeton: Princeton University Press, 1967), 209–10.
108 Lindsay Doulton, "'The Flag That Sets Us Free': Antislavery, Africans, and the Royal Navy in the Western Indian Ocean," in *Indian Ocean Slavery in the Age of Abolition*, ed. Harms, Freamon, and Blight, 101–19.
109 John Oldfield, "After Emancipation: Slavery, Freedom, and the Victorian Empire," in *The Victorian Empire and Britain's Maritime World, 1837–1901: The Sea and Global History*, ed. Miles Taylor (Basingstoke: Palgrave Macmillan, 2013), 55.
110 Hopper, *Slaves of One Master*, 11.
111 On the idea of an "empire of guns," see Priya Satia, *Empire of Guns: The Violent Making of the Industrial Revolution* (London: Penguin, 2018). For a comparable study of arms trafficking in relation to the Ottoman Empire around this period, see Ramazon Hakki Öztan, "Tools of Revolution: Global Military Surplus, Arms Dealers, and Smugglers in the Late Ottoman Balkans, 1878–1908," *Past and Present* 237, no. 1 (2017): 167–95.
112 Robert Crews, "Trafficking in Evil? The Global Arms Trade and the Politics of Disorder," in Gelvin and Green, *Global Muslims in the Age of Steam and Print*, 159–66.
113 On this see Robert Elgood, *The Arms and Armour of Arabia in the 18th, 19th and 20th Centuries* (Aldershot: Scolar Press, 1994).
114 Sükrü Hanioglu, *A Brief History of the Late Ottoman Empire* (Princeton: Princeton University Press, 2008), 29–30.
115 Jonathan A. Grant, *Rulers, Guns, and Money: The Global Arms Trade in the Age of Imperialism* (Cambridge, MA: Harvard University Press, 2007), 4–5.

116 Grant, *Rulers, Guns, and Money*, 37–8.
117 Emrys Chew, *Arming the Periphery: The Arms Trade in the Indian Ocean during the Age of Global Empire* (Basingstoke: Palgrave Macmillan, 2012), 217–19.
118 Agnès Picquart, "Le commerce des armes à Djibouti de 1888 à 1914," *Revue française d'histoire d'outre-mer* 58, no. 4 (1971): 411–12.
119 Chew, *Arming the Periphery*, 109–11.
120 On the Brussels Conference see Grant, *Rulers, Guns, and Money*, 160–8; Chew, *Arming the Periphery*, 110–11.
121 IOR/L/PS/8/62, "Cpt. P.M. Sykes Reports on Arms Traffic to Afghanistan from Persian Gulf," October 1897–March 1898.
122 Chew, *Arming the Periphery*, 100.
123 Archives du Ministère des Affaires étrangères (AMAE), Correspondance politique et commerciale (CPCOM), n.s., Mascate vol. 3 (Le golfe Persique et les puissances, Dossier général, 1896–98), report by Ottavi, April 1896.
124 Chew, *Arming the Periphery*, 100–1.
125 The Lee-Metford rifle was a bolt-action British Army service rifle. It was adopted by the British Army in 1888 but remained in service only briefly. It was replaced by the Lee-Enfield, adopted in 1895, which remained in service until 1957. The Snider-Enfield was a breech-loading rifle used by the British Army until the adoption of the Martini-Henry in the 1870s.
126 Chew, *Arming the Periphery*, 139.
127 FO 539/79/9, Memorandum by general T.E. Gordon on the export of arms to Persia (n.d.); cited in Chew, *Arming the Periphery*, 95.
128 AMAE/ POO180, Tome VII, Laronce to Quai d'Orsay, May 1902.
129 IOR/R/15/5/391, f.20v, July–August 1911; Lorimer, *Gazetteer*, 1:2559.
130 On the *Baluchistan* affair see IOR/L/PS/18/C87/2, Baker to Drummond, 11 February 1898; IOR/L/PS/18/C87/1, exchange of letters between Foreign Office and Fracis, Times & Co., February–March 1898.
131 AMAE CPCOM, n.s., Mascate vol. 19 (Trafic d'armes, Dossier général, 1900–1907), Ottavi to Quai d'Orsay, 18 June 1900.
132 AMAE CPCOM, n.s., Mascate vol. 19 (Trafic d'armes, Dossier général, 1900–1907), Delcassé to Laronce, 14 March 1903.
133 Crew, *Arming the Periphery*, 117.
134 On Fracis, Times & Co. in the Gulf see Lorimer, *Gazetteer*, 1:2557; Chew, *Arming the Periphery*, 153–8.
135 On O'Swald & Co., well established particularly on Madagascar and in East Africa, see the history of the company written by its founder:

William Henry O'Swald, *The Story of the House of O'Swald* (Hamburg: Broschek & Company, 1931). See also J.W. Heldring, *The Killing of Dr Albrecht Roscher: The Story of a Young German Explorer in East Africa 1858–1860* (Kibworth Beauchamp: Upfront Publishing, 2003); and Gwyn Campbell, *An Economic History of Imperial Madagascar, 1750–1895: The Rise and Fall of an Island Empire* (Cambridge: Cambridge University Press, 1995), 175–95. On Hansing see Gaurav Desai, *Commerce with the Universe: Africa, India, and the Afrasian Imagination* (New York: Columbia University Press, 2013), 91, 125; and Heldring, *The Killing of Dr Albrecht Roscher,* 89.

136 Seema Alawi, *Muslim Cosmopolitanism in the Age of Empire* (Cambridge, MA: Harvard University Press, 2015), 76; Chew, *Arming the Periphery*, 139.

137 Matig Keverkoff was a Russian merchant of Armenian origin who operated in Ethiopia. See Goswami, *Globalization before Its Time.*

138 Lorimer, *Gazetteer*, 1:2566.

139 On Goguyer see Guillemette Crouzet, "'A Troublesome Man' ou un Lawrence d'Arabie français? Antonin Goguyer, aventurier et trafiquant d'armes dans le golfe Persique et en Oman au début du XXe siècle," in *Les négociants européens et le monde*, ed. Virginie Chaillou-Atrous, Jean-François Klein, and Antoine Resche (Rennes: Presses Universitaire de Rennes, 2016), 145–56.

140 Herbert H. Austin, *Gun-Running in the Gulf and Other Adventures* (London: John Murray, 1926), 13.

141 Lorimer, *Gazetteer*, 1:2570.

142 IOR/L/PS/18/C87/1, India Office to Foreign Office, 1 December 1897.

143 On the trade in Makran see Lorimer, *Gazetteer*, 1:2572–3.

144 Robert Michael Burrell, "Arms and Afghans in Makran: An Episode of Anglo-Persian Relations, 1905–1912," *Bulletin of the School of Oriental and African Studies* 49, no. 1 (1986): 8–24. For an account of this arms traffic by a contemporary witness see Lovat George Fraser, "Gun-Running in the Persian Gulf," *Proceedings of the Central Asian Society* 33 (1911): 3–16.

145 Alavi, *Muslim Cosmopolitanism*, 75.

146 This was Agha Muhammad Rahim Safar from Persia. See James Onley, "Transnational Merchants in the Nineteenth and Twentieth Century Gulf," in *Transnational Connections and the Arab Gulf*, ed. Madawi Al-Rasheed (London: Routledge, 2004), 64–5.

147 Lorimer, *Gazetteer*, 1:2570.

148 Busch, *Britain and the Persian Gulf*, 272.

149 On Percy M. Sykes, who played an important role for British imperialism in Persia, see Antony Wynn, *Persia in the Great Game: Sir Percy*

Sykes, Explorer, Consul, Soldier, Spy (London: John Murray, 2003); and Denis Wright, "Sir Percy Sykes and Persia," *Central Asian Survey* 12, no. 2 (1993): 217–31. See also Sykes's account of his time in Persia: Percy M. Sykes, *Ten Thousand Miles in Persia* (London: John Murray, 1902).

150 "Cpt P M Sykes: Reports on Arms Traffic to Afghanistan from Persian Gulf and Expenses," IOR/L/PS/8/62, October 1897–March 1898; Lorimer, *Gazetteer*, 1:2574.

151 Lorimer, *Gazetteer*, 1:2573–4. The Afridis are a Pashtun tribe in the Khyber Pass region. See Charles Miller, *Khyber: British India's North West Frontier: The Story of an Imperial Migraine* (London: Macdonald and Jane's, 1977).

152 Lorimer, *Gazetteer*, 1:2574. The Ghilzais are one of the largest Pashtun tribes. They live in Pakistan, Baluchistan, and Afghanistan.

153 See Christine Noelle, *State and Tribe in Nineteenth-Century Afghanistan: The Reign of Amir Dost Muhammad Khan (1826–1863)* (Richmond: Curzon, 1997), 153–5.

154 Lorimer, *Gazetteer*, 1:2574.

155 On this treaty see Robin Bidwell, ed., *British Documents on Foreign Affairs–Reports and Papers from the Foreign Office Confidential Print. Part II, From the First to the Second World War. Series B, Turkey, Iran, and the Middle East, 1918–1939* (Frederick: University Publications of America, 1985), 14.

156 IOR/L/PS/18/B175, f.31v, 1898; f.32r, May 1900. On Mubarak see Ben J. Slot, *Mubarak Al-Sabah, Founder of Modern Kuwait, 1896–1915* (London: Arabian, 2005).

157 J.B. Kelly, "The British Position in the Persian Gulf," *The World Today* 20, no. 6 (1964): 239.

158 Satia, *Empire of Guns*, 384.

159 Lorimer, *Gazetteer*, 1:2586.

160 Jones, Macola, and Welch, *A Cultural History of Firearms*, 173–4.

161 For the Persian Gulf naval blockade see Thomas Tendron Jeans, *Gunboat and Gun-Runner: A Tale of the Persian Gulf* (London: Blackie & Son, 1915); and H. Lyman Stebbins, *British Imperialism in Qajar Iran: Consuls, Agents, and Influence in the Middle East* (London: I.B. Tauris, 2016), 145–6.

162 Busch, *Britain and the Persian Gulf*, 292–7.

163 Hopper, *Slaves of One Master*, 8–9.

164 Sunil Amrith, *Unruly Waters: How Rains, Rivers, Coasts, and Seas Have Shaped Asia's History* (New York: Basic Books, 2018).

Chapter Five

1 J.B. Bewsher, "On Part of Mesopotamia Contained between Sheriat-el-Beytha, on the Tigris, and Tel Ibrahim," *Journal of the Royal Geographical Society of London* 37 (1867): 160–82.
2 Bewsher, "On Part of Mesopotamia," 162.
3 Bewsher, "On Part of Mesopotamia," 167.
4 Bewsher, "On Part of Mesopotamia," 173–6.
5 Halford Lancaster Hoskins, *British Routes to India* (New York: Longmans, Green and Co., 1928). On the Suez Canal see, for instance, Valeska Huber, *Channelling Mobilities: Migration and Globalisation in the Suez Canal Region and Beyond, 1869–1914* (Cambridge: Cambridge University Press, 2013); Hubert Bonin, *History of the Suez Canal Company, 1858–2008: Between Controversy and Utility* (Geneva: Librairie Droz, 2010); and Caroline Piquet, *Histoire du Canal de Suez* (Paris: Perrin, 2009).
6 Hoskins, *British Routes to India*, 85–7.
7 Daniel R. Headrick, *Power over Peoples: Technology, Environments, and Western Imperialism, 1400 to the Present* (Princeton: Princeton University Press, 2010), 189; François Crouzet, *Histoire de l'économie européenne, 1000–2000* (Paris: Albin Michel, 2010), 170–7.
8 Hoskins, *British Routes to India*, 89–95; Jobin M. Kanjirakkat, Gordon McOuat, and Sundar Sarukkai, eds., *Science and Narratives of Nature: East and West* (New Delhi: Routledge, 2015), 273.
9 Satpal Sangwan, "Technology and Imperialism in the Indian Context: The Case of Steamboats, 1819–1839," in *Science, Medicine and Cultural Imperialism*, ed. Teresa A. Meade and Mark Walker (London: Macmillan, 1991), 61–2. William Pitt Amherst was Governor General of India from 1823 to 1828.
10 On this project, see Waghorn's account in Thomas Waghorn, *Overland Mails to India, China, Etc: The Acceleration of Mails, Once a Fortnight, Between England and the East Indies, and Vice Versa* (London: Smith, Elder and Co., 1843). On Waghorn and the "overland" route, see George W. Wheatley, "Some Account of the Late Lt. Waghorn, RN, the Originator of the Overland Route," *Bentley's Miscellany* 27 (1850): 349–57; Philip E. Clunn, *Lt Waghorn, RN, Pioneer of the Overland Route to India* (London: G.W. Wheatley & Co., 1892), 2–14; and Charles R. Low, *History of the Indian Navy (1613–1863)*, 2 vols. (London: R. Bentley and son, 1877), 1:521–30.
11 British Library, London: IOR/F/4/1332/52700, Further papers regarding the proposals of Thomas Waghorn for establishing a steamship service

between England and India, 1829–31; IOR/F/4/1242/40875, Account by Thomas Waghorn, Bengal Pilot Service, of his journey overland to India via the Red Sea, 1829–30.

12 Robert J. Blyth, "Aden, British India, and the Development of Steam Power in the Red Sea," in *Maritime Empires: British Imperial Maritime Trade in the Nineteenth Century*, ed. David Killingray, Margarette Lincoln, and Nigel Rigby (Woodbridge: Boydell, 2004), 74–80.

13 Hoskins, *British Routes to India*, 106–7.

14 IOR/F/4/1354/53792, Further papers regarding steam navigation between Bombay and the Red Sea and between Egypt and England, Jan. 1830–Nov. 1832. On Malcolm's role, see also John Malcolm, *Malcolm: Soldier, Diplomat, Ideologue of British India: The Life of Sir John Malcolm (1769–1833)* (Edinburgh: John Donald, 2014), 108–9; and Hoskins, *British Routes to India*, 108–9.

15 James H. Wilson, *On the Steam Communication between Bombay and Suez with an Account of the Hugh Lindsay's Four Voyages* (Bombay: American Mission Press, 1833), 39–42.

16 Hoskins, *British Routes to India*, 102.

17 Hoskins, *British Routes to India*, 110.

18 Hoskins, *British Routes to India*, 109, 120–1, 125.

19 Hoskins, *British Routes to India*, 20.

20 Edward Ingram, *In Defence of British India: Great Britain in the Middle East, 1775–1842* (London: Cass, 1984), 152–79.

21 See Alexander Mikaberidze, "Turkmanchai, Treaty of," in *Conflict and Conquest in the Islamic World: A Historical Encyclopedia* (Santa Barbara: ABC-CLIO, 2011), 902.

22 Cited in Hoskins, *British Routes to India*, 148.

23 On the Taylor brothers, see J.P. Parry, "Steam Power and British Influence in Baghdad," *Historical Journal* 56, no. 1 (2013): 145–73; and Haim Goren, *Dead Sea Level: Science, Exploration, and Imperial Interests in the Near East* (London: I.B. Tauris, 2010), 59–115.

24 Parry, "Steam Power and British Influence in Baghdad," 152–3.

25 Gordon served as ambassador to the Porte between 1829 and 1831.

26 Hoskins, *British Routes to India*, 149; Dorsey D. Jones, "Chesney Chose the Euphrates Route," *Historian* 5, no. 1 (1942): 6.

27 Letter from Chesney to Gordon, 2 September 1830, printed in Francis R. Chesney, *Reports on the Navigation of the Euphrates* (London: George Taylor, 1833), 52–7; Jones, "Chesney Chose the Euphrates Route," 7–8.

28 Hoskins, *British Routes to India*, 150.

29 Chesney, *Reports on the Navigation of the Euphrates*, 11. On Chesney, see Louise Chesney and Jane O'Donnell, *The Life of the Late General F.K.X. Chesney, by His Wife and Daughter*, ed. Stanley Lane-Poole (London: W.H. Allen & Co., 1885).

30 Jones, "Chesney Chose the Euphrates Route," 10–12.

31 Charles Grant served as president of the India Board between 1830 and 1835.

32 Canning was ambassador to the Ottoman Empire between 1825 and 1828, again in 1832, and once again from 1841 to 1858. On Canning, see Stanley Lane-Poole, *The Life of the Right Honourable Stratford Canning: From His Memoirs and Private and Official Papers*, 2 vols. (New York: AMS Press, 1976); and Steven Richmond, *The Voice of England in the East: Stratford Canning and Diplomacy with the Ottoman Empire* (London: I.B. Tauris, 2014).

33 John B. Kelly, *Britain and the Persian Gulf, 1795–1880* (Oxford: Clarendon Press, 1968), 268. John N. Campbell served as British envoy in Persia between 1830 and 1835. On Campbell, see Edward Ingram, "Family and Faction in the Great Game in Asia: The Struggle over the Persian Mission 1828–1835," *Middle Eastern Studies* 17, no. 3 (1981): 283–309.

34 See Chapter 2.

35 On this alliance, see Edward Ingram, *The British Empire as a World Power* (London: Frank Cass, 2001), 113–14; and Christine M. Philliou, *Biography of an Empire: Governing Ottomans in an Age of Revolution* (Berkeley: University of California Press, 2011), 117–19.

36 Jones, "Chesney Chose the Euphrates Route," 12.

37 *Report from the Select Committee on Steam Navigation* (London: HMSO, 1834), 1. On Peacock and his interests regarding steam navigation, see Headrick, *Power over Peoples*, 191–2.

38 *Report from the Select Committee on Steam Navigation*, 15–20.

39 *Report from the Select Committee on Steam Navigation*, 152.

40 In 1832 Macgregor Laird had built two steamers, one with an iron hull, with which he and his companions explored the lower Niger River. See Headrick, *Power over Peoples*, 192–3.

41 On Laird's contribution to the committee's debates, see Headrick, *Power over Peoples*, 674–85.

42 Hoskins, *British Routes to India*, 158–9.

43 Headrick, *Power over Peoples*, 191–2.

44 Ponsonby served as British ambassador to the Porte from 1832 to 1841.

45 Dorsey D. Jones and J.W. Grissom, "Francis Rawdon Chesney: A Reappraisal of His Work on the Euphrates Route," *Historian* 11, no. 2 (1949): 196.

46 Karkemish is a city located at the border between present-day Syria and Turkey. According to the Bible, an important battle took place between the Babylonian army led by Nebuchadnezzar II and the Egyptian army in the seventh century BC. According to Genesis, the city of Calmeh was founded by King Nimrod. Zenobia reigned over the Palmyrene Empire in the third century AD. Francis R. Chesney, *The Expedition for the Survey of the Rivers Euphrates and Tigris*, 2 vols. (London: Longman, Brown, Green, and Longmans, 1850), 2:250–1.

47 Chesney, *The Expedition for the Survey*, 2:341.

48 Low, *History of the Indian Navy*, 40–1; IOR/Z/E/4/15/C421, Chesney papers.

49 Chesney, *The Expedition for the Survey*, 2:261, 283.

50 Chesney, *The Expedition for the Survey*, 2:306.

51 Jones and Grissom, "Francis Rawdon Chesney," 198.

52 Jones and Grissom, "Francis Rawdon Chesney," 199–200.

53 Hoskins, *British Routes to India*, 175–8.

54 Hoskins, *British Routes to India*, 178.

55 IOR/F/4/1820/75030, Government of India forward to the Bombay Government the bills submitted by Lieutenant Henry Blosse Lynch I.N. on account of the steamer establishment in Mesopotamia for the latter half of 1837, January 1838–June 1839. IOR Mss Eur F213/104, Memorandum of Henry Blosse Lynch regarding the Euphrates expedition, 20 April 1841.

56 See Chapter 2.

57 On the arguments developed in favour of the opening of this steamship line, see Parry, "Steam Power and British Influence in Baghdad," 160.

58 Hoskins, *British Routes to India*, 181.

59 Maharashtra State Archives, Bombay, Comp. 26, vol. 14/1229, "Euphrates, steam flotilla, regarding the latitude to be allowed to commander Lynch in the expenditure required by, and allowances to Mr Powel," 1841; Comp. 149, vol. 15/1342 "Euphrates Expedition Accounts," 1842.

60 Parry, "Steam Power and British Influence in Baghdad," 164. On Rawlinson's time in Iraq, see his autobiography, *A Memoir of Sir Henry Creswicke Rawlinson* (London: Longmans, Green, and Co., 1898).

61 Parry, "Steam Power and British Influence in Baghdad," 170.

62 Thomas K. Lynch, *The Navigation of the Euphrates and Tigris and the Political Rights of England Thereon* (London: Strangeways and Sons,

1884). See also Parry, "Steam Power and British Influence in Baghdad," 163; and Charles Issawi, *The Fertile Crescent 1800–1914: A Documentary Economic History* (Oxford: Oxford University Press, 1988), 216–18, 250.

63 Issawi, *The Fertile Crescent*, 215–16.

64 Henry S. Cooper, *Through Turkish Arabia: A Journey from the Mediterranean to Bombay by the Euphrates and Tigris Valleys and the Persian Gulf* (London: W.H. Allen & Co., 1894), 387–8.

65 On this Ottoman company, see Issawi, *The Fertile Crescent*, 249–50.

66 Stephanie Jones, "The Management of British India Steamers in the Gulf 1862–1945: Gray Mackenzie and the Mesopotamia Persia Corporation," in *The Gulf in the Early 20th Century: Foreign Institutions and Local Responses*, ed. Richard Lawless (Durham: Durham University Centre for Middle Eastern and Islamic Studies, 1986), 25–63; Stephanie Jones, "British India Steamers and the Trade of the Persian Gulf, 1862–1914," *The Great Circle: Journal of the Australian Association for Maritime History* 7, no. 1 (1985): 23–45.

67 Issawi, *The Fertile Crescent*, 257–9.

68 On this, see Camille Cole, "Precarious Empires: A Social and Environmental History of Steam Navigation on the Tigris," *Journal of Social History* 50, no. 1 (2016): 74–101; no. 2: 9–12.

69 Roger Owen, *The Middle East in the World Economy, 1800–1914* (London: I.B. Tauris, 1993), 277–8.

70 On this argument, see David Gange and Michael Ledger-Lomas, "Introduction," in *Cities of God: The Bible and Archaeology in Nineteenth-Century Britain*, ed. David Gange and Michael Ledger-Lomas (Cambridge: Cambridge University Press, 2013), 1–38.

71 On this argument see, for example, Michael Seymour, "Babylon," in Gange and Ledger-Lomas, *Cities of God*, 164–96.

72 Billie Melman, "The Power of the Past: History and Modernity in the Victorian World," in *The Victorian World*, ed. Martin Hewitt (London: Routledge, 2012), 466–84.

73 On British archaeology in Iraq see, for example, Mogens Trolle Larsen, *The Conquest of Assyria: Excavations in an Antique Land, 1840–1860* (New York: Routledge, 1996); Magnus T. Bernhardsson, *Reclaiming a Plundered Past: Archaeology and Nation-Building in Modern Iraq* (Austin: University of Texas Press, 2005), 19–56; and Shawn Malley, *From Archaeology to Spectacle in Victorian Britain: The Case of Assyria* (London: Ashgate, 2012). On the representation of the ancient world in British culture, see for instance Jeffrey Richards, *The Ancient World on the*

Victorian and Edwardian Stage (London: Palgrave Macmillan, 2009); and Jack Green and Emily Teeter, eds., *Picturing the Past: Imagining and Imaging the Ancient Near East* (Chicago: Oriental Institute of the University of Chicago, 2012). For a history of British archaeology in the Middle East in the twentieth century, see Billie Melman, *Empires of Antiquities: Modernity and the Rediscovery of the Ancient Near East, 1914–1950* (Oxford: Oxford University Press, 2020).

74 Claudius J. Rich was the British resident in Baghdad from 1808 to 1820. On the excavations of Babylon, see his *Memoirs on the Ruins of Babylon* (London: Longman, 1816). On Rich himself see, for example, Seymour, "Babylon," 167–71.

75 Holger Hoock, "The British State and the Anglo-French Wars over Antiquities, 1798–1858," *Historical Journal* 50, no. 1 (2007): 49–72; Ian Jenkins, *Archaeologists and Aesthetes: Galleries of the British Museum, 1800–1939* (London: British Museum Press, 1992).

76 Nicole Chevalier, *La Recherche archéologique française au Moyen-Orient: 1842–1947* (Paris: Éd. Recherche sur les Civilisations, 2002).

77 In 1843, Paul-Emile Botta became the first French consul in Mosul. On his excavations at Nineveh, see Paul-Emile Botta, *Monument de Ninive*, 5 vols. (Paris: Imprimerie nationale, 1848–50); and Eugène Flandin, *Monuments de Ninive*, 3 vols. (Paris: Imprimerie Nationale, 1850). On Botta, see Giovanni Bergamini, "'Spoliis Orientis Onustus,' Paul-Émile Botta et la redécouverte de la civilisation assyrienne," in *De Khorsabad à Paris: la découverte des Assyriens*, ed. Élisabeth Fontan and Nicole Chevalier (Paris: Réunion des musées nationaux, 1994), 68–85; and Béatrice André-Salvini, "Introduction aux publications de P.E. Botta et de V. Place," in Fontan and Chevalier, *De Khorsabad à Paris*, 166–75. On the reception of Assyria in France, see Frederick N. Bohrer, *Orientalism and Visual Culture: Imagining Mesopotamia in Nineteenth-Century Europe* (Cambridge: Cambridge University Press, 2003), 66–97.

78 On Layard see, for example, Larsen, *The Conquest of Assyria*; and Shawn Malley, "Layard Enterprise: Victorian Archaeology and Informal Imperialism in Mesopotamia," *International Journal of Middle East Studies* 40, no. 4 (2008): 623–46.

79 Frederick N. Bohrer, "Monumental Nationalism: Layard's Assyrian Discoveries and the Formation of British National Identity," in *Cultural Identities and the Aesthetics of Britishness*, ed. Dana Arnold (Manchester: Manchester University Press, 2004), 101–2.

80 On Rawlinson's role in British archaeology in the region, see Lesley Adkins, *Empires of the Plain: Henry Rawlinson and the Lost Languages of Babylon* (London: HarperCollins, 2003).

81 On the importance of Rassam for the discovery of Assyrian ruins, see Julian Reade, "Hormuzd Rassam and His Discoveries," *Iraq* 55 (1993): 39–62.

82 The discovery of this wall and its reliefs depicting in very realistic detail the siege and destruction of Lachish by Sennacherib in 701 BC was a milestone not only in the history of British archaeology in the Orient but also in the development of an *imaginaire* of Mesopotamia in Britain. See Melman, *Empires of Antiquities*, 129–30.

83 Austen H. Layard, *Nineveh and its Remains*, 2 vols. (London: John Murray, 1849); Layard, *A Popular Account of Discoveries at Nineveh* (London: John Murray, 1851).

84 Malley, *From Archaeology to Spectacle*, 15–44; Bohrer, *Orientalism and Visual Culture*, 98–105.

85 Victor Place held the post in Mosul from 1852 to 1855. On his excavations at Khorsabad, see Victor Place, *Ninive et l'Assyrie, avec des essais de restauration par Félix Thomas. Ouvrage publié d'après les ordres de l'Empereur*, 3 vols. (Paris: Imprimerie impériale, 1867–70). On Place, see Nicole Chevalier, "Des consuls en Iraq," in *Cités disparues*, ed. Michel Baud (Paris: Autrement, 1991); Maurice Pillet, *Un pionnier de l'assyriologie: Victor Place, consul de France à Mossoul* (Paris: Imprimerie nationale, 1962); and Nicole Chevalier, "Victor Place: consul et archéologue," in Fontan and Chevalier, *De Khorsabad à Paris*, 94–101.

86 Maurice Pillet, *Khorsabad, les découvertes de Victor Place en Assyrie* (Paris: E. Leroux, 1918).

87 Seymour, "Babylon," 187.

88 Layard published a number of accounts of his archaeological adventures in Mesopotamia. See, for example, Austen H. Layard, *Nineveh and its Remains*; Layard, *A Popular Account of Discoveries at Nineveh*; Layard, *Discoveries among the Ruins of Nineveh and Babylon* (New York: G.P. Putnam and Co., 1853). On the success of the publication of Layard's accounts, see Bohrer, *Orientalism and Visual Culture*, 142–54.

89 On the emergence of this discourse, see Gange and Ledger-Lomas, "Introduction," in Gange and Ledger-Lomas, *Cities of God*, 1–3. For further elements on this narrative see, for example, Diana K. Davis, *Resurrecting the Granary of Rome: Environmental History and French Colonial Expansion in North Africa* (Athens: Ohio University Press, 2007).

90 On the Crimean War and the Great Game see, for example, Edward Ingram, *The Beginnings of the Great Game in Asia* (Oxford: Clarendon, 1979), 328–36; and Alexander L. Macfie, *The Eastern Question 1774–1923* (London: Longman, 1989), 27–33. On the risk of a Russian invasion of India during the Crimean War, see Garry J. Adler, "India and the Crimean War," *Journal of Imperial and Commonwealth History* 2, no. 1 (1973): 15–37.

91 Christine Noelle, *State and Tribe in Nineteenth-Century Afghanistan: The Reign of Amir Dost Muhammad Kahn (1826–1863)* (Richmond: Curzon, 1997), 248–51. On the role of Herat in Anglo-Persian relations, see Garry J. Adler, "The Key to India? Britain and the Herat Problem, 1838–1863 – Part I," *Middle Eastern Studies* 10, no. 2 (1974): 186–209.

92 The fall of Herat led the Governor General of India to declare war on Persia on behalf of Britain in November. A response to Persia's invasion was quickly organized, and the British attacked Qajar positions in the Gulf. In December, troops sent from Bombay launched an assault on Kharg Island, which surrendered. From Kharg, Anglo-Indian troops led an operation against Bushire, which quickly capitulated. In February 1857, with further contingents sent from India, the expedition under the command of James Outram crushed the Qajar army at the battle of Koosh-Ab. In March 1857, Britain and Persia signed a peace treaty. Naser al-Din Shah promised to withdraw his troops from Herat and to refrain from further interference in the affairs of the Afghan state. On the Anglo-Persian war of 1856–57 see, for instance, Kelly, *Britain and the Persian Gulf*, 452–99; J.F. Standish, "The Persian War of 1856–57," *Middle Eastern Studies* 3, no. 1 (1966): 18–45; Abbas Amanat, *Iran: A Modern History* (New Haven: Yale University Press, 2017), 262–4, 312–13; Mikhail Volodarsky, "Persia and the Great Powers, 1856–1869," *Middle Eastern Studies* 19, no. 1 (1983): 75–92; and Pirouz Mojtahed-Zadeh, *Small Players of the Great Game: The Settlement of Iran's Eastern Borderlands* (London: Routledge, 2004), 145–7.

93 François Crouzet, *L'économie de la Grande-Bretagne victorienne* (Paris: Belin, 2009), 203–22; Ralph Harrington, "The Railway Journey and the Neuroses of Modernity," in *Pathologies of Travel*, ed. Richard Wrigley and George Revill (Amsterdam: Rodopi, 2000), 229–59; Robert Kubicek, "British Expansion, Empire, and Technological Change," in *The Oxford History of the British Empire*, ed. Andrew Porter, 5 vols. (Oxford: Oxford University Press, 1999), 3:247–69.

94 Francis R. Chesney, *Report on the Euphrates Valley Railway* (London: Smith, Elder & Co. 65, Cornhill, 1857), 1–4.

95 William P. Andrew, *The Scinde Railway and Its Relations to the Euphrates Valley, and Other Routes to India* (London: W.H. Allen & Co., 1856), 2, 4–5, 16–18.

96 William P. Andrew, *Euphrates Valley Route to India, in Connection with the Central Asian and Egyptian Questions* (London: W.H. Allen & Co., 1882); Andrew, *Indian Railways as Connected with British Empire in the East* (London: W.H. Allen & Co., 1884); Andrew, *The Scinde Railway*; and Andrew, *Memoir on the Euphrates Valley Route to India: With Official Correspondence and Maps* (London: W.H. Allen & Co., 1857).

97 On Stephenson's project, see Hoskins, *British Routes to India*, 328–9.

98 Andrew, *Euphrates Valley Route to India*, 11; on the disadvantages of the "overland" route, see 4, 6, 17.

99 Andrew, *Euphrates Valley Route to India*, 14, 211; Andrew, *The Scinde Railway*, 33–6.

100 Andrew, *Memoir on the Euphrates Valley Route to India*, xi, 4, 33–4, 164.

101 Andrew, *The Scinde Railway*, 57–9.

102 Andrew, *The Scinde Railway*, 20–30, 45; Andrew, *Memoir on the Euphrates Valley Route to India*, 143.

103 Andrew, *Euphrates Valley Route to India*, 3.

104 Andrew, *Euphrates Valley Route to India*, 2, 30: "The ancient route of the Euphrates – the route of the Emperors Trajan and Julian, in whose steps, in more recent times, the Great Napoleon intended to follow, when the Russian campaign turned his energies in another direction" (12).

105 Sheil served as British envoy from 1844 to 1854. The supporters of the project, among whom was Chesney, signed the following letter, addressed to Palmerston: *Letter to Viscount Palmerston, K.G., on the Political Importance of the Euphrates Valley Railway, and the Necessity of the Financial Support of Her Majesty's Government* (London: W.H. Allen & Co., 1857).

106 Prospectus of the Euphrates Valley Railway Company, repr. in Andrew, *Memoir on the Euphrates Valley Route to India*, 175.

107 National Archives, London: FO 78/1711, Euphrates Valley Railway, vol. 1 (1854–62); BT 41/232/1302, Euphrates Valley Railway Company Ltd. (1844–c.1860).

108 Hoskins, *British Routes to India*, 334.

109 Hoskins, *British Routes to India*, 339, 341–2.

110 Soli Shahvar, "Concession Hunting in the Age of Reform: British Companies and the Search for Government Guarantees; Telegraph Concessions through Ottoman Territories, 1855–1858," *Middle Eastern Studies* 38, no. 4 (2002): 169–93.

Chapter Six

1 Archives du Ministère des Affaires étrangères (AMAE), Correspondance politique et commerciale (CPCOM), n.s., Mascate vol. 3 (Le golfe Persique et les puissances, Dossier général, 1896–98), report by Ottavi, April 1896.

2 Christopher A. Bayly, *The Birth of the Modern World, 1780–1914: Global Connections and Comparisons* (Malden: Blackwell, 2004), 227–9.

3 Bayly, *The Birth of the Modern World*, 229–33.

4 See, for example, Mostafa Minawi, *The Ottoman Scramble for Africa: Empire and Diplomacy in the Sahara and the Hijaz* (Stanford: Stanford University Press, 2016), 1–18.

5 A graduate of the *École des Langues Orientales*, Ottavi arrived in Oman having already held several positions in the French diplomatic service, successively in Beirut, Aleppo, Zanzibar, and Mogador: *Annuaire diplomatique et consulaire de la République française pour 1904 et 1905* (Paris: Berger-Levrault, 1905), 250.

6 Jeremy Jones and Nicholas Ridout, *A History of Modern Oman* (Cambridge: Cambridge University Press, 2015), 33–8.

7 Robert Oddos, "Deux siècles de relations franco-omanaises (1735–1920). Aperçu historique," *Revue historique* 599, no. 2 (1996): 87.

8 Beatrice Nicolini, *Makran, Oman, and Zanzibar: Three-Terminal Cultural Corridor in the Western Indian Ocean, 1799–1856*, trans. Penelope-Jane Watson (Leiden: Brill, 2004), 87.

9 [Sultan] Muhammad Al-Qasimi, *Les relations entre Oman et la France (1715–1905)*, trans. Abdeljelil and Mireille Temimi (Paris: L'Harmattan, 1995), 73–83. On Badr bin Sayf, see Jones and Ridout, *A History of Modern Oman*, 45–6.

10 Joseph A. Kechichian, *Oman and the World: The Emergence of an Independent Foreign Policy* (Santa Monica: Rand, 1995), 135–6.

11 Jones and Ridout, *A History of Modern Oman*, 33–8. On the treaty with France, see Al-Qasimi, *Les relations entre Oman et la France*, 1; and Charles Brunet-Million, *Les boutriers de la mer des Indes, affaires de Zanzibar et de Mascate* (Paris: A. Pedone, 1910), 79–80.

12 Robert Bennett, "France and Zanzibar, 1844 to the 1860s," *International Journal of African Historical Studies* 6, no. 4 (1973): 602–32; Jean-François Rispal, "Zanzibar et la politique française dans l'océan Indien (1776–1904)," *Rahia. Recherches en anthropologie et en histoire de l'Afrique* 15 (2005): 35–6.

13 Briton C. Busch, *Britain and the Persian Gulf, 1894–1914* (Berkeley: University of California Press, 1967), 49–50.
14 See Rispal, "Zanzibar et la politique française," 34.
15 Henri Brunschwig, "Une colonie inutile: Obock (1862–1888)," *Cahiers d'études africaines* 8, no. 29 (1968): 32–47.
16 Colette Dubois, *Djibouti, 1888–1967: Héritage ou frustration* (Paris: L'Harmattan, 1997); Ioan M. Lewis, *The Modern History of Somaliland: From Nation to State* (London: Weidenfeld and Nicolson, 1965), 35, 43–8.
17 Italy developed an imperial presence on the Red Sea from the late 1860s: Mark I. Choate, "From Territorial to Ethnographic Colonies and Back Again: The Politics of Italian Expansion 1890–1912," *Modern Italy* 8, no. 1 (2003): 65–75.
18 Jones and Ridout, *A History of Modern Oman*, 77–8.
19 Hussein Ghubash, *Oman, une démocratie islamique millénaire: la tradition de l'imâma, l'histoire politique moderne (1500–1970)* (Paris: Maisonneuve and Larose, 1998), 215–17; and Husain M. Al-Baharna, *The Legal Status of the Arabian Gulf States: A Study of Their Treaty Relations and Their International Problems* (Manchester: Manchester University Press, 1968), 50, 69–70, 98.
20 Bruno Le Cour Grandmaison, *Le Sultanat d'Oman* (Paris: Karthala, 2000), 134–5.
21 See, for example, Darrell Bates, *The Fashoda Incident of 1898: Encounter on the Nile* (Oxford: Oxford University Press, 1984).
22 British Library, London: IOR/L/PS/18/B119, Memorandum by Sir W. Lee-Warner on the Lease to France of a Coaling Station in Muskat Territory, f.91, 1899. On the crisis, see Y.A. Al-Ghailani, "Oman and the Franco-British Colonial Rivalry: The Bandar al-Jissah Crisis 1898–1900," ADAB: *Journal of the Faculty of Arts, University of Khartoum* 27 (2009): 1–17.
23 On Delcassé, one of the main instigators of the Entente Cordiale, see Christopher Andrew, *Théophile Delcassé and the Making of the Entente Cordiale: A Reappraisal of a Foreign Policy, 1889–1889* (London: Macmillan, 1968).
24 Brunschwig, "Une colonie inutile," 45–6.
25 Alain Gascon, "Djibouti: Singapour sur mer Rouge. Un confetti d'Empire futur dragon africain," *Outre-Terre* 2, no. 11 (2005): 453.
26 IOR/R/15/1/400, f.25, Fagan to Foreign Department, Calcutta, 17 Jan. 1899. See also Busch, *Britain and the Persian Gulf*, 70.
27 For discussion of complaints from Faisal about the British failure to respect the sovereignty of Oman, see IOR/R/15/1/401, f.11, Fagan to Meade,

21 January 1899. For the 1862 treaty itself, see J.A. Kieran, "The Origins of the Zanzibar Guarantee Treaty of 1862," *Canadian Journal of African Studies / Revue Canadienne des Études Africaines* 2, no. 2 (1968): 147–66.

28 Busch, *Britain and the Persian Gulf*, 78, 90–2.

29 Busch, *Britain and the Persian Gulf*, 73–7. See also IOR/R/15/1/401, f.117, translated note from Faysal to "all who may see this on behalf of the British Government," 13 February 1899; and f.138, Meade to Faysal, 14 February 1899.

30 IOR/R/15/1/401, ff.122–123, Meade to Douglas, 15 February 1899.

31 Busch, *Britain and the Persian Gulf*, 77–8.

32 Busch, *Britain and the Persian Gulf*, 83–5.

33 Curzon to Hamilton, 2 March 1899, ctd in Busch, *Britain and the Persian Gulf*, 85.

34 Busch, *Britain and the Persian Gulf*, 86.

35 IOR Mss Eur D510/1, Curzon to Hamilton, 9 March 1899.

36 For these interventions, see Busch, *Britain and the Persian Gulf*, 86–7.

37 Brunet-Millon, *Les boutriers de la mer des Indes*, 103–11.

38 Fahad Ahmad Bishara, "'No Country But the Ocean': Reading International Law from the Deck of an Indian Ocean Dhow, ca. 1900," *Comparative Studies in Society and History* 60, no. 2 (2018): 345.

39 Bishara, "'No Country But the Ocean,'" 346–7. See also Lauren Benton, "Legal Spaces of Empire: Piracy and the Origins of Ocean Regionalism," *Comparative Studies in Society and History* 47, no. 4 (2005): 700–24.

40 Paul Boiteau, *Les traités de commerce* (Paris: Guillaumin, 1863), 464–8.

41 Brunet-Million, *Les boutriers de la mer des Indes*, 342.

42 Johan Mathew, *Margins of the Market: Trafficking and Capitalism across the Arabian Sea* (Berkeley: University of California Press, 2016), 35–6; Brunet-Million, *Les boutriers de la mer des Indes*, 79–80.

43 Boleslaw A. Boczek, *Flags of Convenience: An International Legal Study* (Cambridge, MA: Harvard University Press, 1962); Rodney Carlisle, *Sovereignty for Sale: The Origins and Evolution of the Panamanian and Liberian Flags of Convenience* (Annapolis: Naval Institute Press, 1982).

44 John G. Lorimer, *Gazetteer of the Persian Gulf, Oman, and Central Arabia*, 2 vols. (Calcutta: Superintendent Government Printing, India, 1908–15; Gerrards Cross: Archive Editions, 1986, 6 vols.), 1:2498.

45 Lorimer, *Gazetteer*, 1:2499.

46 Translated letter qtd in AMAE CPCOM, n.s., Mascate, October 1898.

47 Raphaël Chériaux, "The French Flag in Zanzibar Waters 1860s–1900s: Abolition and Imperial Rivalry in the Western Indian Ocean," *Journal of Imperial and Commonwealth History* 49, no. 1 (2021): 44–69.

48 Ottavi to Hanotaux, 30 June 1897, ctd in Brunet-Million, *Les boutriers de la mer des Indes*, 112.
49 See Percy C. Cox, "Some Excursions in Oman," *Geographical Journal* 66, no. 3 (1925): 193–221. On Cox's larger Middle East career, see John Townsend, *Proconsul to the Middle East: Sir Percy Cox and the End of Empire* (London: I.B. Tauris, 2010).
50 Faysal declaration, 12 June 1900, ctd in Busch, *Britain and the Persian Gulf*, 159–60.
51 See Busch, *Britain and the Persian Gulf*, 160.
52 Curzon minute, 18 June 1900, ctd in Busch, *Britain and the Persian Gulf*, 160.
53 IOR/R/15/1/403, f.152, Cox to Kemball, 3 April 1901.
54 AMAE CPCOM, n.s., Mascate, Ottavi to Faysal, 28 August 1901.
55 François Crouzet, "Entente cordiale: réalités et mythes d'un siècle de relations franco-britanniques," *Etudes anglaises* 57, no. 3 (2004): 310–20.
56 Richard Mayne, Douglas Johnson, and Robert Tombs, eds., *Cross-Channel Currents: 100 Years of the Entente Cordiale* (London: Routledge, 2004); Maurice Vaïsse, *L'Entente cordiale de Fachoda à la Grande Guerre dans les archives du Quai d'Orsay* (Bruxelles: Editions Complexe, 2004).
57 Guillemette Crouzet, "A Second 'Fashoda'? Britain, India, and a French 'Threat' in Oman at the End of the Nineteenth Century," in *British and French Colonialism in Africa, Asia, and the Middle East*, ed. James R. Fichter (Basingstoke: Palgrave Macmillan, 2019), 131–50; Busch, *Britain and the Persian Gulf*, 180.
58 Rodney Carlisle, "The Muscat Dhow Case in Historical Perspective," *Northern Mariner* 24, no. 1 (2014): 23–40.
59 IOR/R/15/1/406, Muscat Dhows Arbitration, f.3r, 1905.
60 *The Muscat Dhows Case (France v. Great Britain), Hague Court Reports* 93 (1905): 93–109.
61 IOR/R/15/1/406, f.21.
62 *Muscat Dhows Case*, 96.
63 IOR/R/15/1/406, ff.27r–29v.
64 Suzanne Miers, "The Brussels Conference of 1889–1890," in *Britain and Germany in Africa: Imperial Rivalry and Colonial Rule*, ed. Prosser Gifford and W.M. Roger Louis (New Haven: Yale University Press, 1967), 83–118.
65 *Muscat Dhows Case*, 99; Carlisle, "The Muscat Dhow Case," 36.
66 Brunet-Millon, *Les boutriers de la mer des Indes*, 326–44; Maurice Bessonnet, "L'arbitrage franco–anglais dans l'affaire des boutres de Mascate," *Revue internationale de droit international public* 13 (1906): 145–64.

67 Lorimer, *Gazetteer*, 1:2566.

68 See also Guillemette Crouzet, "'A Troublesome Man' ou un Lawrence d'Arabie français? Antonin Goguyer, aventurier et trafiquant d'armes dans le Golfe Persique et en Oman au début du XXe siècle," in *Les négociants européens et le monde: histoire d'une mise en connexion*, ed. Virginie Chaillou-Atrous, Jean-François Klein, and Antoine Resche (Rennes: Presses universitaires de Rennes, 2016), 145–56; Henri d'Orléans, *Une visite à l'empereur Ménélik. Notes et impressions de route* (Paris: Dentu, 1898), 196–7.

69 On Ettinghausen, see Guillemette Crouzet, *Genèses du Moyen-Orient. Le Golfe Persique à l'âge des imperialismes (vers 1800–vers 1914)* (Ceyzérieux: Champ Vallon, 2015), 482.

70 Goguyer had a long-standing interest in steam railways. Antonin Goguyer, *A M. le ministre résident général de France à Tunis, supériorité du chemin de fer de Gafsa à Gabès sur celui de Gafsa à Sfax* (Tunis: Picard, 1895).

71 AMAE CPCOM, n.s., Mascate vol. 46 (Affaire Goguyer, 1899–1909).

72 AMAE CPCOM, n.s., Mascate, Ottavi to Quai d'Orsay, 12 February 1900.

73 Herbert H. Austin, *Gun-Running in the Gulf and Other Adventures* (London: John Murray, 1926), 13.

74 Lorimer, *Gazetteer*, 1:341.

75 Emrys Chew, *Arming the Periphery: The Arms Trade in the Indian Ocean during the Age of Global Empire* (Basingstoke: Palgrave Macmillan, 2012), 139.

76 AMAE CPCOM, n.s., Mascate, Laronce to Quai d'Orsay, 20 September 1903.

77 AMAE CPCOM, n.s., Mascate vol. 46 (Affaire Goguyer, 1899–1909).

78 IOR/R/15/1/403, f.202, Cox to Dane, 22 August 1903; Alain Rouaud, *Casimir Mondon-Vidailhet, pionnier de l'amitié franco-éthiopienne* (Addis Ababa: Centre Français des Etudes Ethiopiennes, 1997), 39–40; Lorimer, *Gazetteer*, 1:339.

79 Lorimer, *Gazetteer*, 1:340–2.

80 AMAE CPCOM, n.s., Mascate, Beguin-Billecocq to Quai d'Orsay, March 1906; Lorimer, *Gazetteer*, 1:342.

81 On Jean Beguin-Billecocq, see Xavier Beguin-Billecocq, *Un Consul de France à Mascate* (Paris: privately printed, 1991).

82 AMAE CPCOM, n.s., Mascate vol. 46 (Affaire Goguyer, 1899–1909), letter from Léon Michel de la Croix, 24 October 1909.

83 Jon E. Mandaville, "The Ottoman Province of al-Hasa in the Sixteenth and Seventeenth Centuries," *Journal of the American Oriental Society* 90,

no. 3 (1970): 486–513; Salih Özbaran, "A Note on the Ottoman Administration in Arabia in the Sixteenth Century," *International Journal of Turkish Studies* 3, no. 1 (1985): 93–9; Salih Özbaran, *Ottoman Expansion towards the Indian Ocean in the 16th Century* (Istanbul: Bilgi University Press, 2009).

84 The Tanzimat (meaning "reorganization") period lasted from 1839 to 1876. Abdülhamid then continued reforms from 1876 until the Young Turk Revolution in 1908.

85 Zekeriya Kursun, *The Ottomans in Qatar: A History of Anglo-Ottoman Conflicts in the Persian Gulf* (Istanbul: Isis Press, 2002); Gökhan Cetinsaya, *Ottoman Administration of Iraq, 1890–1908* (London: Routledge, 2006); Selim Deringil, "They Live in a State of Nomadism and Savagery: The Late Ottoman Empire and the Post-Colonial Debate," *Comparative Studies in Society and History* 45, no. 2 (2003): 311–42.

86 On Midhat, see Ebubekir Ceylan, *The Ottoman Origins of Modern Iraq: Political Reform, Modernization, and Development in the Nineteenth-Century Middle East* (London: I.B. Tauris, 2011); and Zekeriya Kursun, *The Ottomans in Qatar*, 49–61.

87 Frederick F. Anscombe, *The Ottoman Gulf: The Creation of Kuwait, Saudi Arabia, and Qatar* (New York: Columbia University Press, 1997), 50; John B. Kelly, *Britain and the Persian Gulf, 1795–1880* (Oxford: Clarendon, 1968), 729–30.

88 Kelly, *Britain and the Persian Gulf*, 718–24.

89 Anscombe, *The Ottoman Gulf*, 70–1.

90 Penelope Tuson and Emma Quick, eds., *Arabian Treaties, 1600–1960*, 4 vols. (Slough: Archive Editions, 1992), 2:5; James Onley, "Britain's Informal Empire in the Gulf," *Journal of Social Affairs* 87 (2005): 30–2.

91 James Onley, *The Arabian Frontier of the Raj: Merchants, Rulers, and the British in the Nineteenth-Century Gulf* (Oxford: Oxford University Press, 2007), 121–2.

92 Sir Charles Wood to Sir George Clerk, 18 February 1861, ctd in Kelly, *Britain and the Persian Gulf*, 525.

93 Kelly, *Britain and the Persian Gulf*, 731.

94 Al-Baharna, *The Legal Status of the Arabian Gulf States*, 313–14.

95 Anscombe, *The Ottoman Gulf*, 60.

96 Tuson and Quick, *Arabian Treaties*, 2:65.

97 David Roberts, "The Consequences of the Exclusive Treaties: A British View," in *The Arab Gulf and the West*, ed. Brian R. Pridham (London: Croom Helm, 1985), 1–14; Husain M. Al-Baharna, "The Consequences of

Britain's Exclusive Treaties: A Gulf View," in *The Arab Gulf and the West*, ed. Pridham, 15–37.

98 Haldun Gülalp and Günter Seufert, *Religion, Identity, and Politics: Germany and Turkey in Interaction* (London: Routledge, 2013); Wolfgang G. Schwanitz, "The German Middle Eastern Policy, 1871–1945," in *Germany and the Middle East, 1871–1945*, ed. Wolfgang G. Schwanitz (Princeton: Marcus Wiener, 2004), 1–24.

99 Jonathan McMurray, *Distant Ties: Germany, the Ottoman Empire, and the Construction of the Baghdad Railway* (Westport: Praeger, 2001), 31.

100 Sebastian Conrad, *German Colonialism: A Short History* (Cambridge: Cambridge University Press, 2012).

101 Murat Özyüksel, *The Berlin–Baghdad Railway and the Ottoman Empire: Industrialization, Imperial Germany, and the Middle East* (London: I.B. Tauris, 2016); McMurray, *Distant Ties*; Sean McMeekin, *The Berlin–Baghdad Express: The Ottoman Empire and Germany's Bid for World Power* (Cambridge, MA: Belknap Press of Harvard University Press, 2010).

102 Necla Geyikdaği, *Foreign Investment in the Ottoman Empire: International Trade and Relations 1854–1914* (London: Tauris Academic Studies, 2011), 58–60; Aryeh Yodfat and Mordechai Abir, *In the Direction of the Persian Gulf: The Soviet Union and the Persian Gulf* (London: Cass, 1977), 24–5.

103 Briton C. Busch, "Britain and the Status of Kuwayt 1896–1899," *Middle East Journal* 21, no. 2 (1967): 187–98.

104 Alan Rush, *Al-Sabah: History and Genealogy of Kuwait's Ruling Family, 1752–1987* (London: Ithaca Press, 1987); Anscombe, *The Ottoman Gulf*, 92–112; Salwa Alghanim, *The Reign of Mubarak al-Sabah: Shaikh of Kuwait, 1896–1915* (London: I.B. Tauris, 1998), 39–81; Souad M. Al-Sabah, *Abdullah Mubarak Al-Sabah: The Transformation of Kuwait* (London: I.B. Tauris, 2015).

105 Busch, *Britain and the Persian Gulf*, 99–101.

106 IOR/R/15/1/472, ff.6–7, Meade to Foreign Department, 30 December 1898.

107 Elihu Lauterpacht et al., eds., *The Kuwait Crisis: Basic Documents* (Cambridge: Grotius, 1991), 3–7. On the Ottoman reaction to the treaty, see Anscombe, *The Ottoman Gulf*, 121–42.

108 John B. Kelly, "Salisbury, Curzon, and the Kuwait agreement of 1899," in *Studies in International History: Essays Presented to W. Norton Medlicott*, ed. K. Bourne and D.C. Watt (London: Longmans, 1967), 259–90.

109 Qtd in Townsend, *Proconsul to the Middle East*, 13.

110 Busch, *Britain and the Persian Gulf*, 109.

111 Anscombe, *The Ottoman Gulf*, 109–12.

112 Lorimer, *Gazetteer*, 1:327; National Archives, London, FO 60/733, vol. 1, enclosure 2, India Office to Foreign Office, 1 November 1900; Busch, *Britain and the Persian Gulf*, 128–32.

113 The German consulate in Baghdad was established in 1897, and that in Bushire in 1894. Edward Mead Earle, *Turkey, the Great Powers, and the Bagdad Railway: A Study in Imperialism* (London: Macmillan, 1923), 109–10. On von Stemrich in the Gulf, see John Albert White, *Transition to Global Rivalry: Alliance Diplomacy and the Quadruple Entente, 1907* (Cambridge: Cambridge University Press, 1995), 49–50; and Ulrich Trumpener, "Germany and the End of the Ottoman Empire," in *The Great Powers and the End of the Ottoman Empire*, ed. Marian Kent (London: George Allen and Unwin, 1984), 110–12.

114 J.A. Saldanha, *Précis of Correspondence on International Rivalry and British Policy in the Persian Gulf. 1872–1905* (n.p.: s.i., 1906), 4–5. On the system of "native agents," see James Onley, "Britain's Native Agents in Arabia and Persia in the Nineteenth Century," *Comparative Studies of South Asia, Africa and the Middle East* 24, no. 1 (2004): 129–37.

115 Lorimer, *Gazetteer*, 1:330–1. See also Pirouz Mojahed-Zadeh, *Security and Territoriality in the Persian Gulf: A Maritime Political Geography* (London: Curzon, 1998), 194–5.

116 National Archives, London, CAB 38/3/46, Possible railway from Russian (Trans-Caucasian) frontier of Persia to a Persian port in the Arabian Sea, June 1903; Lorimer, *Gazetteer*, 1:367–9; Richard I. Lawless, ed., *The Gulf in the Early Twentieth Century: Foreign Institutions and Local Responses* (Durham: University of Durham Centre for Middle Eastern and Islamic Studies, 1986), 167–9.

117 Lorimer, *Gazetteer*, 1:332–4; Edward G. Browne, *The Persian Revolution of 1905–1909* (Cambridge: Cambridge University Press, 1910), 104; FO 368/38/46, ff.361–80, Cox to Foreign Office, 18 March 1906. Founded in 1856, the Russian Steam Navigation and Trading Company was one of the most powerful companies in Tsarist Russia.

118 Saldanha, *Précis of Correspondence*, 35.

119 E.A. Rezvan, *Russian Ships in the Gulf, 1899–1903* (Reading: Ithaca Press, 1993); Lorimer, *Gazetteer*, 1:329, 376; White, *Transition to Global Rivalry*, 57-8.

120 AMAE CPCOM, n.s., Mascate vol. 10 (Le Golfe Persique et les puissances, Dossier général, November 1903 to April 1904), Dorville to Quai d'Orsay, 22 August 1903.

121 On Curzon, see David Gilmour, *Curzon, Imperial Statesman, 1859–1925* (London: John Murray, 2003). Curzon expounded his frontier theories in a series of publications, notably *Frontiers: The Romanes Lecture* (Oxford: Clarendon Press, 1907); *Persia and the Persian Question* (London: Longmans, Green & Co, 1892); *Problems of the Far East* (London: Longmans, Green & Co, 1894); and *Russia in Central Asia* (London: Longmans, Green & Co, 1889).

122 IOR Mss Eur D510/8, f.32, Curzon to Hamilton, 22 May 1901.

123 Lorimer, *Gazetteer*, 1:2627–8.

124 On the 1903 coronation *durbar*, see David Cannadine, *Aspects of Aristocracy: Grandeur and Decline in Modern Britain* (New Haven: Yale University Press, 1994); and Julie F. Codell, ed., *Power and Resistance: The Delhi Coronation Durbars* (Delhi: Mapin, 2012).

125 AMAE CPCOM, n.s., Mascate vol. 19 (Trafic d'armes, Dossier général, 1900–1907), Laronce to Ministère des Affaires étrangères, 22 November 1903.

126 Lorimer, *Gazetteer*, 1:2628.

127 On Arthur H. Hardinge, see his *A Diplomatist in the East* (London: Jonathan Cape, 1928), 256–350.

128 Bernard S. Cohn, "Representing Authority in Victorian India," in *The Invention of Tradition*, ed. Eric Hobsbawm and Terence Ranger (Cambridge: Cambridge University Press, 1983), 165–211; Codell, ed., *Power and Resistance*.

129 Lorimer, *Gazetteer*, 1:2632–6.

130 IOR Mss Eur F111/162, f.411, Curzon to Secretary of Indian Foreign Department, 21 November 1903. Lus Beyla (or Las Bela) and Kelat were two princely states in Baluchistan.

131 On princely states and indirect rule see, for instance, Michael H. Fisher, "Indirect Rule in the British Empire: The Foundations of the Residency System in India (1764–1858)," *Modern Asian Studies* 18, no. 3 (1984): 393–428; Fisher, *Indirect Rule in India: Residents and Residency System, 1764–1858* (Delhi: Oxford University Press, 1998); and Barbara N. Ramusack, *The Indian Princes and Their States* (Cambridge: Cambridge University Press, 2004).

132 Kristopher Radford, "Curzon's Cruise: The Pomp and Circumstances of Indian Indirect Rule of the Persian Gulf," *International History Review* 35, no. 4 (2013): 893–96.

133 Radford, "Curzon's Cruise," 884–95.

134 For a similar argument regarding Yemen, see John M. Willis, "Making Yemen Indian: Rewriting the Boundaries of Imperial Arabia," *International Journal of Middle East Studies* 41, no. 1 (2009): 23–38.

135 Lorimer, *Gazetteer*, 1:2637.
136 For Curzon's speech, see Lorimer, *Gazetteer*, 1:2638–9.
137 Jerome A. Saldanha, *The Persian Gulf Précis*, 18 vols. (Calcutta: Superintendent Government Printing, 1903–1908; Gerrards Cross: Archive Editions, 1986, 8 vols.).
138 Saldanha, *The Persian Gulf Précis*, 1:2644.
139 "Address of Lord Curzon to the British Residents at Bushire, 2 December 1903," qtd in Paul J. Rich, *Creating the Arabian Gulf: The British Raj and the Invasions of the Gulf* (Lanham: Lexington Books, 2009), 274–7.

Conclusion

1 Roderic H. Davison, "Where Is the Middle East?," *Foreign Affairs* 38, no. 4 (1960): 665–75 at 665.
2 Nile Green, "Rethinking the 'Middle East' after the Oceanic Turn," *Comparative Studies of South Asia, Africa, and the Middle East* 34, no. 3 (2014): 556–64; see also Green, "The View from the Edge: The Indian Ocean's Middle East," *International Journal of Middle East Studies* 48, no. 4 (2016): 746–49.
3 For a recent study on informal imperialism in the nineteenth century see David Todd, *A Velvet Empire: French Informal Imperialism in the Nineteenth Century* (Princeton: Princeton University Press, 2021). On the concept of informal imperialism for the case of the British Empire see John Gallagher and Ronald Robinson, "The Imperialism of Free Trade," *Economic History Review*, New Series 6, no. 1 (1953): 1–15; and Wm Roger Louis, ed., *Imperialism: The Robinson and Gallagher Controversy* (New York: New Viewpoints, 1976). Studies on the concept's validity for other regions include for instance Andrew Thompson, "Informal Empire? An Exploration in the History of Anglo-Argentine Relations, 1810–1914," *Journal of Latin American Studies* 24, no. 2 (1992): 419–36; and Anthony G. Hopkins, "Informal Empire in Argentina: An Alternative View," *Journal of Latin American Studies* 26, no. 2 (1994): 469–84.
4 The expression was used by Curzon. Qtd in Briton C. Busch, *Britain and the Persian Gulf, 1894–1914* (Berkeley: University of California Press, 1967), 258.
5 James Onley, *The Arabian Frontier of the Raj: Merchants, Rulers, and the British in the Nineteenth-Century Gulf* (Oxford: Oxford University Press, 2007).
6 Christopher A. Bayly, *Imperial Meridian: The British Empire and the World, 1780–1830* (London: Longman, 1989).

7 On the importance of the Middle East for the British Empire during the First World War and the interwar years see Priya Satia, *Spies in Arabia: The Great War and the Cultural Foundations of Britain's Covert Empire in the Middle East* (Oxford: Oxford University Press, 2008).

8 On British imperialism in the Middle East during the interwar years and after the Second World War, see for instance John Darwin, *Britain, Egypt and the Middle East: Imperial Policy in the Aftermath of War, 1918–1922* (London: Macmillan, 1981); and William Roger Lewis, *The British Empire in the Middle East, 1945–1951: Arab Nationalism, the United States, and Postwar Imperialism* (Oxford: Clarendon Press, 1985).

9 On British imperial policy in the mandates, see the following two studies: Jacob Norris, *Land of Progress: Palestine in the Age of Colonial Development, 1905–1948* (Oxford: Oxford University Press, 2013); and Robert Fletcher, *British Imperialism and "The Tribal Question": Desert Administration and Nomadic Societies in the Middle East, 1919–1936* (Oxford: Oxford University Press, 2015).

10 Marian Kent, *Moguls and Mandarins: Oil, Imperialism, and the Middle East in British Policy* (London: Frank Cass, 1993); Roger Adelson, *London and the Invention of the Middle East: Money, Power, and War, 1902–1922* (New Haven: Yale University Press, 1995).

INDEX

Note: Page numbers in *italics* denote figures.

www.ingramcontent.com/pod-product-compliance
Lightning Source LLC
LaVergne TN
LVHW041400090826
845264LV00023B/217
* 9 7 8 0 2 2 8 0 1 4 0 6 5 *